Skip·Beat!

Shojo Beat

Skip·Beat!

12
Story & Art by Yoshiki Nakamura

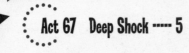

Skip·Beat!

Volume 12

CONTENTS

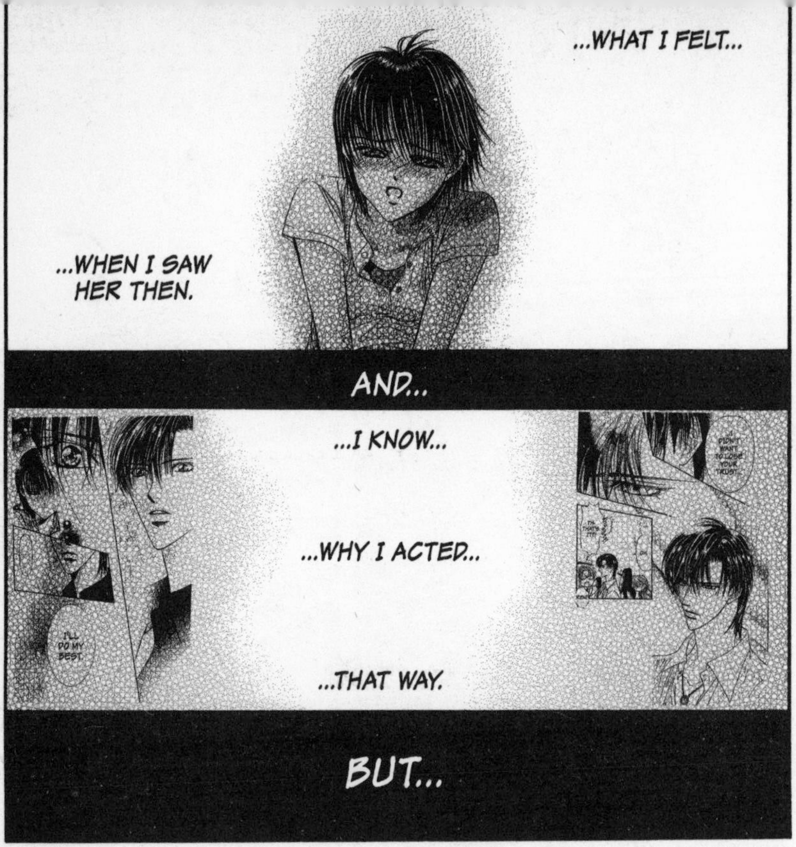
...WHAT I FELT...
...WHEN I SAW HER THEN.
AND...
...I DIDN'T WANT TO LOSE YOUR TRUST...
TH-THAT'S IT!!
...I KNOW...
...WHY I ACTED...
...THAT WAY.
I'LL DO MY BEST.
BUT...

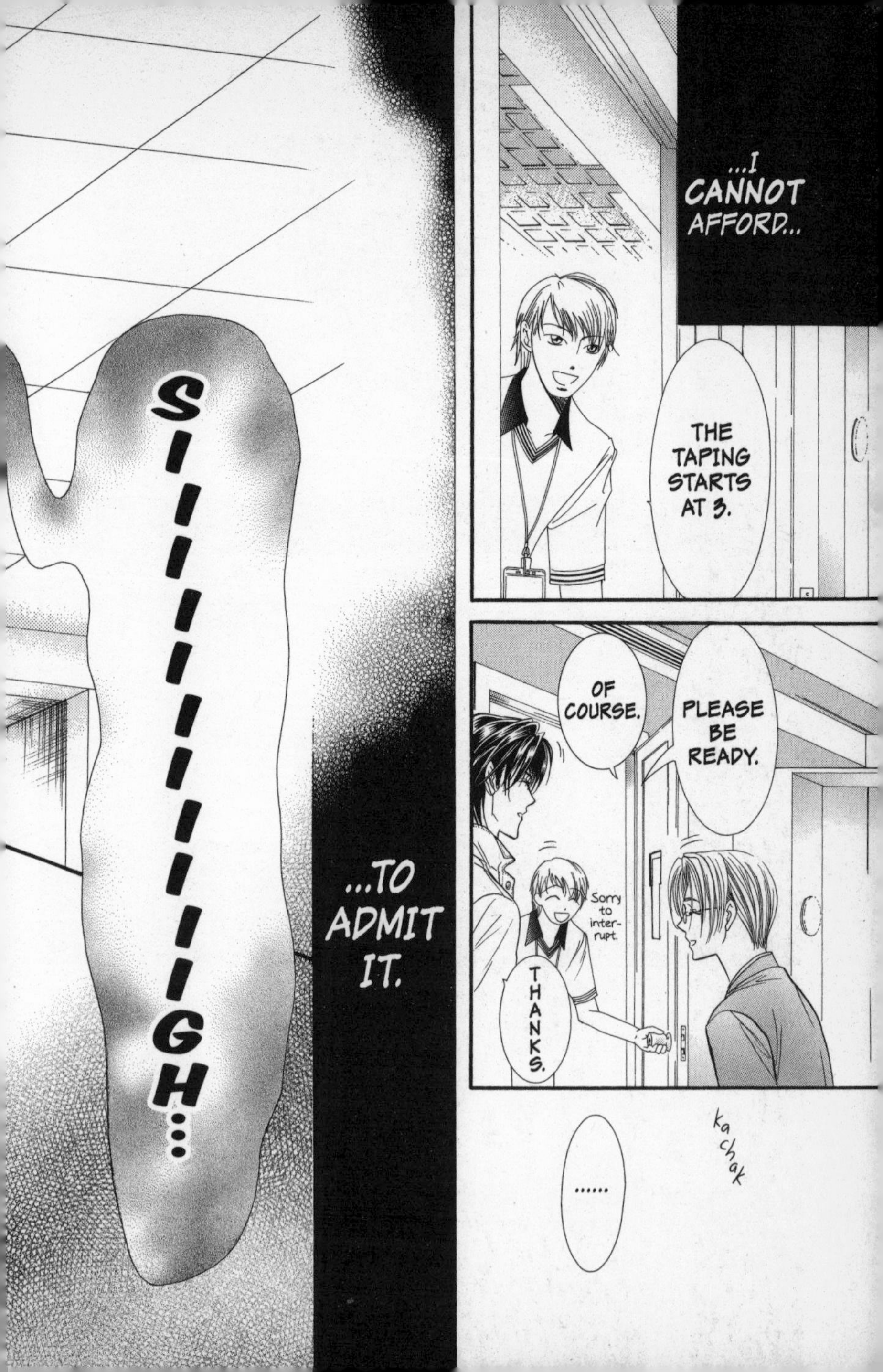
...I CANNOT AFFORD...
THE TAPING STARTS AT 3.
PLEASE BE READY.
OF COURSE.
Sorry to interrupt.
THANKS.
ka chak
......
SIIIIIIIIIGH...
...TO ADMIT IT.

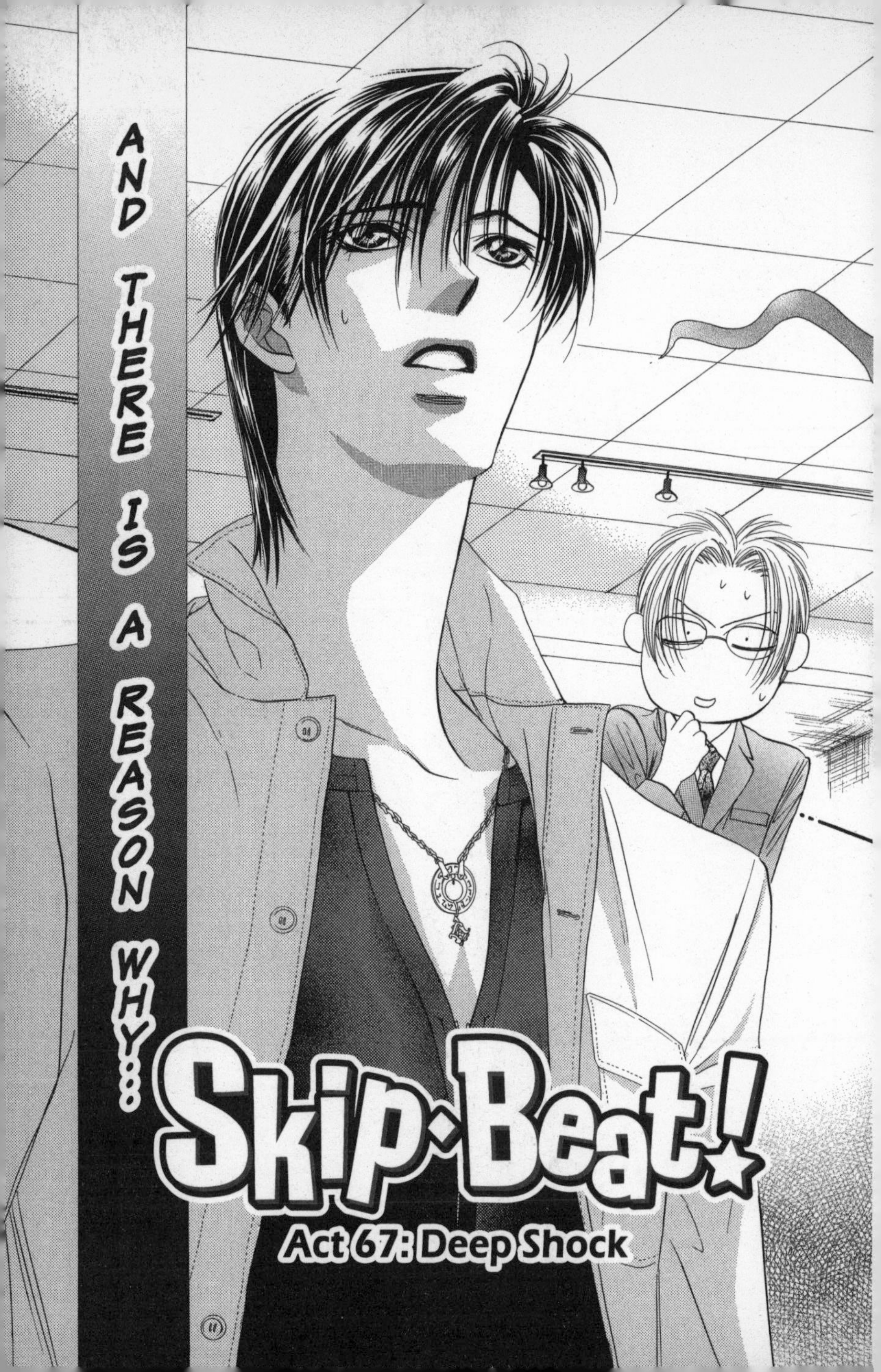
AND THERE IS A REASON WHY...
Skip·Beat!
Act 67: Deep Shock

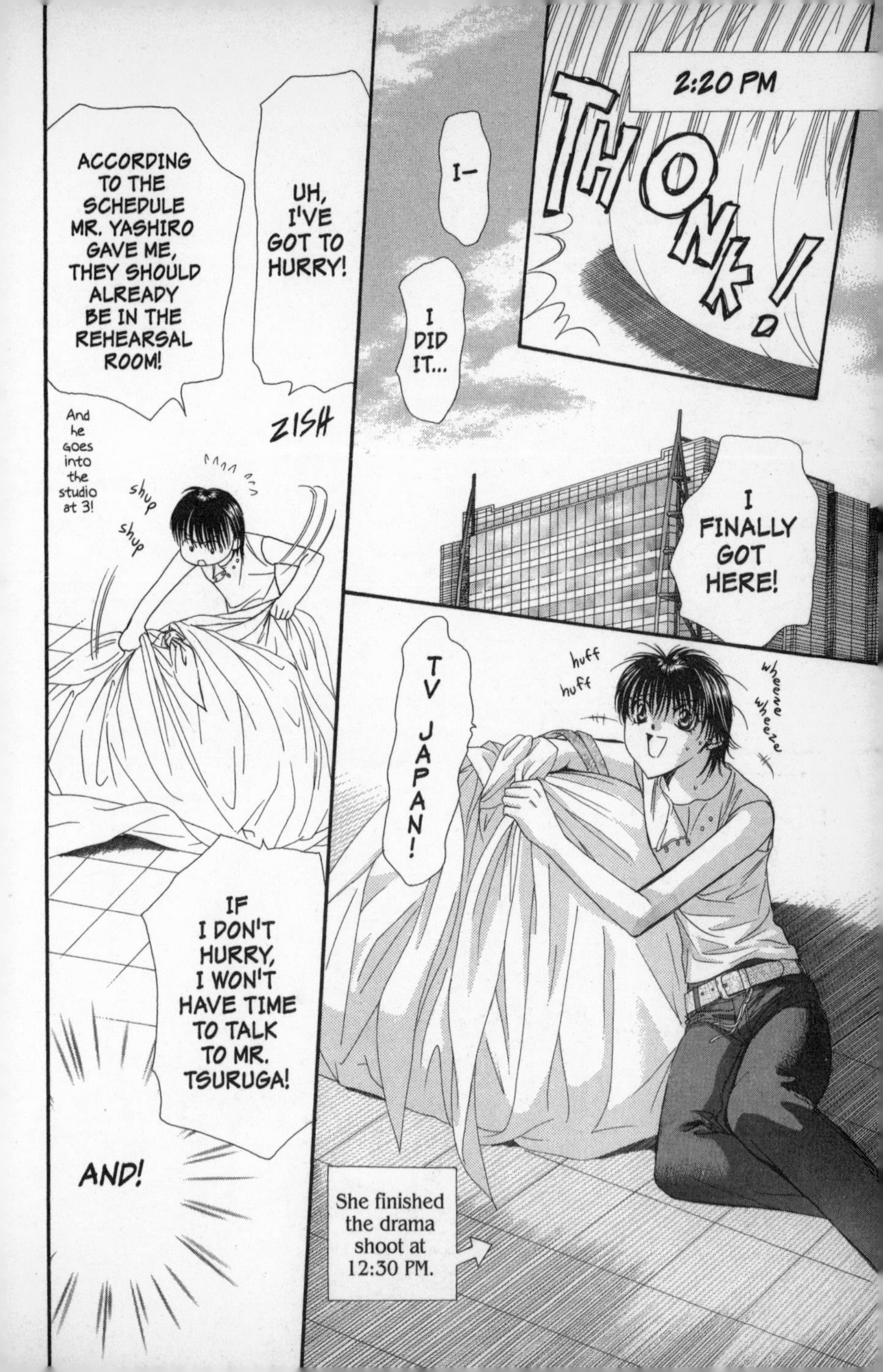
2:20 PM
THONK!
I—
I DID IT...
I FINALLY GOT HERE!
TV JAPAN!
huff huff
wheeze wheeze
She finished the drama shoot at 12:30 PM.
UH, I'VE GOT TO HURRY!
ACCORDING TO THE SCHEDULE MR. YASHIRO GAVE ME, THEY SHOULD ALREADY BE IN THE REHEARSAL ROOM!
ZISH
And he goes into the studio at 3!
shup shup
IF I DON'T HURRY, I WON'T HAVE TIME TO TALK TO MR. TSURUGA!
AND!

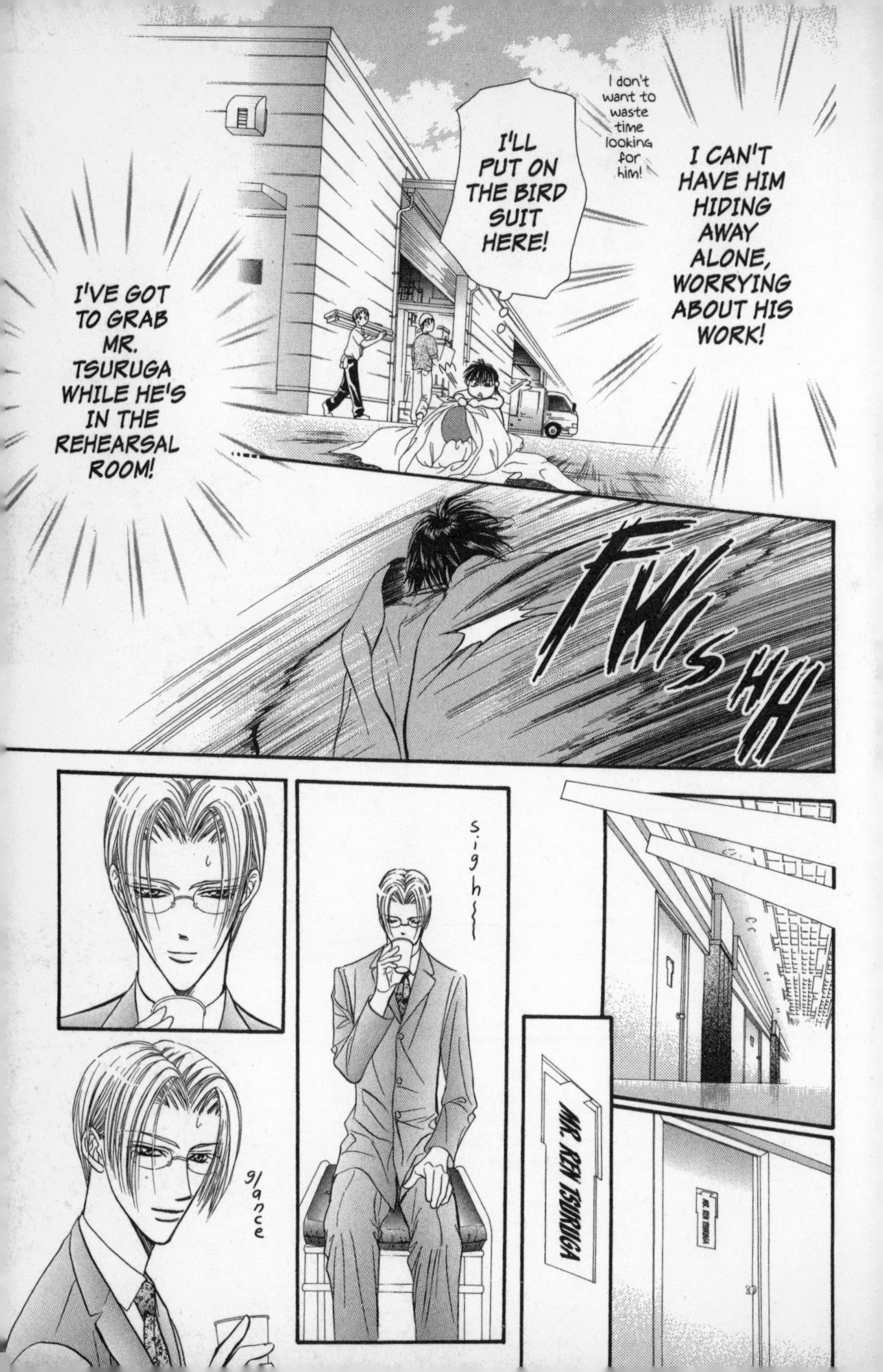
I CAN'T HAVE HIM HIDING AWAY ALONE, WORRYING ABOUT HIS WORK!
I don't want to waste time looking for him!
I'LL PUT ON THE BIRD SUIT HERE!
I'VE GOT TO GRAB MR. TSURUGA WHILE HE'S IN THE REHEARSAL ROOM!
FWISHH
MR. REN TSURUGA
MR. REN TSURUGA
sigh~
glance

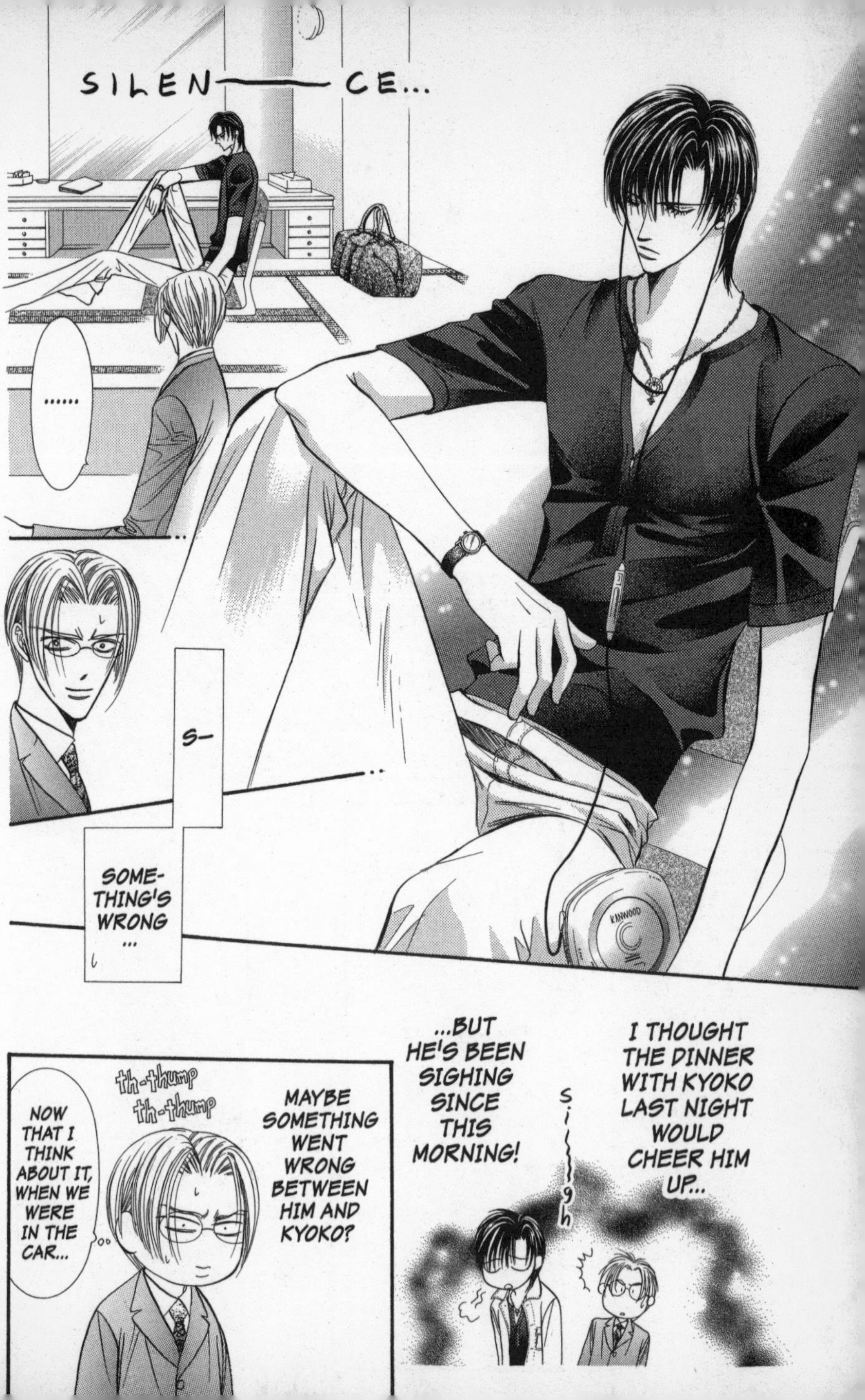
SILEN——CE...
......
S—
SOME-THING'S WRONG...
I THOUGHT THE DINNER WITH KYOKO LAST NIGHT WOULD CHEER HIM UP...
...BUT HE'S BEEN SIGHING SINCE THIS MORNING!
S-i-g-h
MAYBE SOMETHING WENT WRONG BETWEEN HIM AND KYOKO?
th-thump th-thump
NOW THAT I THINK ABOUT IT, WHEN WE WERE IN THE CAR...

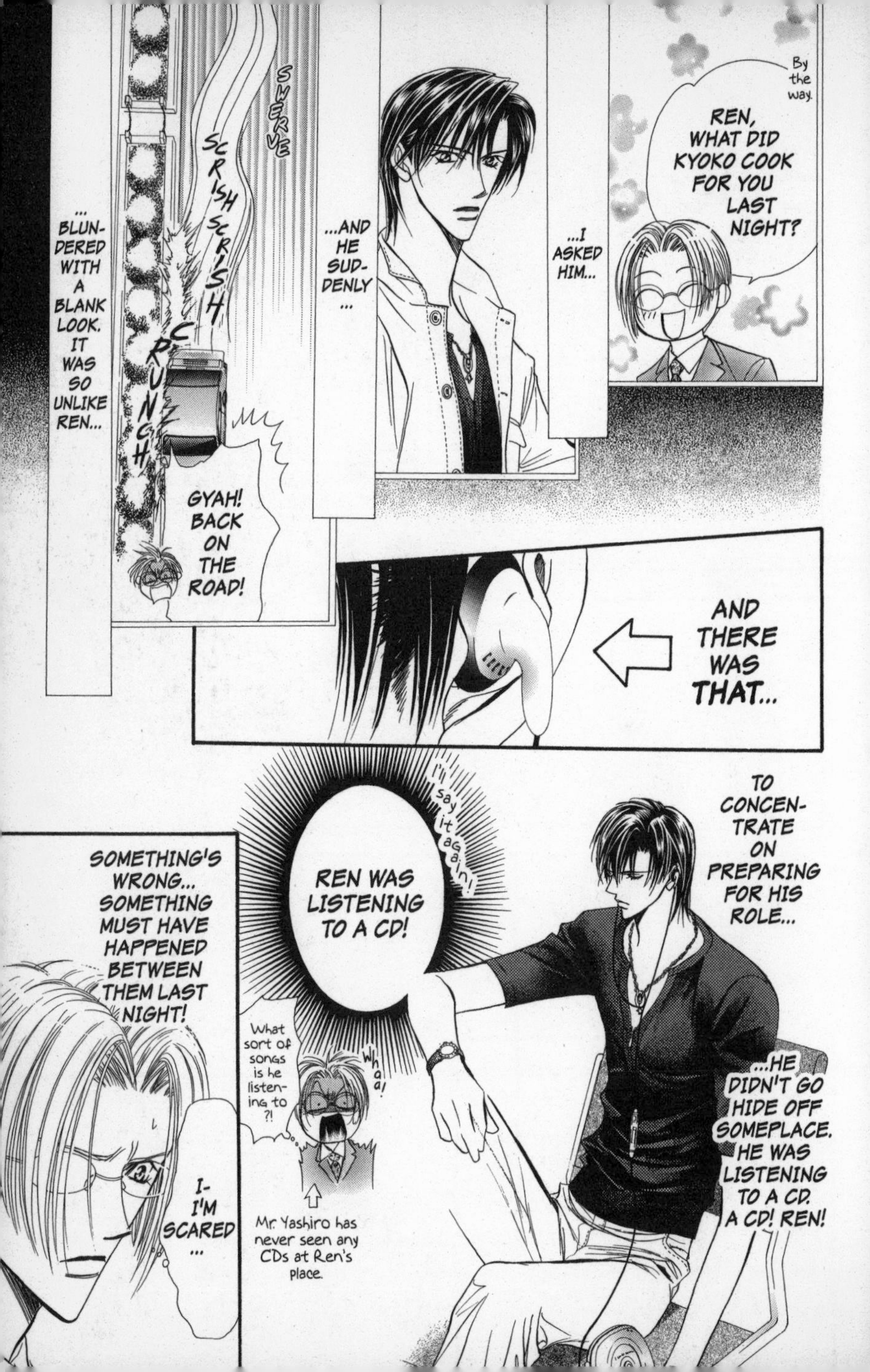
By the way.
REN, WHAT DID KYOKO COOK FOR YOU LAST NIGHT?
...I ASKED HIM...
...AND HE SUDDENLY...
SWERVE
SCRISH SCRISH
CRUNCH
GYAH! BACK ON THE ROAD!
...BLUNDERED WITH A BLANK LOOK. IT WAS SO UNLIKE REN...
AND THERE WAS THAT...
TO CONCENTRATE ON PREPARING FOR HIS ROLE...
...HE DIDN'T GO HIDE OFF SOMEPLACE. HE WAS LISTENING TO A CD. A CD! REN!
I'll say it again!
REN WAS LISTENING TO A CD!
Whaa!
What sort of songs is he listening to?!
Mr. Yashiro has never seen any CDs at Ren's place.
SOMETHING'S WRONG... SOMETHING MUST HAVE HAPPENED BETWEEN THEM LAST NIGHT!
I-I'M SCARED...

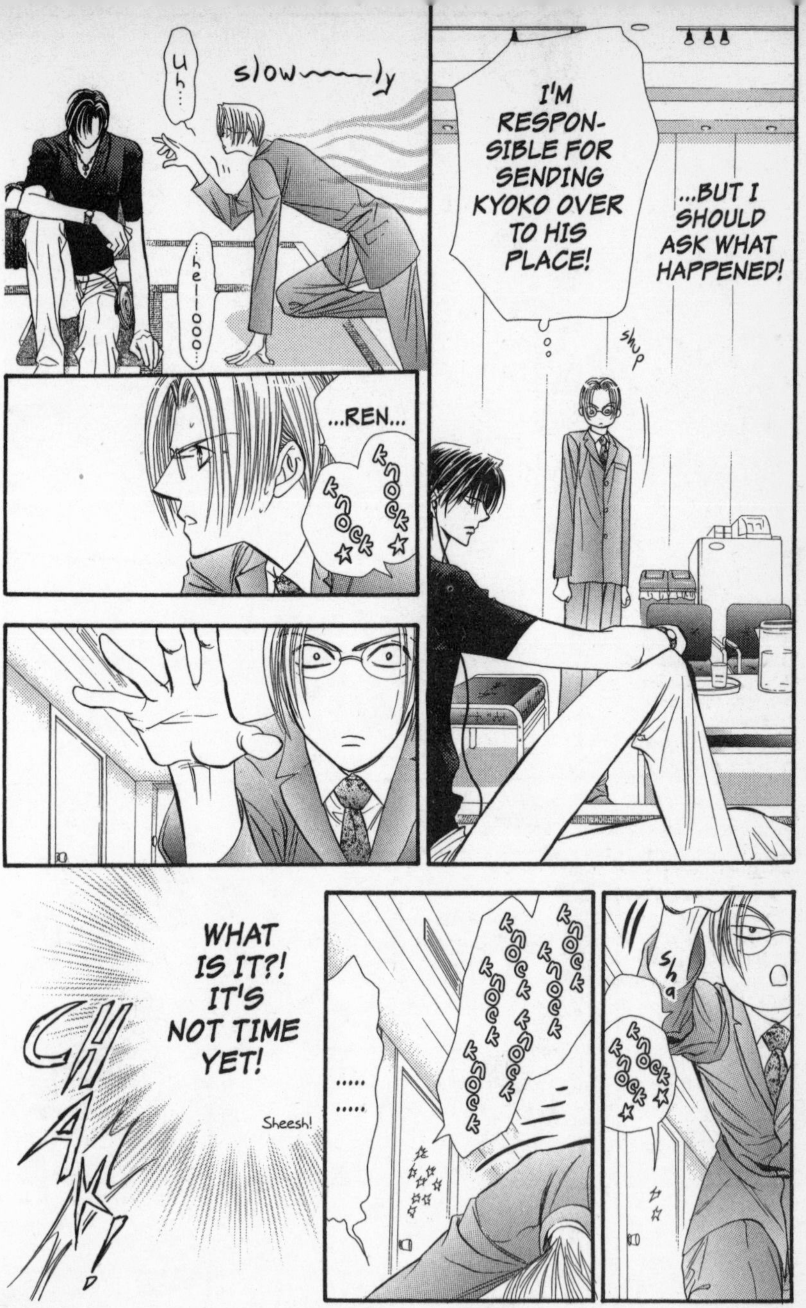
I'M RESPONSIBLE FOR SENDING KYOKO OVER TO HIS PLACE!
...BUT I SHOULD ASK WHAT HAPPENED!
shup
slow~~~ly
Uh...
...hellooo...
...REN...
knock knock ☆
knock knock ☆
Sha
knock knock knock ☆
knock knock knock knock knock knock
.....
.....
WHAT IS IT?! IT'S NOT TIME YET!
Sheesh!
CHAMK!

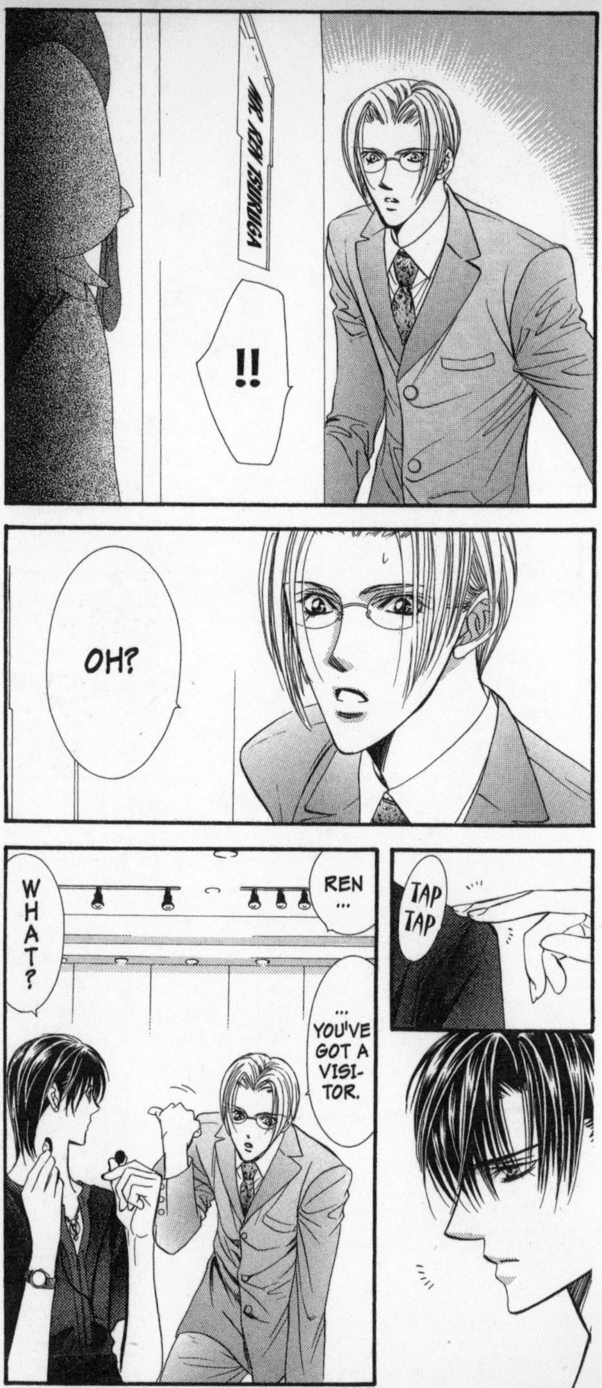
MR. REN TSURUGA
!!
OH?
TAP TAP
REN ...
... YOU'VE GOT A VISITOR.
WHAT?

Greetings

Thank you for reading this volume of Skip♦Beat! too.

At last the Dark Moon arc is about to enter the climax...eh heh heh... It...took...a...long... time...!!

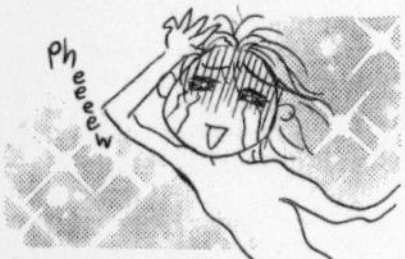
Pheeeew

I knew it. Yes, I knew it. From the time I thought of drawing the Tsukigomori and Dark Moon arc, I knew it was probably going to be long...! Yes...!! I felt faint before I even began and was sighing...!!

↑

(This is why I had a far-away look last time and the time before that...) Still, I felt that I'd handled Kyoko and Ogata pretty well, and I was at ease... the problem is that guy...the guy that always gives me trouble...!! Yes, I'm still desperately struggling to draw that guy...(when will I get used to drawing him...?) Ren Tsuruga... it's you...

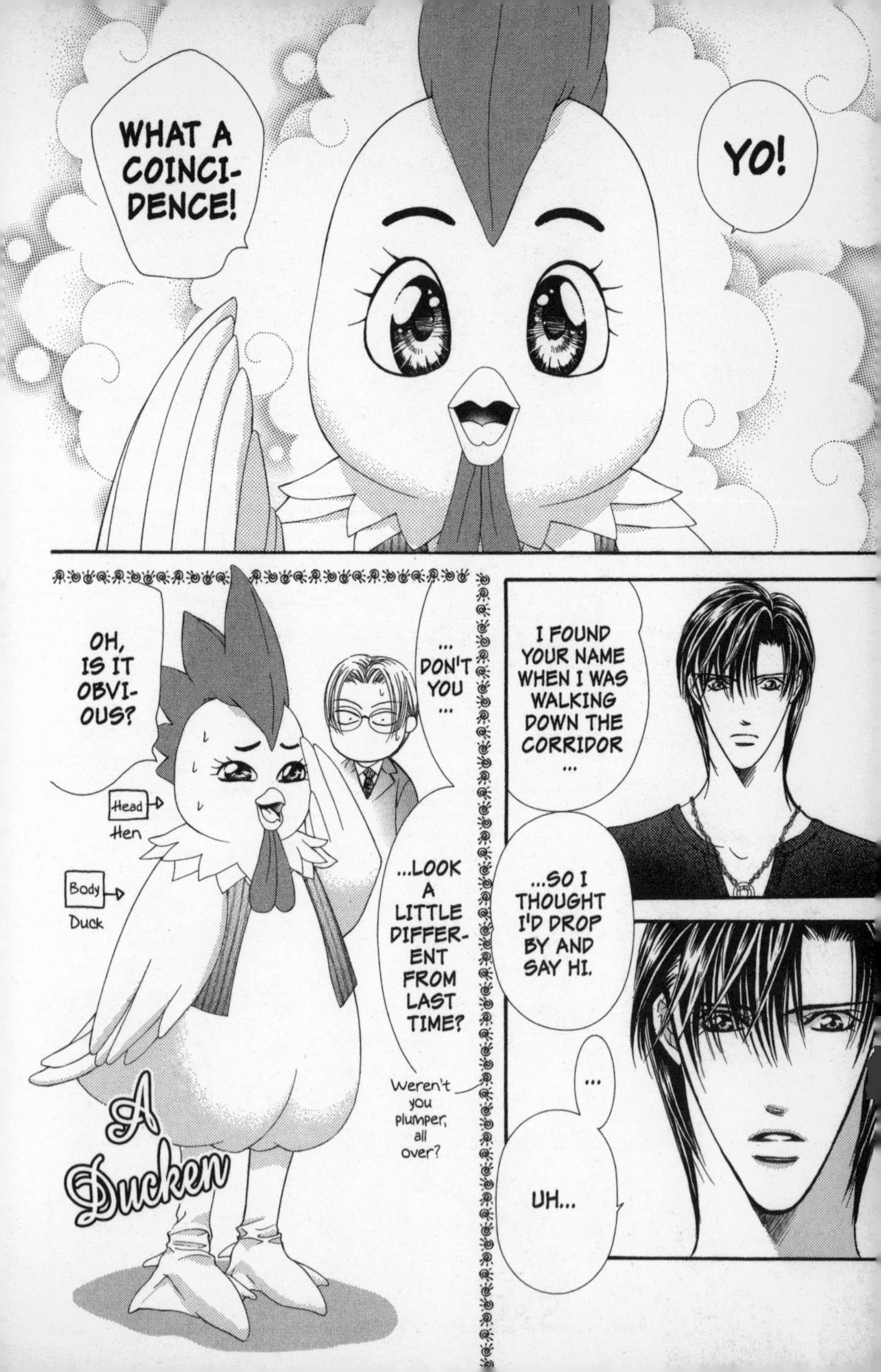
YO!
WHAT A COINCI-DENCE!
I FOUND YOUR NAME WHEN I WAS WALKING DOWN THE CORRIDOR ...
...SO I THOUGHT I'D DROP BY AND SAY HI.
...
UH...
... DON'T YOU ...
...LOOK A LITTLE DIFFER-ENT FROM LAST TIME?
Weren't you plumper, all over?
OH, IS IT OBVI-OUS?
Head
Hen
Body
Duck
A Ducken

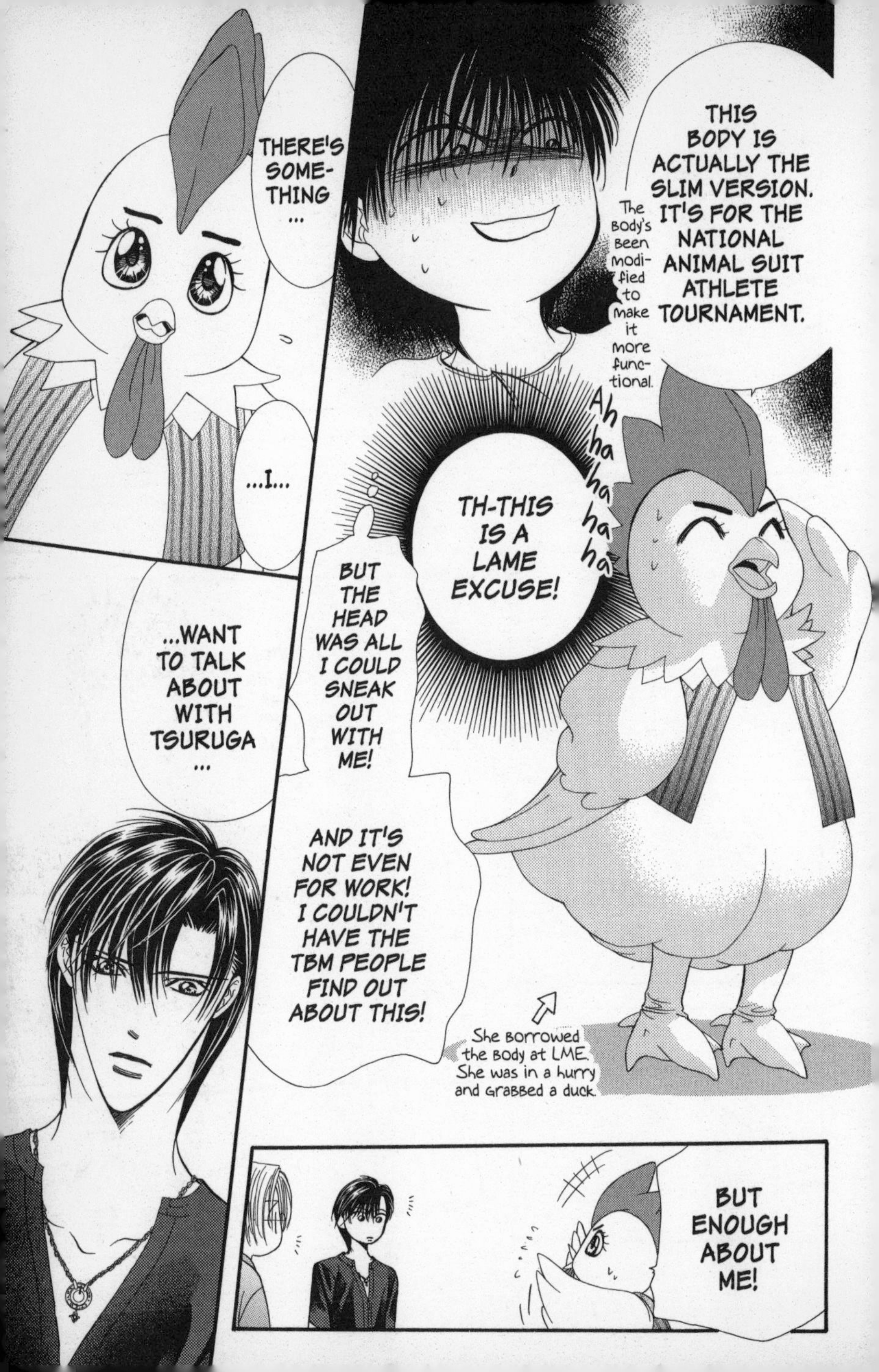
THIS BODY IS ACTUALLY THE SLIM VERSION. IT'S FOR THE NATIONAL ANIMAL SUIT ATHLETE TOURNAMENT.
The body's been modi-fied to make it more func-tional.
Ah ha ha ha ha ha
TH-THIS IS A LAME EXCUSE!
BUT THE HEAD WAS ALL I COULD SNEAK OUT WITH ME!
AND IT'S NOT EVEN FOR WORK! I COULDN'T HAVE THE TBM PEOPLE FIND OUT ABOUT THIS!
She borrowed the body at LME. She was in a hurry and grabbed a duck.
THERE'S SOME-THING ...
...I...
...WANT TO TALK ABOUT WITH TSURUGA ...
BUT ENOUGH ABOUT ME!

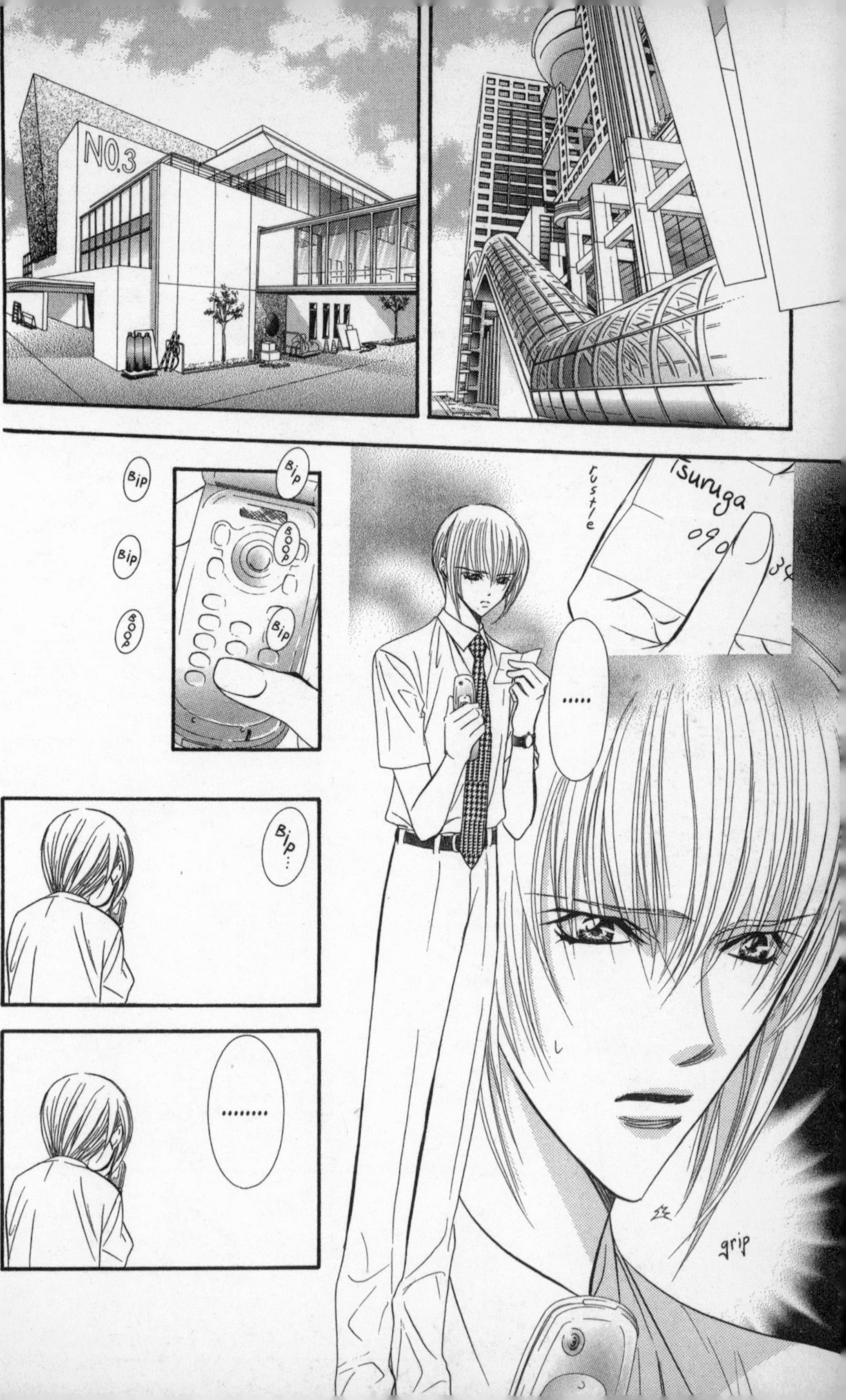
NO.3
rustle
Tsuruga
090 34
......
grip
Bip
Bip
BOOP
Bip
BOOP
Bip
Bip...
....

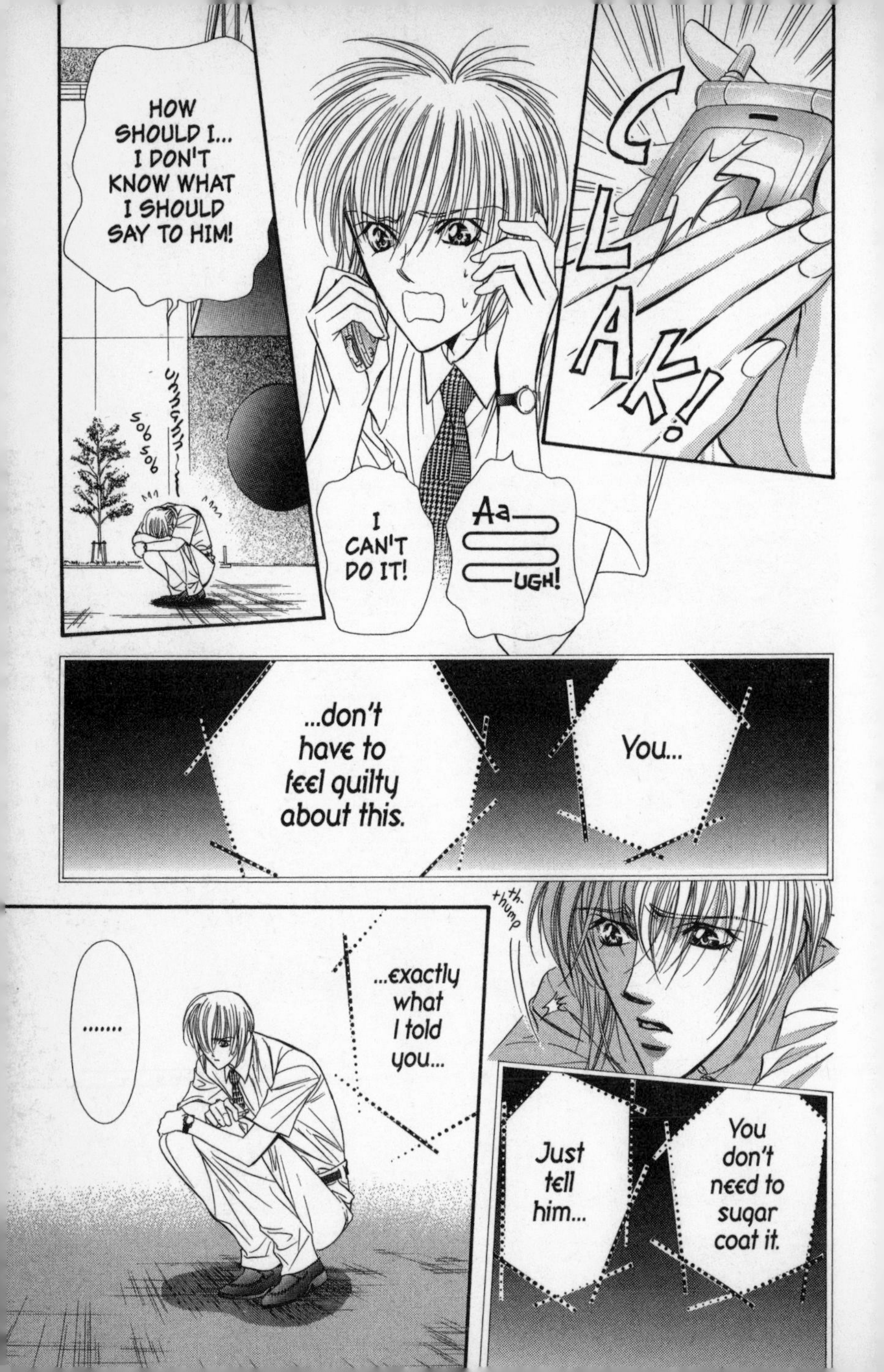
CLAK!
Aa———UGH!
I CAN'T DO IT!
HOW SHOULD I... I DON'T KNOW WHAT I SHOULD SAY TO HIM!
unnghhh~
sob sob
You...
...don't have to feel guilty about this.
th-thump
You don't need to sugar coat it.
Just tell him...
...exactly what I told you...
....

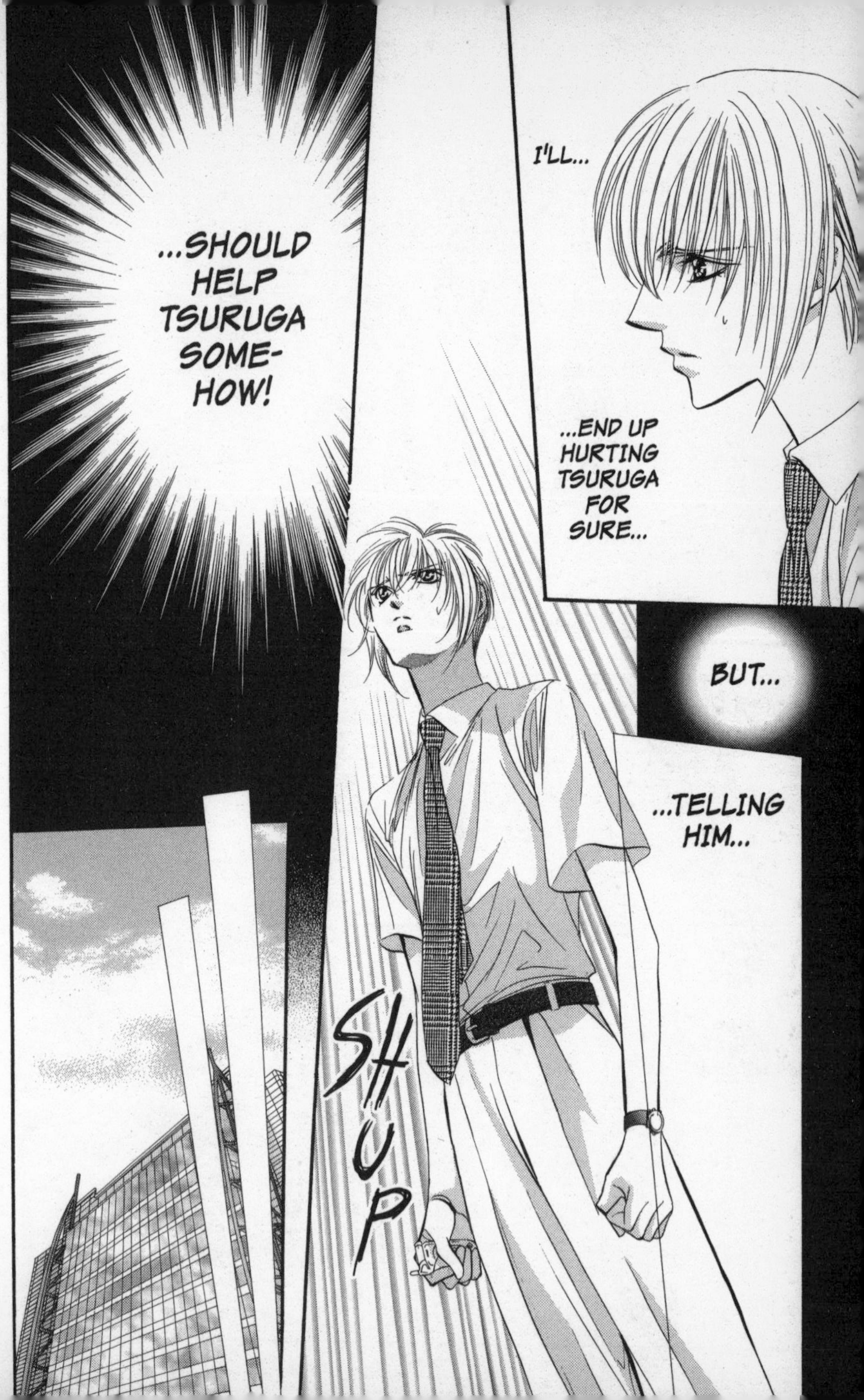
I'LL...
...END UP HURTING TSURUGA FOR SURE...
BUT...
...TELLING HIM...
...SHOULD HELP TSURUGA SOME-HOW!
SHUP

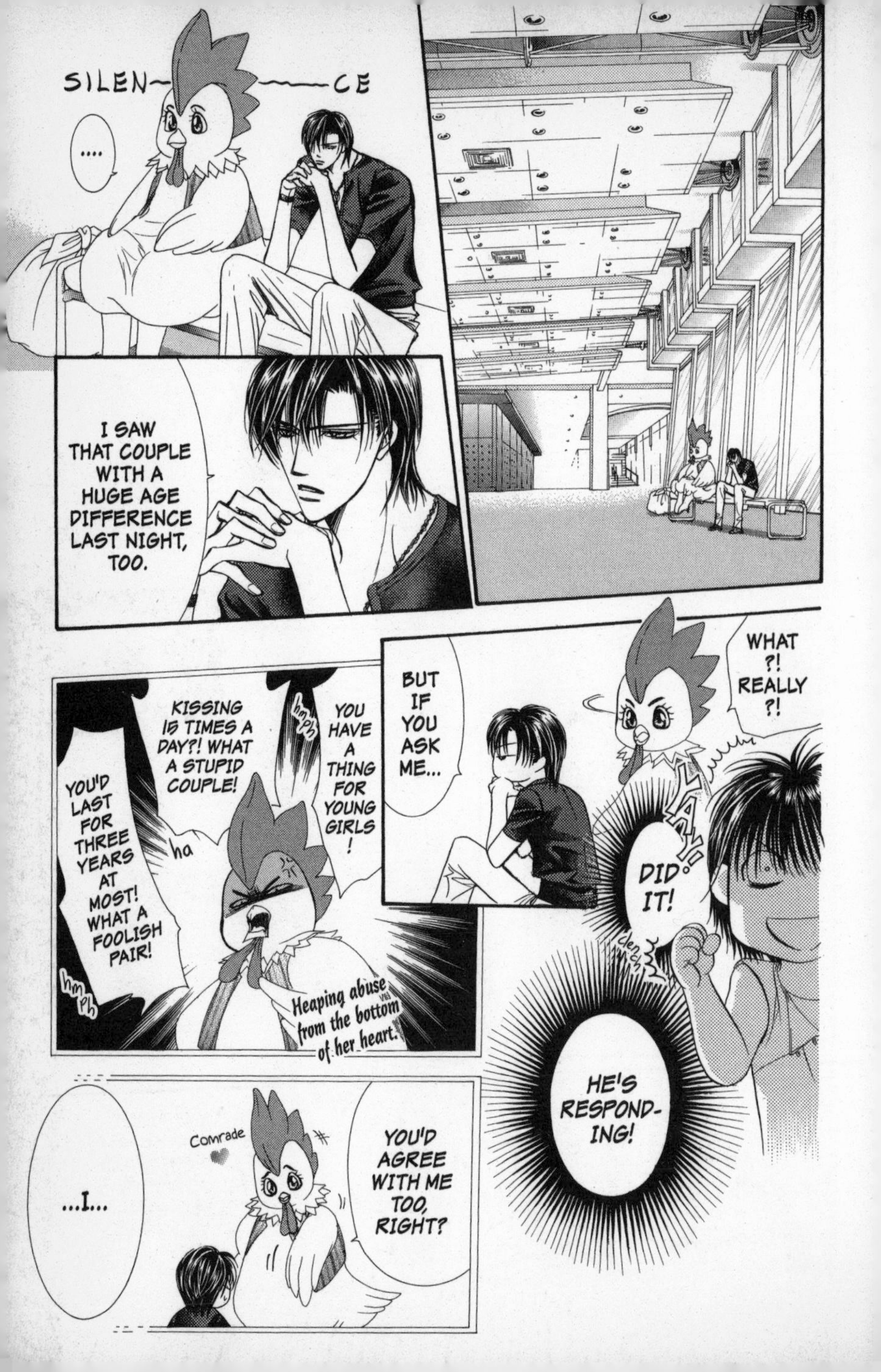
SILEN~ ~~~CE
.....
I SAW THAT COUPLE WITH A HUGE AGE DIFFERENCE LAST NIGHT, TOO.
WHAT ?! REALLY ?!
BUT IF YOU ASK ME...
YAY!!
DID IT!
clench
HE'S RESPOND-ING!
YOU HAVE A THING FOR YOUNG GIRLS!
hmph
KISSING 15 TIMES A DAY?! WHAT A STUPID COUPLE!
YOU'D LAST FOR THREE YEARS AT MOST! WHAT A FOOLISH PAIR!
ha
hmph
Heaping abuse from the bottom of her heart.
YOU'D AGREE WITH ME TOO, RIGHT?
Comrade
...I...

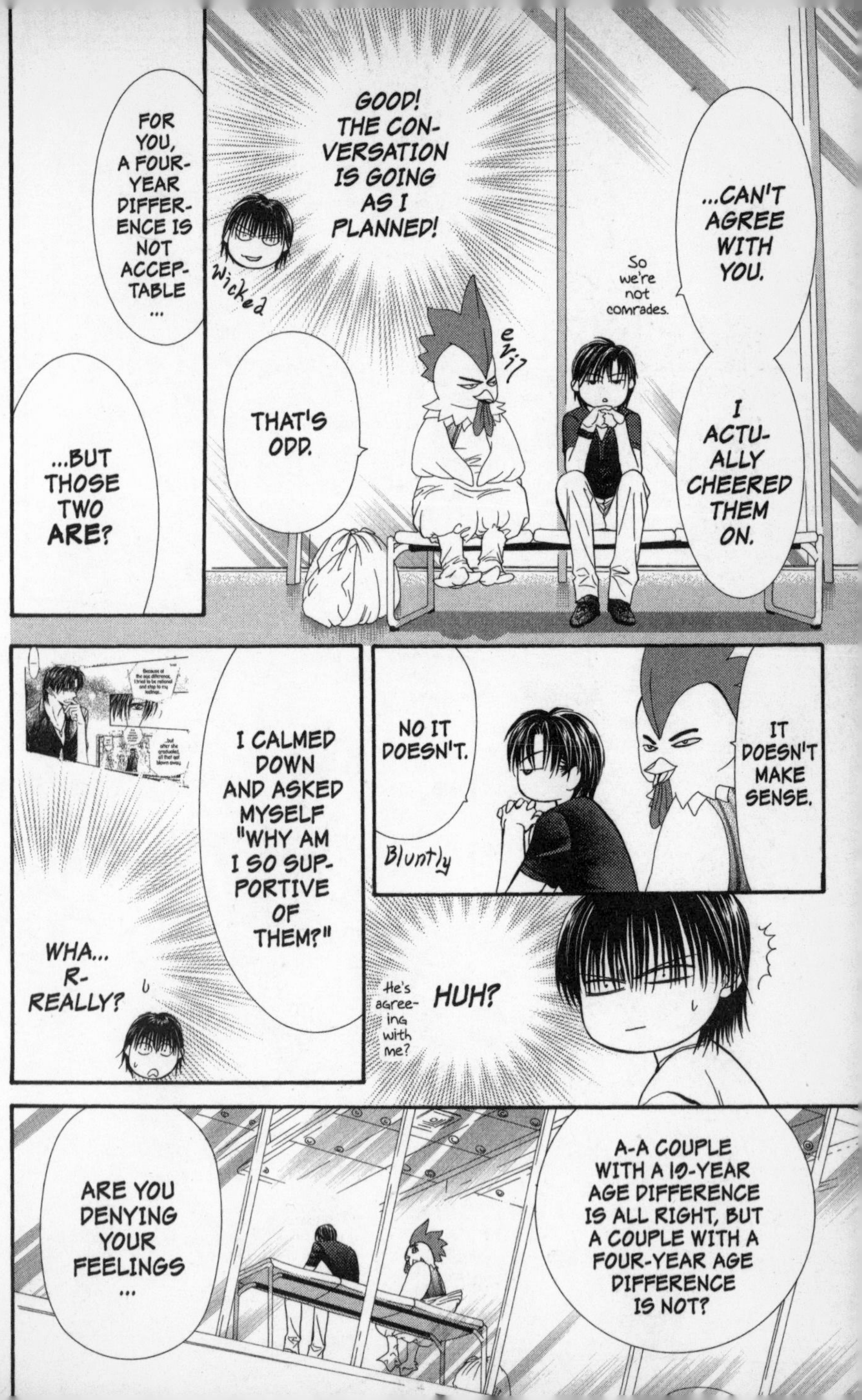
...CAN'T AGREE WITH YOU.
I ACTUALLY CHEERED THEM ON.
So we're not comrades.
GOOD! THE CON-VERSATION IS GOING AS I PLANNED!
Wicked
evil
THAT'S ODD.
FOR YOU, A FOUR-YEAR DIFFER-ENCE IS NOT ACCEP-TABLE ...
...BUT THOSE TWO ARE?
IT DOESN'T MAKE SENSE.
NO IT DOESN'T.
Bluntly
HUH?
He's agree-ing with me?
I CALMED DOWN AND ASKED MYSELF "WHY AM I SO SUP-PORTIVE OF THEM?"
WHA... R-REALLY?
A-A COUPLE WITH A 19-YEAR AGE DIFFERENCE IS ALL RIGHT, BUT A COUPLE WITH A FOUR-YEAR AGE DIFFERENCE IS NOT?
ARE YOU DENYING YOUR FEELINGS ...

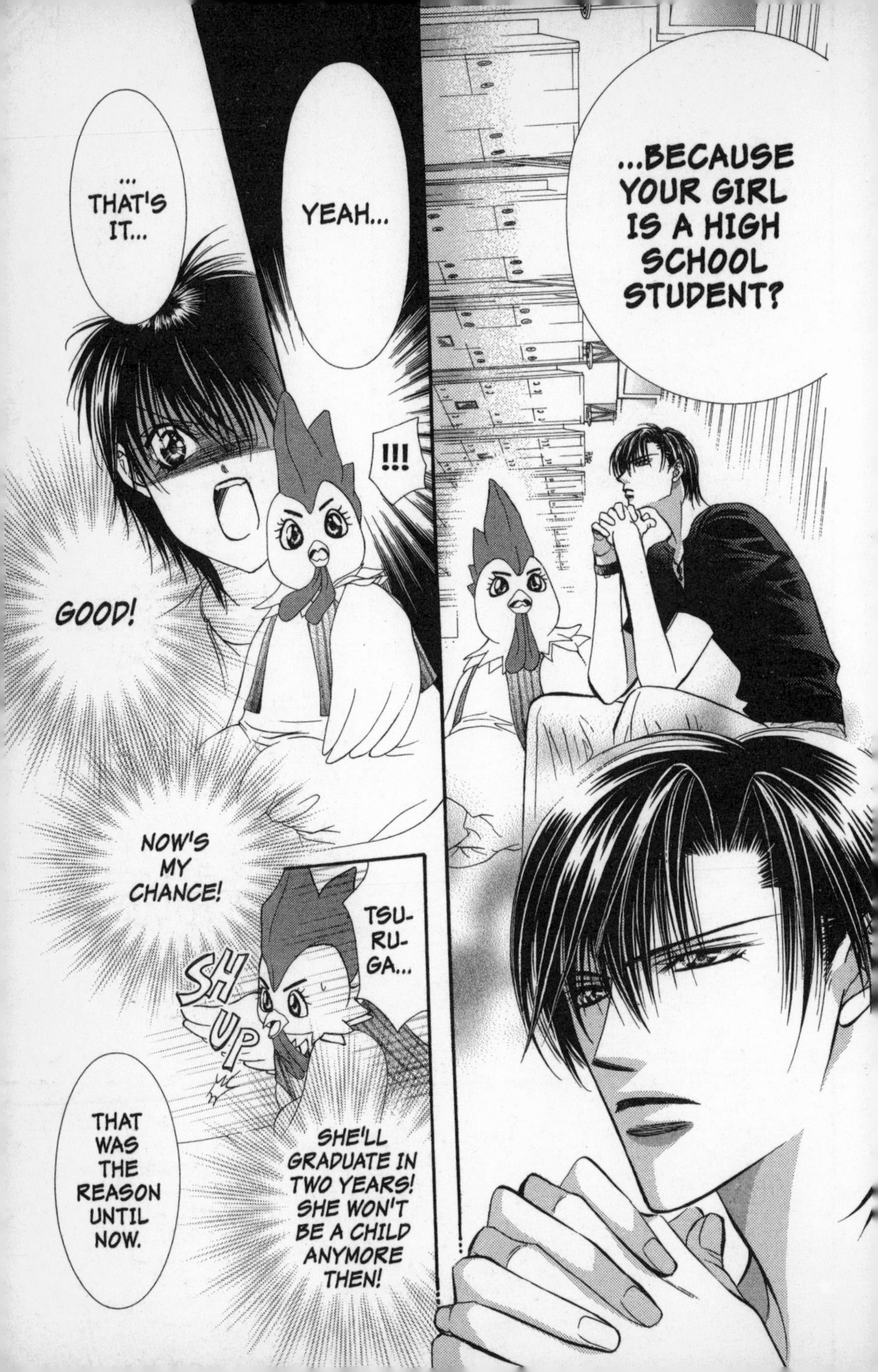
...BECAUSE YOUR GIRL IS A HIGH SCHOOL STUDENT?
YEAH...
... THAT'S IT...
!!!
GOOD!
NOW'S MY CHANCE!
TSU-RU-GA...
SHUP
SHE'LL GRADUATE IN TWO YEARS! SHE WON'T BE A CHILD ANYMORE THEN!
THAT WAS THE REASON UNTIL NOW.

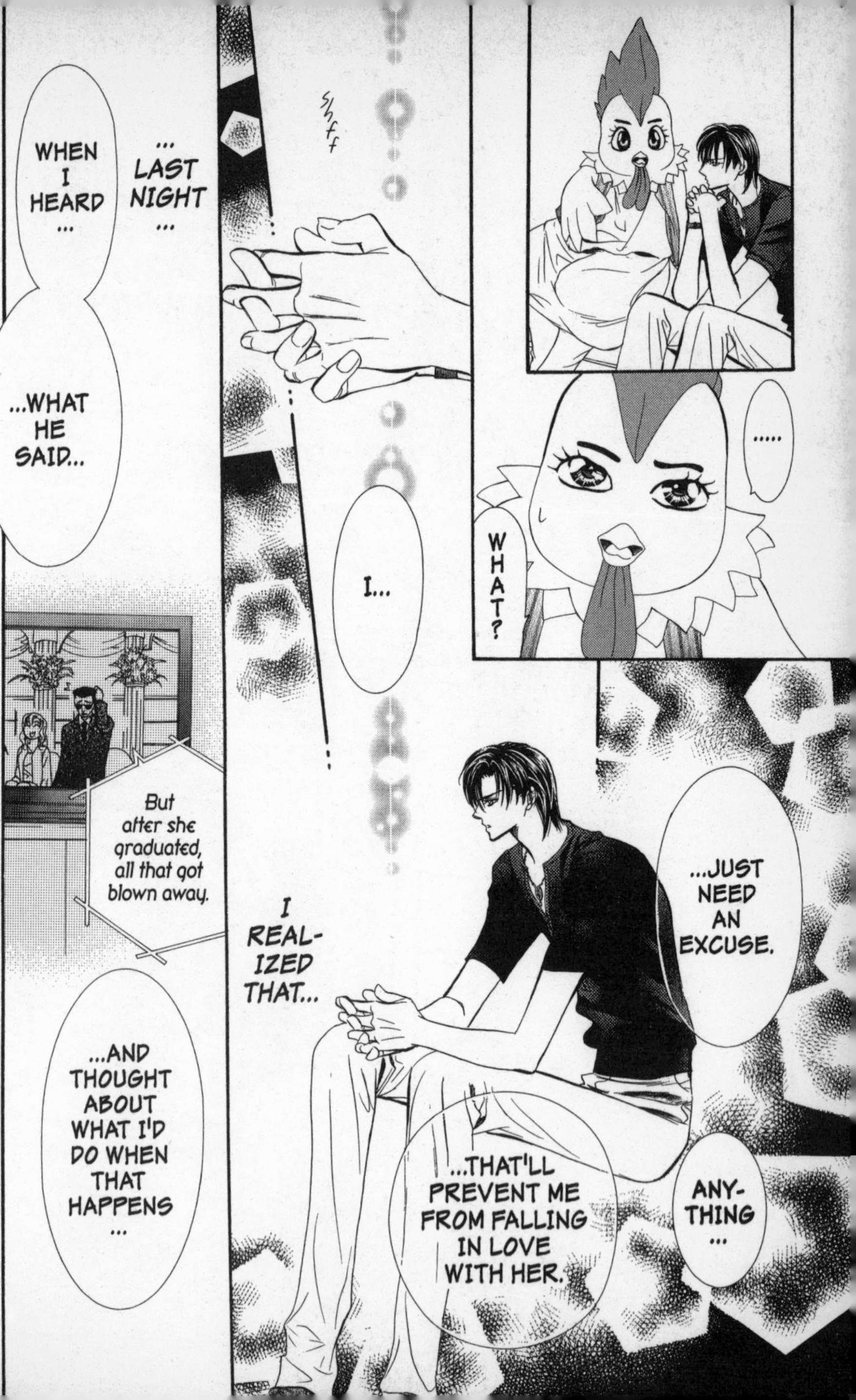
.....
WHAT?
shff
I...
...LAST NIGHT...
WHEN I HEARD...
...WHAT HE SAID...
But after she graduated, all that got blown away.
I REAL-IZED THAT...
...AND THOUGHT ABOUT WHAT I'D DO WHEN THAT HAPPENS...
...JUST NEED AN EXCUSE.
ANY-THING...
...THAT'LL PREVENT ME FROM FALLING IN LOVE WITH HER.

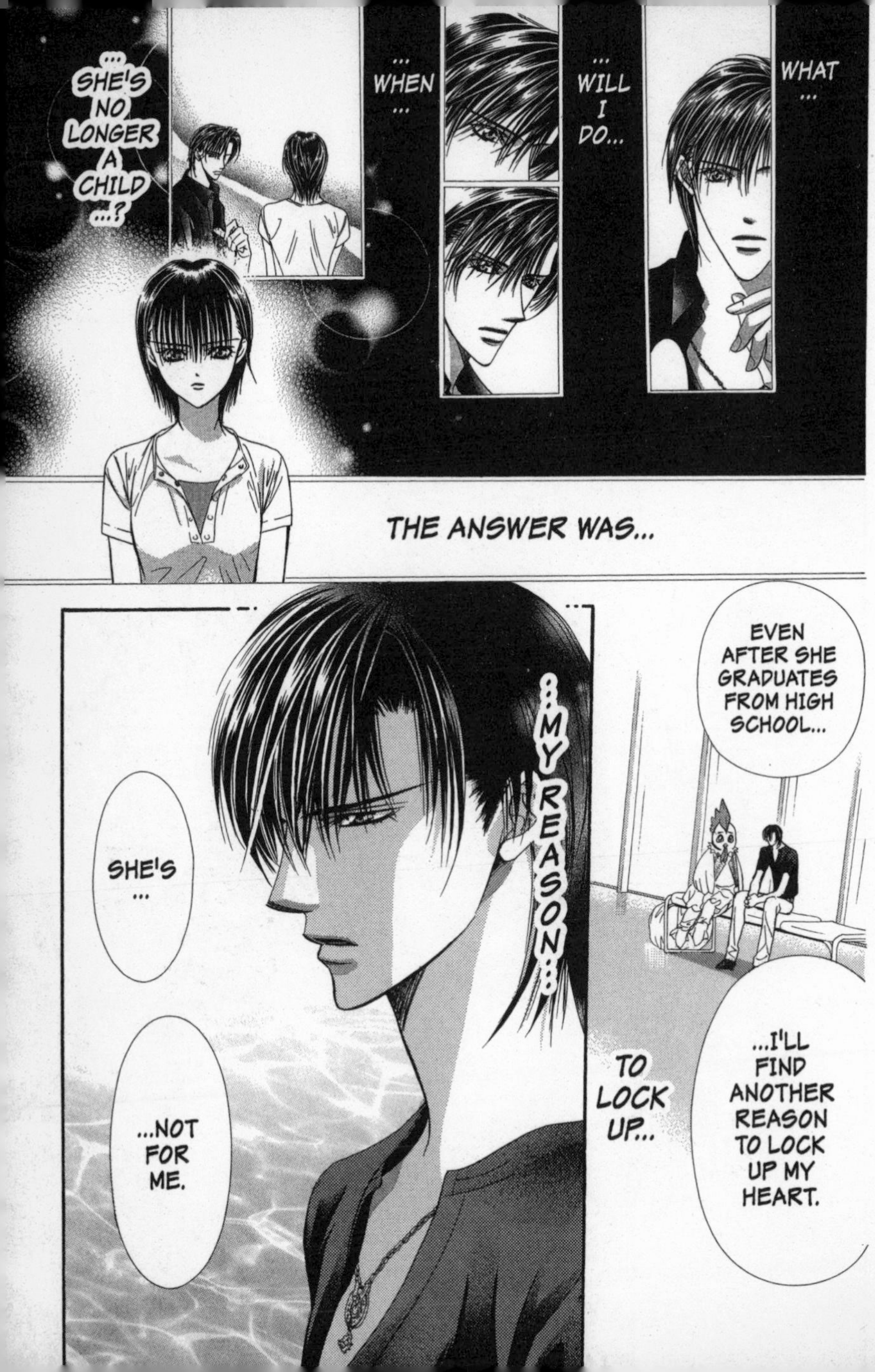
WHAT...
...WILL I DO...
...WHEN...
...SHE'S NO LONGER A CHILD...?
THE ANSWER WAS...
EVEN AFTER SHE GRADUATES FROM HIGH SCHOOL...
...I'LL FIND ANOTHER REASON TO LOCK UP MY HEART.
TO LOCK UP...
...MY REASON...
SHE'S...
...NOT FOR ME.

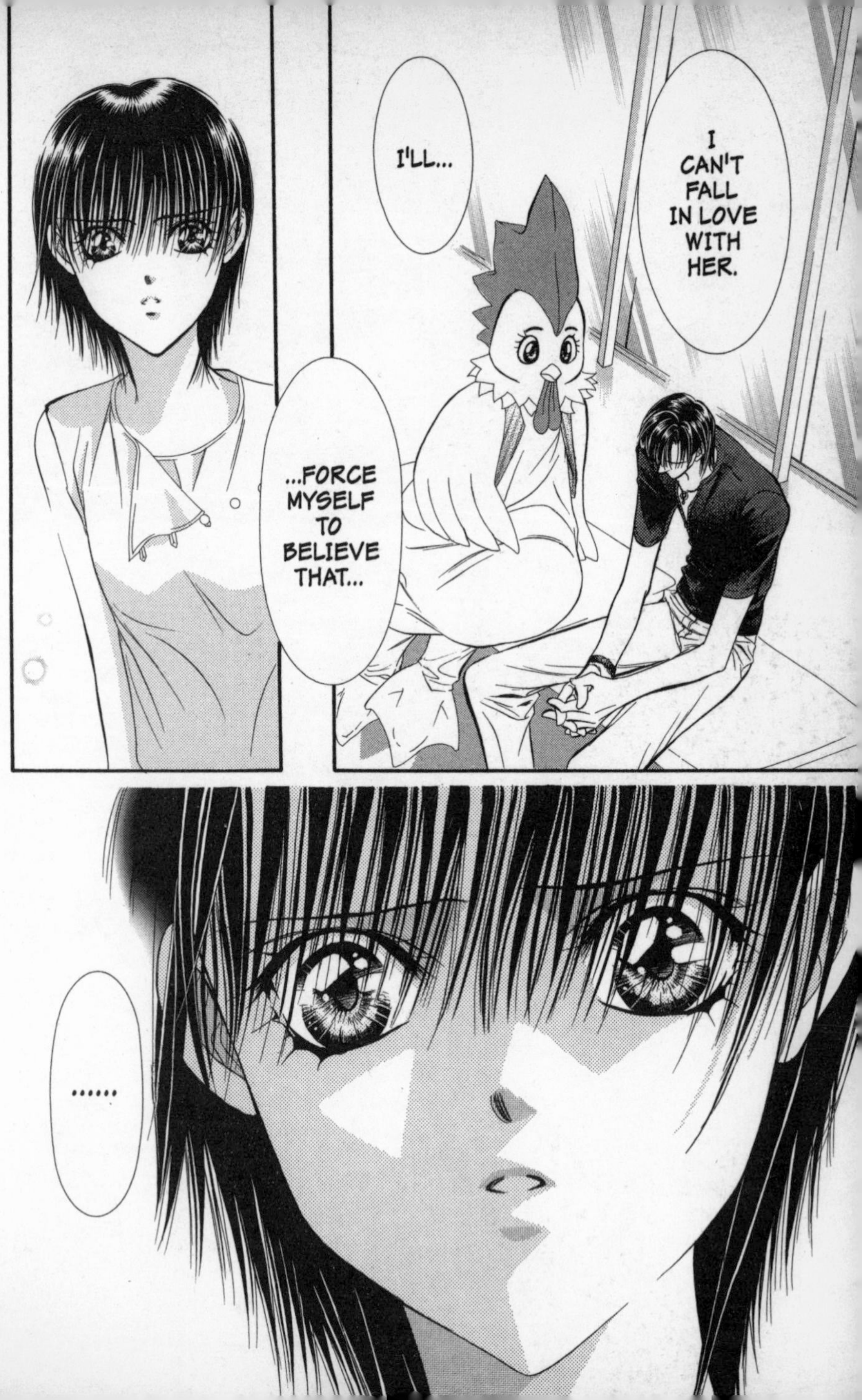
I CAN'T FALL IN LOVE WITH HER.
I'LL...
...FORCE MYSELF TO BELIEVE THAT...
......

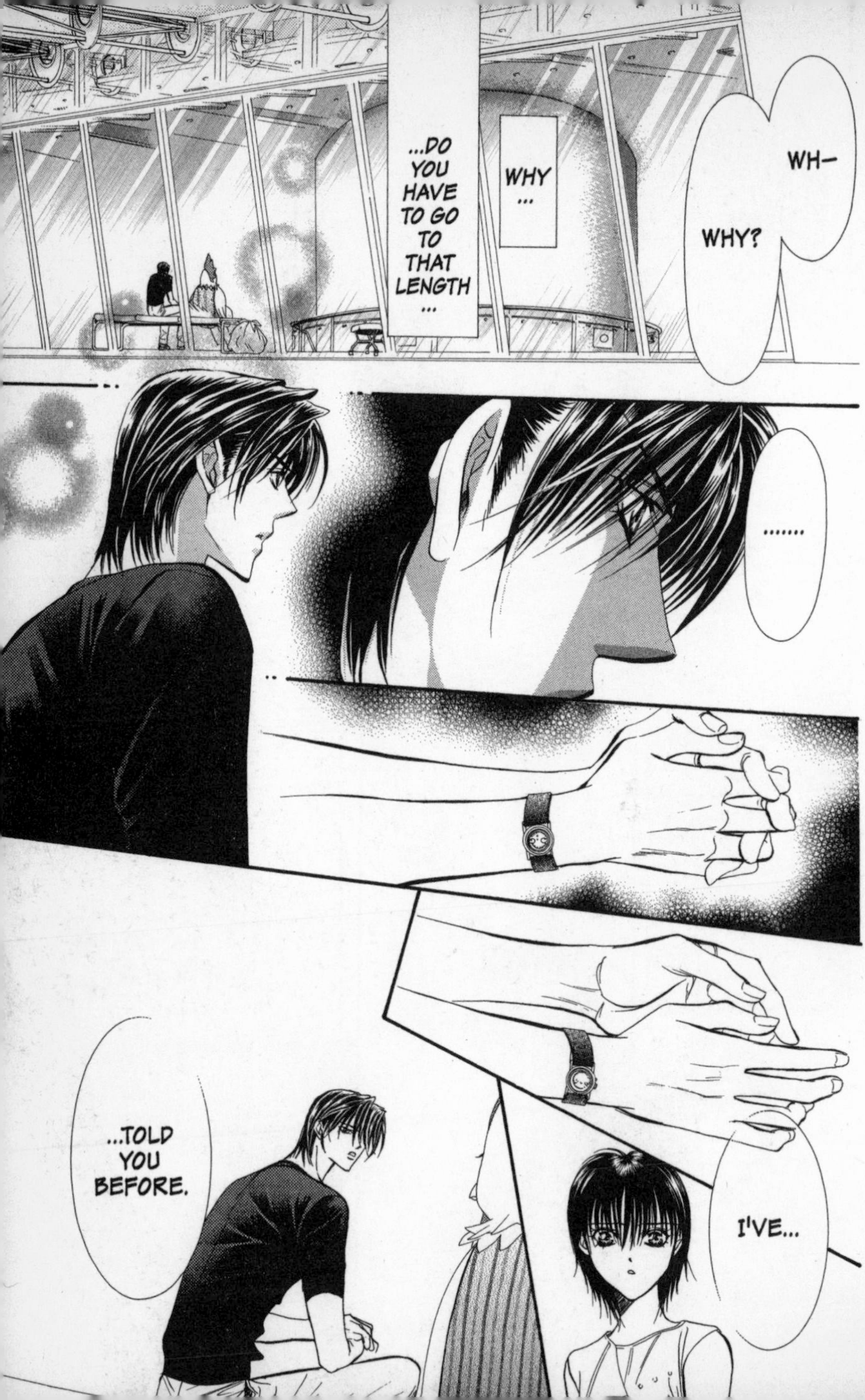
WH— WHY?
WHY ...
...DO YOU HAVE TO GO TO THAT LENGTH ...
....
I'VE...
...TOLD YOU BEFORE.

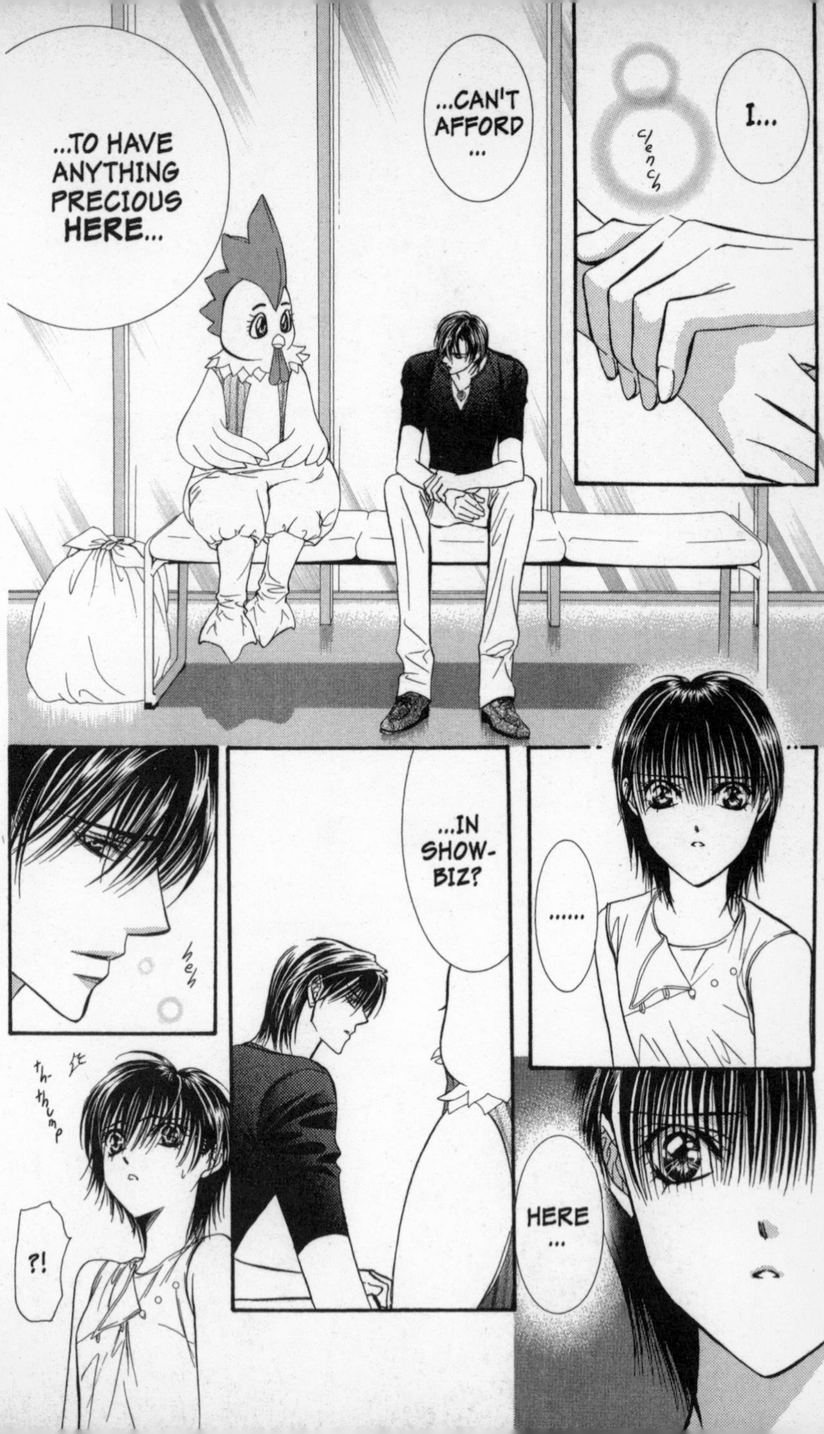
I...
clench
...CAN'T AFFORD ...
...TO HAVE ANYTHING PRECIOUS HERE...
......
...IN SHOW-BIZ?
heh
HERE ...
th-thump
?!

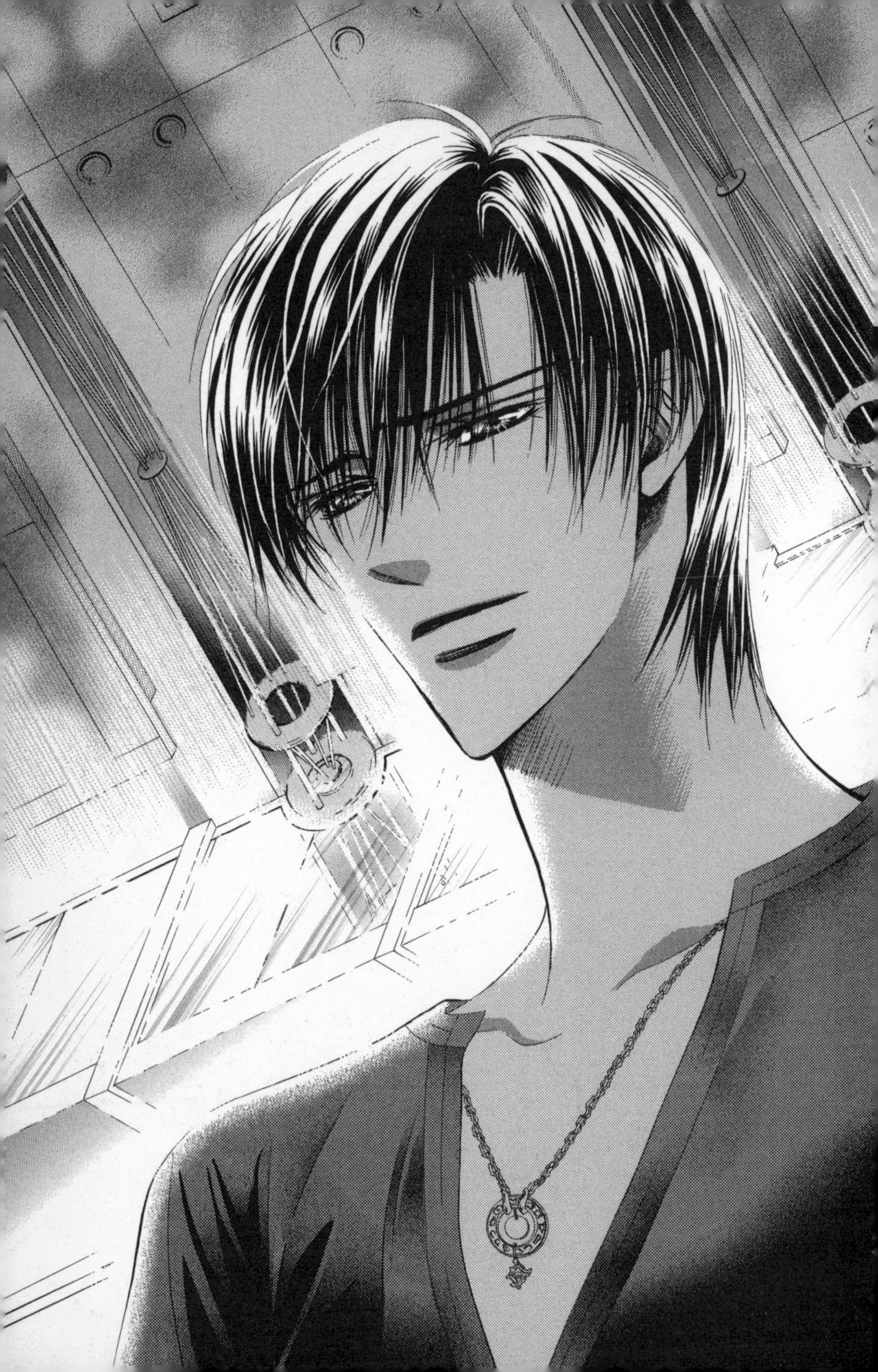

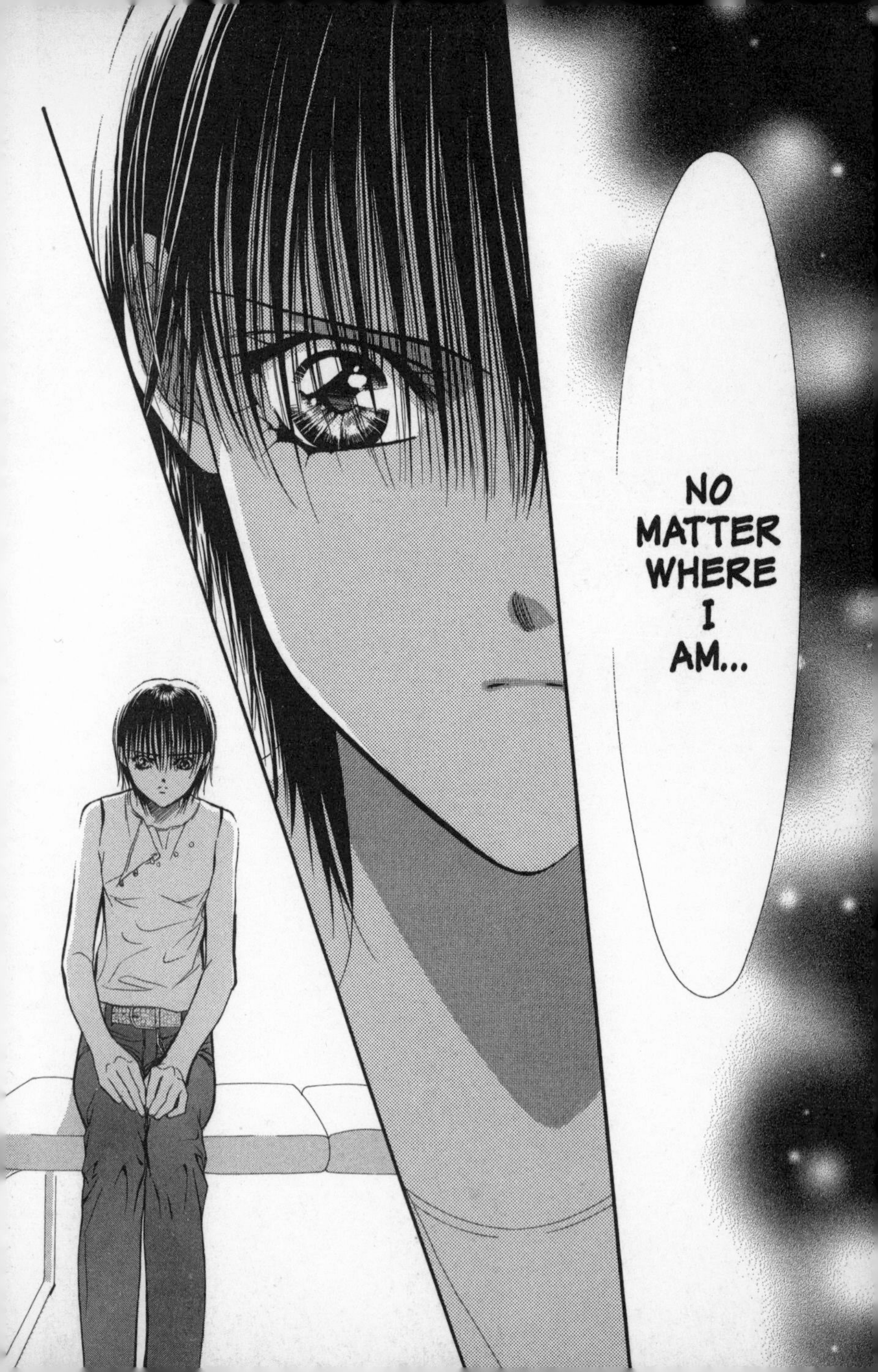
NO MATTER WHERE I AM...

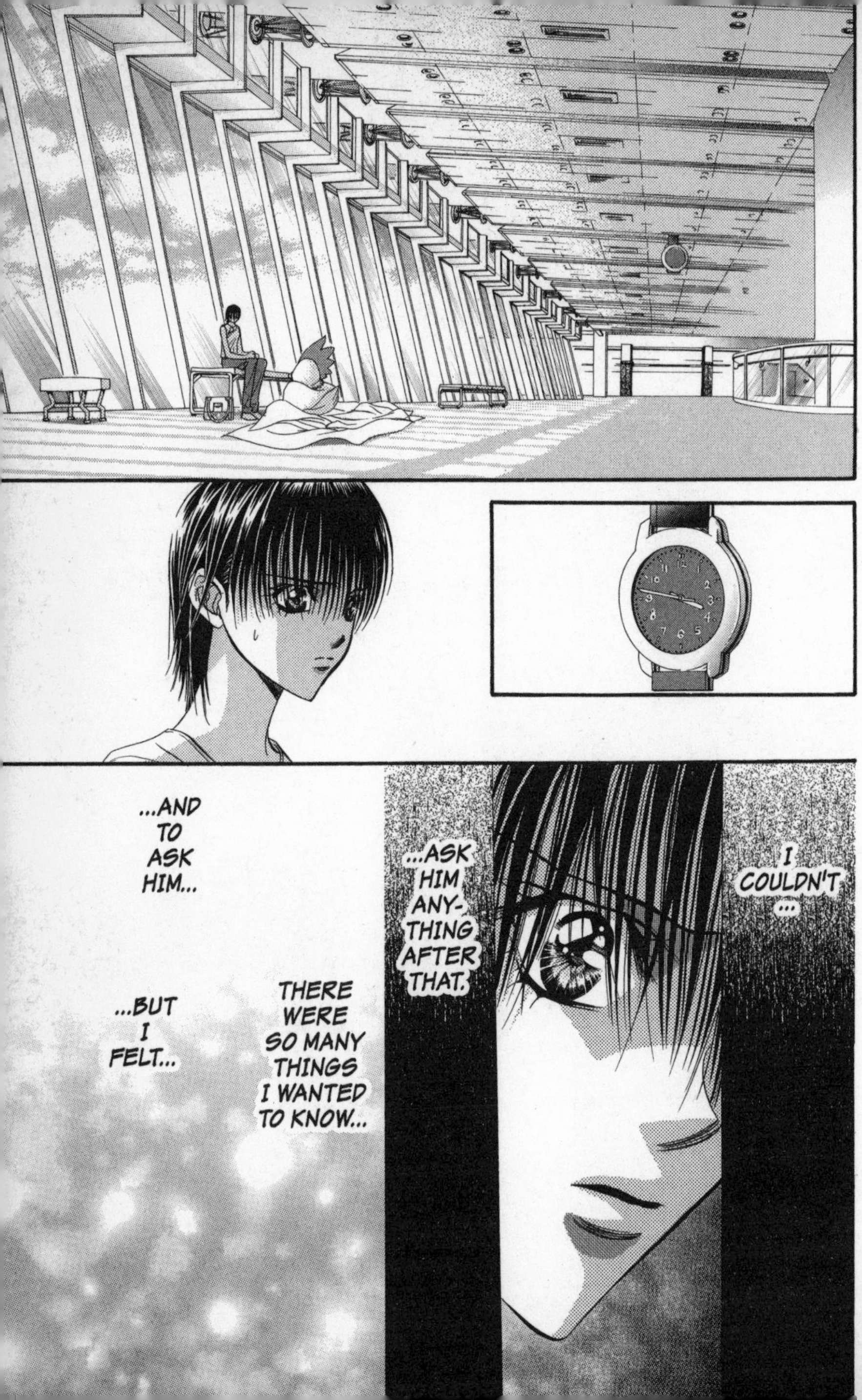
I COULDN'T ...
...ASK HIM ANY-THING AFTER THAT.
THERE WERE SO MANY THINGS I WANTED TO KNOW...
...AND TO ASK HIM...
...BUT I FELT...

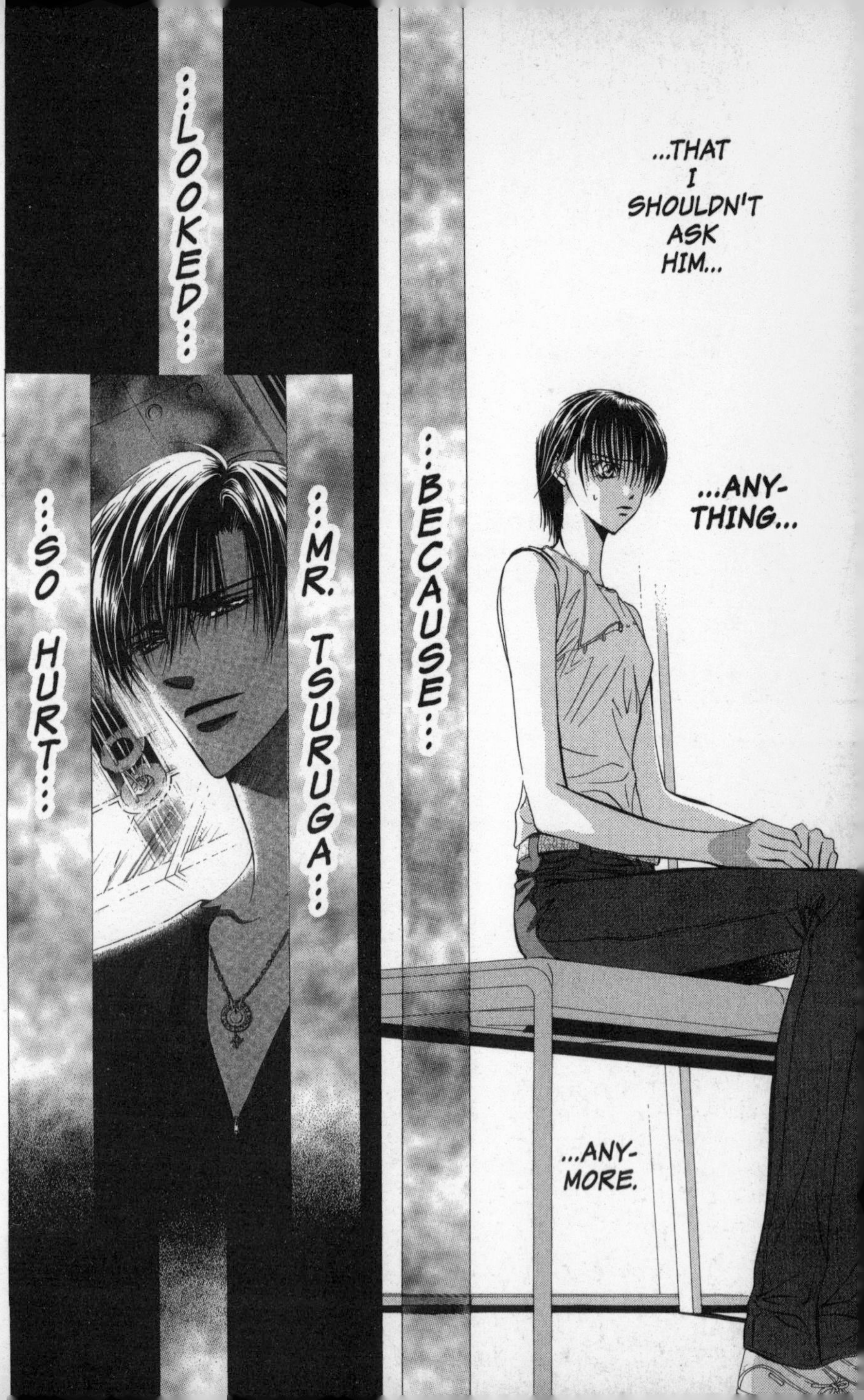
...THAT I SHOULDN'T ASK HIM...
...ANY-THING...
...ANY-MORE.
...BECAUSE...
...MR. TSURUGA...
...LOOKED...
...SO HURT...

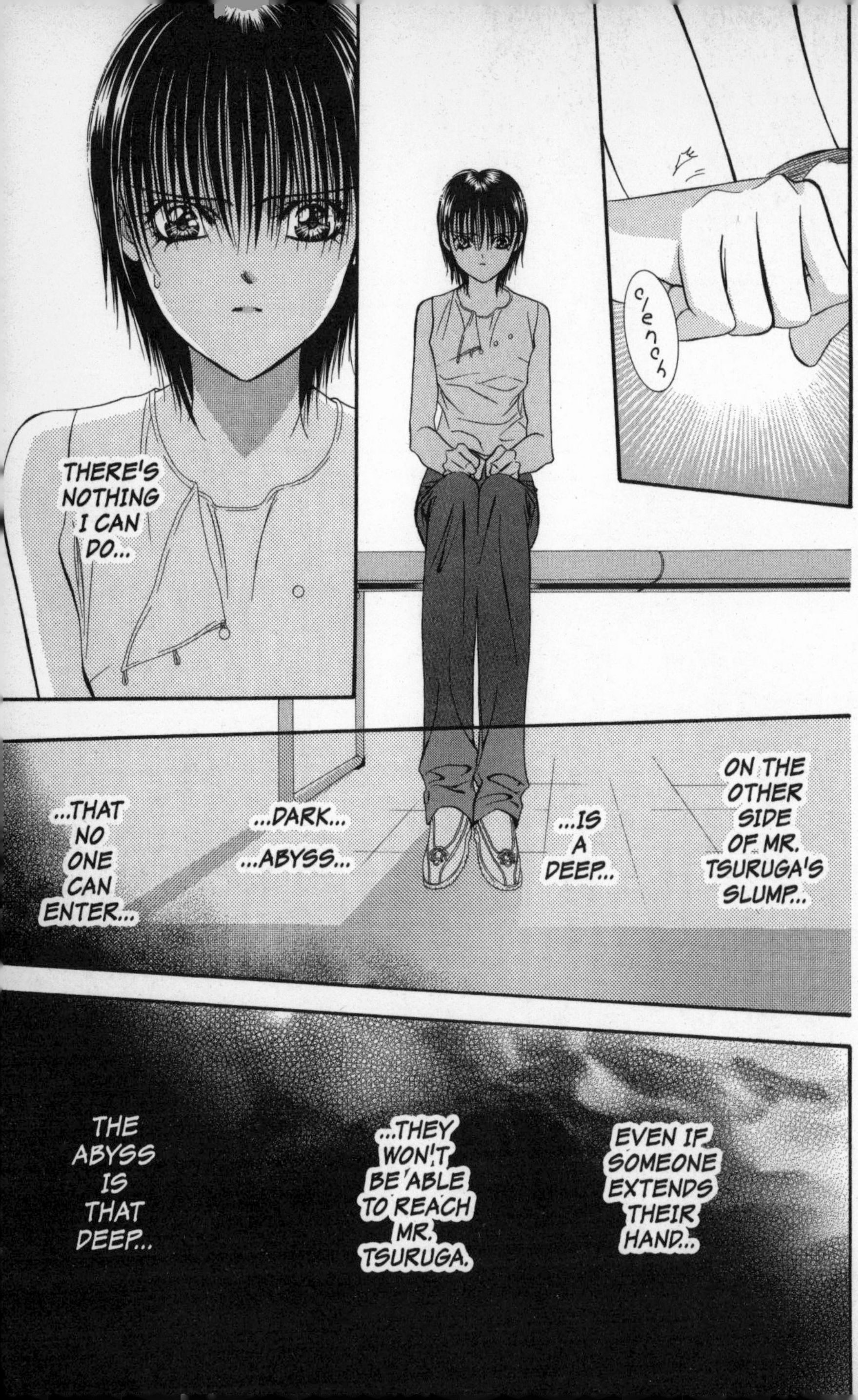
clench
THERE'S NOTHING I CAN DO...
ON THE OTHER SIDE OF MR. TSURUGA'S SLUMP...
...IS A DEEP...
...DARK...
...ABYSS...
...THAT NO ONE CAN ENTER...
EVEN IF SOMEONE EXTENDS THEIR HAND...
...THEY WON'T BE ABLE TO REACH MR. TSURUGA.
THE ABYSS IS THAT DEEP...

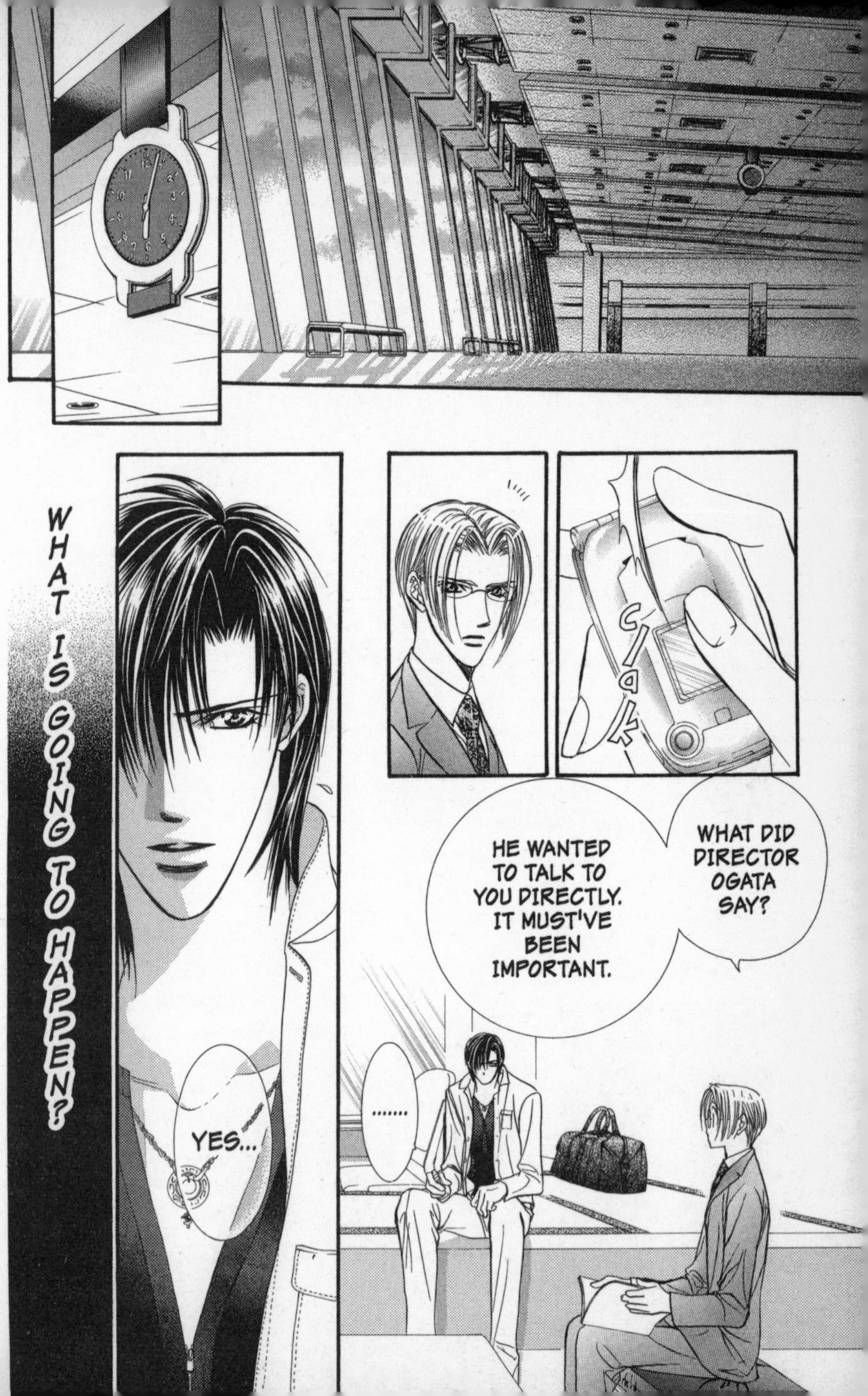
CLAK
WHAT DID DIRECTOR OGATA SAY?
HE WANTED TO TALK TO YOU DIRECTLY. IT MUST'VE BEEN IMPORTANT.
....
YES...
WHAT IS GOING TO HAPPEN?

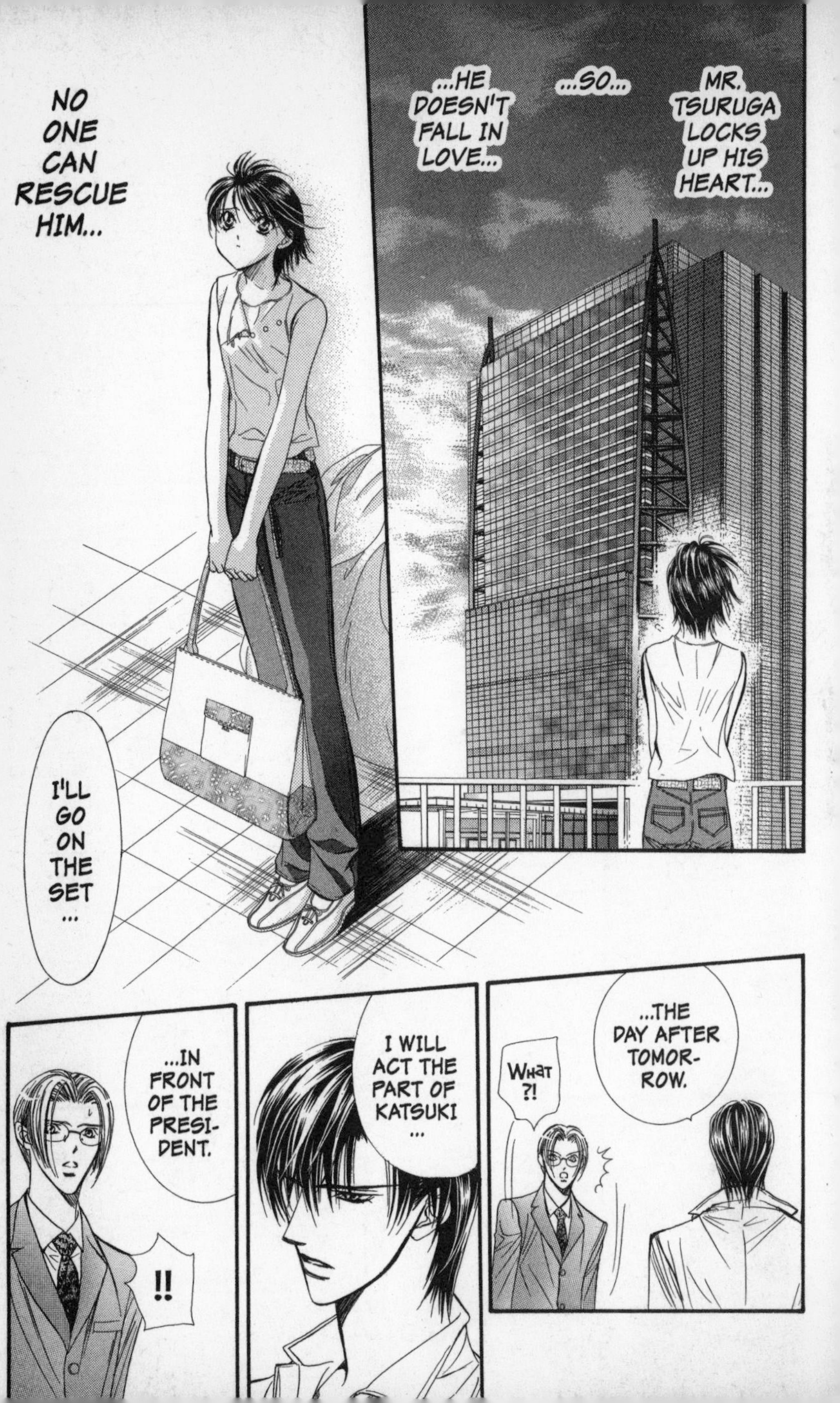
MR. TSURUGA LOCKS UP HIS HEART...
...SO...
...HE DOESN'T FALL IN LOVE...
NO ONE CAN RESCUE HIM...
I'LL GO ON THE SET ...
...THE DAY AFTER TOMOR-ROW.
WHAT ?!
I WILL ACT THE PART OF KATSUKI ...
...IN FRONT OF THE PRESI-DENT.
!!

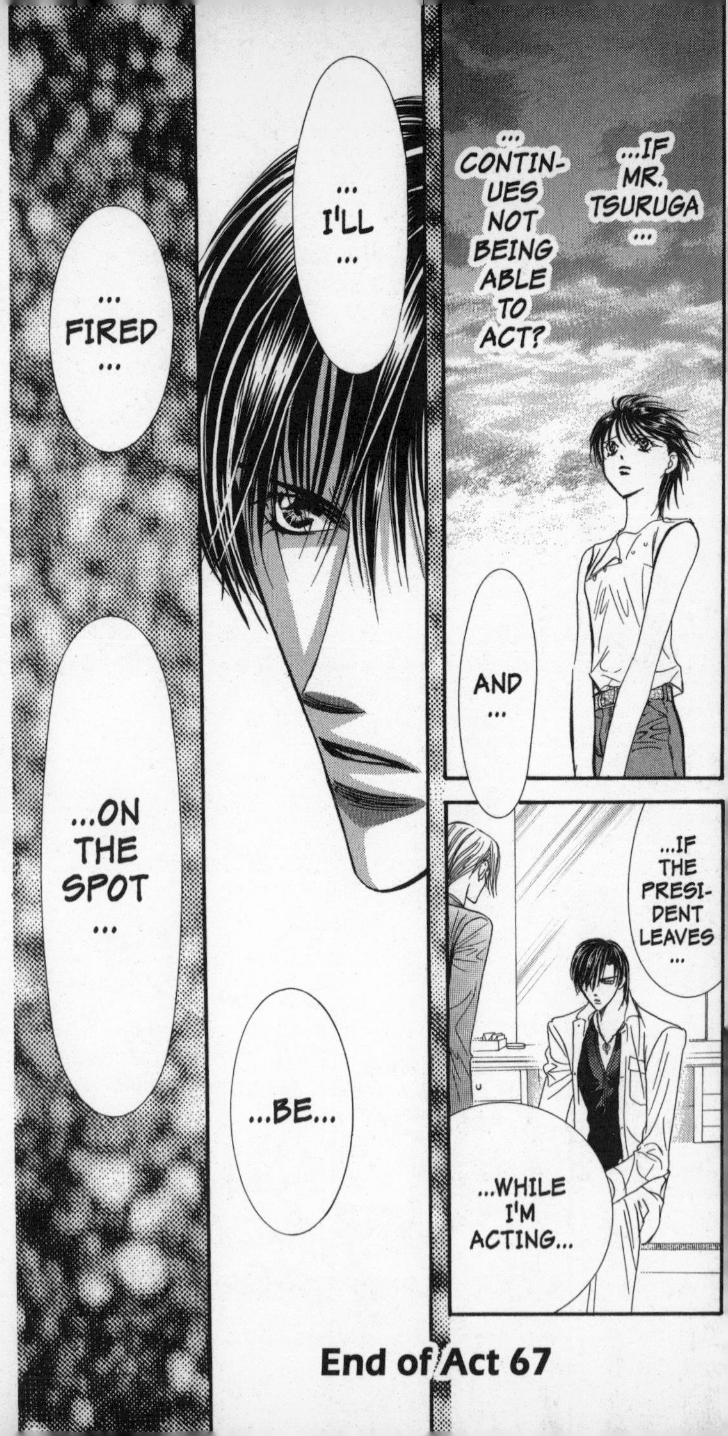
...IF MR. TSURUGA...
...CONTINUES NOT BEING ABLE TO ACT?
AND...
...IF THE PRESIDENT LEAVES...
...WHILE I'M ACTING...
...I'LL...
...BE...
...FIRED...
...ON THE SPOT...

End of Act 67

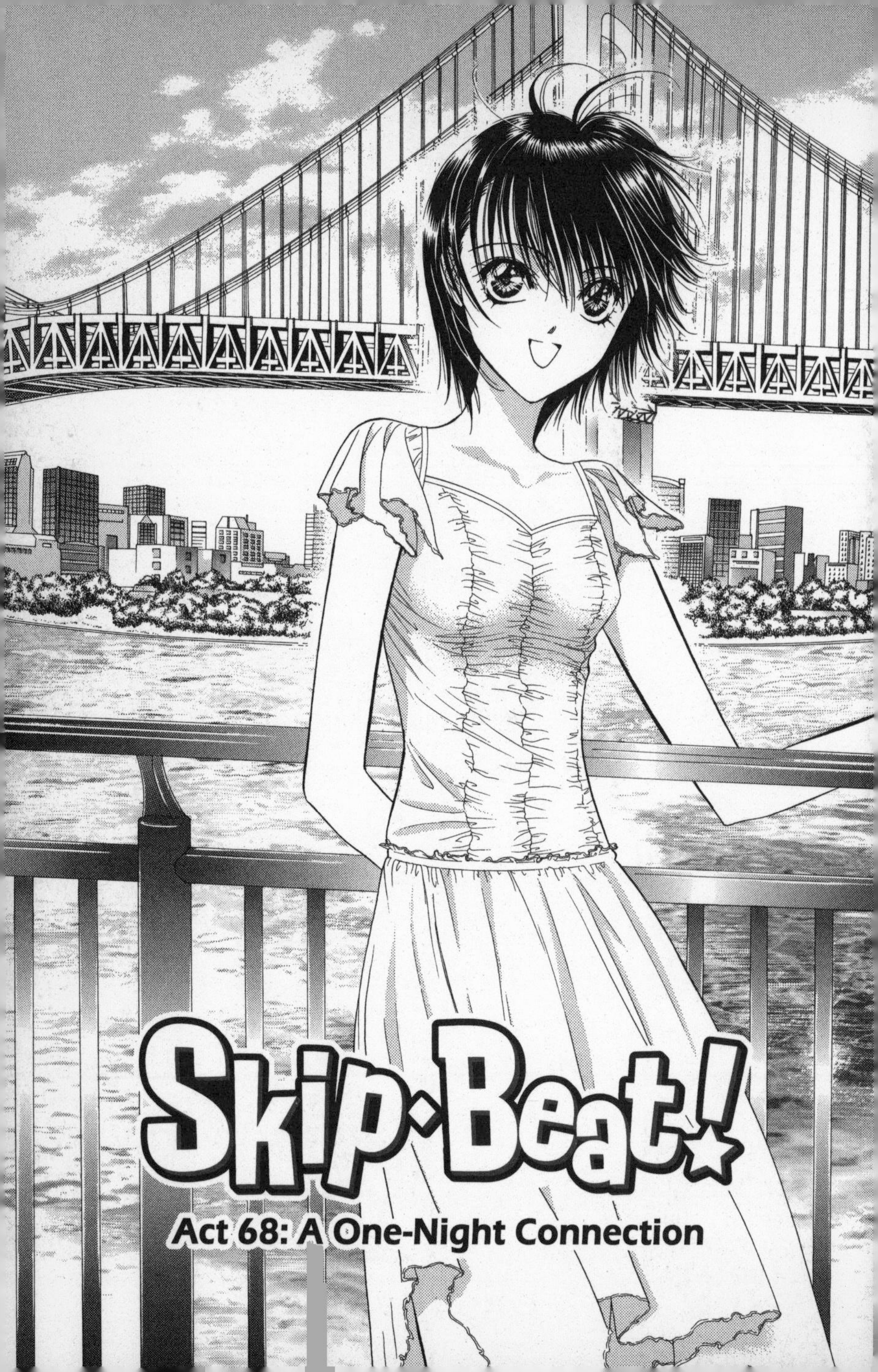
Skip·Beat!
Act 68: A One-Night Connection

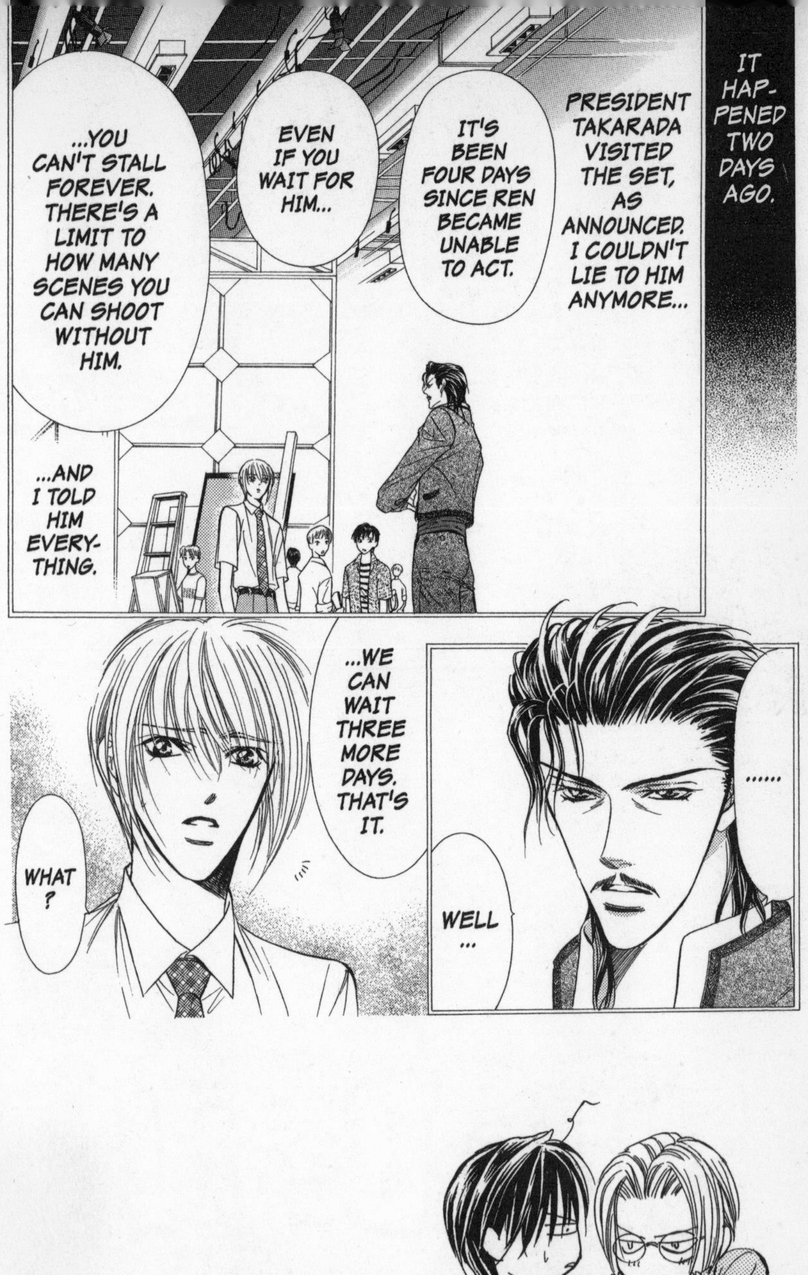
IT HAPPENED TWO DAYS AGO.
PRESIDENT TAKARADA VISITED THE SET, AS ANNOUNCED. I COULDN'T LIE TO HIM ANYMORE...
IT'S BEEN FOUR DAYS SINCE REN BECAME UNABLE TO ACT.
EVEN IF YOU WAIT FOR HIM...
...YOU CAN'T STALL FOREVER. THERE'S A LIMIT TO HOW MANY SCENES YOU CAN SHOOT WITHOUT HIM.
...AND I TOLD HIM EVERYTHING.
......
WELL ...
...WE CAN WAIT THREE MORE DAYS. THAT'S IT.
WHAT ?

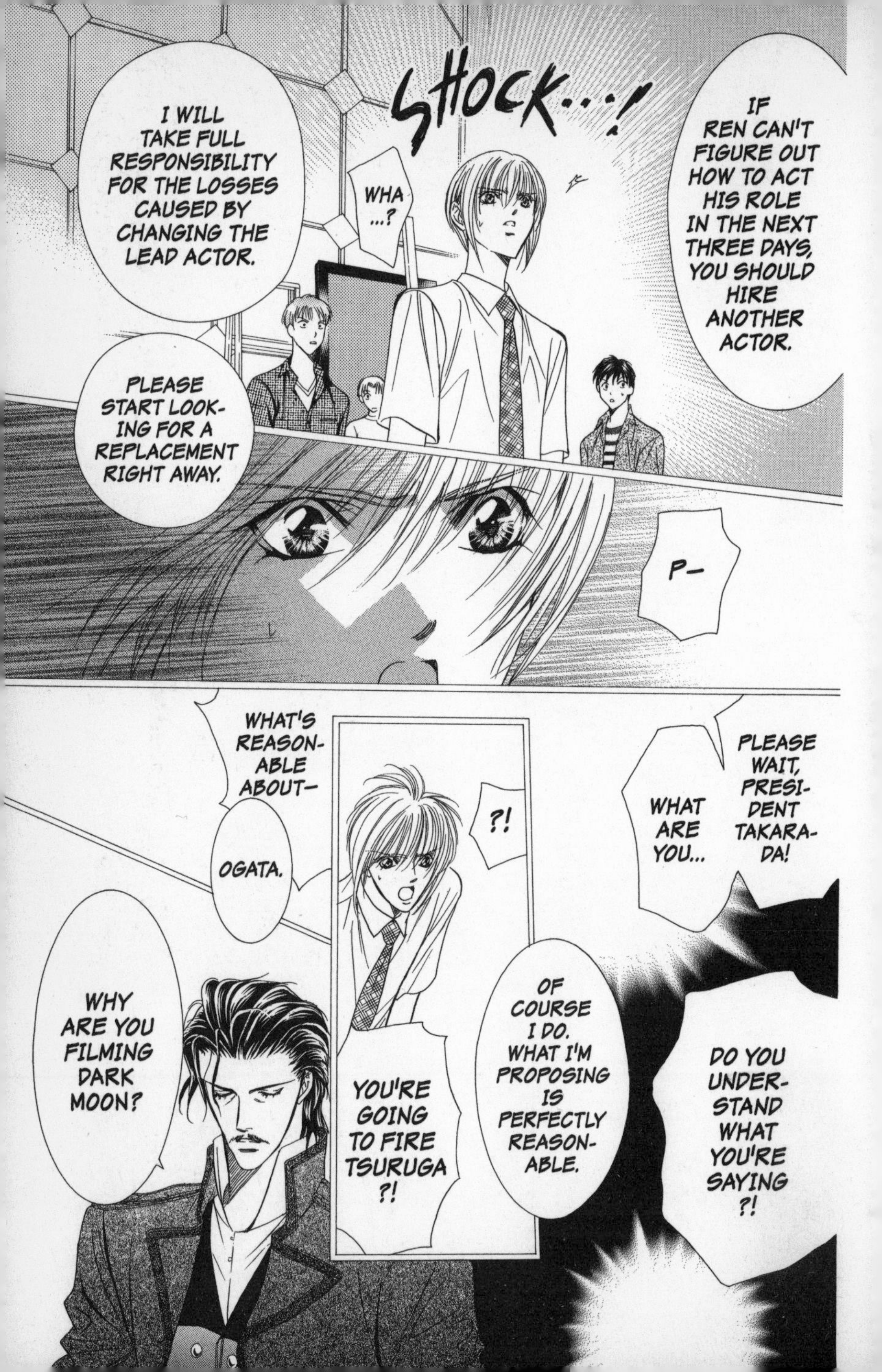
IF REN CAN'T FIGURE OUT HOW TO ACT HIS ROLE IN THE NEXT THREE DAYS, YOU SHOULD HIRE ANOTHER ACTOR.
SHOCK...!
WHA ...?
I WILL TAKE FULL RESPONSIBILITY FOR THE LOSSES CAUSED BY CHANGING THE LEAD ACTOR.
PLEASE START LOOK-ING FOR A REPLACEMENT RIGHT AWAY.
P–
PLEASE WAIT, PRESI-DENT TAKARA-DA!
WHAT ARE YOU...
?!
WHAT'S REASON-ABLE ABOUT–
OGATA.
DO YOU UNDER-STAND WHAT YOU'RE SAYING ?!
OF COURSE I DO. WHAT I'M PROPOSING IS PERFECTLY REASON-ABLE.
YOU'RE GOING TO FIRE TSURUGA ?!
WHY ARE YOU FILMING DARK MOON?

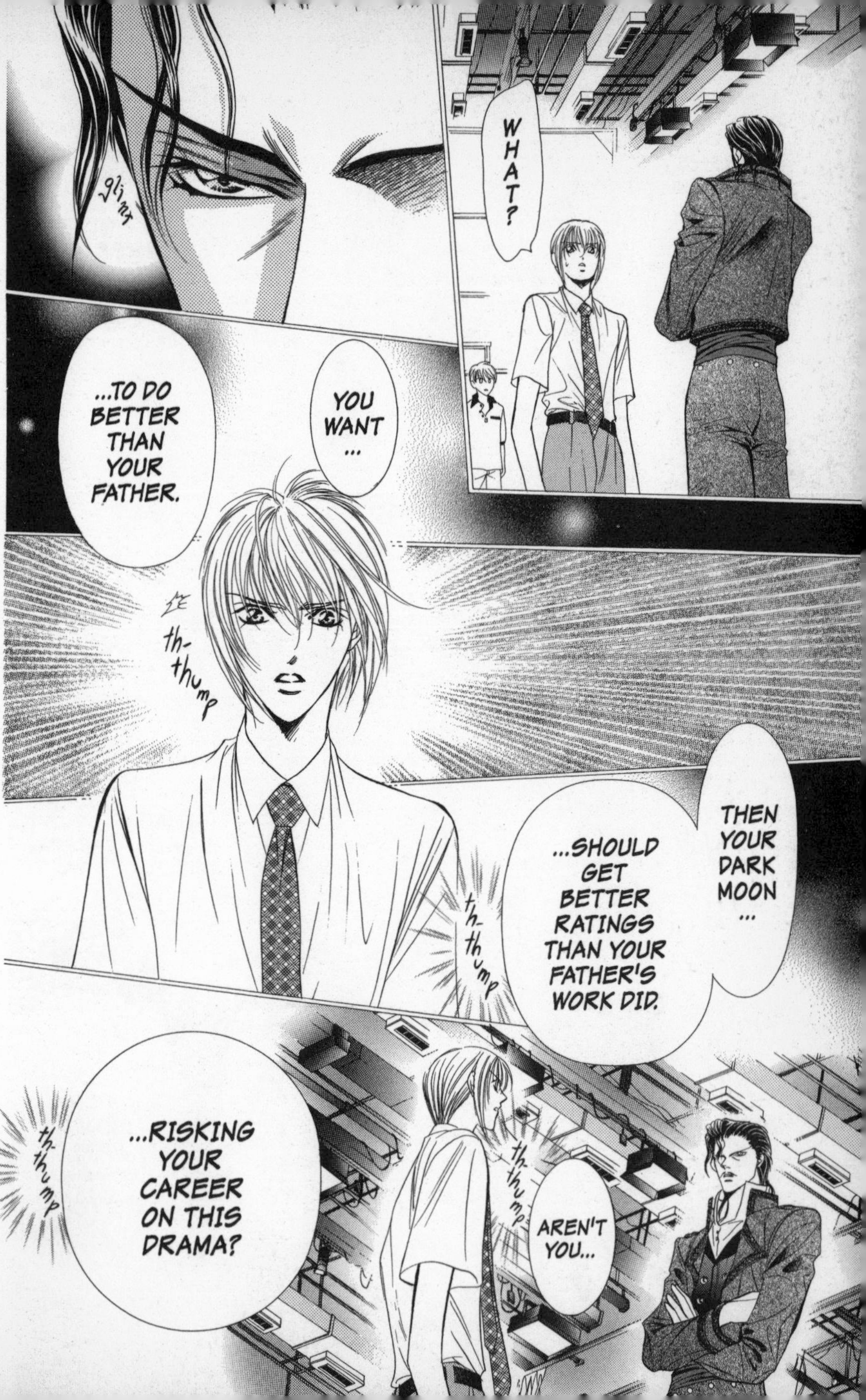
WHAT?
glint
YOU WANT...
...TO DO BETTER THAN YOUR FATHER.
th-thump
THEN YOUR DARK MOON...
...SHOULD GET BETTER RATINGS THAN YOUR FATHER'S WORK DID.
th-thump
AREN'T YOU...
th-thump
...RISKING YOUR CAREER ON THIS DRAMA?
th-thump

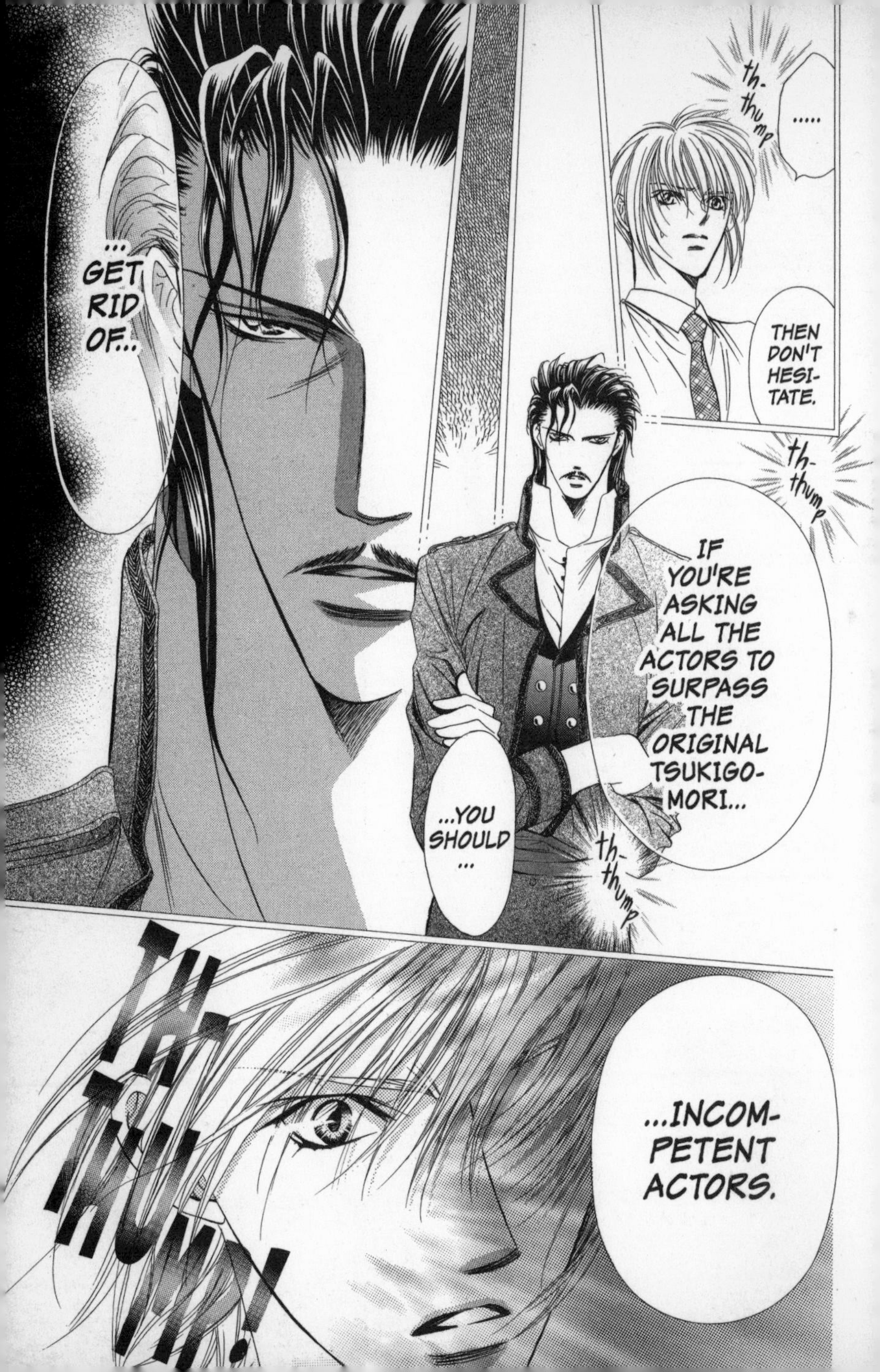
th-thump
.....
THEN DON'T HESITATE.
th-thump
IF YOU'RE ASKING ALL THE ACTORS TO SURPASS THE ORIGINAL TSUKIGO-MORI...
...YOU SHOULD ...
th-thump
... GET RID OF...
...INCOM-PETENT ACTORS.

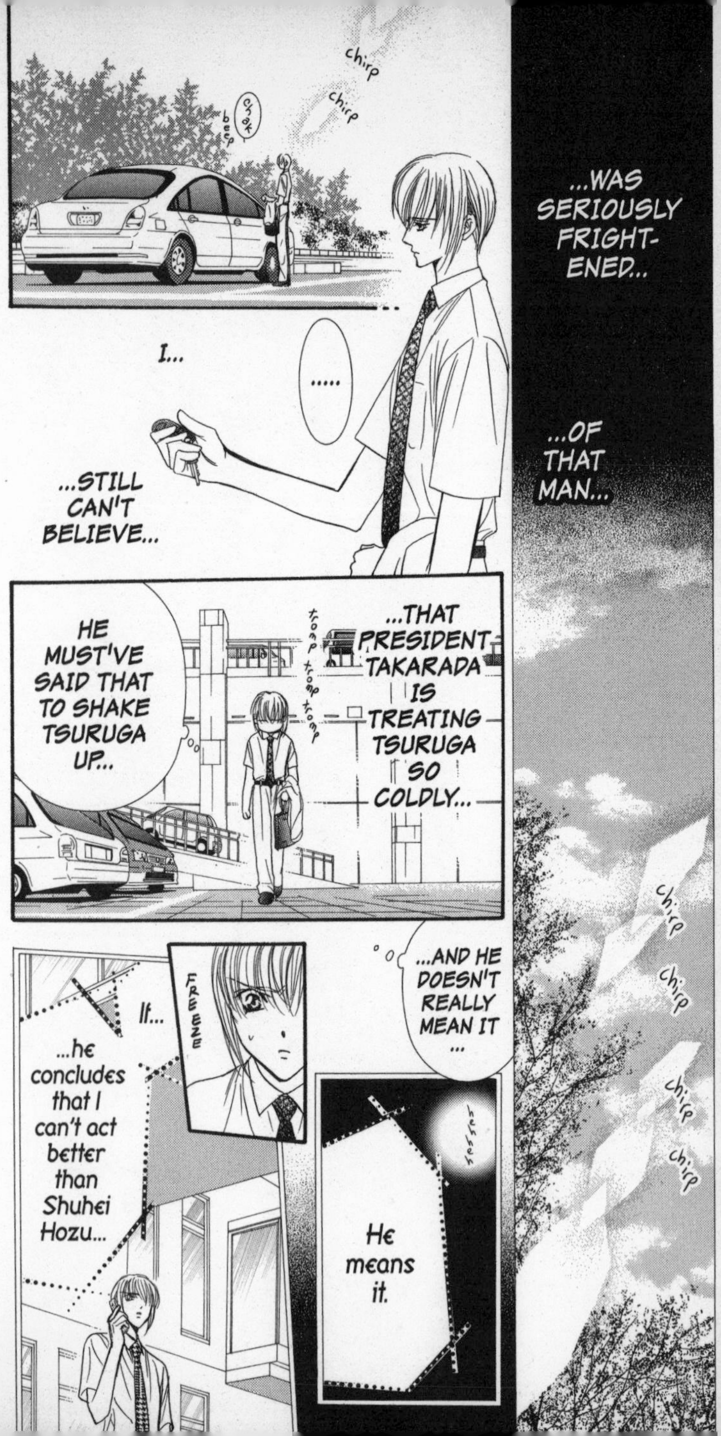

...WAS SERIOUSLY FRIGHT-ENED...
...OF THAT MAN...
chirp
chirp
chirp
chirp
chirp
chirp
chak
beep
I...
.....
...STILL CAN'T BELIEVE...
...THAT PRESIDENT TAKARADA IS TREATING TSURUGA SO COLDLY...
tromp tromp tromp
HE MUST'VE SAID THAT TO SHAKE TSURUGA UP...
...AND HE DOESN'T REALLY MEAN IT...
FREEZE
If...
...he concludes that I can't act better than Shuhei Hozu...
heh heh
He means it.

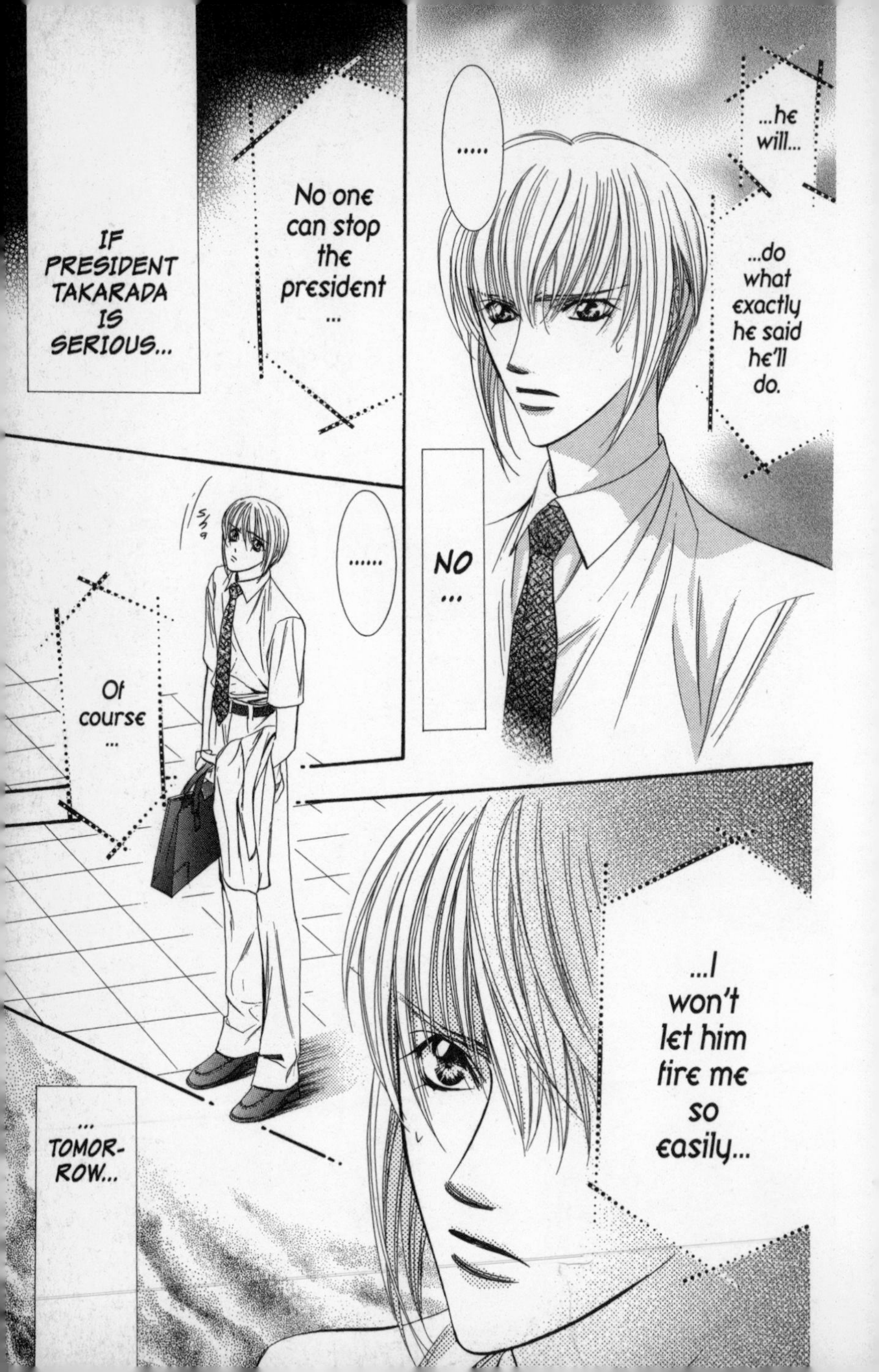
.....
...he will...
...do what exactly he said he'll do.
NO ...
IF PRESIDENT TAKARADA IS SERIOUS...
No one can stop the president ...
......
Of course ...
... TOMORROW...
...I won't let him fire me so easily...

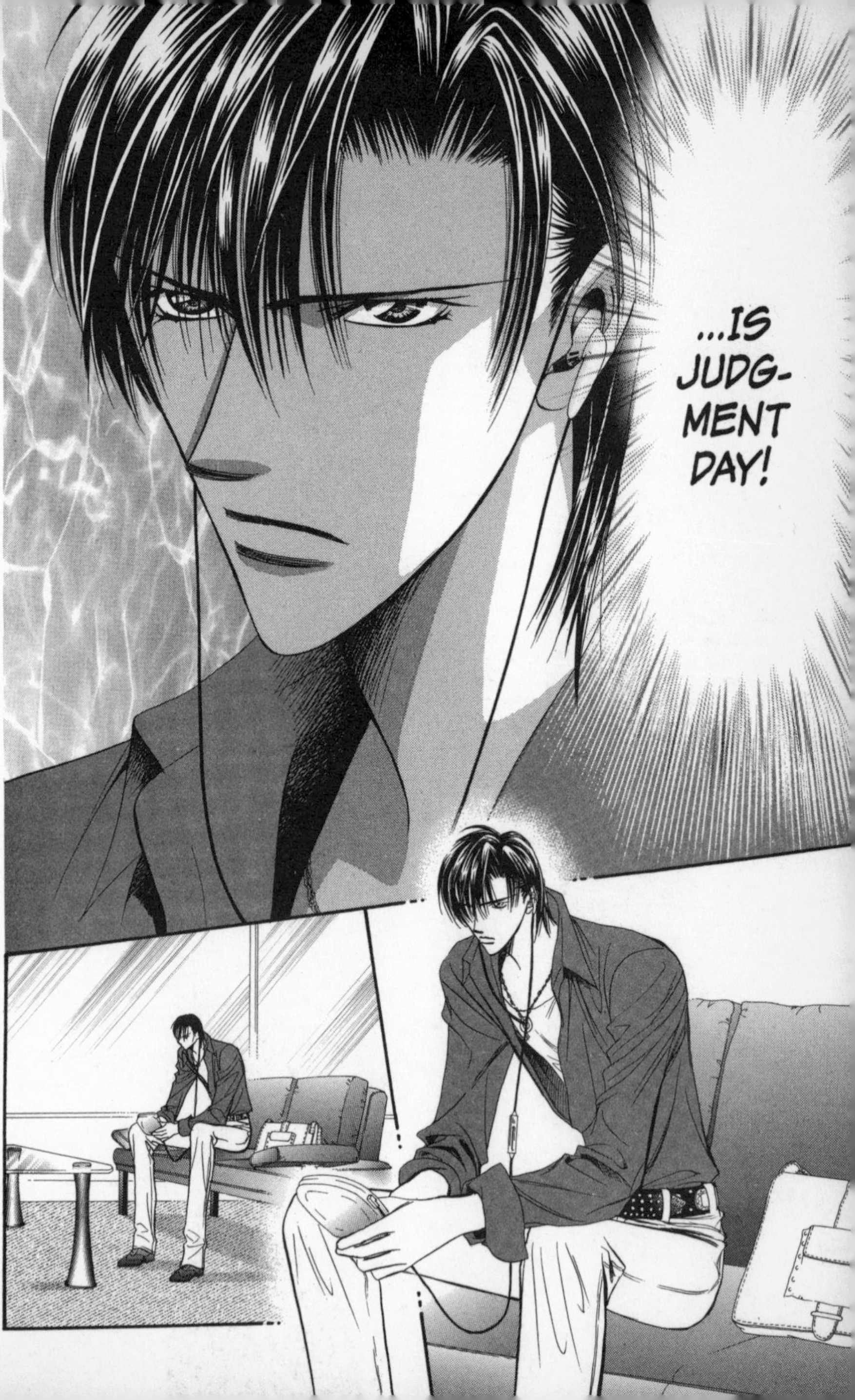
...IS JUDGMENT DAY!

The Truth Was...

So anyway, I could not make Ren's story progress as fast as I wanted to. As a result, the Tsukigomori arc itself seemed drawn out, and to tell the truth, I wanted to give up while working on it...

I was driven into a corner. So...I thought of removing the episode about Kyoko and Ren rehearsing Dark Moon at Ren's place. And I'd planned to include this episode when I started the Tsukigomori arc... Yes...I was going to remove it entirely... ...no...all I wanted to do was to just get the story moving... when I was working on my storyboards, I told my editor "I think I won't draw the Dark Moon rehearsal scene." And I worked on some storyboards where Ren gets to understand Katsuki's feelings without having to rehearse Dark Moon...but...it was boring... I just wasted time working on storyboards that never got used...

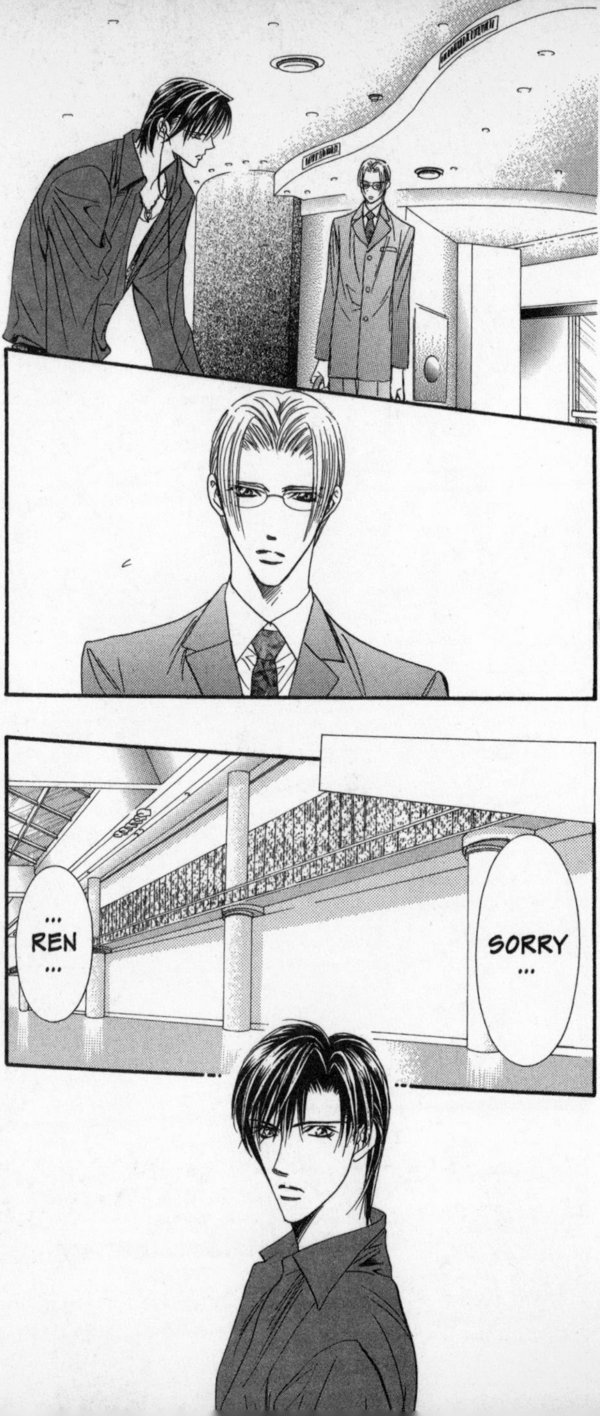
SORRY...
...REN...

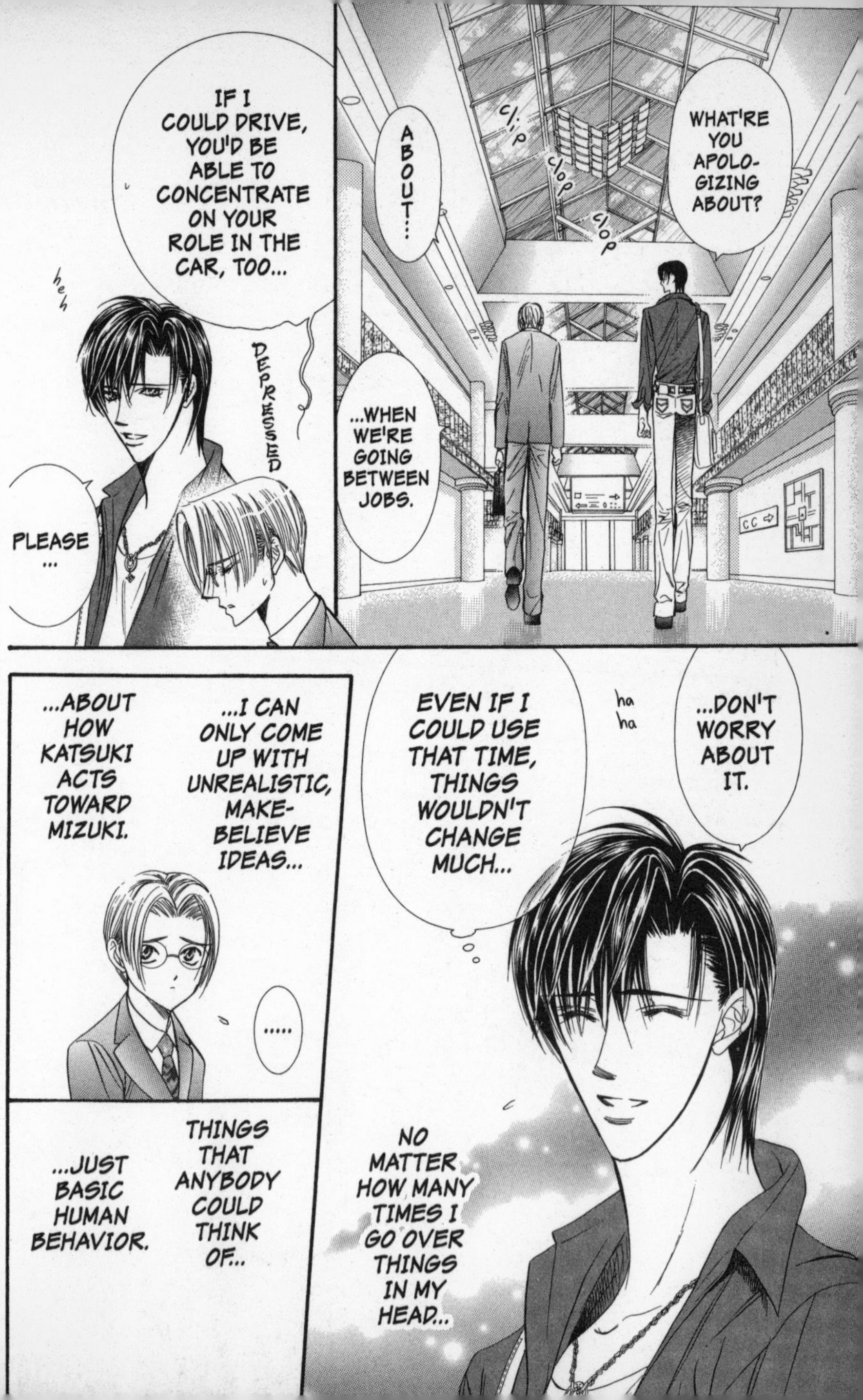
WHAT'RE YOU APOLOGIZING ABOUT?
clip
clop
clop
ABOUT...
...WHEN WE'RE GOING BETWEEN JOBS.
IF I COULD DRIVE, YOU'D BE ABLE TO CONCENTRATE ON YOUR ROLE IN THE CAR, TOO...
heh
DEPRESSED
PLEASE...
...DON'T WORRY ABOUT IT.
ha ha
EVEN IF I COULD USE THAT TIME, THINGS WOULDN'T CHANGE MUCH...
NO MATTER HOW MANY TIMES I GO OVER THINGS IN MY HEAD...
...I CAN ONLY COME UP WITH UNREALISTIC, MAKE-BELIEVE IDEAS...
...ABOUT HOW KATSUKI ACTS TOWARD MIZUKI.
......
THINGS THAT ANYBODY COULD THINK OF...
...JUST BASIC HUMAN BEHAVIOR.

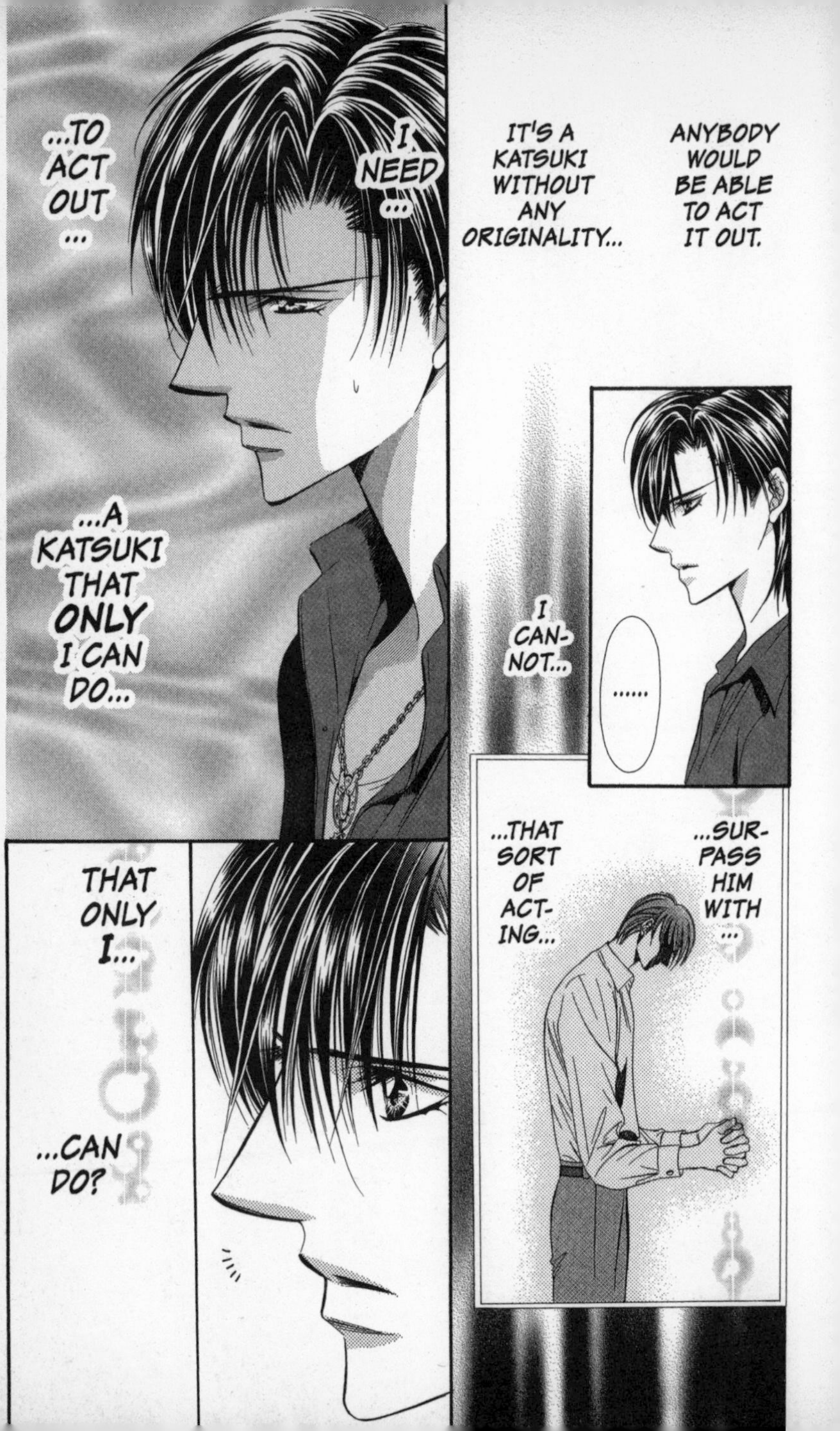
ANYBODY WOULD BE ABLE TO ACT IT OUT.
IT'S A KATSUKI WITHOUT ANY ORIGINALITY...
......
I CAN-NOT...
...SUR-PASS HIM WITH...
...THAT SORT OF ACT-ING...
I NEED...
...TO ACT OUT...
...A KATSUKI THAT ONLY I CAN DO...
THAT ONLY I...
...CAN DO?

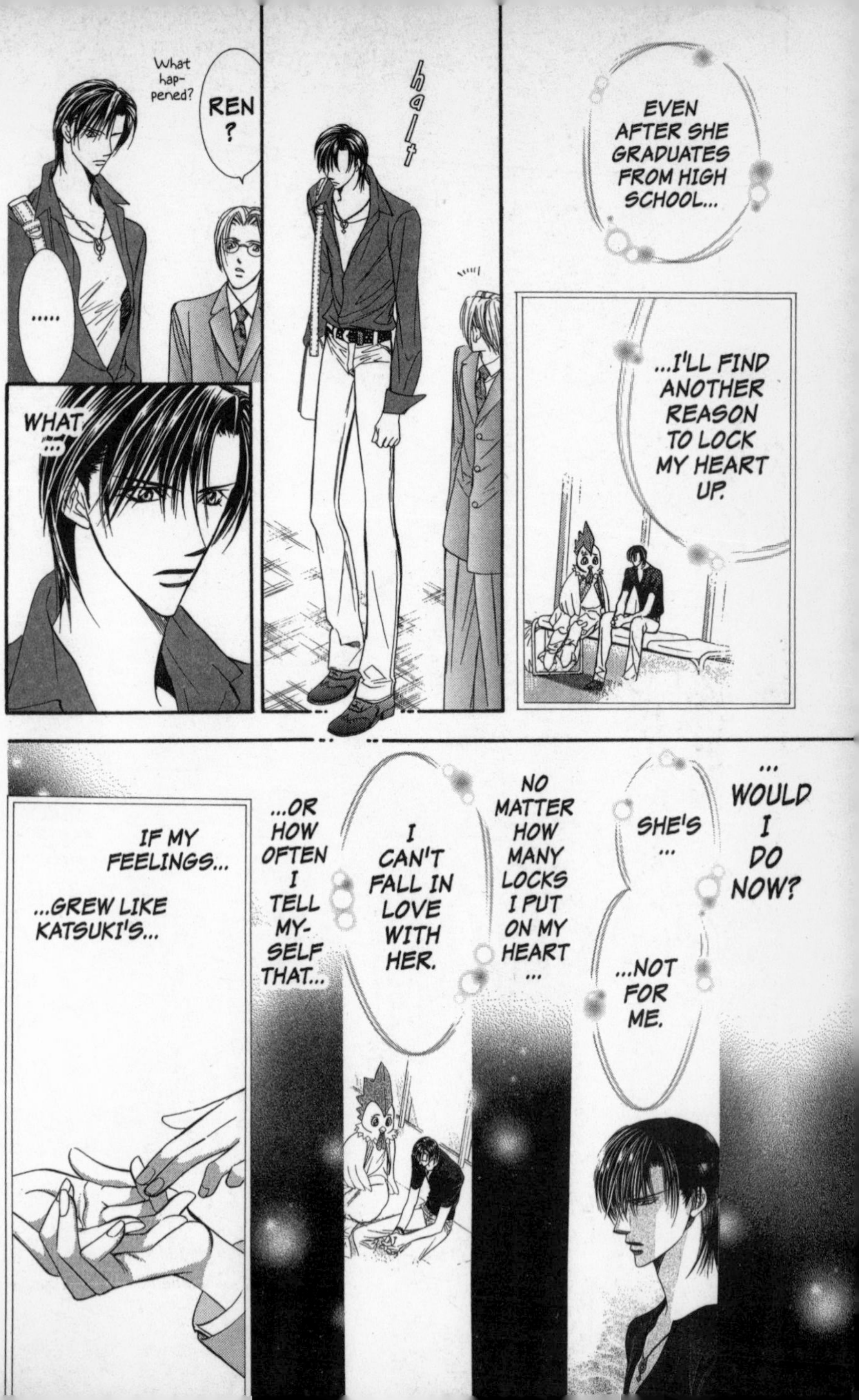
EVEN AFTER SHE GRADUATES FROM HIGH SCHOOL...
...I'LL FIND ANOTHER REASON TO LOCK MY HEART UP.
halt
What happened?
REN?
.....
WHAT ...
... WOULD I DO NOW?
SHE'S ...
...NOT FOR ME.
NO MATTER HOW MANY LOCKS I PUT ON MY HEART ...
I CAN'T FALL IN LOVE WITH HER.
...OR HOW OFTEN I TELL MY-SELF THAT...
IF MY FEELINGS...
...GREW LIKE KATSUKI'S...

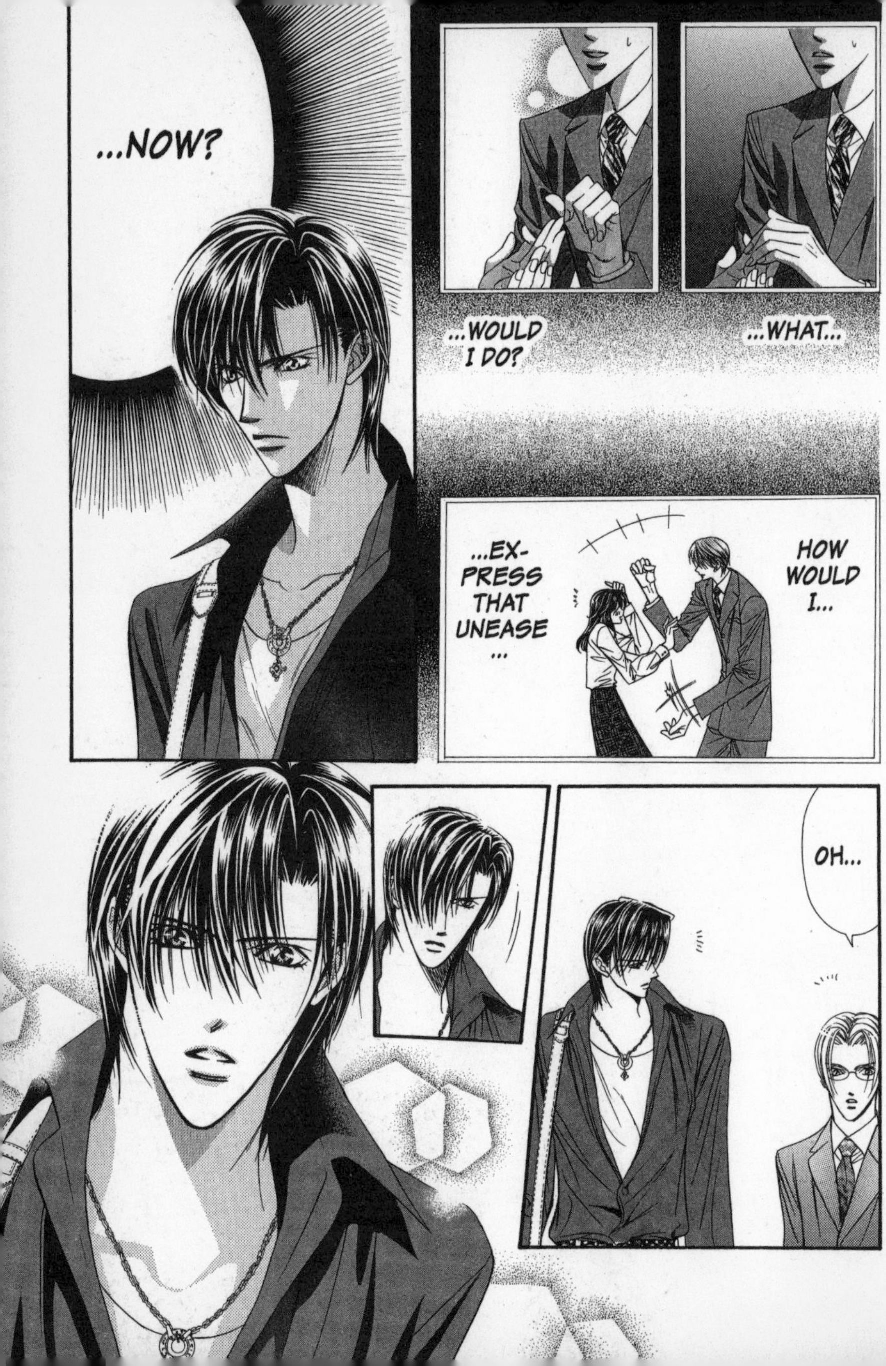
...WHAT...
...WOULD I DO?
HOW WOULD I...
...EX-PRESS THAT UNEASE ...
...NOW?
OH...

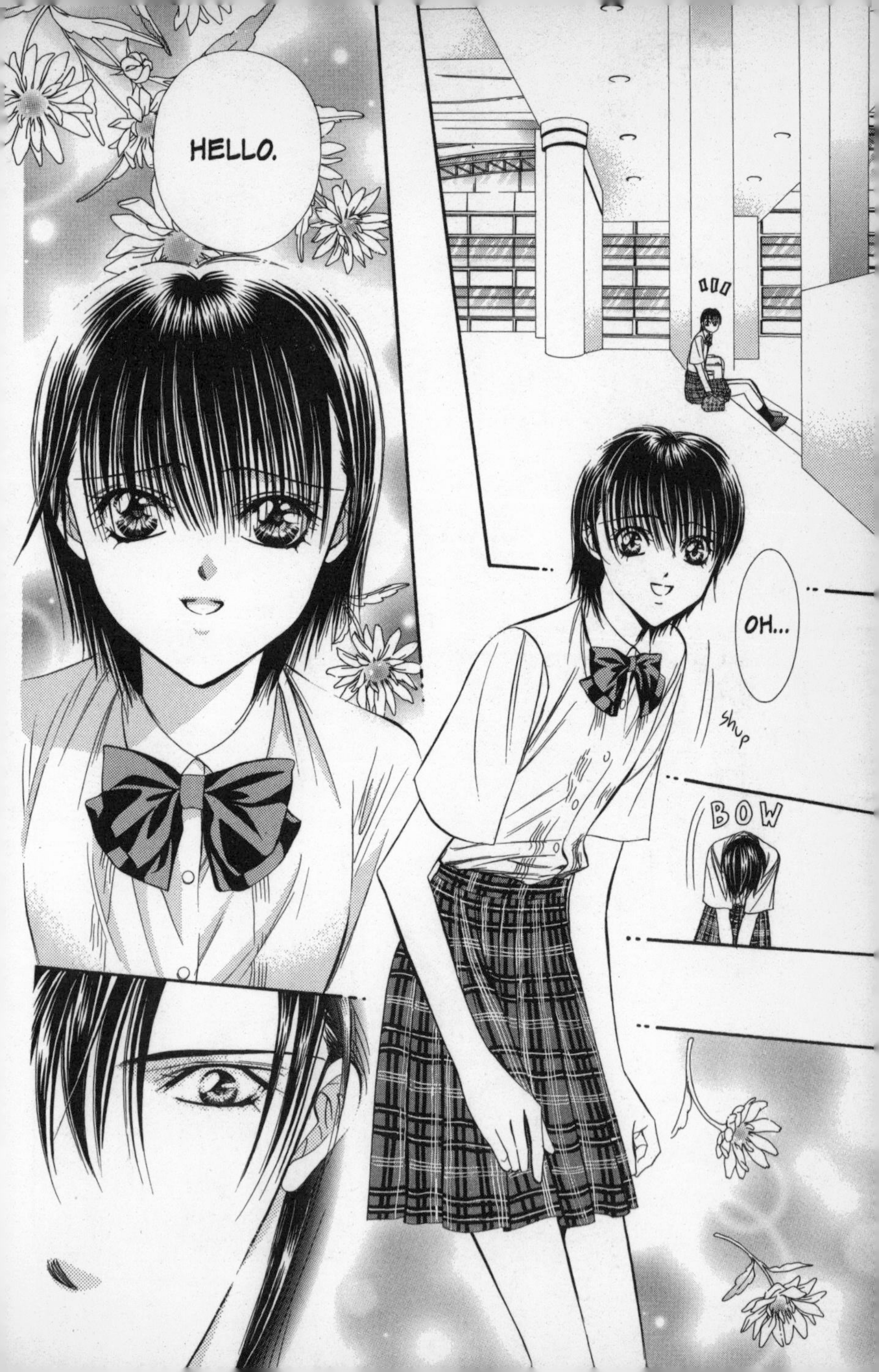
OH...
shup
BOW
HELLO.

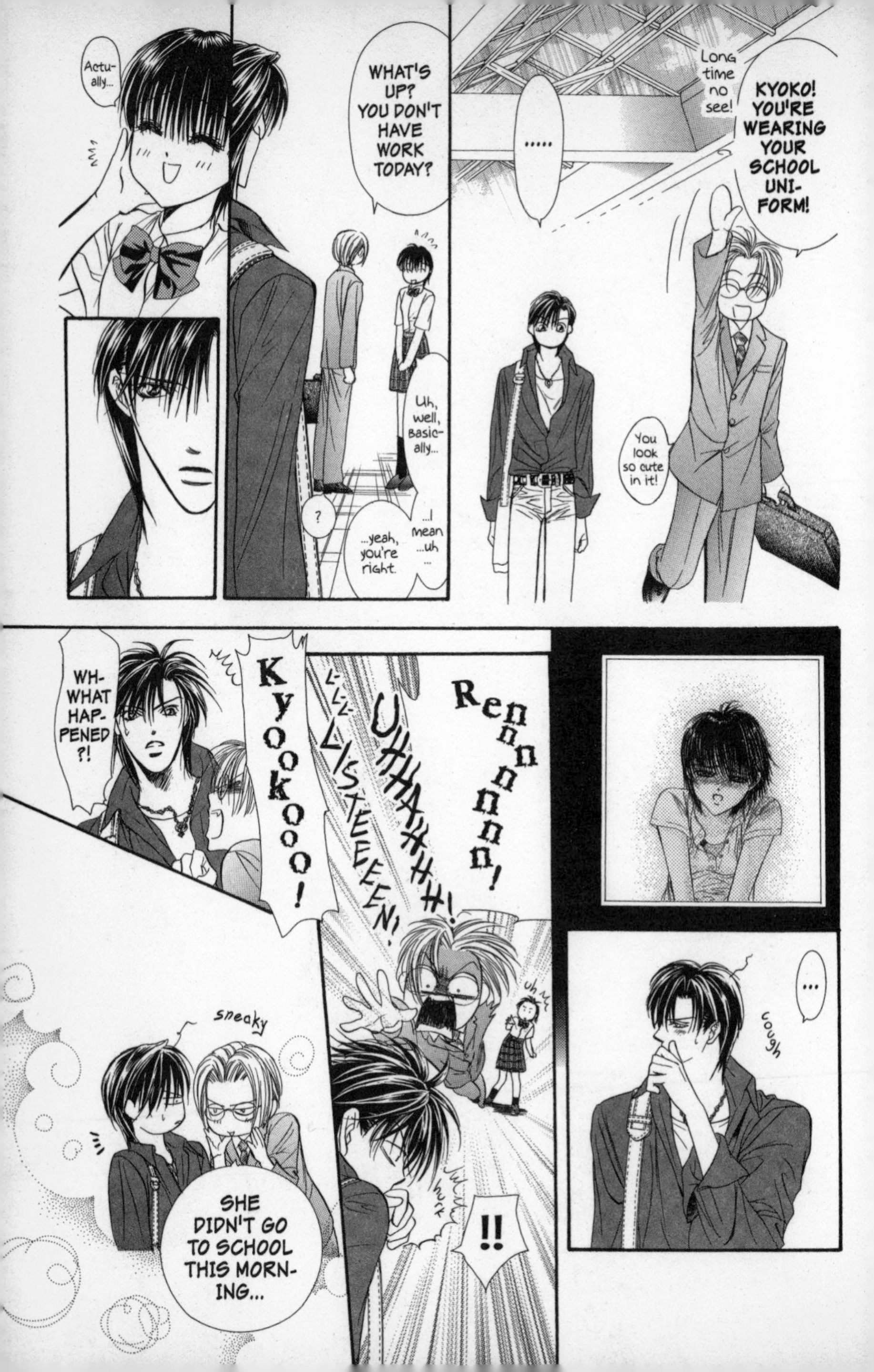
KYOKO! YOU'RE WEARING YOUR SCHOOL UNI-FORM!
Long time no see!
You look so cute in it!
.....
WHAT'S UP? YOU DON'T HAVE WORK TODAY?
Uh, well, basic-ally...
...I mean ...uh ...
...yeah, you're right.
?
Actu-ally...
...
cough
Rennnnnnnn!
UHHAHHHH!
L-L-L-LISTEEEEN!
Kyoooooo!
uh
!!
hurk
WH-WHAT HAP-PENED?!
sneaky
SHE DIDN'T GO TO SCHOOL THIS MORN-ING...

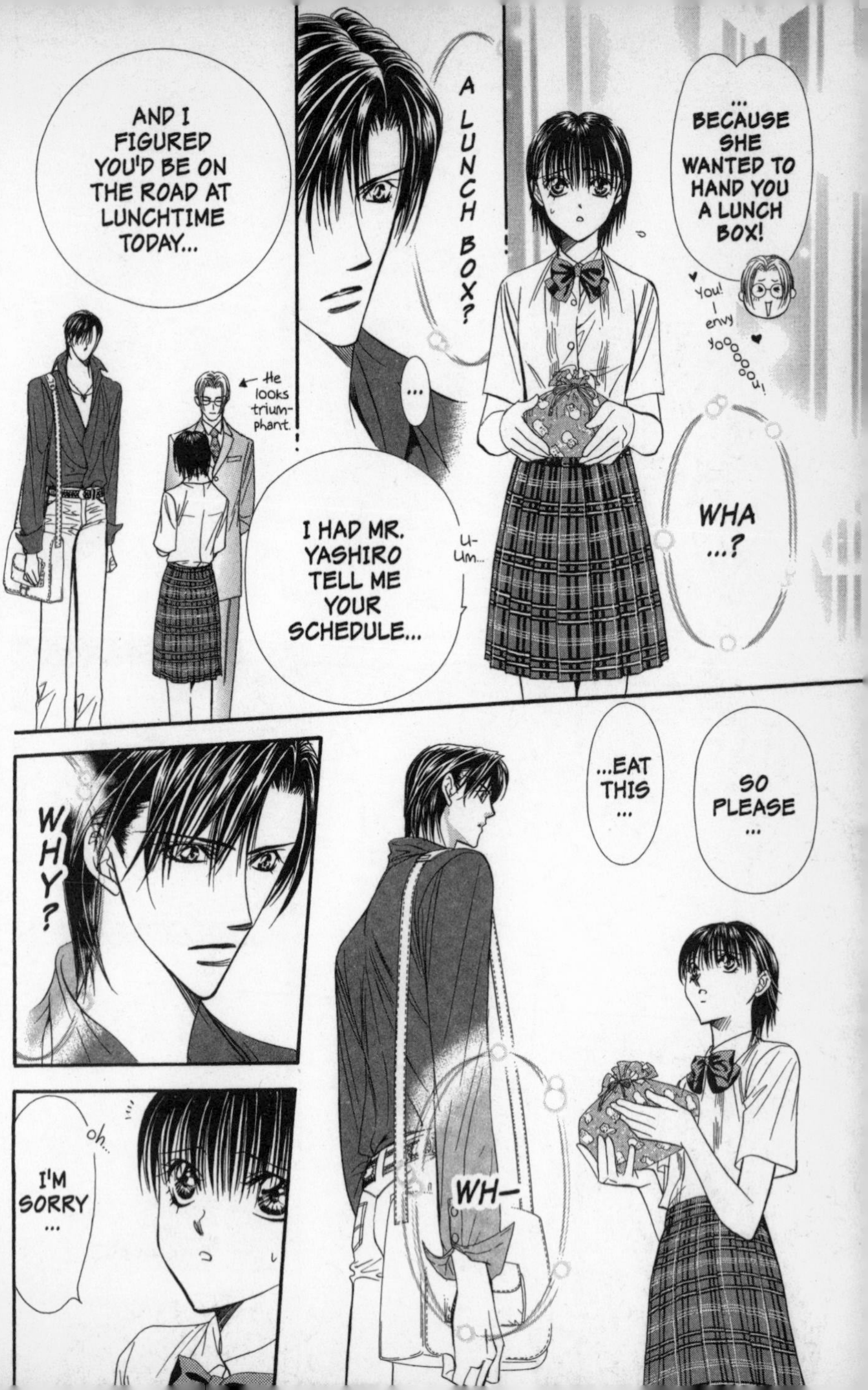
...BECAUSE SHE WANTED TO HAND YOU A LUNCH BOX!
You! I envy yoooooou!
WHA...?
A LUNCH BOX?
...
U-Um...
I HAD MR. YASHIRO TELL ME YOUR SCHEDULE...
AND I FIGURED YOU'D BE ON THE ROAD AT LUNCHTIME TODAY...
He looks triumphant.
SO PLEASE...
...EAT THIS...
WH—
WHY?
oh...
I'M SORRY...

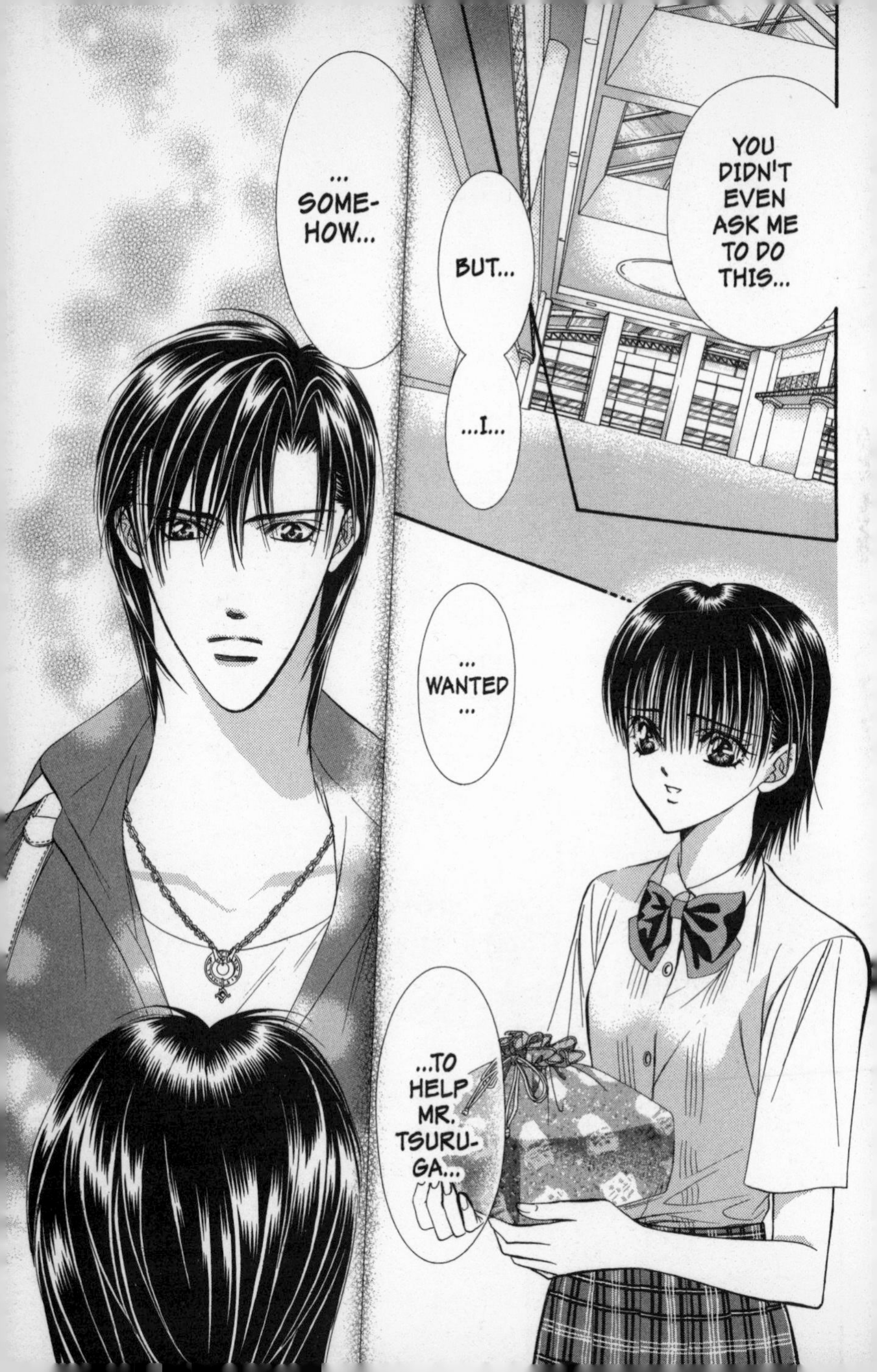
YOU DIDN'T EVEN ASK ME TO DO THIS...
BUT...
...I...
...WANTED...
...TO HELP MR. TSURUGA...
...SOME-HOW...

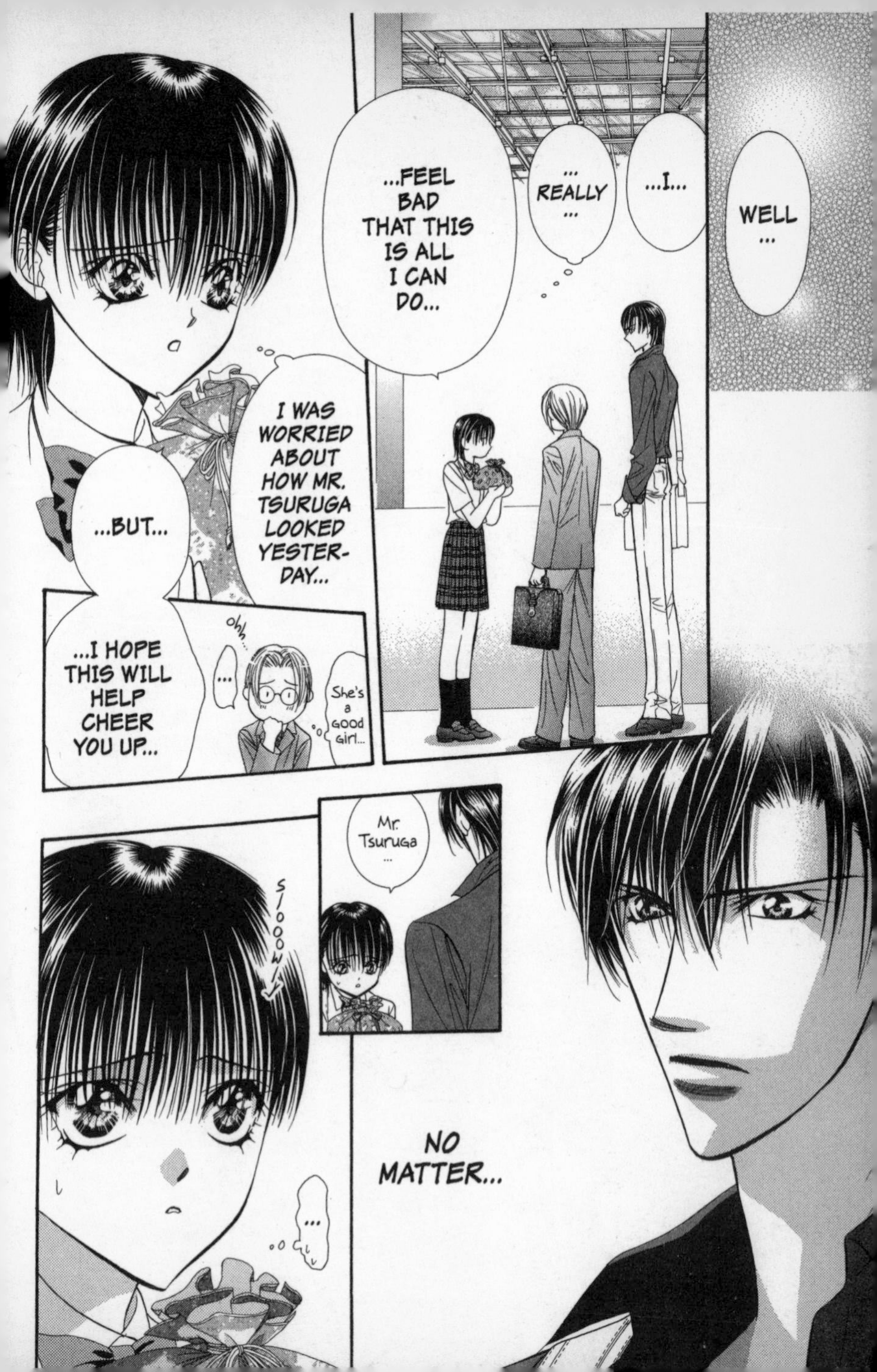
WELL...
...I...
...REALLY...
...FEEL BAD THAT THIS IS ALL I CAN DO...
I WAS WORRIED ABOUT HOW MR. TSURUGA LOOKED YESTERDAY...
...BUT...
...I HOPE THIS WILL HELP CHEER YOU UP...
She's a Good Girl...
ohh...
...
NO MATTER...
Mr. Tsuruga...
SLOOOW
...

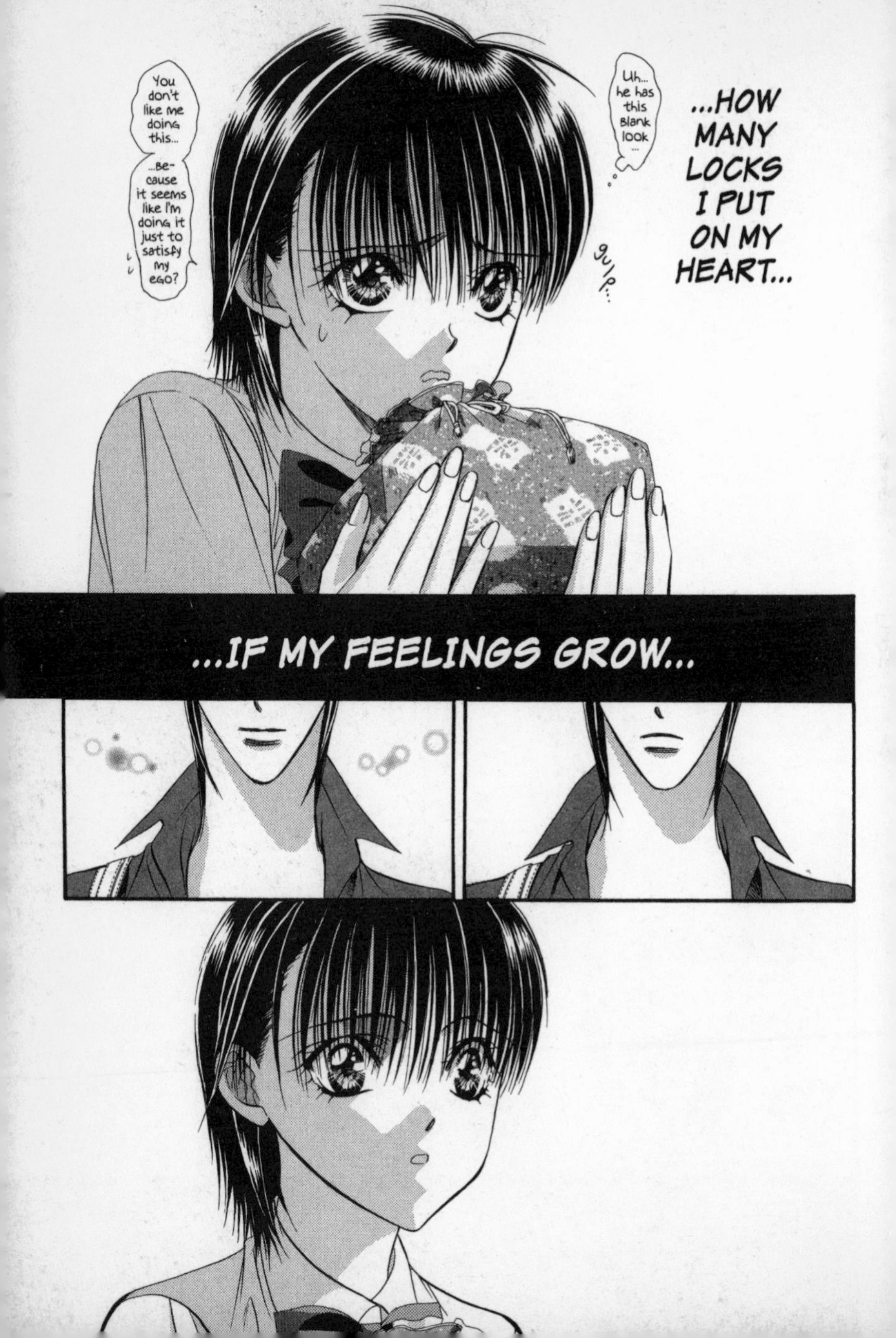
...HOW MANY LOCKS I PUT ON MY HEART...
Uh... he has this blank look ...
gulp...
You don't like me doing this...
...Be-cause it seems like I'm doing it just to satisfy my ego?
...IF MY FEELINGS GROW...

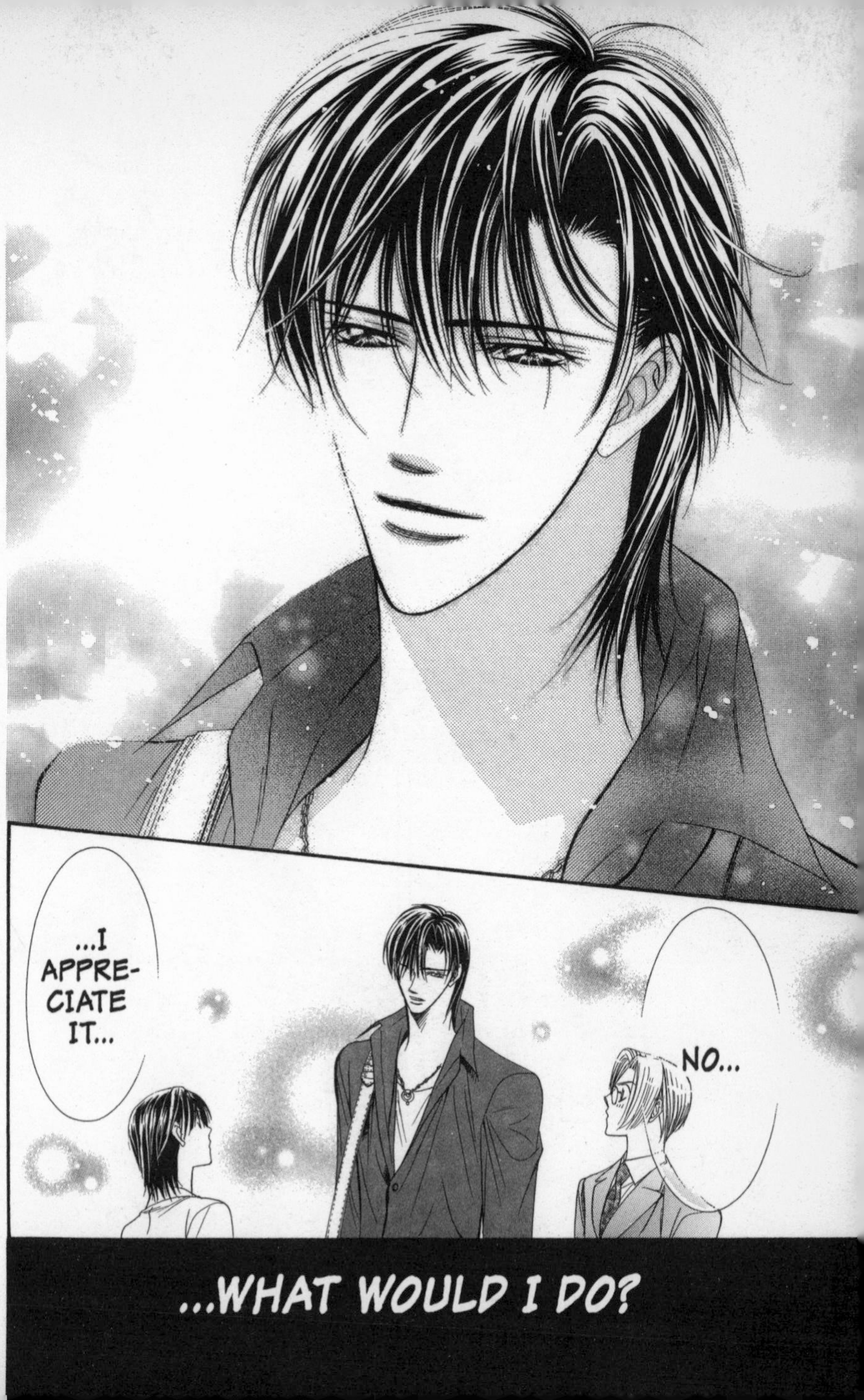
NO...
...I APPRECIATE IT...
...WHAT WOULD I DO?

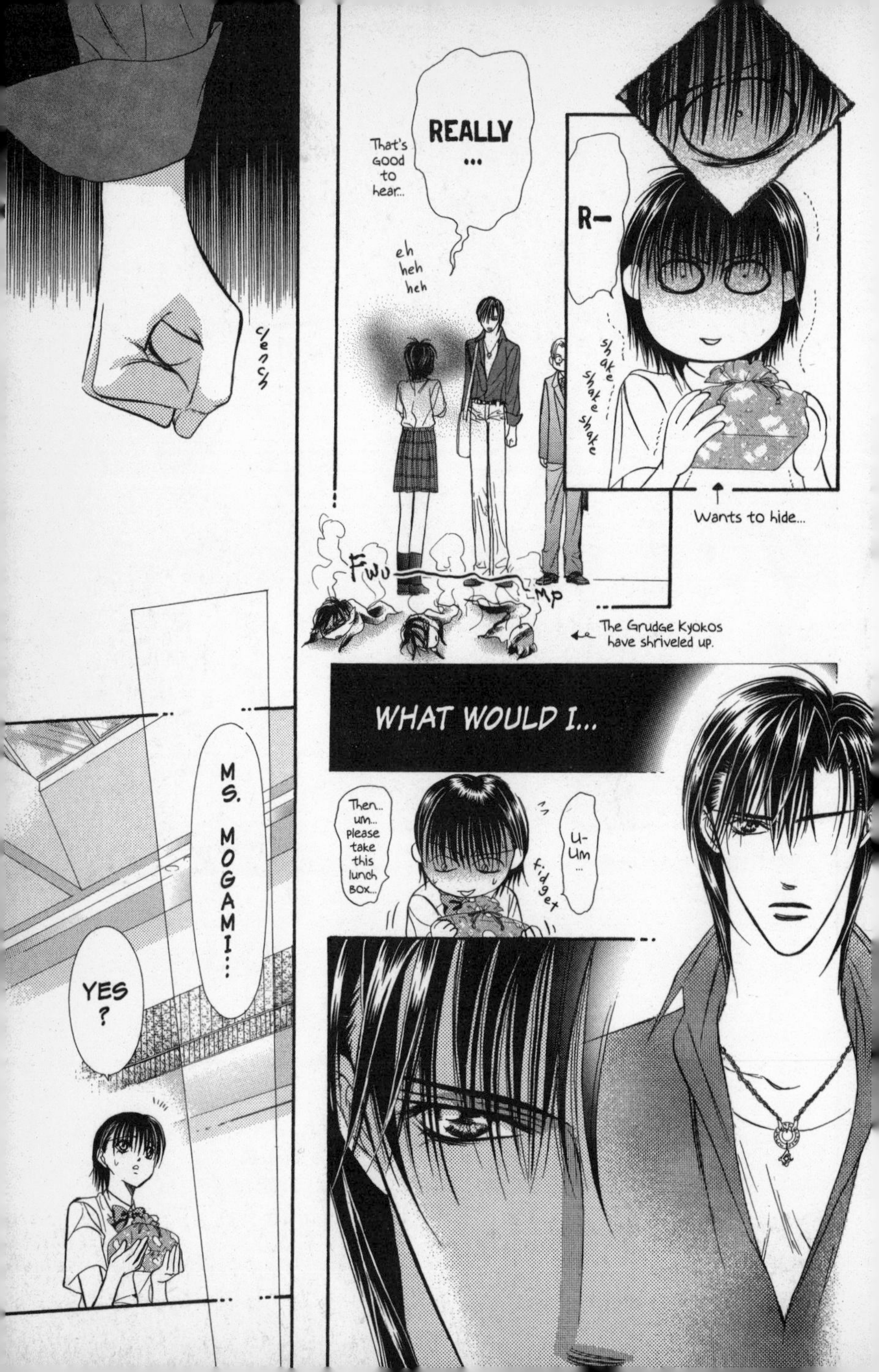
R–
shake shake shake shake
Wants to hide...
REALLY ...
That's good to hear...
eh heh heh
Fwump
The Grudge Kyokos have shriveled up.
WHAT WOULD I...
Then.. um... please take this lunch box...
U-Um ...
fidget
clench
MS. MOGAMI...
YES ?

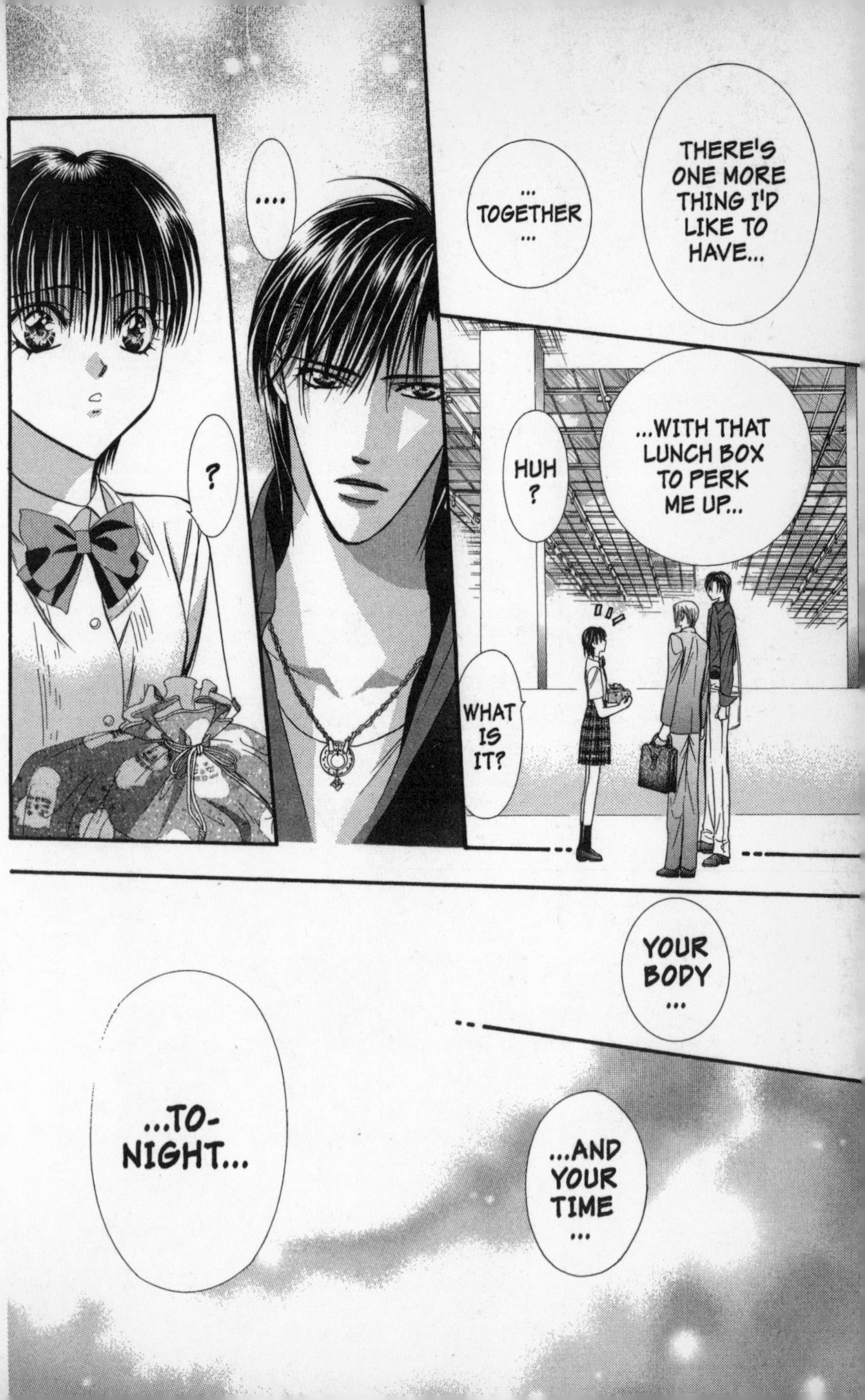
THERE'S ONE MORE THING I'D LIKE TO HAVE...
...WITH THAT LUNCH BOX TO PERK ME UP...
HUH ?
WHAT IS IT?
... TOGETHER ...
....
?
YOUR BODY ...
...AND YOUR TIME ...
...TO-NIGHT...

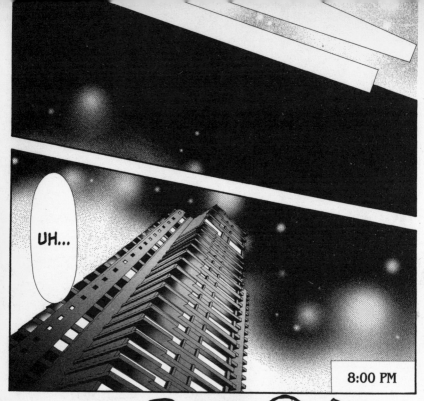

UH...

8:00 PM

DO OM

...DON'T SAY THINGS LIKE THAT.

...PLEASE...

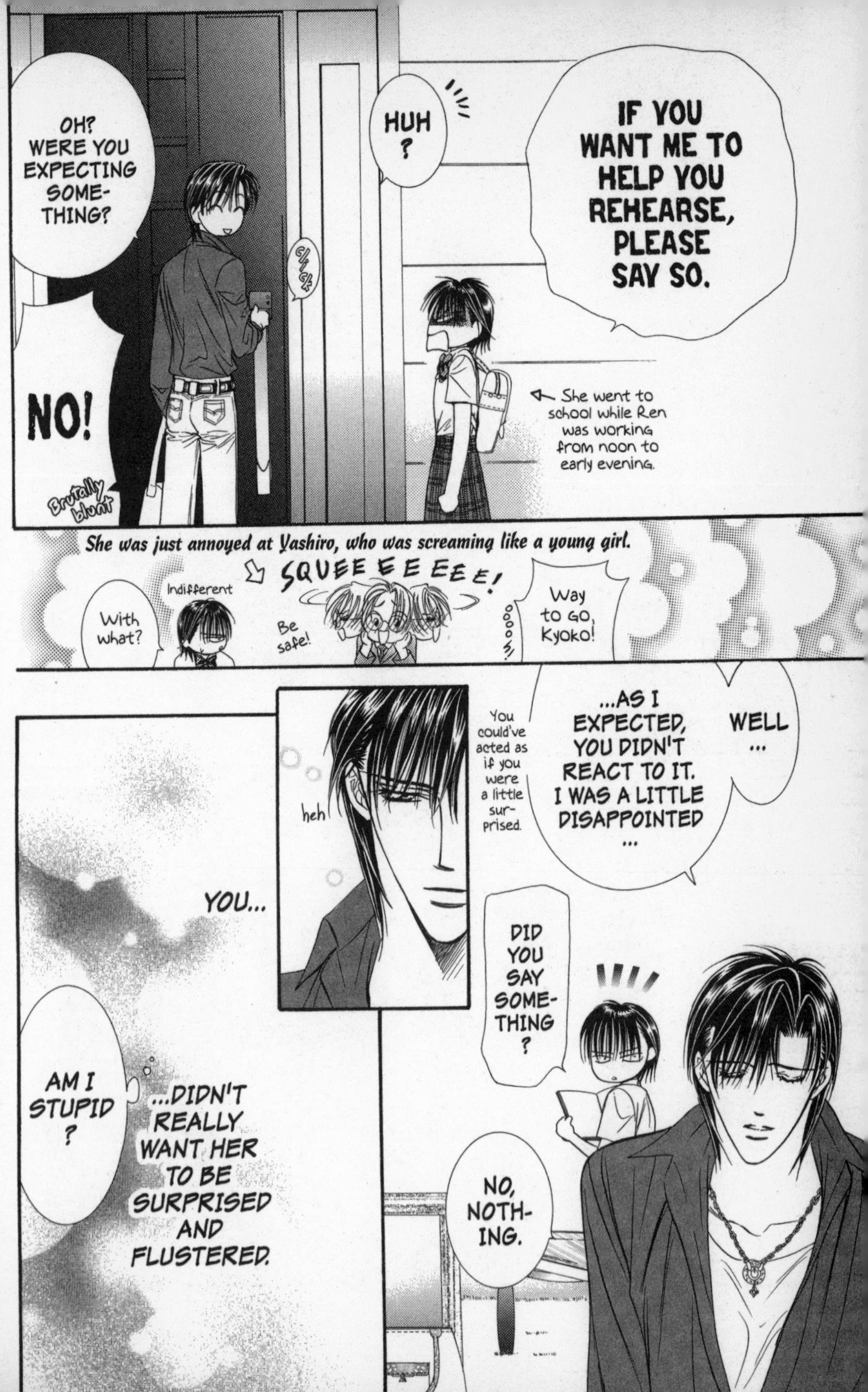
IF YOU WANT ME TO HELP YOU REHEARSE, PLEASE SAY SO.
HUH?
She went to school while Ren was working from noon to early evening.
Click
OH? WERE YOU EXPECTING SOME-THING?
NO!
Brutally blunt
She was just annoyed at Yashiro, who was screaming like a young girl.
Way to go, Kyoko!
Ooooh!
SQUEEEEEEEE!
Be safe!
Indifferent
With what?
WELL...
...AS I EXPECTED, YOU DIDN'T REACT TO IT. I WAS A LITTLE DISAPPOINTED...
You could've acted as if you were a little sur-prised.
heh
DID YOU SAY SOME-THING?
NO, NOTH-ING.
YOU...
...DIDN'T REALLY WANT HER TO BE SURPRISED AND FLUSTERED.
AM I STUPID?

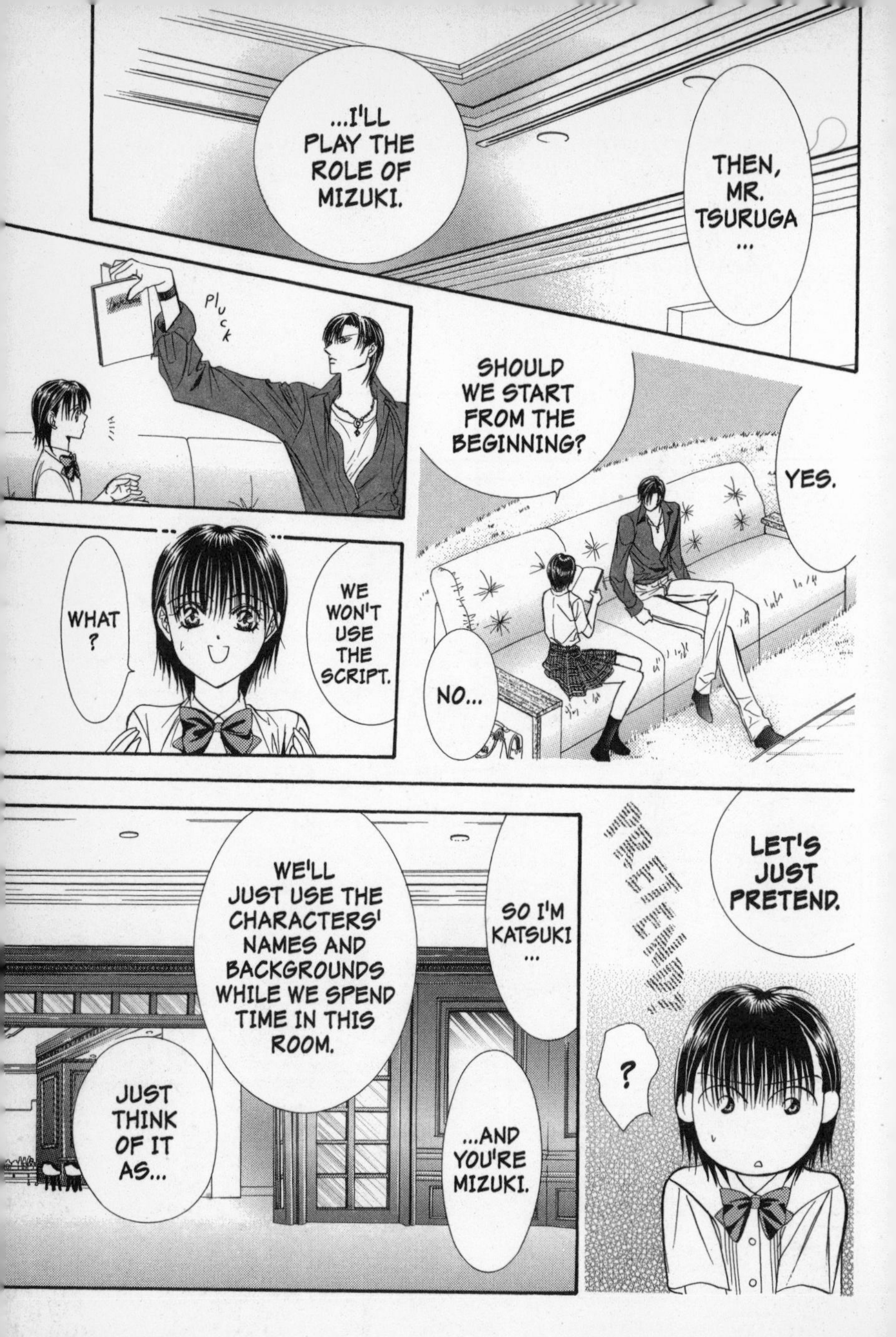
THEN, MR. TSURUGA...
...I'LL PLAY THE ROLE OF MIZUKI.
SHOULD WE START FROM THE BEGINNING?
YES.
NO...
PLUCK
WE WON'T USE THE SCRIPT.
WHAT?
LET'S JUST PRETEND.
?
SO I'M KATSUKI...
WE'LL JUST USE THE CHARACTERS' NAMES AND BACKGROUNDS WHILE WE SPEND TIME IN THIS ROOM.
...AND YOU'RE MIZUKI.
JUST THINK OF IT AS...

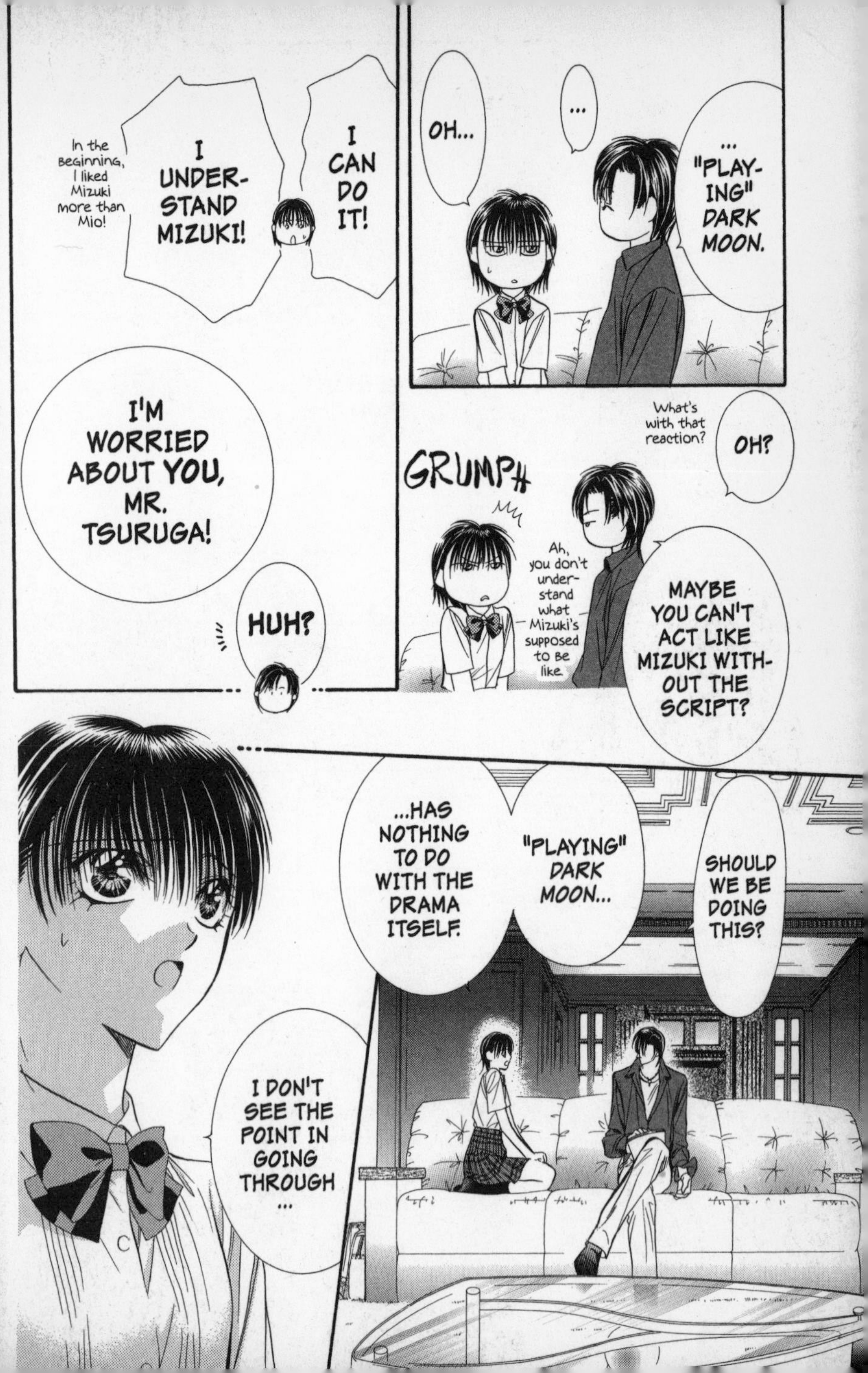

..."PLAYING" DARK MOON.
...
OH...
I CAN DO IT!
I UNDERSTAND MIZUKI!
In the beginning, I liked Mizuki more than Mio!
OH?
What's with that reaction?
GRUMPH
MAYBE YOU CAN'T ACT LIKE MIZUKI WITHOUT THE SCRIPT?
Ah, you don't understand what Mizuki's supposed to be like.
I'M WORRIED ABOUT YOU, MR. TSURUGA!
HUH?
...
...
SHOULD WE BE DOING THIS?
"PLAYING" DARK MOON...
...HAS NOTHING TO DO WITH THE DRAMA ITSELF.
I DON'T SEE THE POINT IN GOING THROUGH ...

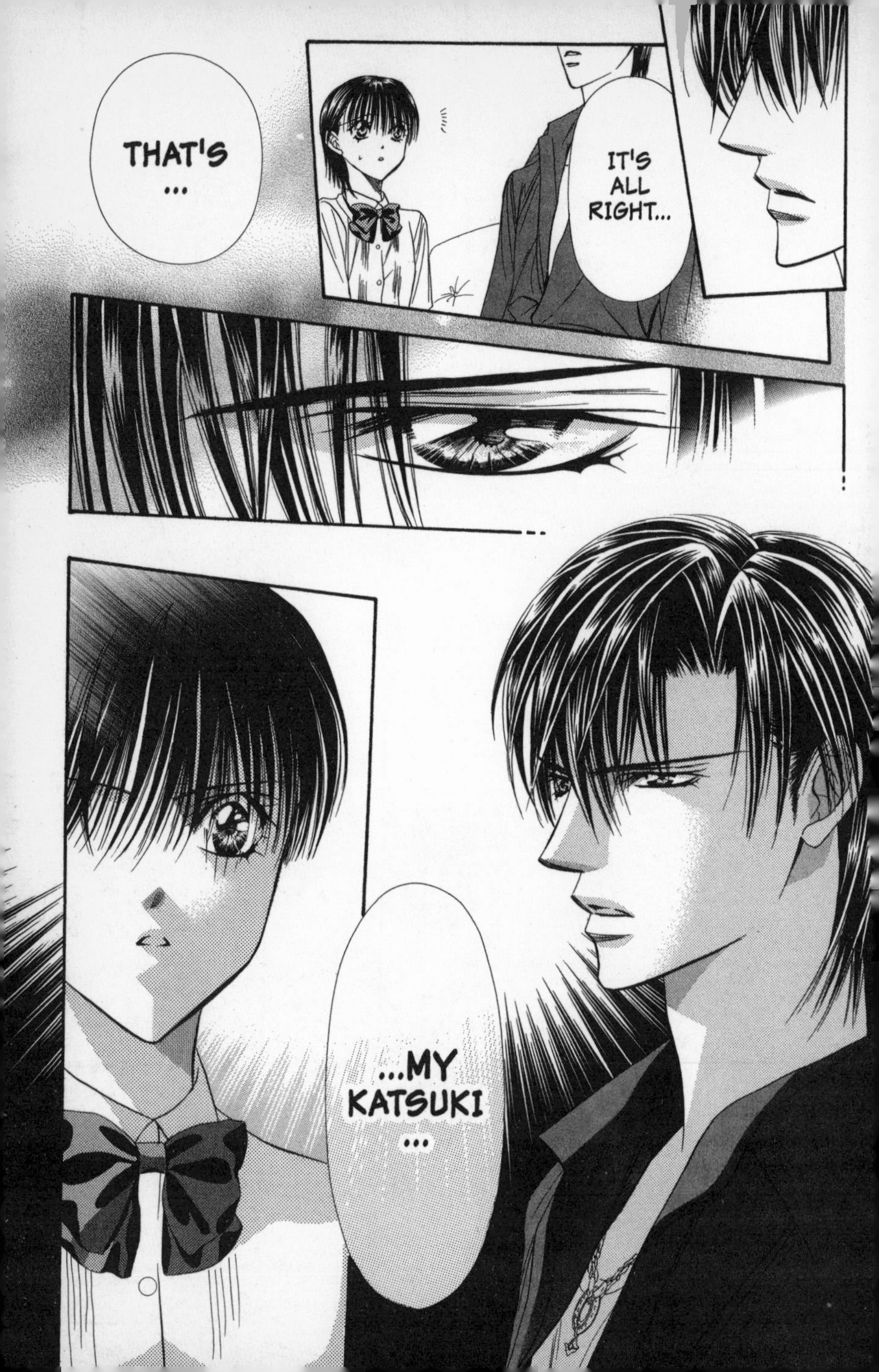
IT'S ALL RIGHT...
THAT'S ...
...MY KATSUKI ...

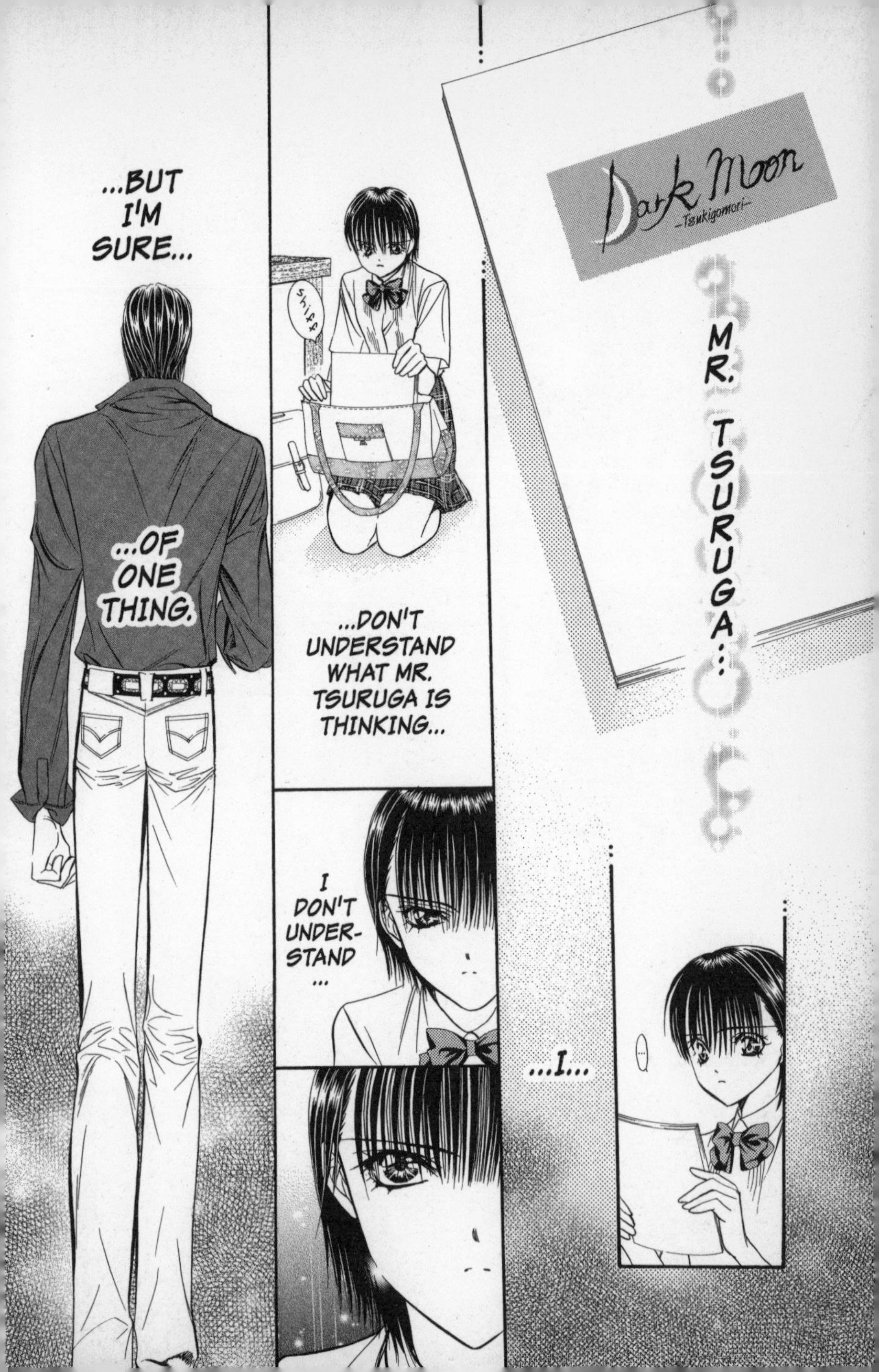
Dark Moon
-Tsukigomori-
MR. TSURUGA...
...
...I...
sniff
...DON'T UNDERSTAND WHAT MR. TSURUGA IS THINKING...
I DON'T UNDER-STAND...
...BUT I'M SURE...
...OF ONE THING.

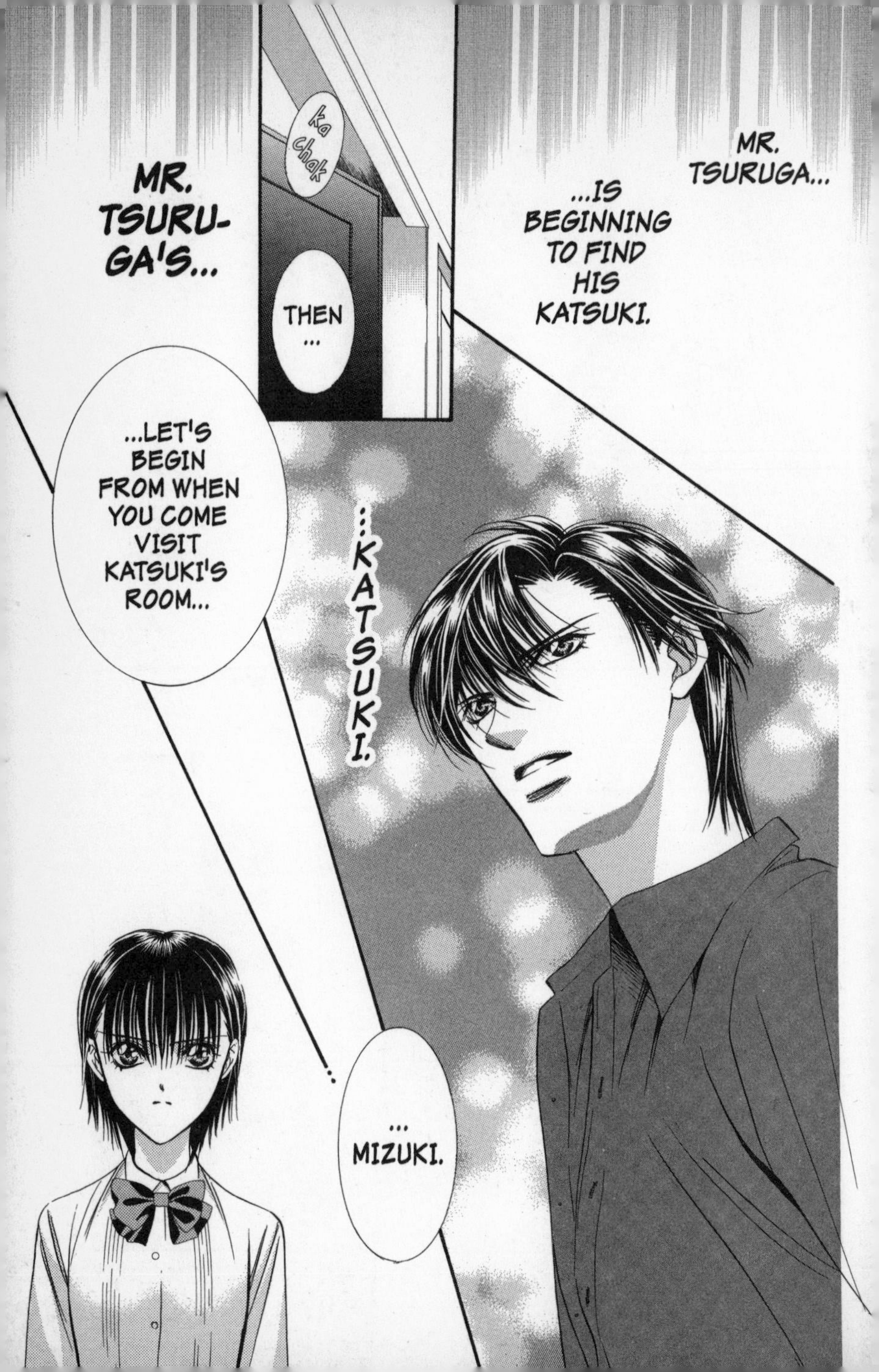
MR. TSURUGA...
...IS BEGINNING TO FIND HIS KATSUKI.
ka chak
THEN ...
MR. TSURU-GA'S...
...KATSUKI.
...LET'S BEGIN FROM WHEN YOU COME VISIT KATSUKI'S ROOM...
... MIZUKI.

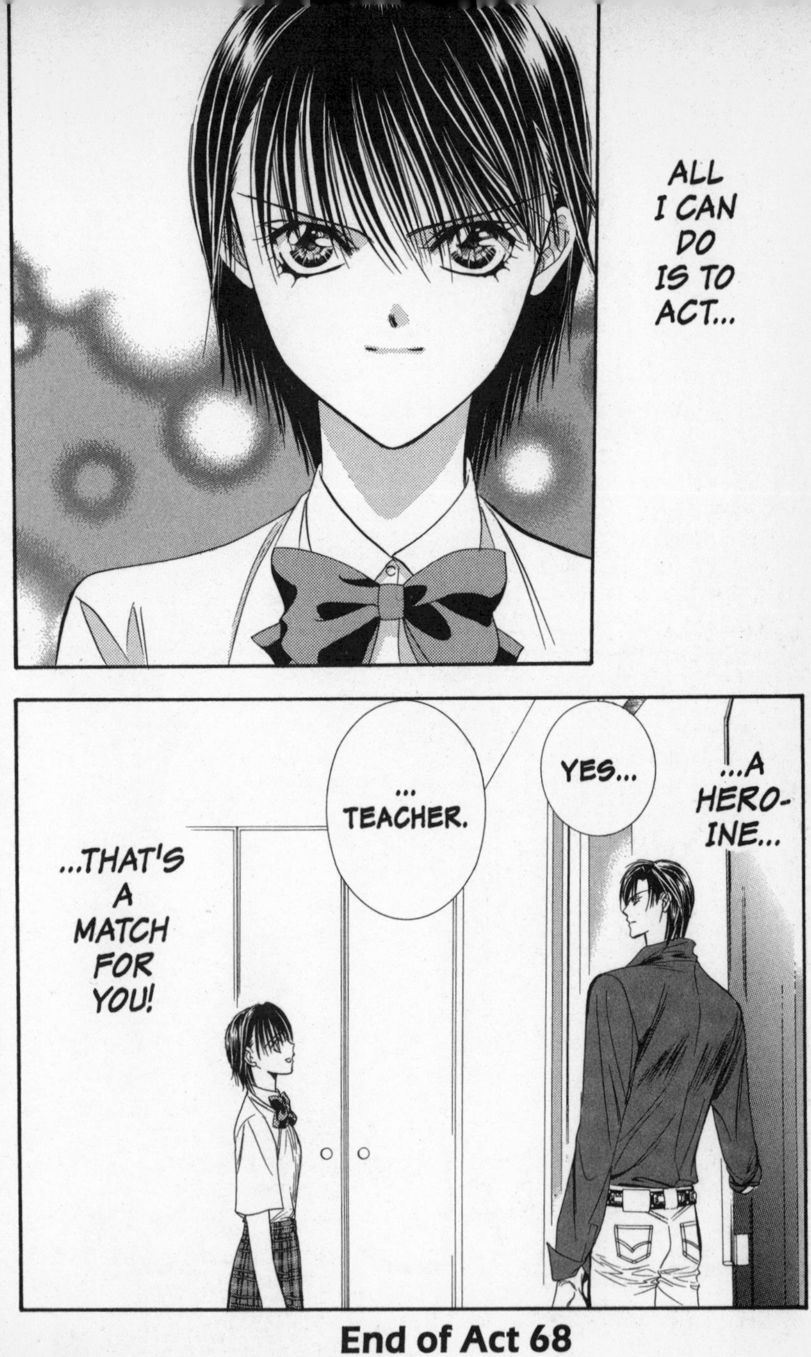
ALL I CAN DO IS TO ACT...
...A HERO-INE...
YES...
... TEACHER.
...THAT'S A MATCH FOR YOU!

End of Act 68

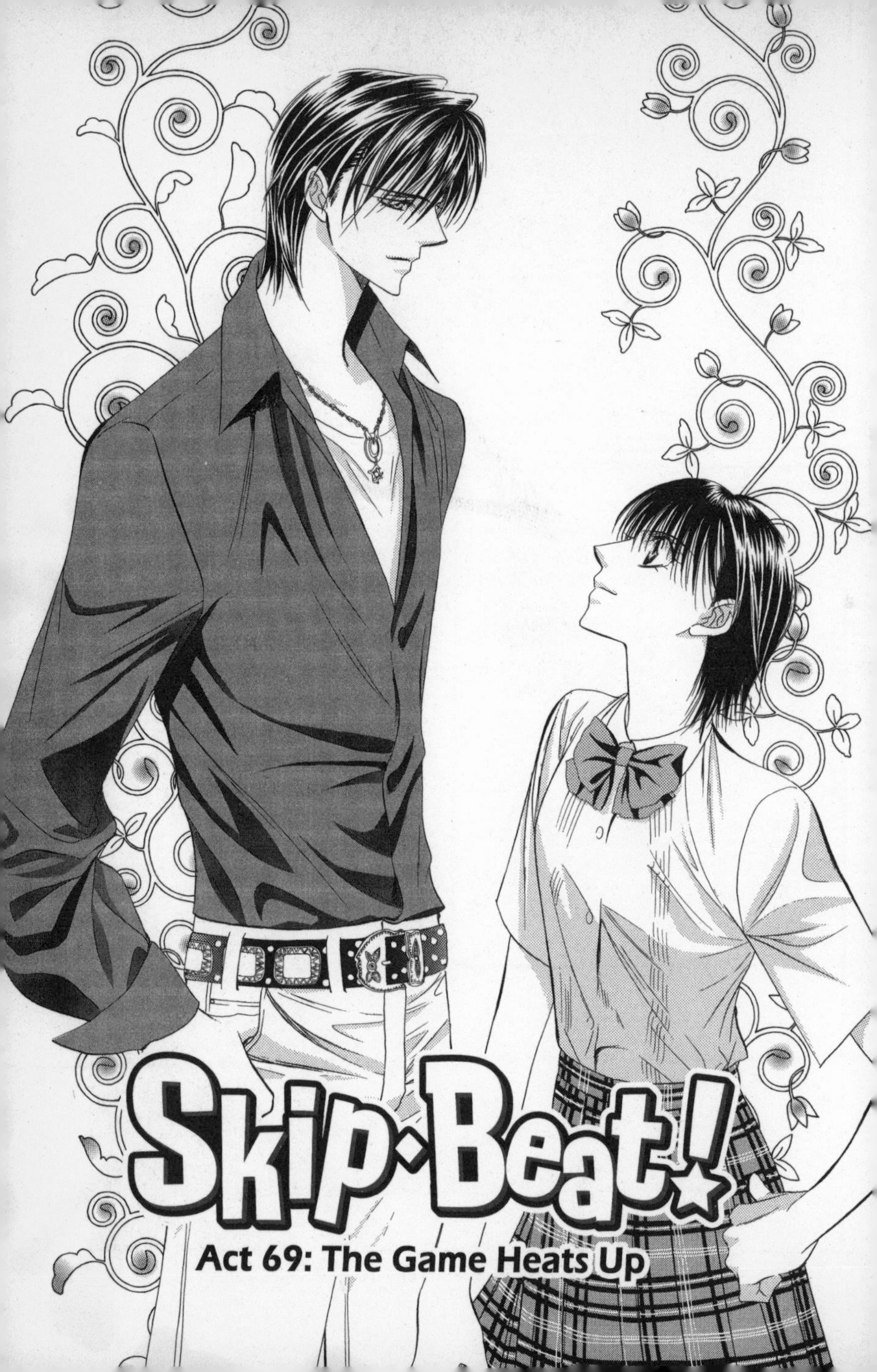
Skip·Beat!
Act 69: The Game Heats Up

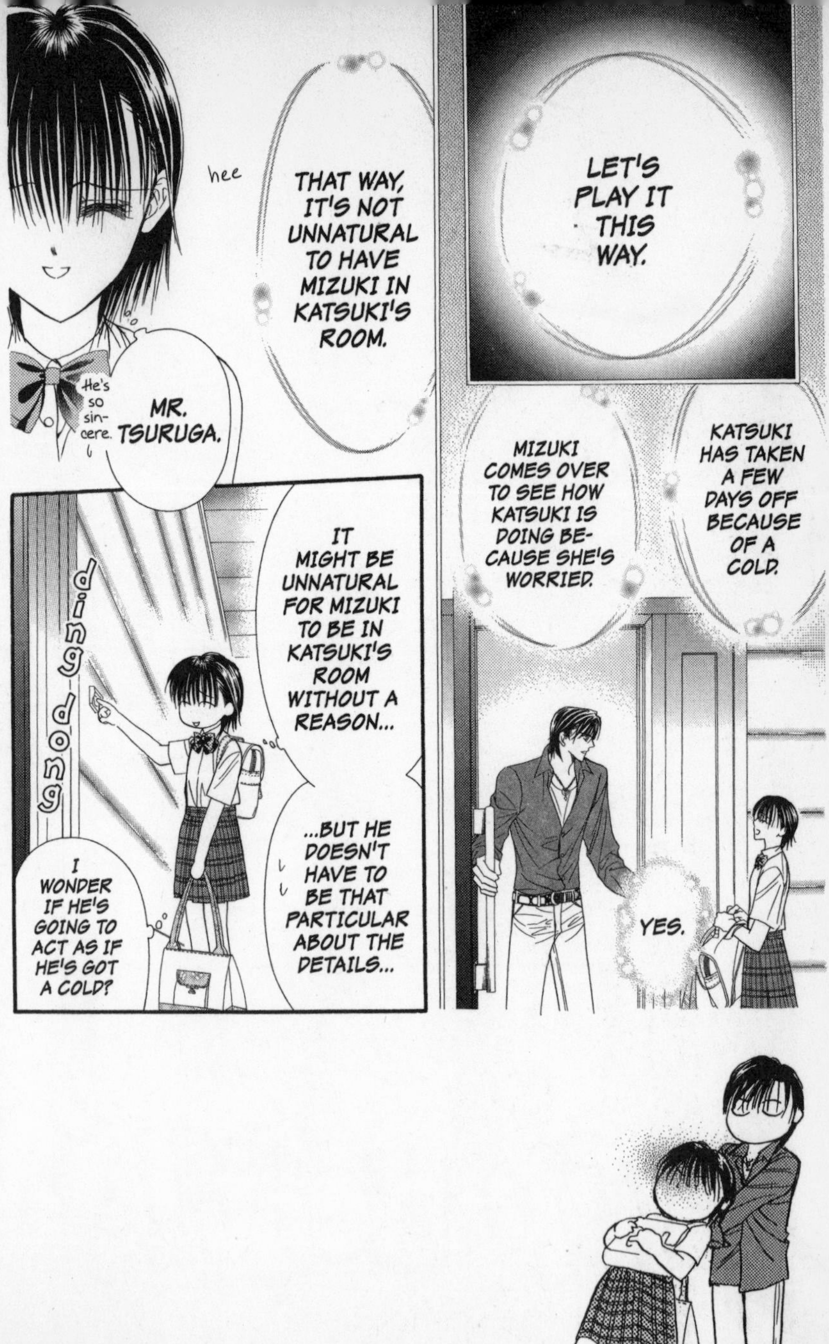
LET'S PLAY IT THIS WAY.
THAT WAY, IT'S NOT UNNATURAL TO HAVE MIZUKI IN KATSUKI'S ROOM.
hee
MR. TSURUGA.
He's so sin-cere.
KATSUKI HAS TAKEN A FEW DAYS OFF BECAUSE OF A COLD.
MIZUKI COMES OVER TO SEE HOW KATSUKI IS DOING BE-CAUSE SHE'S WORRIED.
YES.
IT MIGHT BE UNNATURAL FOR MIZUKI TO BE IN KATSUKI'S ROOM WITHOUT A REASON...
...BUT HE DOESN'T HAVE TO BE THAT PARTICULAR ABOUT THE DETAILS...
ding-dong
I WONDER IF HE'S GOING TO ACT AS IF HE'S GOT A COLD?

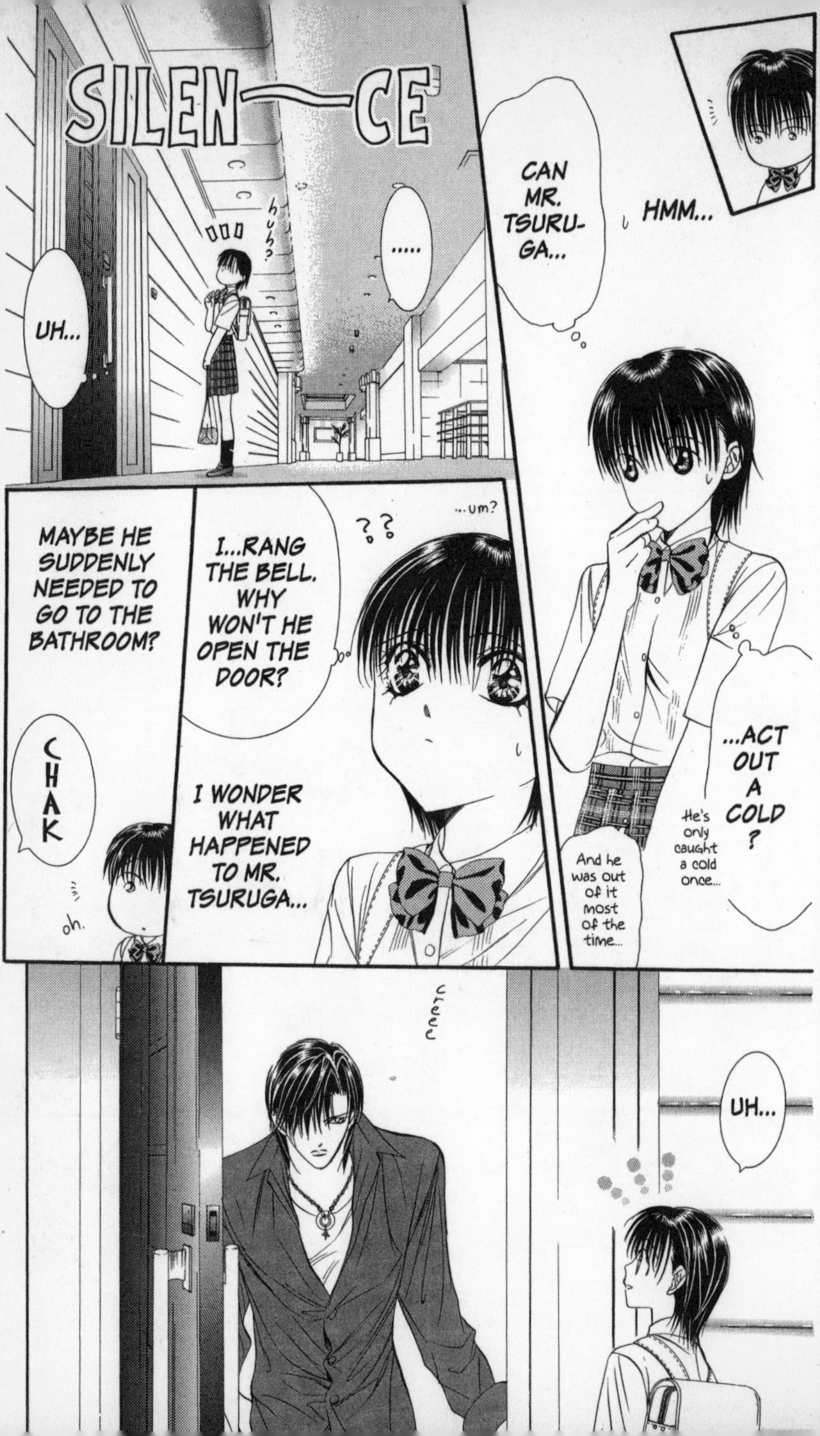
HMM...
CAN MR. TSURUGA...
...ACT OUT A COLD?
He's only caught a cold once...
And he was out of it most of the time...
.....
huh?
UH...
SILEN—CE
...um?
I...RANG THE BELL. WHY WON'T HE OPEN THE DOOR?
I WONDER WHAT HAPPENED TO MR. TSURUGA...
MAYBE HE SUDDENLY NEEDED TO GO TO THE BATHROOM?
CHAK
oh.
creee
UH...

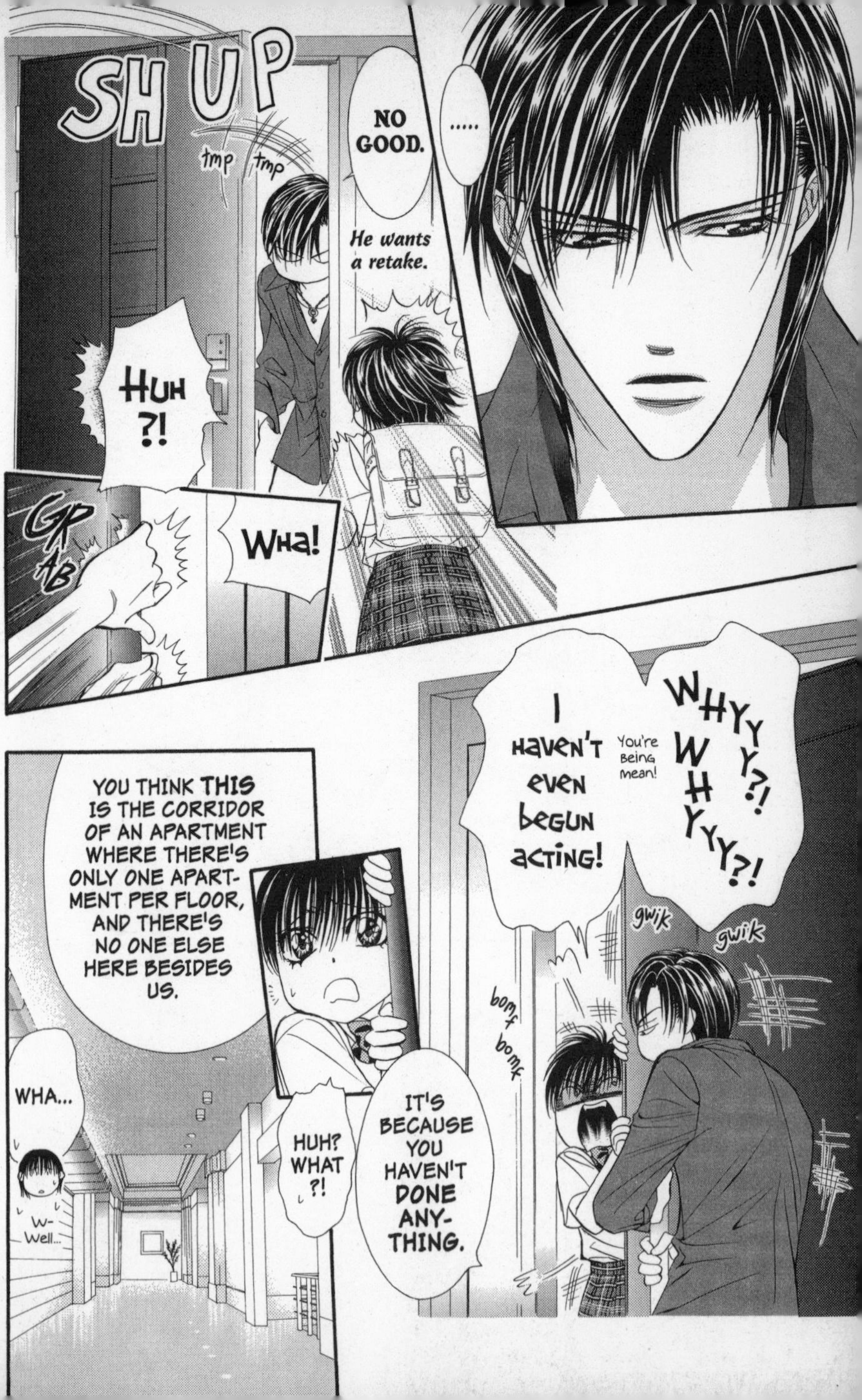
.....
NO GOOD.
SH UP
tmp tmp
He wants a retake.
HUH?!
GRAB
Wha!
WHYYY WHY?! WHYYY?!
I haven't even begun acting!
You're being mean!
gwik gwik
bomf bomf
IT'S BECAUSE YOU HAVEN'T DONE ANYTHING.
YOU THINK THIS IS THE CORRIDOR OF AN APARTMENT WHERE THERE'S ONLY ONE APARTMENT PER FLOOR, AND THERE'S NO ONE ELSE HERE BESIDES US.
HUH? WHAT?!
WHA...
W-Well...

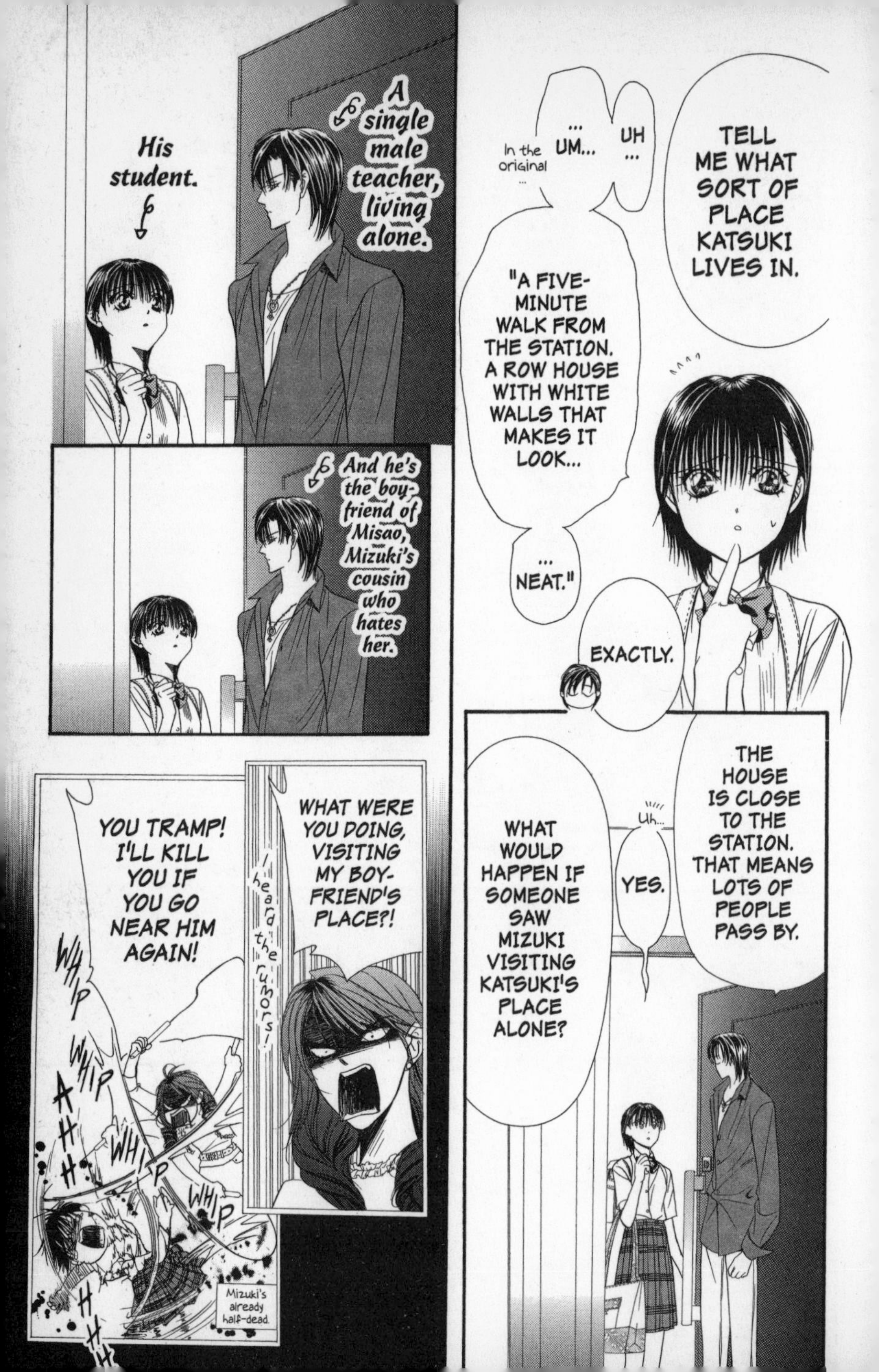

TELL ME WHAT SORT OF PLACE KATSUKI LIVES IN.
UH ...
... UM...
In the original ...
"A FIVE-MINUTE WALK FROM THE STATION. A ROW HOUSE WITH WHITE WALLS THAT MAKES IT LOOK...
... NEAT."
EXACTLY.
THE HOUSE IS CLOSE TO THE STATION. THAT MEANS LOTS OF PEOPLE PASS BY.
Uh...
YES.
WHAT WOULD HAPPEN IF SOMEONE SAW MIZUKI VISITING KATSUKI'S PLACE ALONE?
A single male teacher, living alone.
His student.
And he's the boy-friend of Misao, Mizuki's cousin who hates her.
WHAT WERE YOU DOING, VISITING MY BOY-FRIEND'S PLACE?!
I heard the rumors!
YOU TRAMP! I'LL KILL YOU IF YOU GO NEAR HIM AGAIN!
WHIP
WHIP
AHHHHHH
WHIP
WHIP
Mizuki's already half-dead.

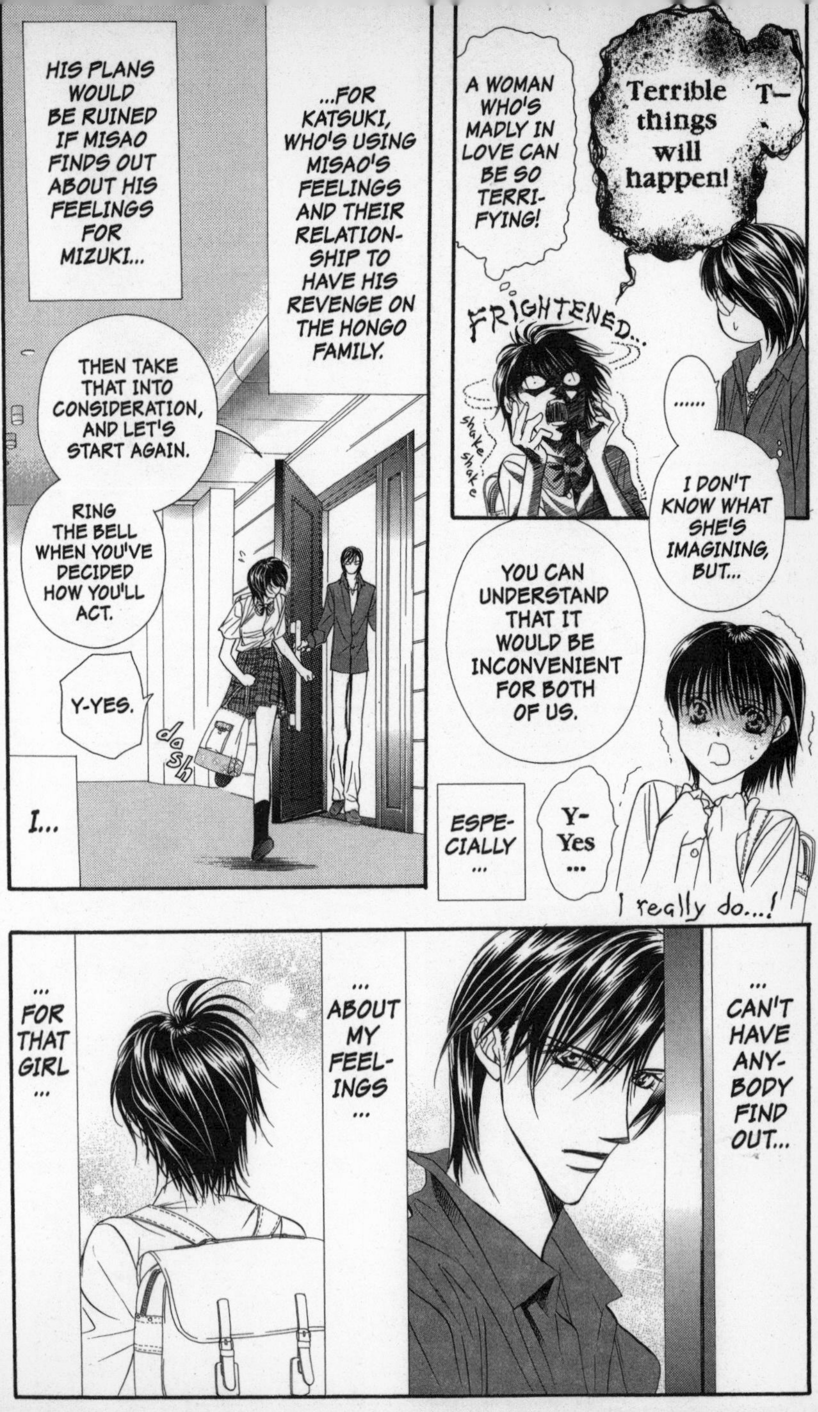
T—
Terrible things will happen!
A WOMAN WHO'S MADLY IN LOVE CAN BE SO TERRIFYING!
FRIGHTENED...
shake shake
......
I DON'T KNOW WHAT SHE'S IMAGINING, BUT...
YOU CAN UNDERSTAND THAT IT WOULD BE INCONVENIENT FOR BOTH OF US.
Y-Yes...
ESPECIALLY...
I really do...!
...FOR KATSUKI, WHO'S USING MISAO'S FEELINGS AND THEIR RELATIONSHIP TO HAVE HIS REVENGE ON THE HONGO FAMILY.
HIS PLANS WOULD BE RUINED IF MISAO FINDS OUT ABOUT HIS FEELINGS FOR MIZUKI...
THEN TAKE THAT INTO CONSIDERATION, AND LET'S START AGAIN.
RING THE BELL WHEN YOU'VE DECIDED HOW YOU'LL ACT.
Y-YES.
dash
I...
...CAN'T HAVE ANYBODY FIND OUT...
...ABOUT MY FEELINGS...
...FOR THAT GIRL...

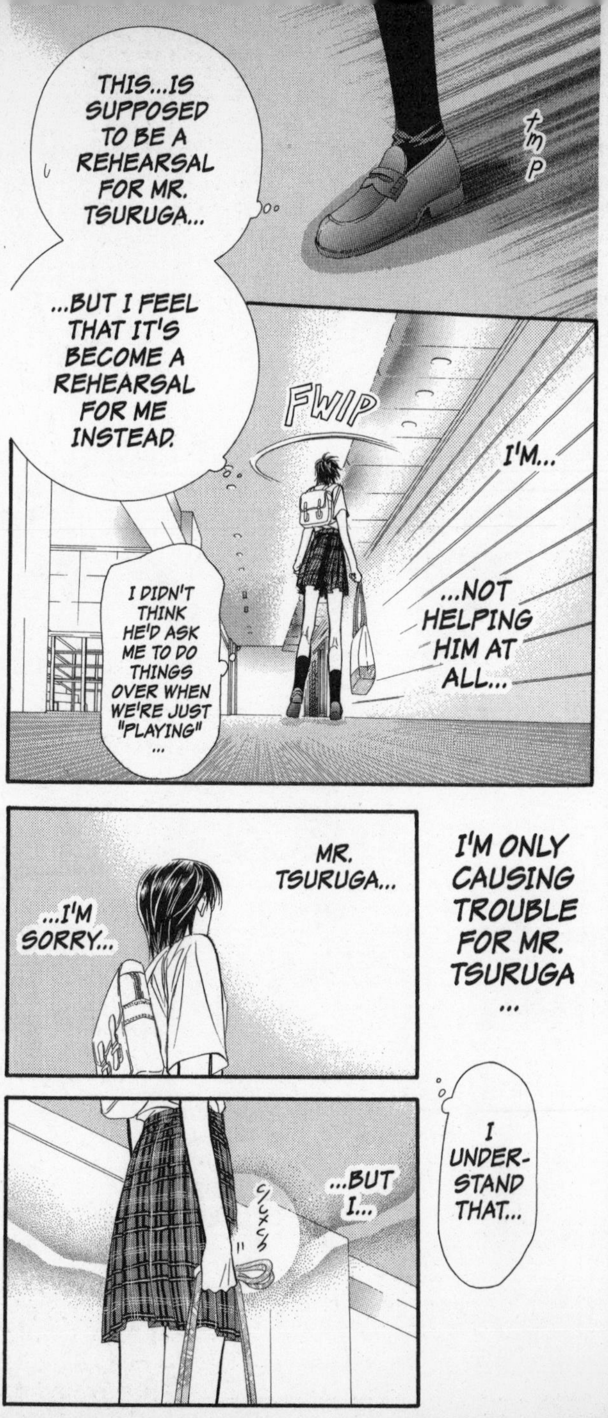
tmp
THIS...IS SUPPOSED TO BE A REHEARSAL FOR MR. TSURUGA...
...BUT I FEEL THAT IT'S BECOME A REHEARSAL FOR ME INSTEAD.
FWIP
I'M...
...NOT HELPING HIM AT ALL...
I DIDN'T THINK HE'D ASK ME TO DO THINGS OVER WHEN WE'RE JUST "PLAYING" ...
I'M ONLY CAUSING TROUBLE FOR MR. TSURUGA ...
MR. TSURUGA...
...I'M SORRY...
I UNDER-STAND THAT...
...BUT I...

I'm Really Glad...

Having Ren and Kyoko, just the two of them "playing" Dark Moon at Ren's place is a delicious episode that's a must for Ren + Kyoko readers...I pondered again and decided to have Ren realize how Katsuki should be played by "playing" Dark Moon.. I was really glad I didn't cut the episode when I read the readers' comments. The readers liked Ren being the King of the Night quite a bit (?), and I'm happy...

Ooh...I'm really glad I drew it...

Ren being King of the Night will probably appear again...I have a hunch that it will appear somewhere in the future...
It's not planned?

Of course, that won't be in this Dark Moon arc.. Well...I don't know when that will actually happen...

...Speaking of King of the Night, there's a TV drama called *Yaoh* which is based on the night business...

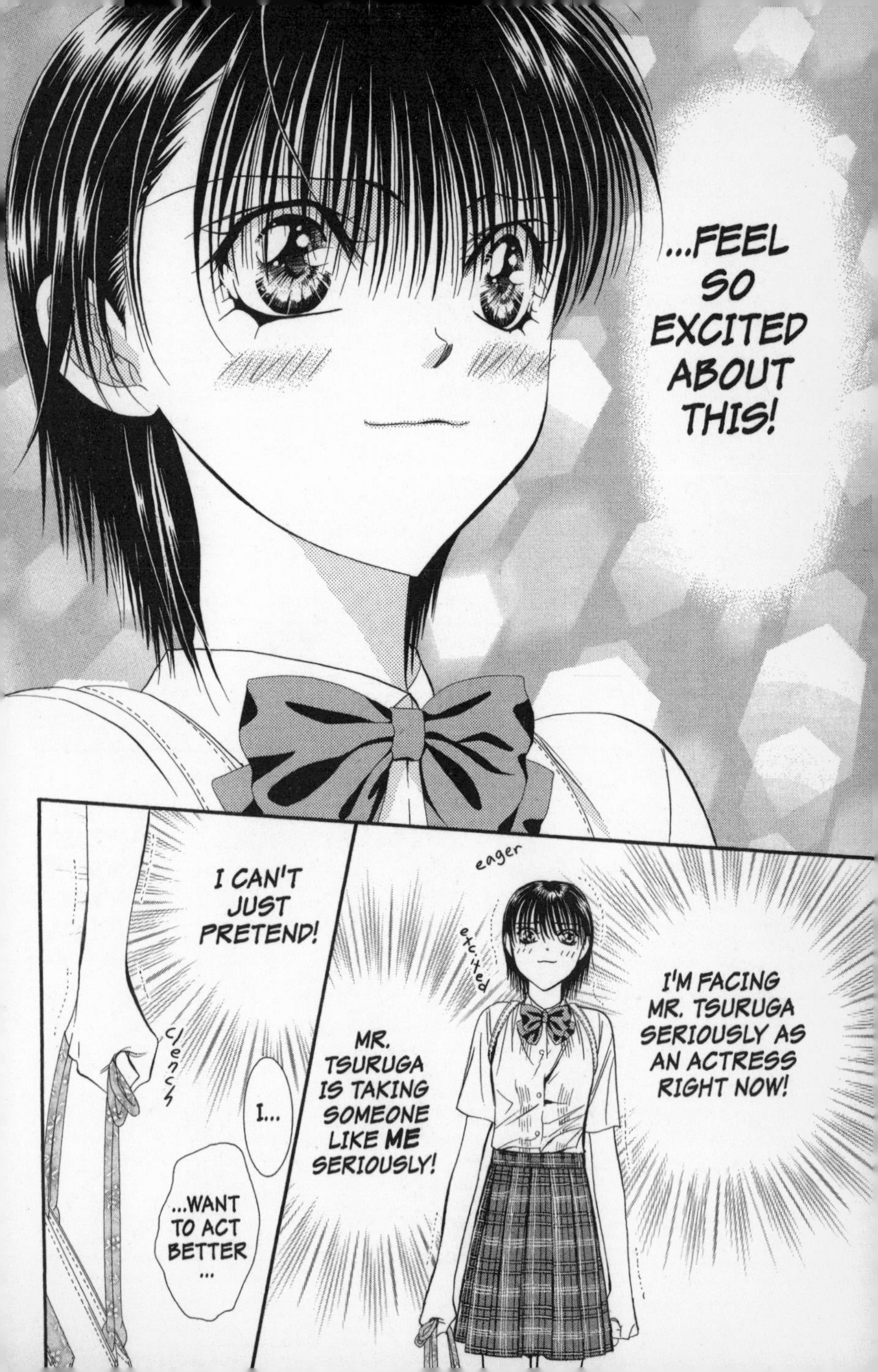
...FEEL SO EXCITED ABOUT THIS!
eager
excited
I'M FACING MR. TSURUGA SERIOUSLY AS AN ACTRESS RIGHT NOW!
MR. TSURUGA IS TAKING SOMEONE LIKE **ME** SERIOUSLY!
I CAN'T JUST PRETEND!
clench
I...
...WANT TO ACT BETTER ...

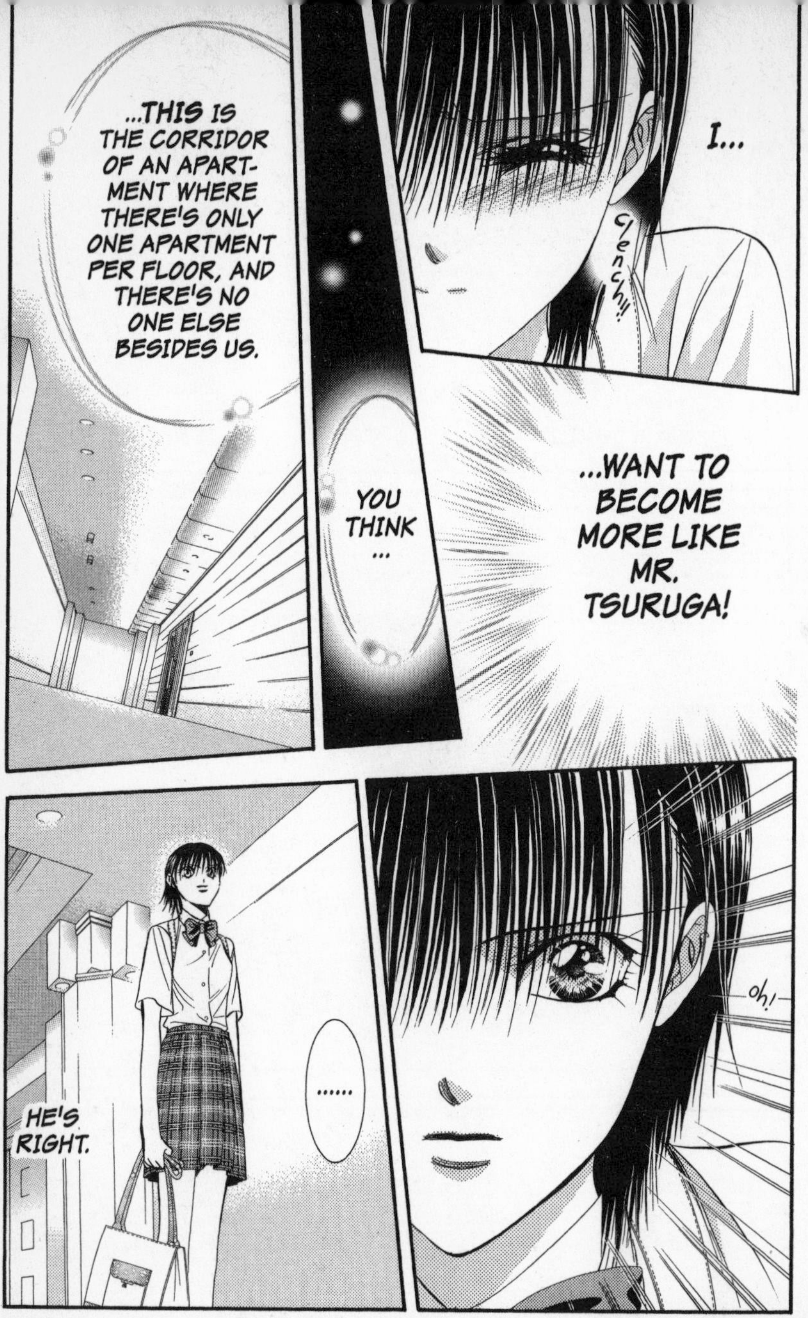
I...
Clench!!
...WANT TO BECOME MORE LIKE MR. TSURUGA!
YOU THINK ...
...THIS IS THE CORRIDOR OF AN APARTMENT WHERE THERE'S ONLY ONE APARTMENT PER FLOOR, AND THERE'S NO ONE ELSE BESIDES US.
oh!
......
HE'S RIGHT.

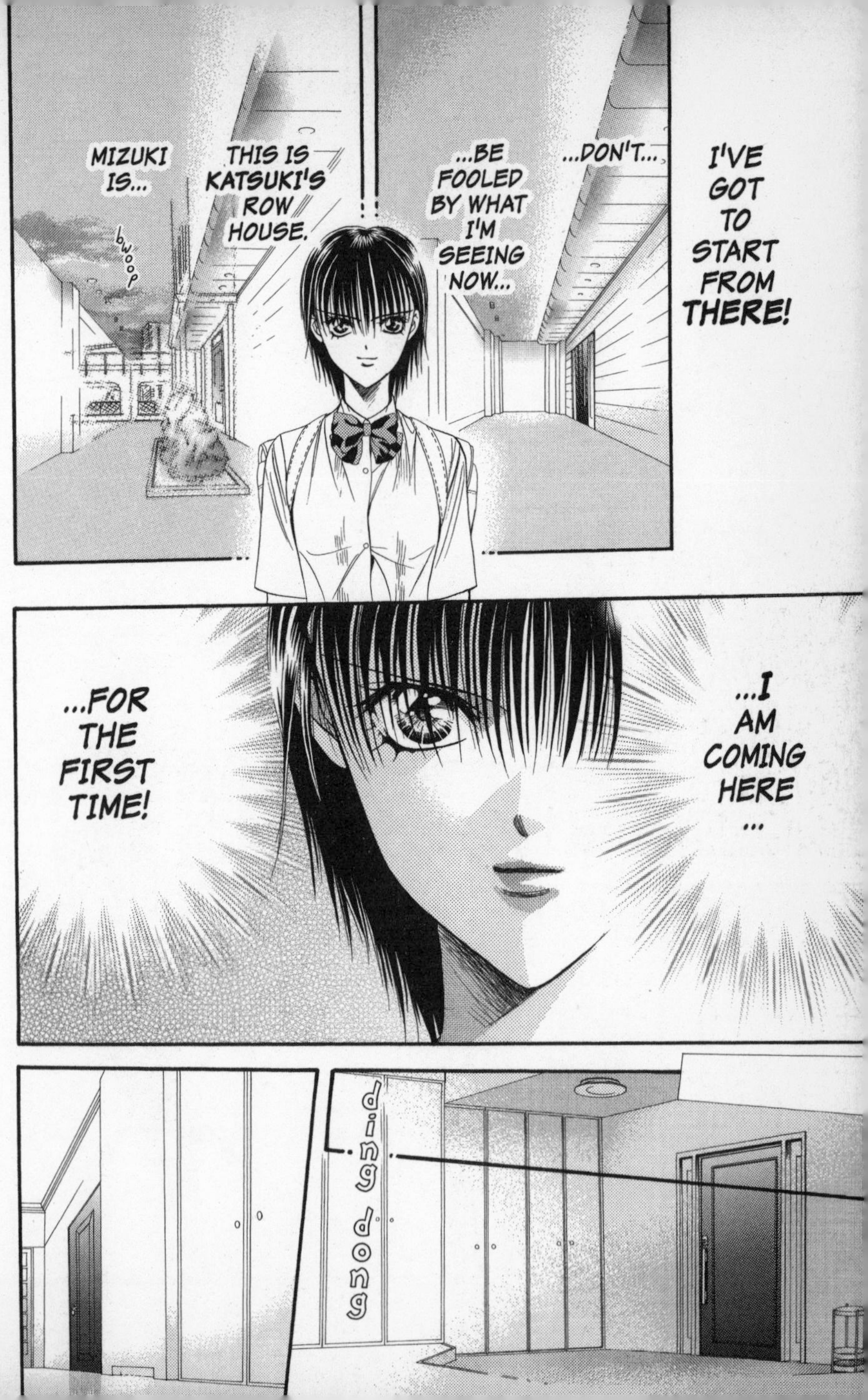
I'VE GOT TO START FROM THERE!
...DON'T...
...BE FOOLED BY WHAT I'M SEEING NOW...
THIS IS KATSUKI'S ROW HOUSE.
MIZUKI IS...
bwoop
...I AM COMING HERE ...
...FOR THE FIRST TIME!
ding dong

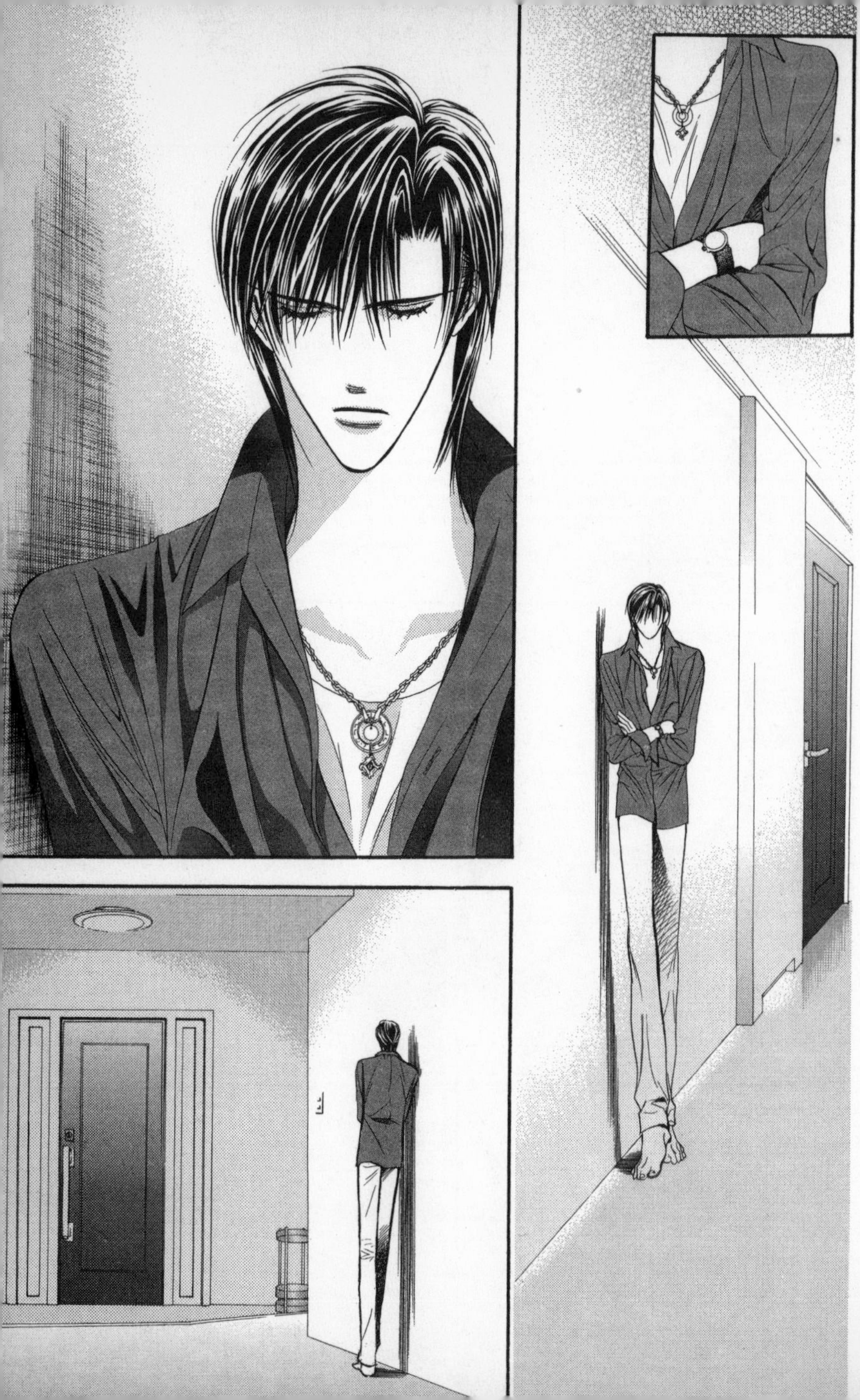

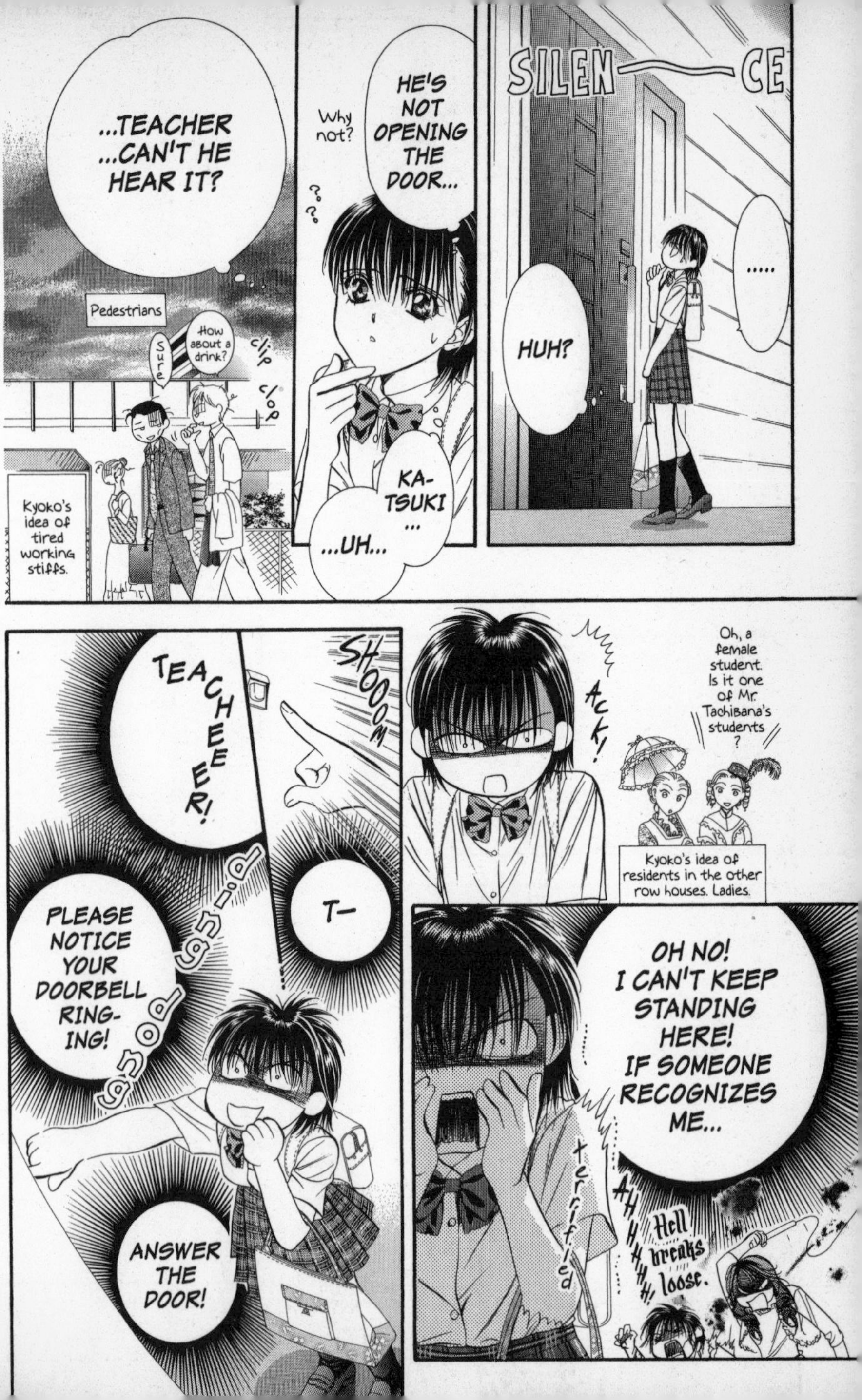
SILEN—CE
.....
HUH?
HE'S NOT OPENING THE DOOR...
Why not?
? ?
KA-TSUKI...
...UH...
...TEACHER ...CAN'T HE HEAR IT?
Pedestrians
How about a drink?
Sure
clip clop
Kyoko's idea of tired working stiffs.
ACK!
Oh, a female student. Is it one of Mr. Tachibana's students?
Kyoko's idea of residents in the other row houses. Ladies.
OH NO! I CAN'T KEEP STANDING HERE! IF SOMEONE RECOGNIZES ME...
terrified
AHHHHH!
Hell breaks loose.
TEACHEEEER!
SHOOOOM
T–
PLEASE NOTICE YOUR DOORBELL RINGING!
ding dong
ANSWER THE DOOR!

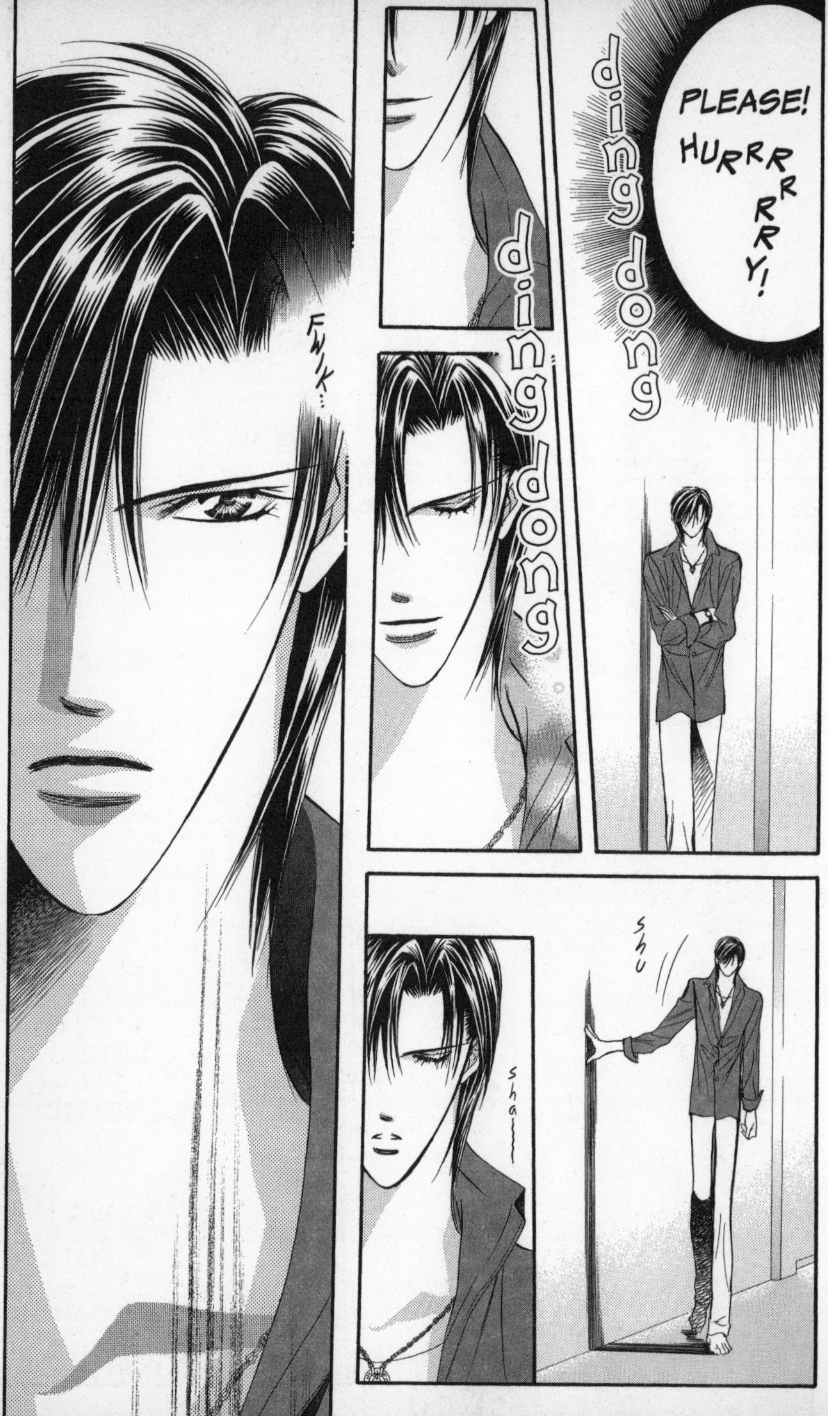
PLEASE! HURRRRRRY!
ding dong
ding dong
shu
sha
FWIK...

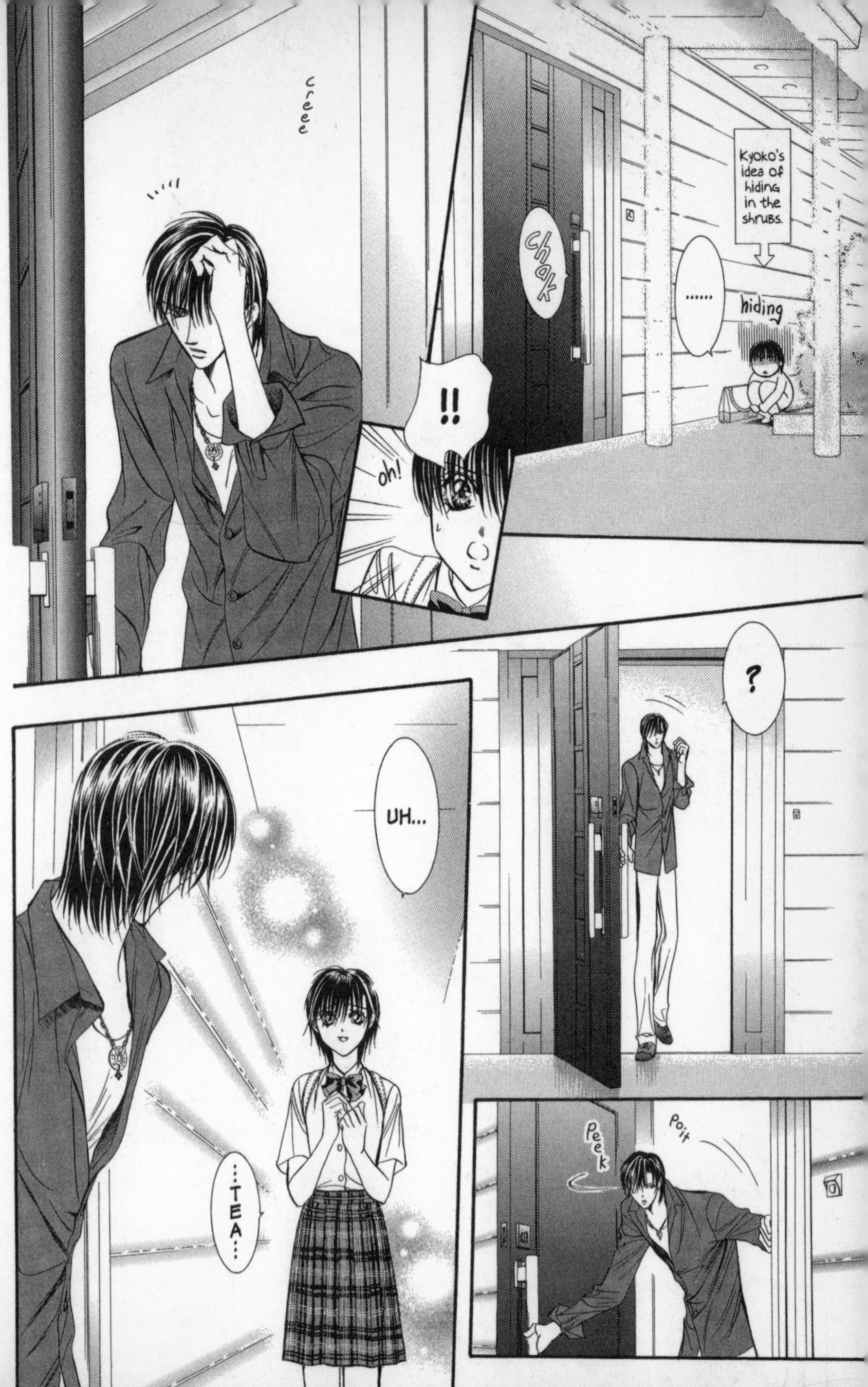
Kyoko's idea of hiding in the shrubs.
......
hiding
Chak
!!
oh!
creee
?
Poit
Peek
UH...
...TEA...

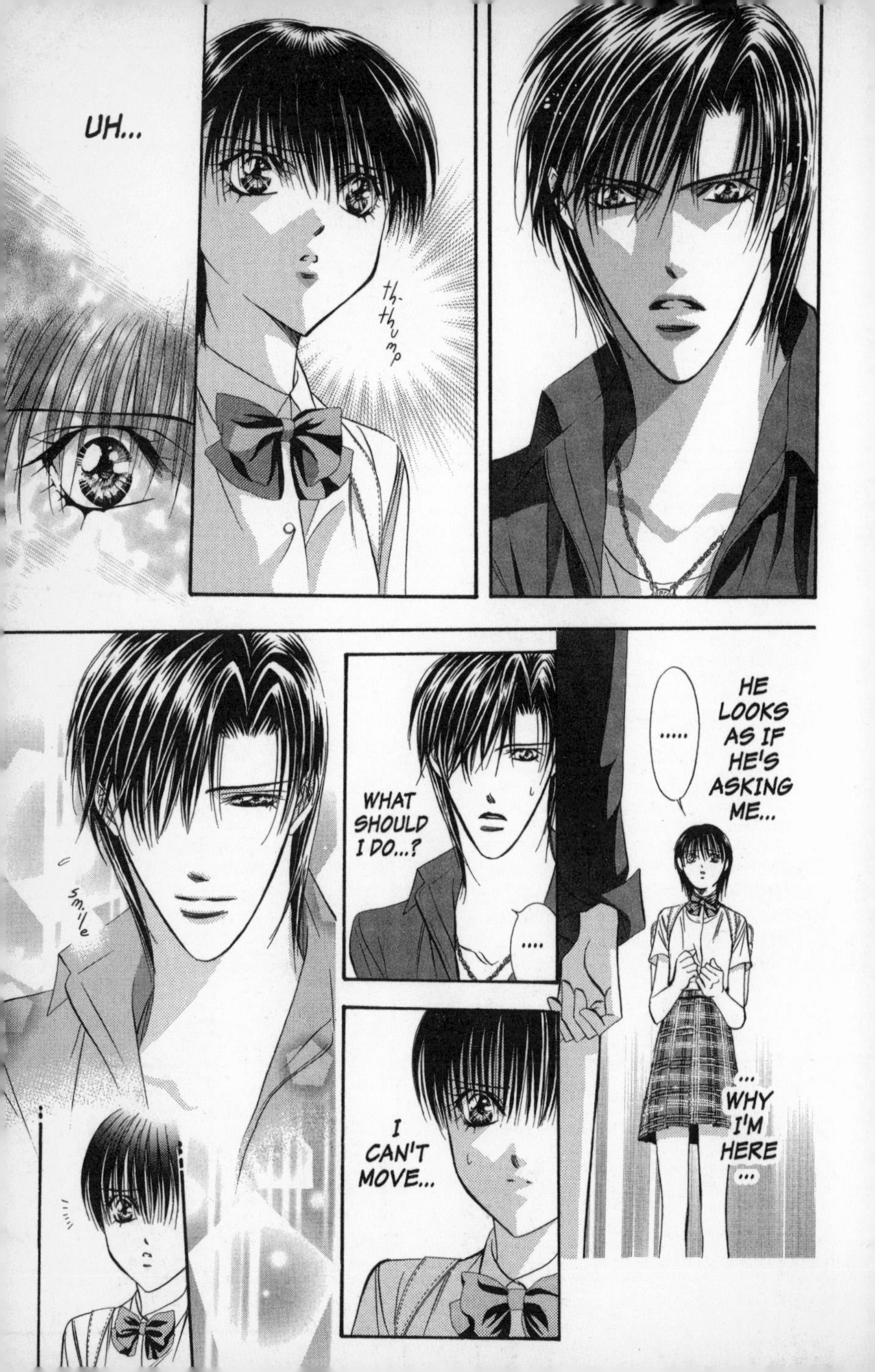
th-thump
UH...
.....
HE LOOKS AS IF HE'S ASKING ME...
... WHY I'M HERE ...
WHAT SHOULD I DO...?
....
I CAN'T MOVE...
smile

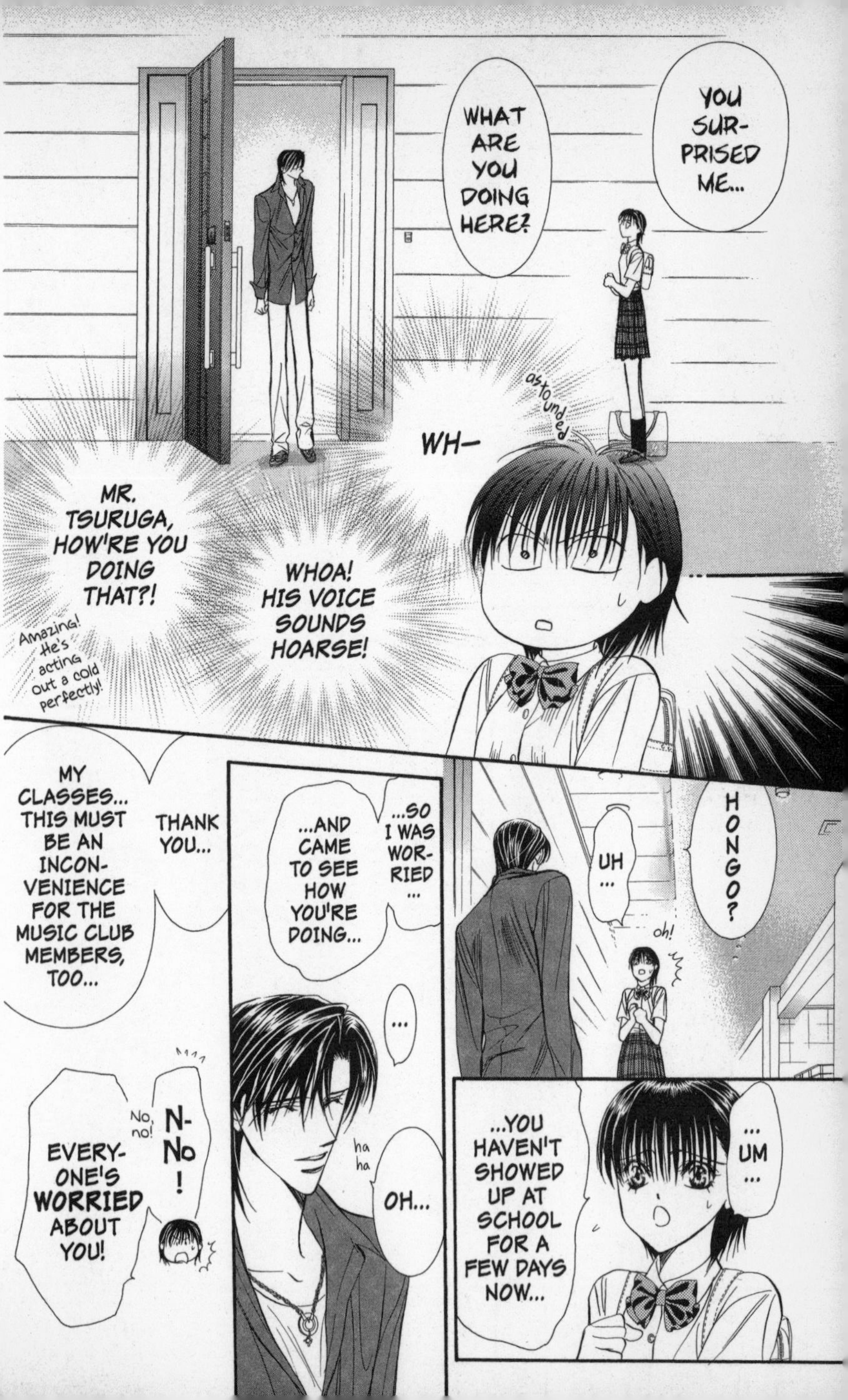
YOU SUR-PRISED ME...
WHAT ARE YOU DOING HERE?
astounded
WH—
WHOA! HIS VOICE SOUNDS HOARSE!
MR. TSURUGA, HOW'RE YOU DOING THAT?!
Amazing! He's acting out a cold perfectly!
HONGO?
UH...
oh!
...UM...
...YOU HAVEN'T SHOWED UP AT SCHOOL FOR A FEW DAYS NOW...
...SO I WAS WOR-RIED...
...AND CAME TO SEE HOW YOU'RE DOING...
...
OH...
ha ha
THANK YOU...
MY CLASSES... THIS MUST BE AN INCON-VENIENCE FOR THE MUSIC CLUB MEMBERS, TOO...
N-No!
No, no!
EVERY-ONE'S WORRIED ABOUT YOU!

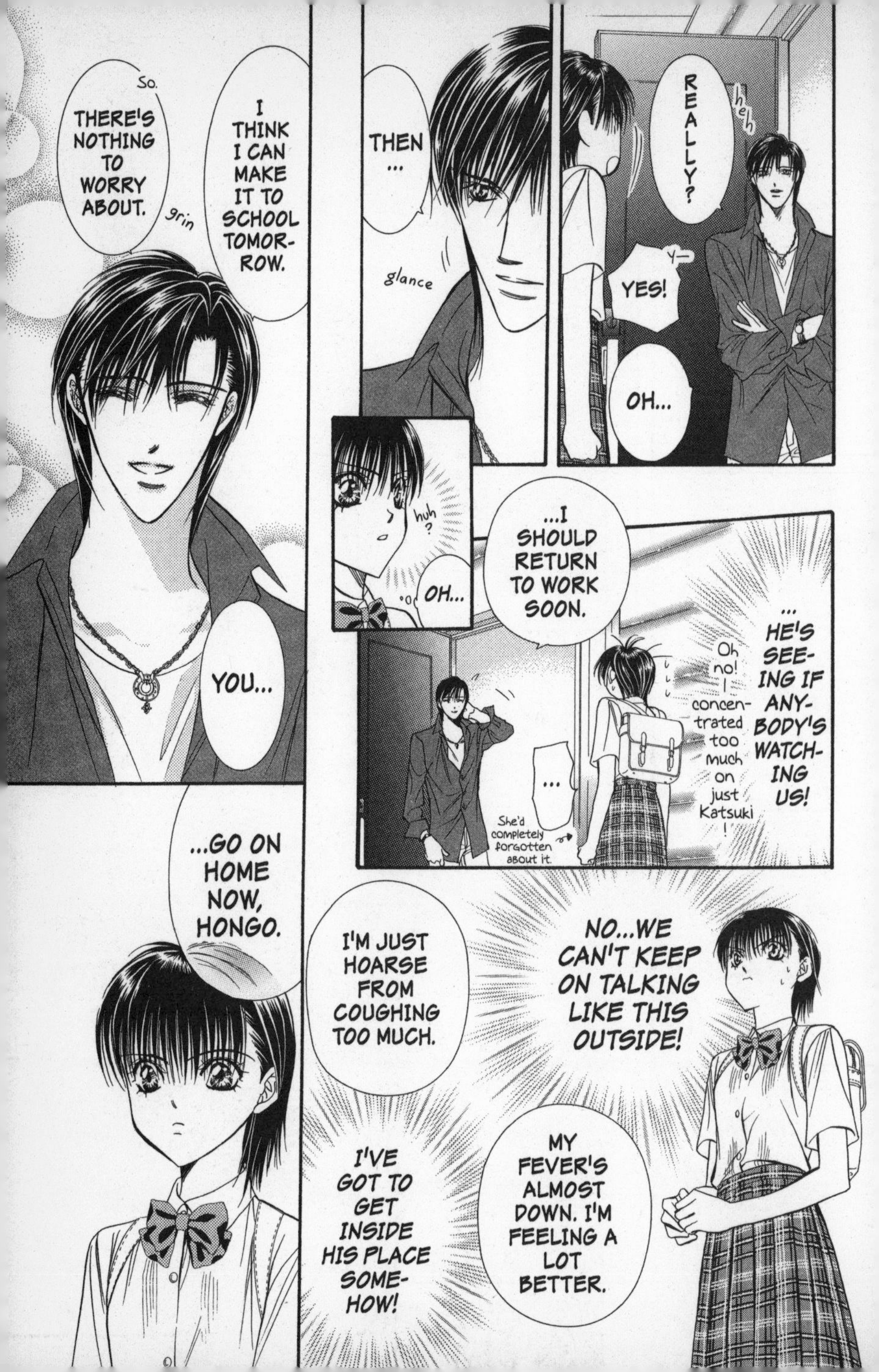
REALLY?
heh
y—
YES!
OH...
THEN...
glance
...I SHOULD RETURN TO WORK SOON.
huh?
OH...
... HE'S SEEING IF ANYBODY'S WATCHING US!
Oh no! I concentrated too much on just Katsuki!
...
She'd completely forgotten about it.
I THINK I CAN MAKE IT TO SCHOOL TOMORROW.
So. THERE'S NOTHING TO WORRY ABOUT.
grin
YOU...
...GO ON HOME NOW, HONGO.
NO...WE CAN'T KEEP ON TALKING LIKE THIS OUTSIDE!
I'M JUST HOARSE FROM COUGHING TOO MUCH.
MY FEVER'S ALMOST DOWN. I'M FEELING A LOT BETTER.
I'VE GOT TO GET INSIDE HIS PLACE SOMEHOW!

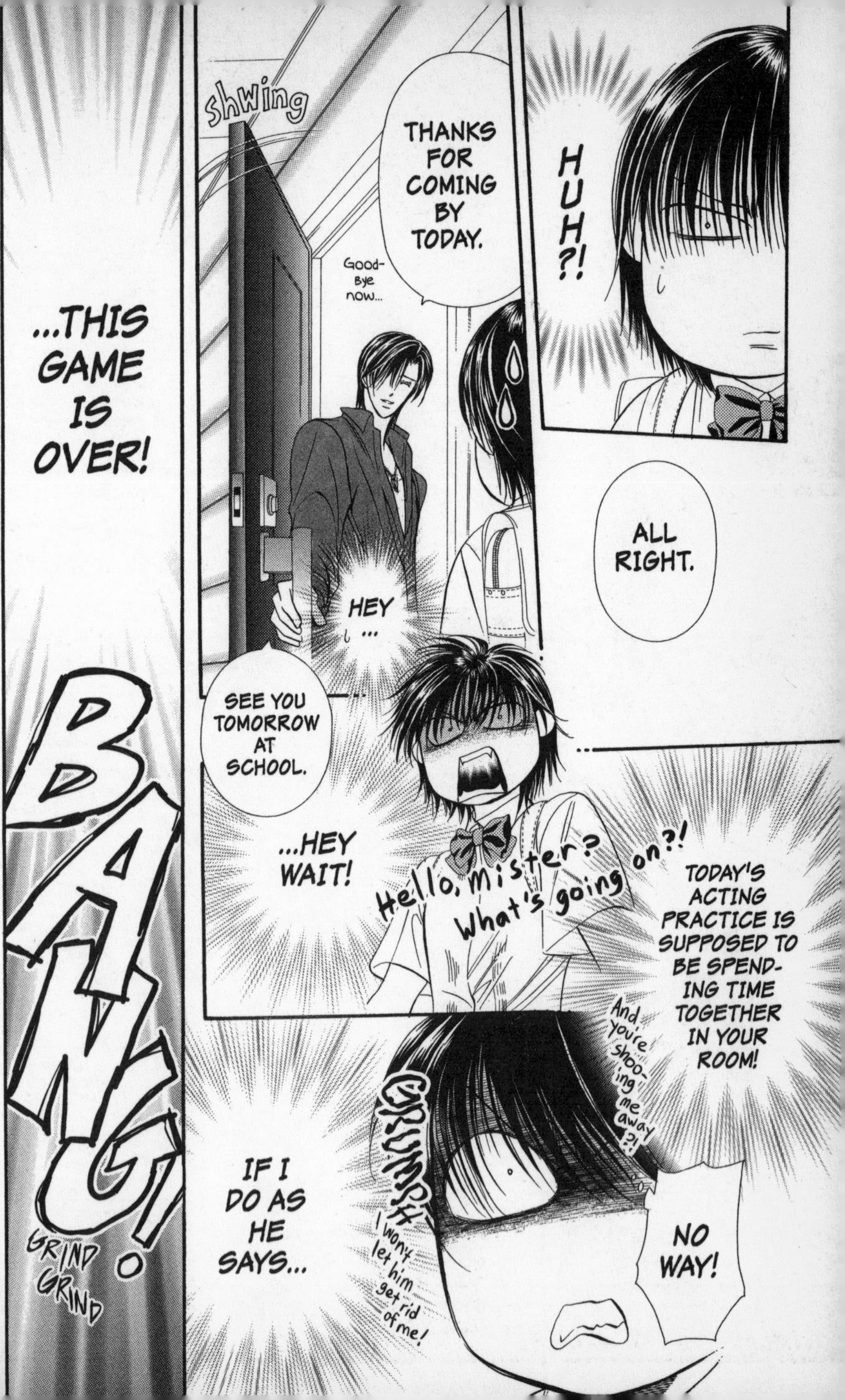
HUH?!
ALL RIGHT.
THANKS FOR COMING BY TODAY.
Good-bye now...
shwing
HEY ...
SEE YOU TOMORROW AT SCHOOL.
...HEY WAIT!
Hello, mister? What's going on?!
TODAY'S ACTING PRACTICE IS SUPPOSED TO BE SPEND-ING TIME TOGETHER IN YOUR ROOM!
And you're shoo-ing me away?!
NO WAY!
I won't let him get rid of me!
GRUMPH
IF I DO AS HE SAYS...
...THIS GAME IS OVER!
BANG!
GRIND GRIND

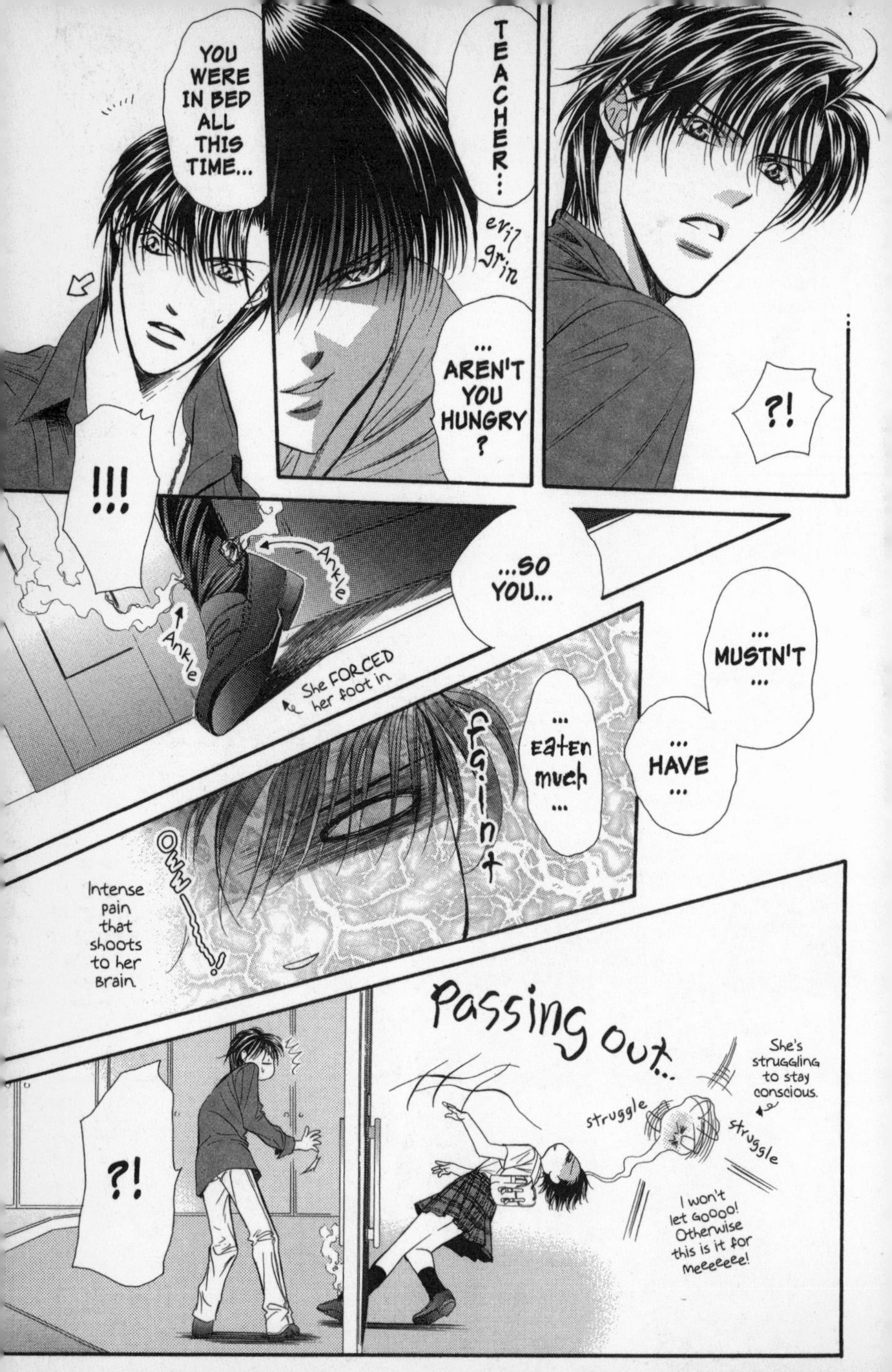
?!
TEACHER...
evil grin
...AREN'T YOU HUNGRY?
YOU WERE IN BED ALL THIS TIME...
!!!
...SO YOU...
Ankle
Ankle
She FORCED her foot in.
...MUSTN'T...
...HAVE...
...eaten much...
faint
OWW——!
Intense pain that shoots to her brain.
Passing out...
She's struggling to stay conscious.
struggle
struggle
I won't let GOOOO! Otherwise this is it for meeeeeee!
?!

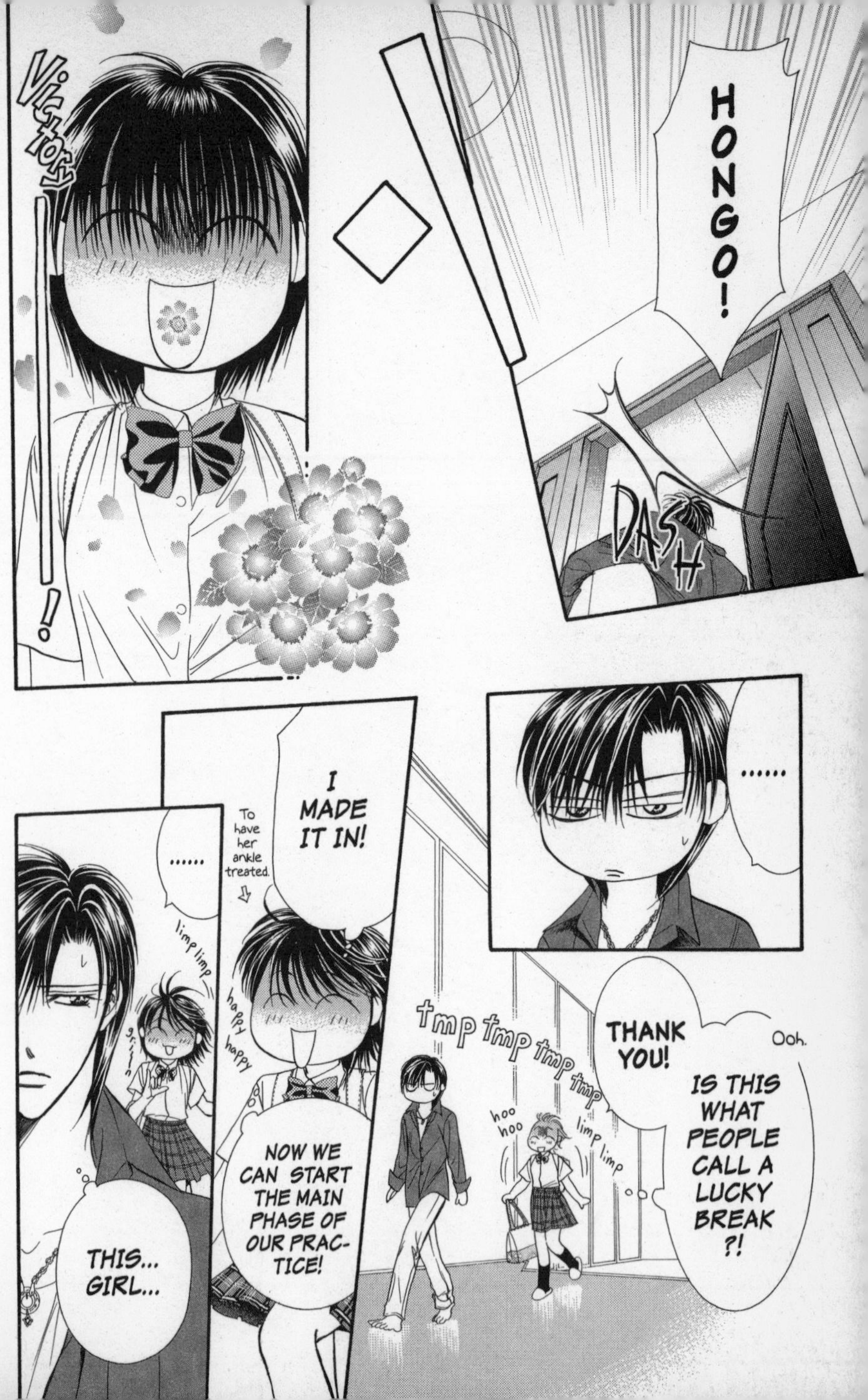
HONGO!
DASH
Victory
!
......
THANK YOU!
tmp tmp tmp tmp
hoo hoo
limp limp
Ooh.
IS THIS WHAT PEOPLE CALL A LUCKY BREAK?!
I MADE IT IN!
To have her ankle treated.
NOW WE CAN START THE MAIN PHASE OF OUR PRAC-TICE!
happy happy
......
limp limp
gri-n
THIS... GIRL...

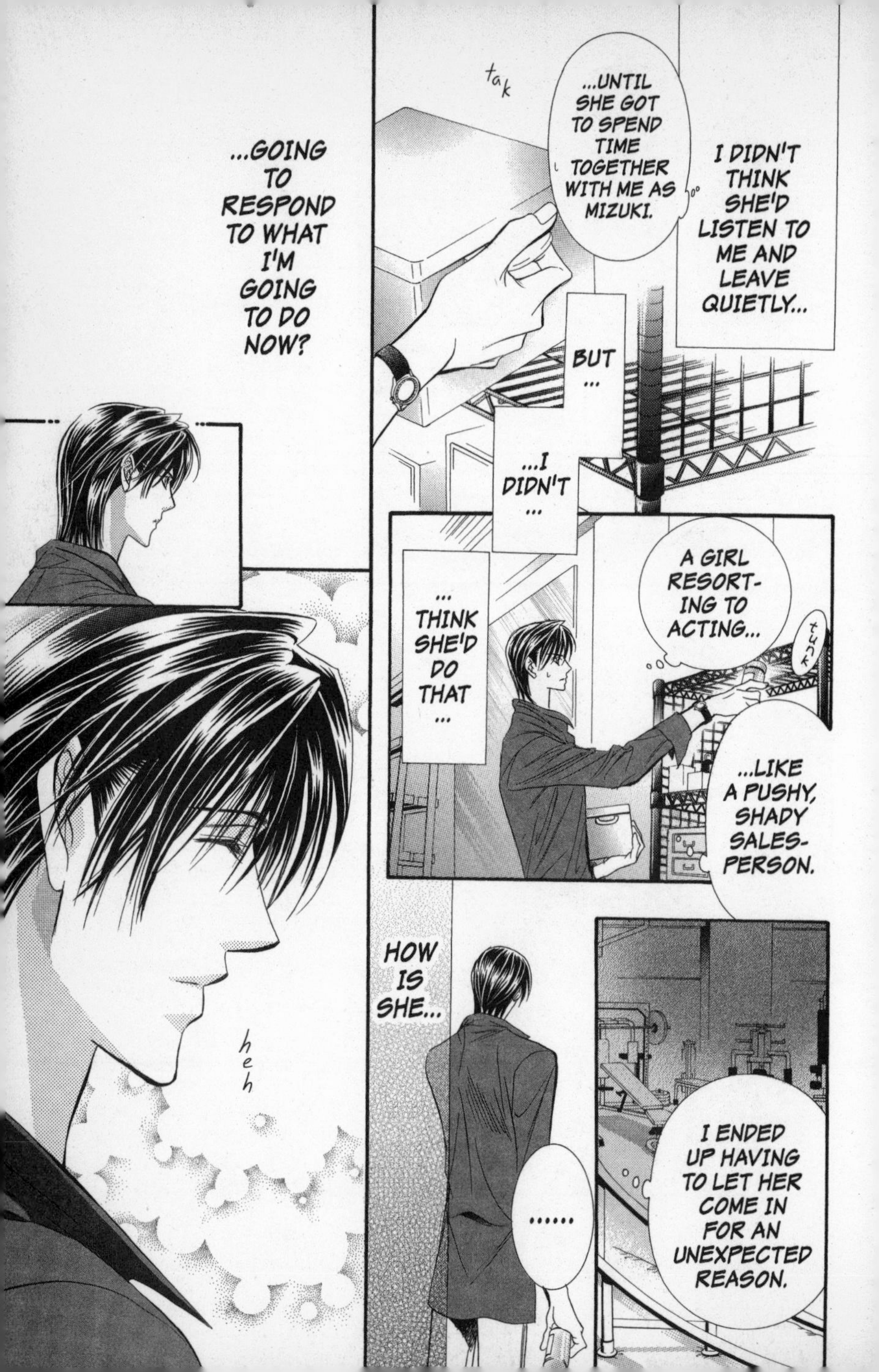
I DIDN'T THINK SHE'D LISTEN TO ME AND LEAVE QUIETLY...
...UNTIL SHE GOT TO SPEND TIME TOGETHER WITH ME AS MIZUKI.
tak
BUT ...
...I DIDN'T ...
A GIRL RESORT-ING TO ACTING...
tunk
...LIKE A PUSHY, SHADY SALES-PERSON.
... THINK SHE'D DO THAT ...
I ENDED UP HAVING TO LET HER COME IN FOR AN UNEXPECTED REASON.
......
HOW IS SHE...
...GOING TO RESPOND TO WHAT I'M GOING TO DO NOW?
heh

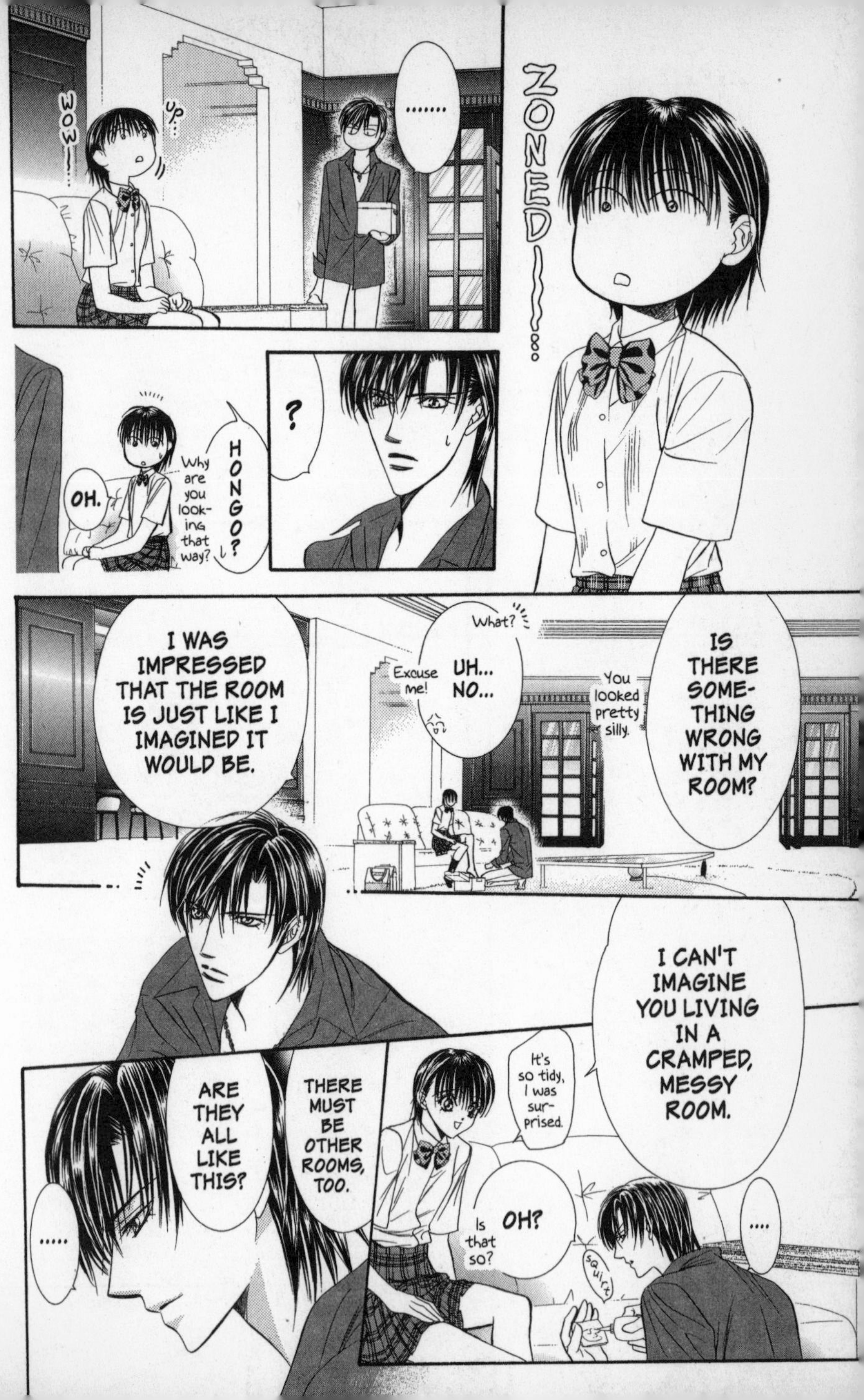
ZONED...!!
....
up...
WOW...!!
?
HONGO?
Why are you looking that way?
OH.
IS THERE SOMETHING WRONG WITH MY ROOM?
What?
You looked pretty silly.
UH... NO...
Excuse me!
I WAS IMPRESSED THAT THE ROOM IS JUST LIKE I IMAGINED IT WOULD BE.
I CAN'T IMAGINE YOU LIVING IN A CRAMPED, MESSY ROOM.
It's so tidy, I was surprised.
....
OH?
Is that so?
squirt
THERE MUST BE OTHER ROOMS, TOO.
ARE THEY ALL LIKE THIS?
.....

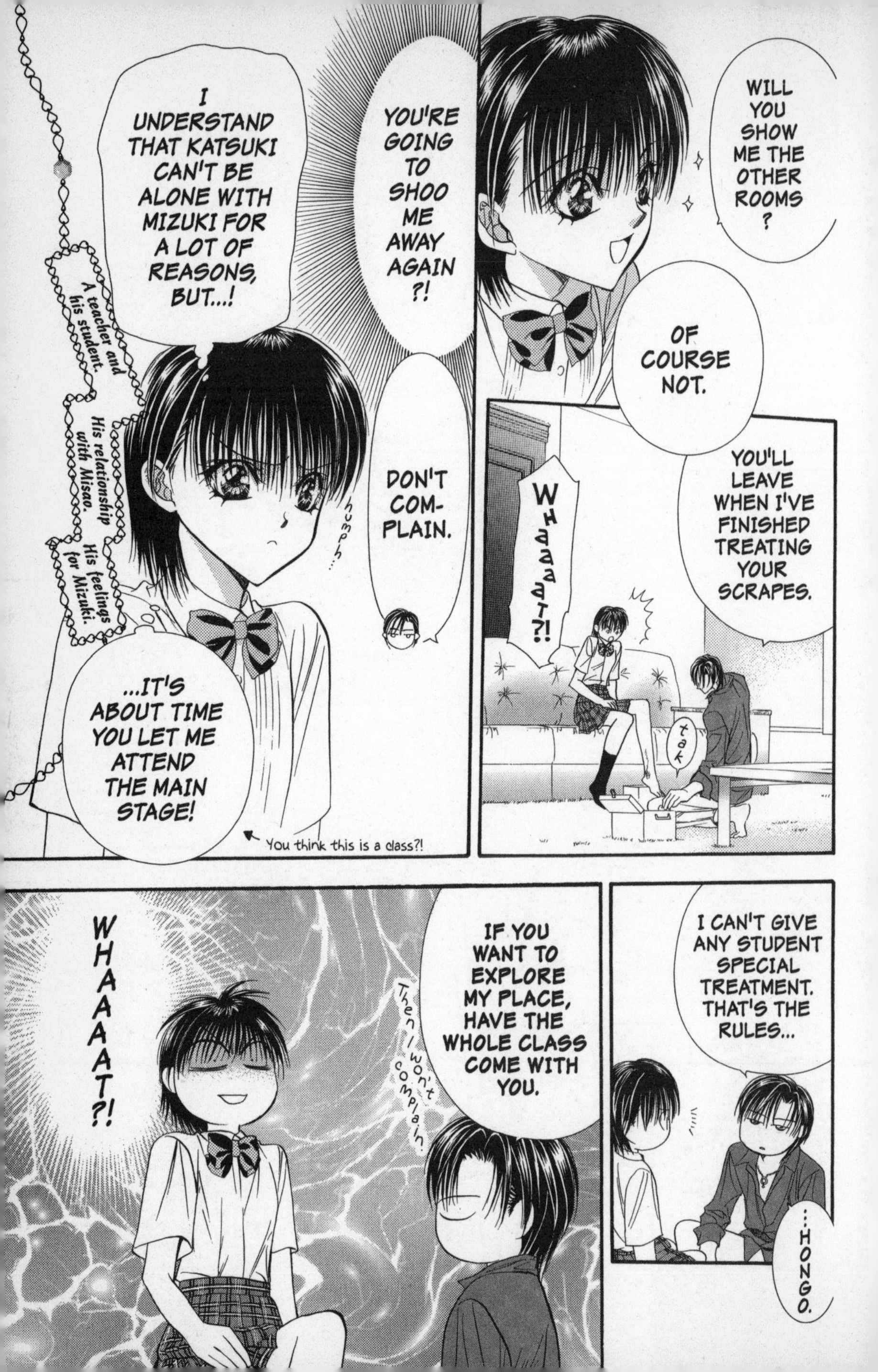
WILL YOU SHOW ME THE OTHER ROOMS?
OF COURSE NOT.
YOU'LL LEAVE WHEN I'VE FINISHED TREATING YOUR SCRAPES.
WHaaaaT?!
tak
YOU'RE GOING TO SHOO ME AWAY AGAIN?!
DON'T COM-PLAIN.
humph...
I UNDERSTAND THAT KATSUKI CAN'T BE ALONE WITH MIZUKI FOR A LOT OF REASONS, BUT...!
A teacher and his student.
His relationship with Misao.
His feelings for Mizuki.
...IT'S ABOUT TIME YOU LET ME ATTEND THE MAIN STAGE!
You think this is a class?!
I CAN'T GIVE ANY STUDENT SPECIAL TREATMENT. THAT'S THE RULES...
...HONGO.
IF YOU WANT TO EXPLORE MY PLACE, HAVE THE WHOLE CLASS COME WITH YOU.
Then I won't complain.
WHAAAAT?!

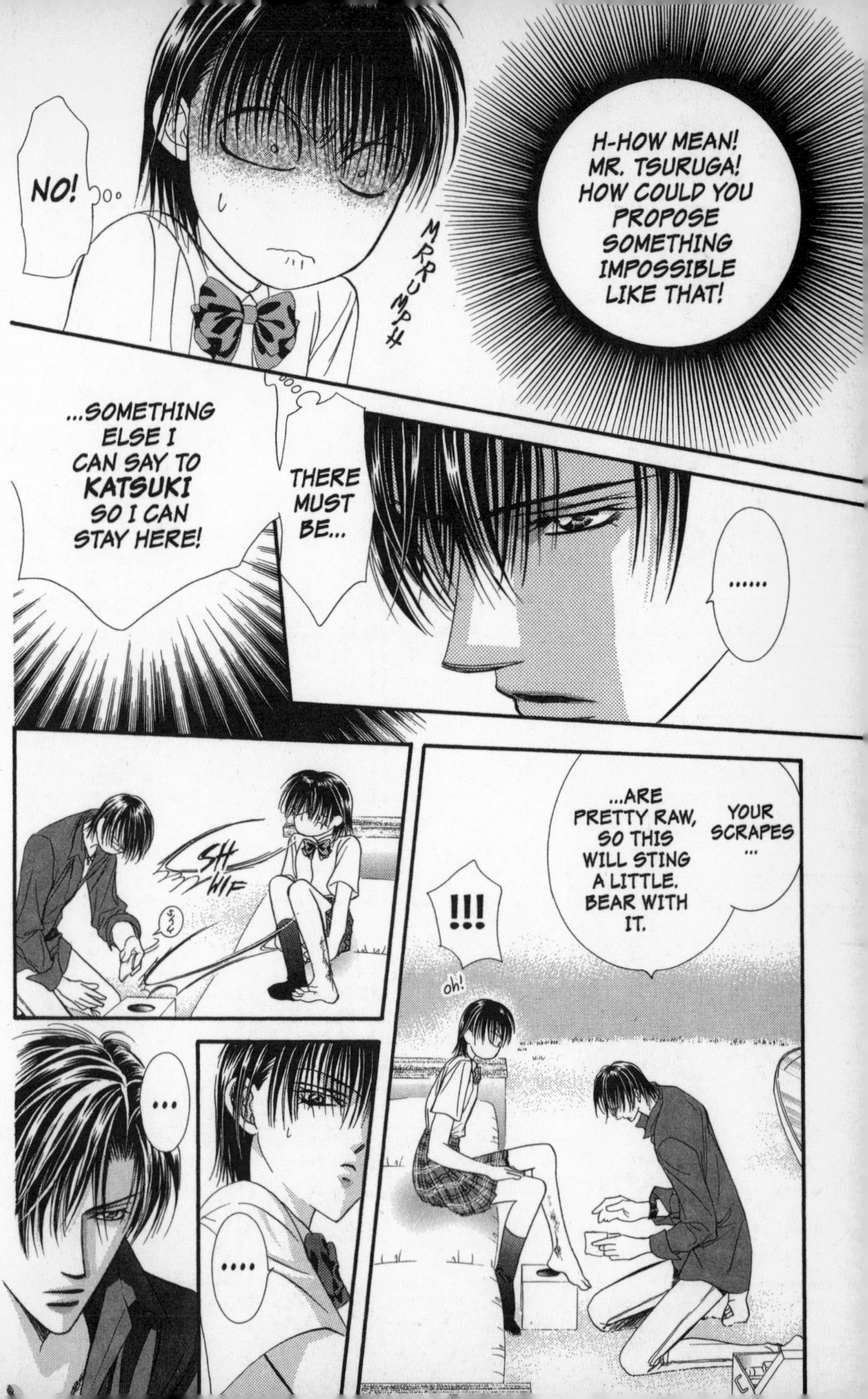

H-HOW MEAN! MR. TSURUGA! HOW COULD YOU PROPOSE SOMETHING IMPOSSIBLE LIKE THAT!
MRRUMPH
NO!
......
THERE MUST BE...
...SOMETHING ELSE I CAN SAY TO KATSUKI SO I CAN STAY HERE!
YOUR SCRAPES ...
...ARE PRETTY RAW, SO THIS WILL STING A LITTLE. BEAR WITH IT.
!!!
oh!
SHWIF
....
...

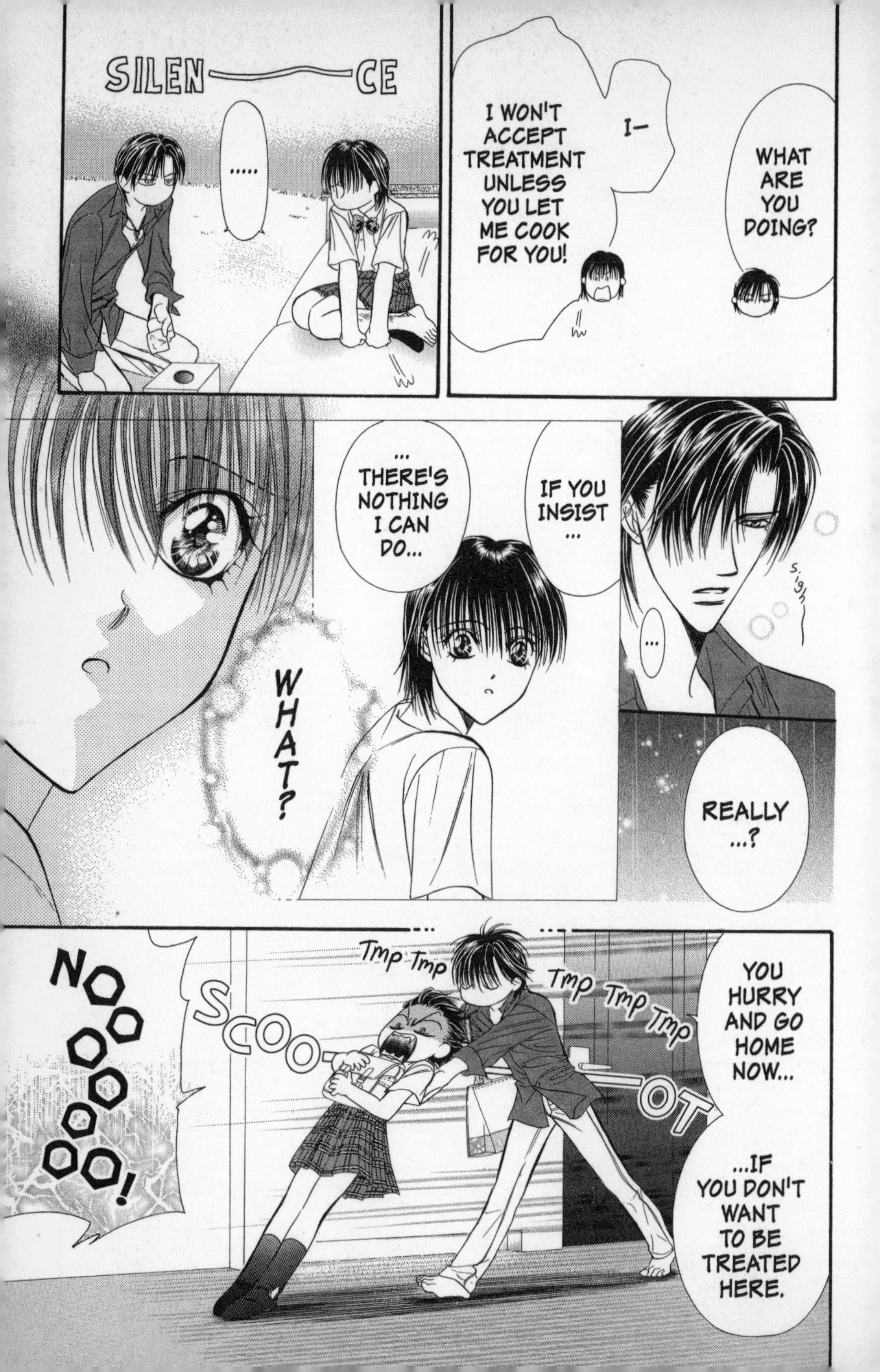
WHAT ARE YOU DOING?
I—
I WON'T ACCEPT TREATMENT UNLESS YOU LET ME COOK FOR YOU!
SILEN——CE
.....
...
Sigh
REALLY ...?
IF YOU INSIST ...
... THERE'S NOTHING I CAN DO...
WHAT?
YOU HURRY AND GO HOME NOW...
...IF YOU DON'T WANT TO BE TREATED HERE.
Tmp Tmp Tmp
Tmp Tmp
SCOO—OT
NOOOOOOOO!

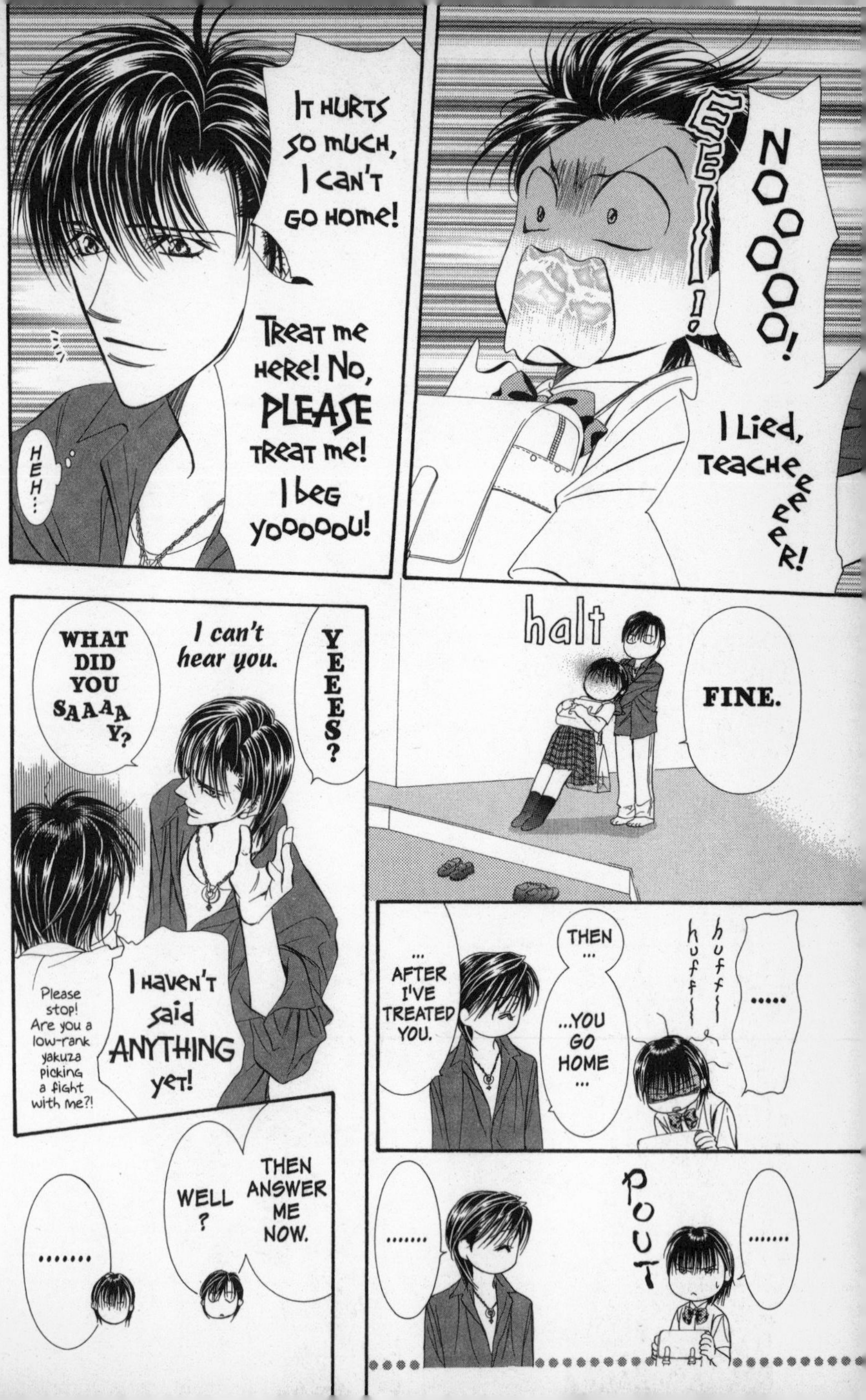
NOOOOO!
EE—!
I lied, teacheeeeer!
It hurts so much, I can't go home!
Treat me here! No, PLEASE treat me! I beg yoooooou!
HEH...
FINE.
halt
YEEES?
I can't hear you.
WHAT DID YOU SAAAAY?
I haven't said ANYTHING yet!
Please stop! Are you a low-rank yakuza picking a fight with me?!
.....
huff huff
THEN... ...YOU GO HOME...
... AFTER I'VE TREATED YOU.
THEN ANSWER ME NOW.
WELL?
....
....
POUT
....

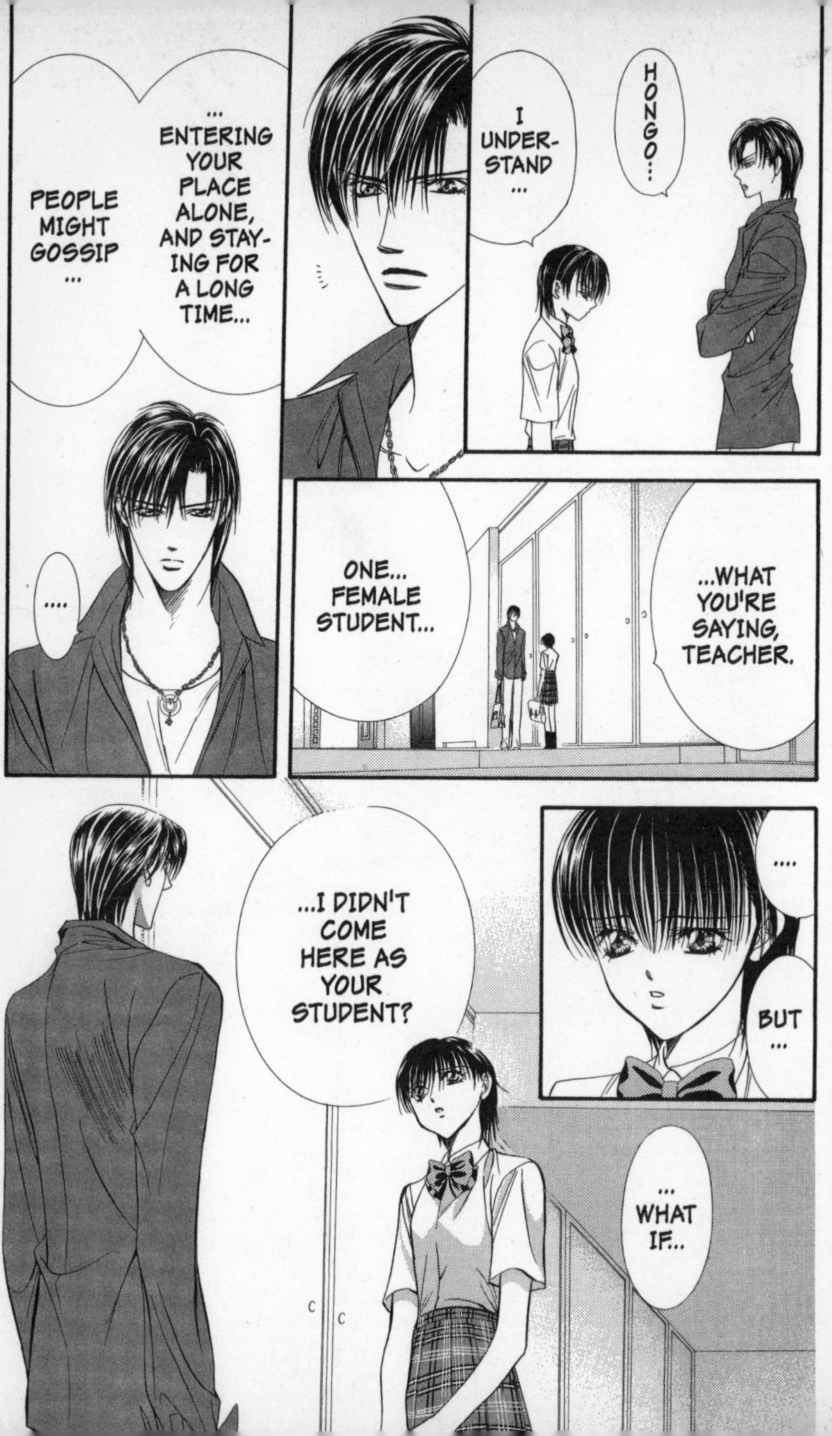
HONGO...
I UNDER-STAND ...
...WHAT YOU'RE SAYING, TEACHER.
ONE... FEMALE STUDENT...
... ENTERING YOUR PLACE ALONE, AND STAY-ING FOR A LONG TIME...
PEOPLE MIGHT GOSSIP ...
....
....
BUT ...
... WHAT IF...
...I DIDN'T COME HERE AS YOUR STUDENT?

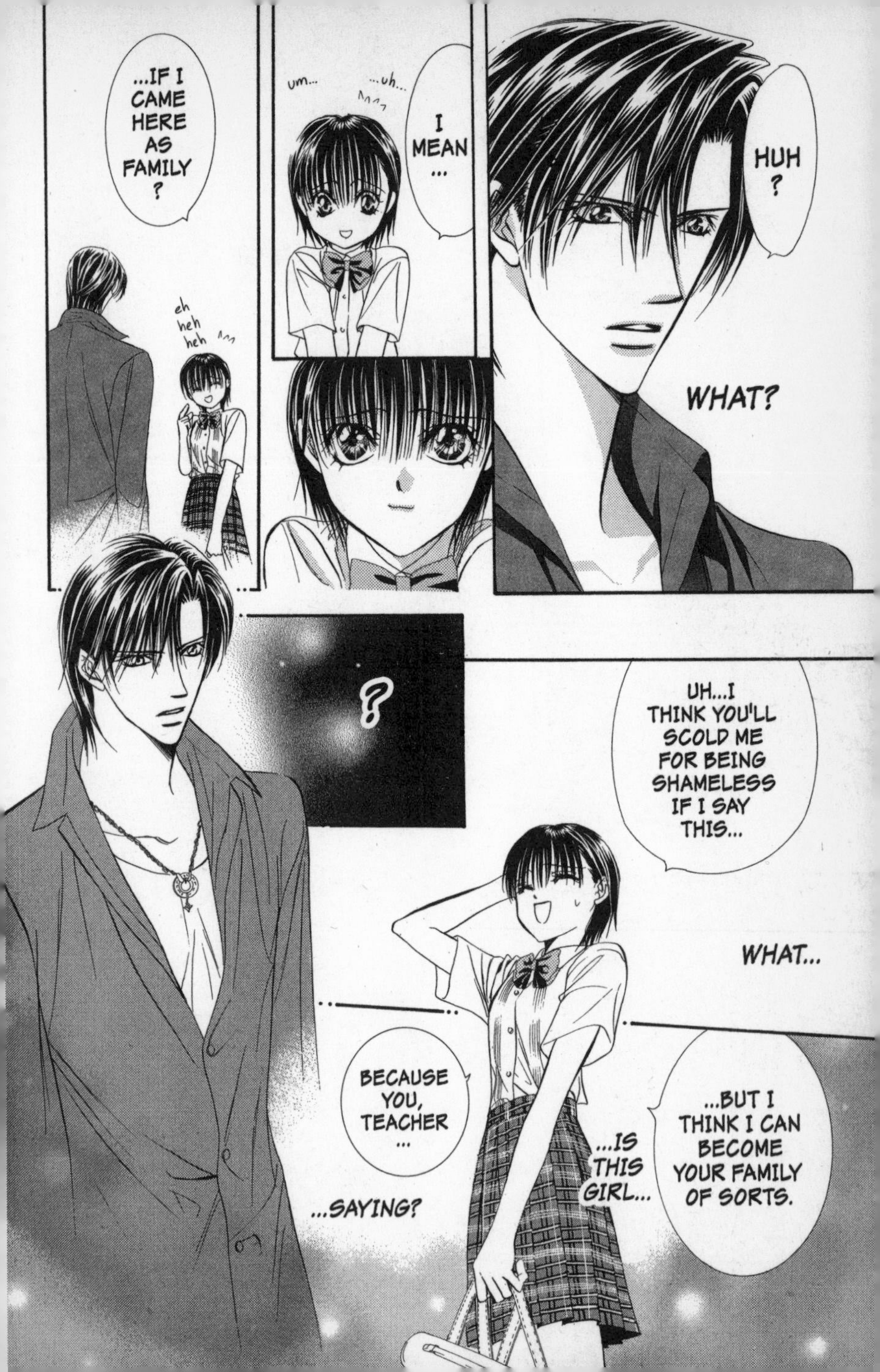
HUH?
WHAT?
I MEAN...
...uh...
um...
...IF I CAME HERE AS FAMILY?
eh heh heh
UH...I THINK YOU'LL SCOLD ME FOR BEING SHAMELESS IF I SAY THIS...
?
WHAT...
...BUT I THINK I CAN BECOME YOUR FAMILY OF SORTS.
...IS THIS GIRL...
BECAUSE YOU, TEACHER...
...SAYING?

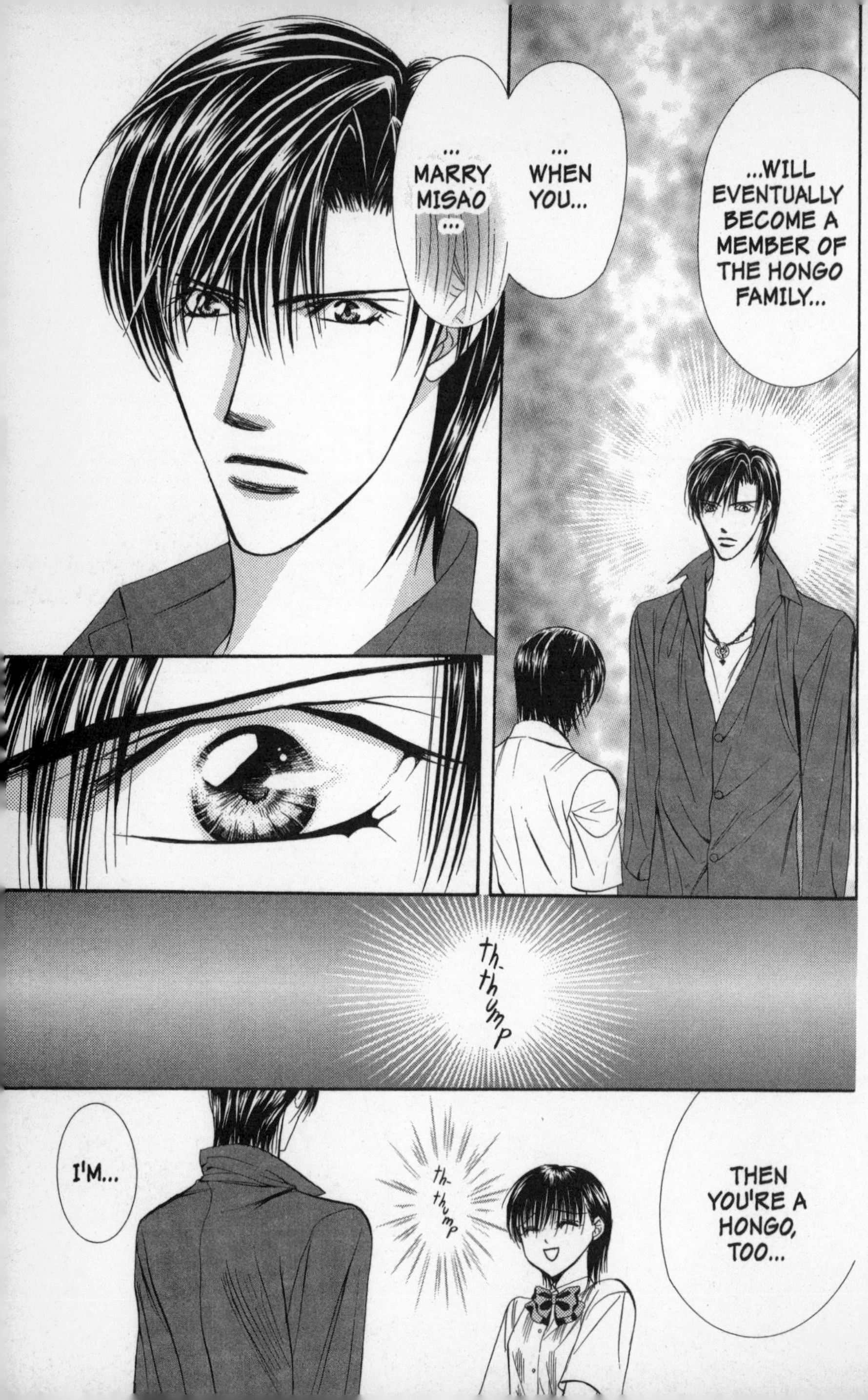
...WILL EVENTUALLY BECOME A MEMBER OF THE HONGO FAMILY...
... WHEN YOU...
... MARRY MISAO ...
th-thump
THEN YOU'RE A HONGO, TOO...
th-thump
I'M...

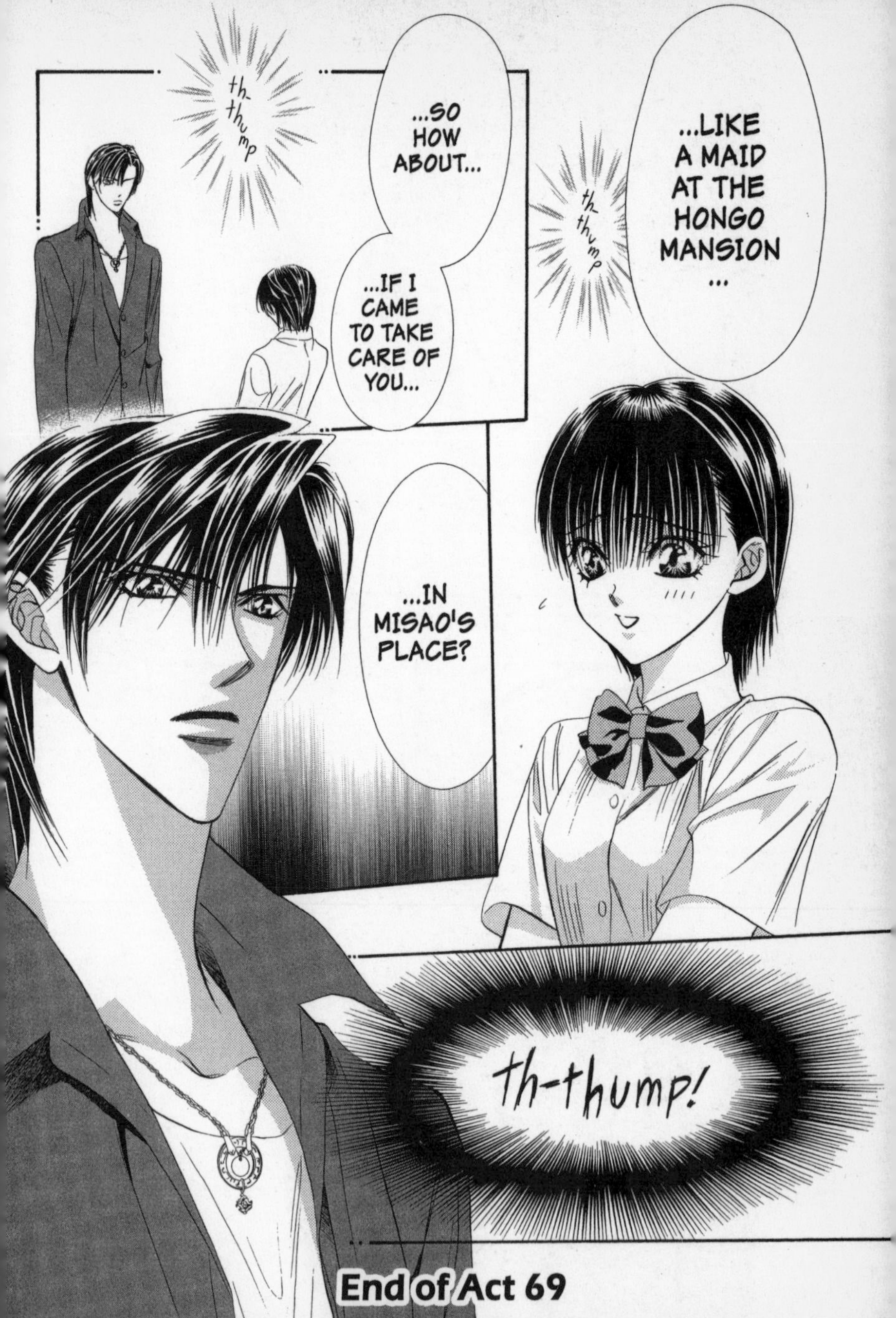
...LIKE A MAID AT THE HONGO MANSION ...
th-thump
...SO HOW ABOUT...
...IF I CAME TO TAKE CARE OF YOU...
th-thump
...IN MISAO'S PLACE?
th-thump!
End of Act 69

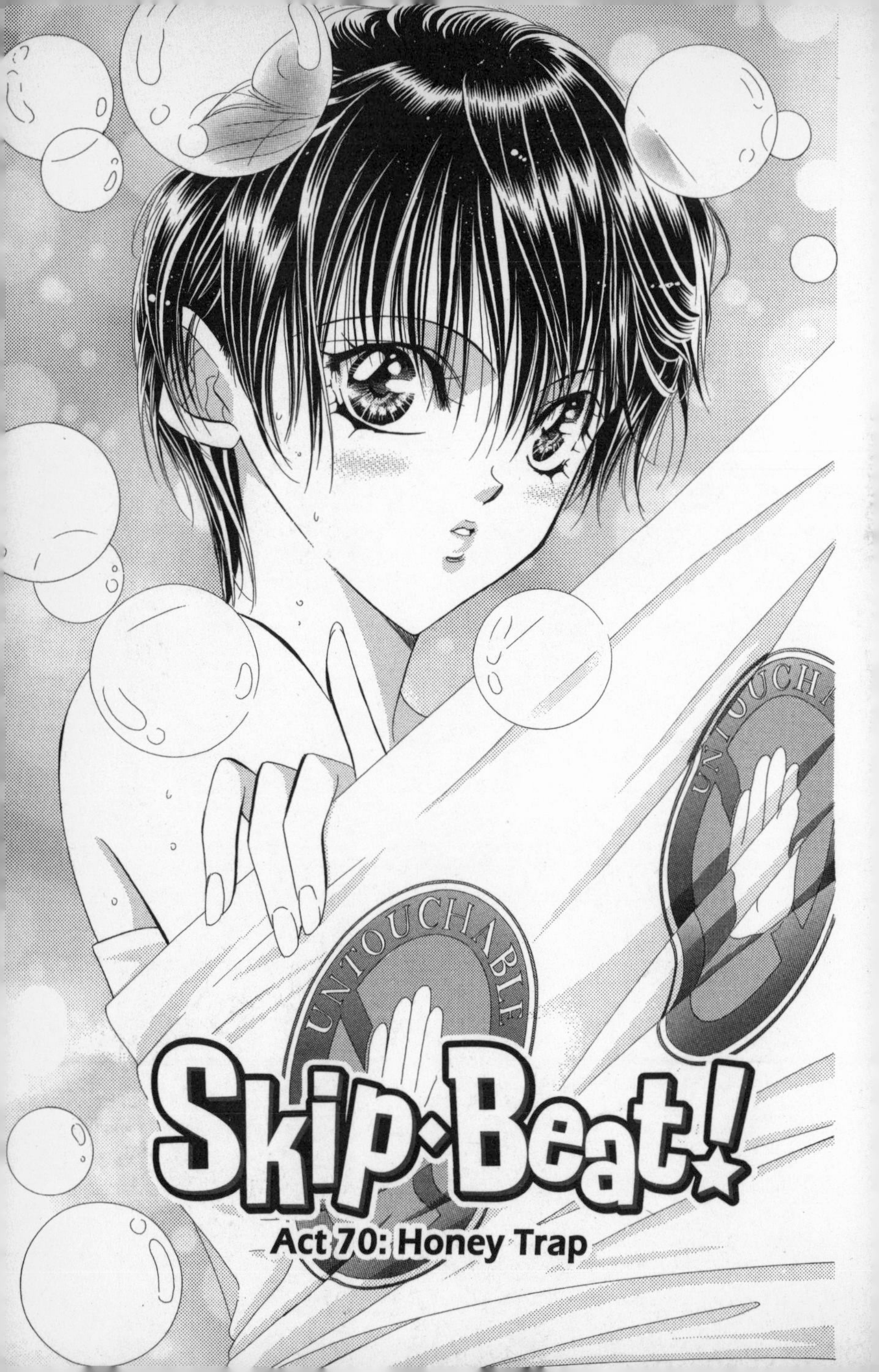
UNTOUCHABLE
UNTOUCHA
Skip·Beat!
Act 70: Honey Trap

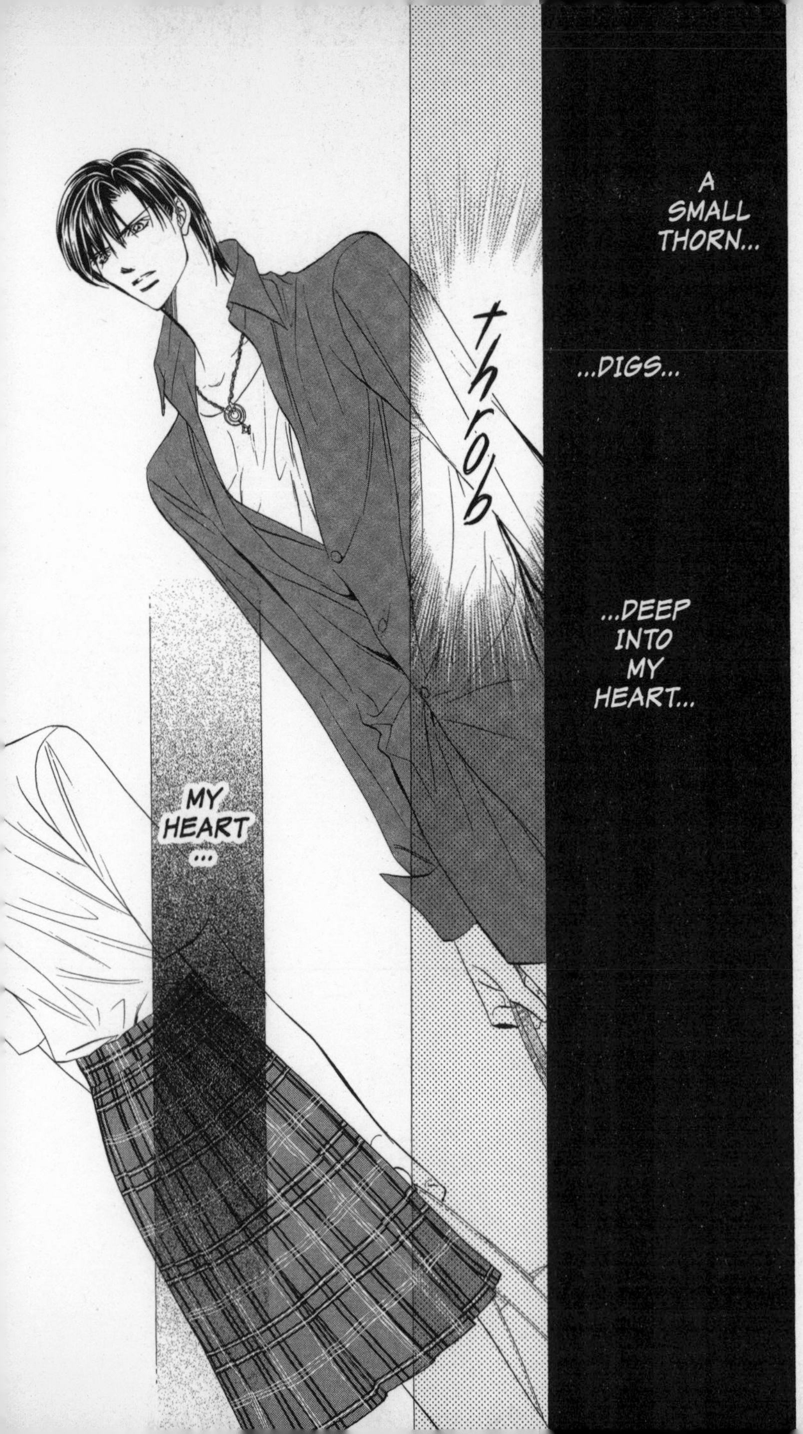
A SMALL THORN...
...DIGS...
...DEEP INTO MY HEART...
throb
MY HEART...

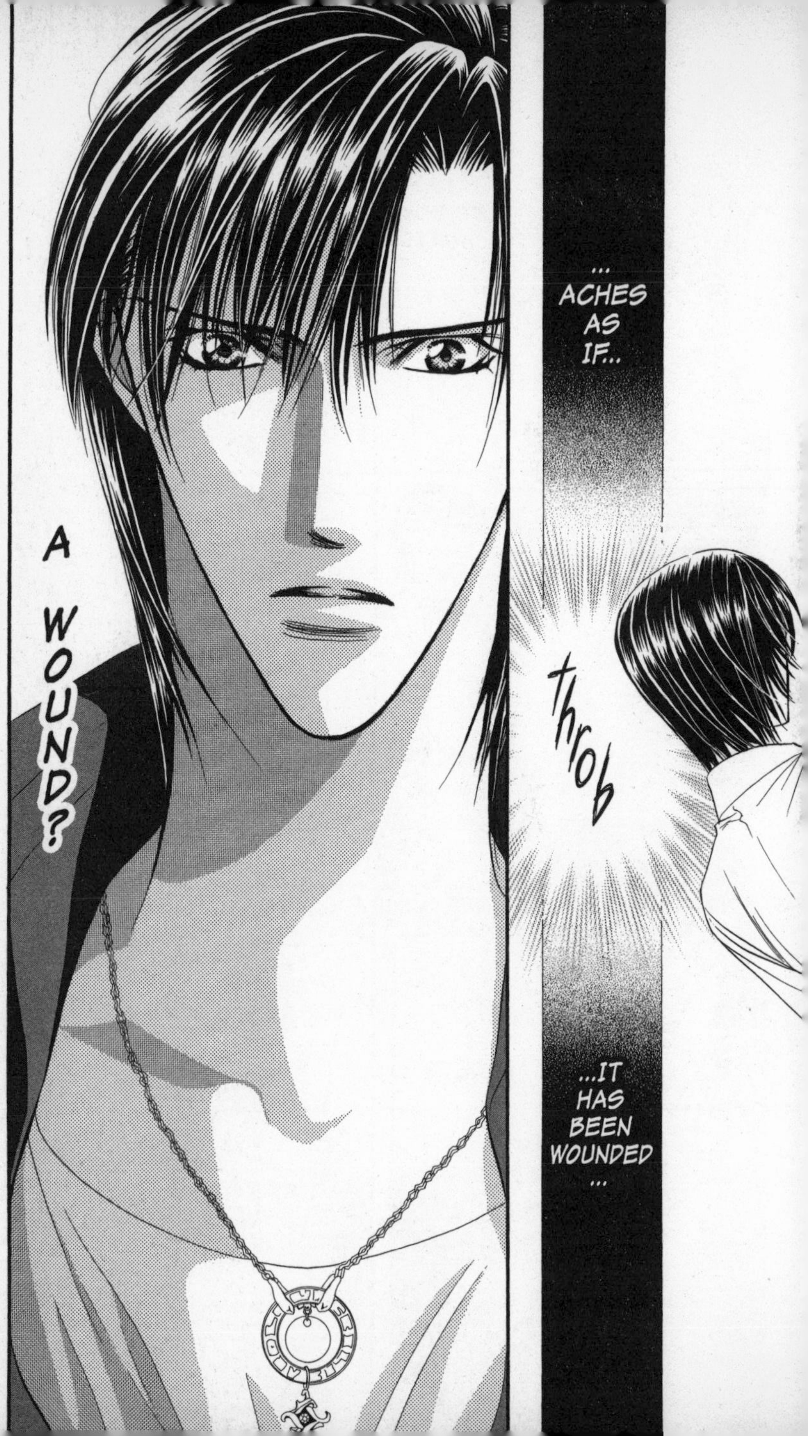
...ACHES AS IF...
throb
...IT HAS BEEN WOUNDED...
A WOUND?

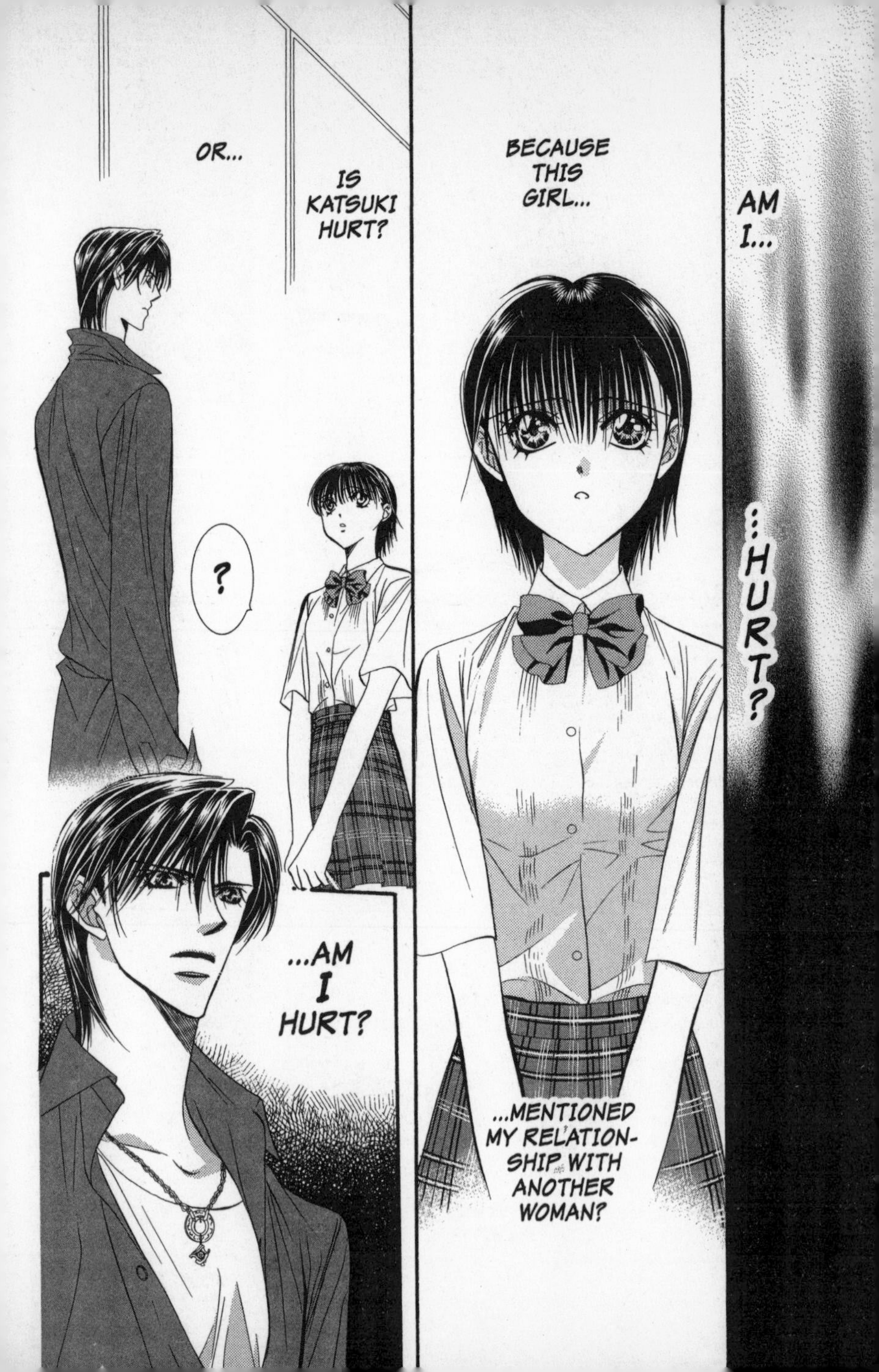
AM I...
...HURT?
BECAUSE THIS GIRL...
...MENTIONED MY RELATION-SHIP WITH ANOTHER WOMAN?
OR...
IS KATSUKI HURT?
?
...AM I HURT?

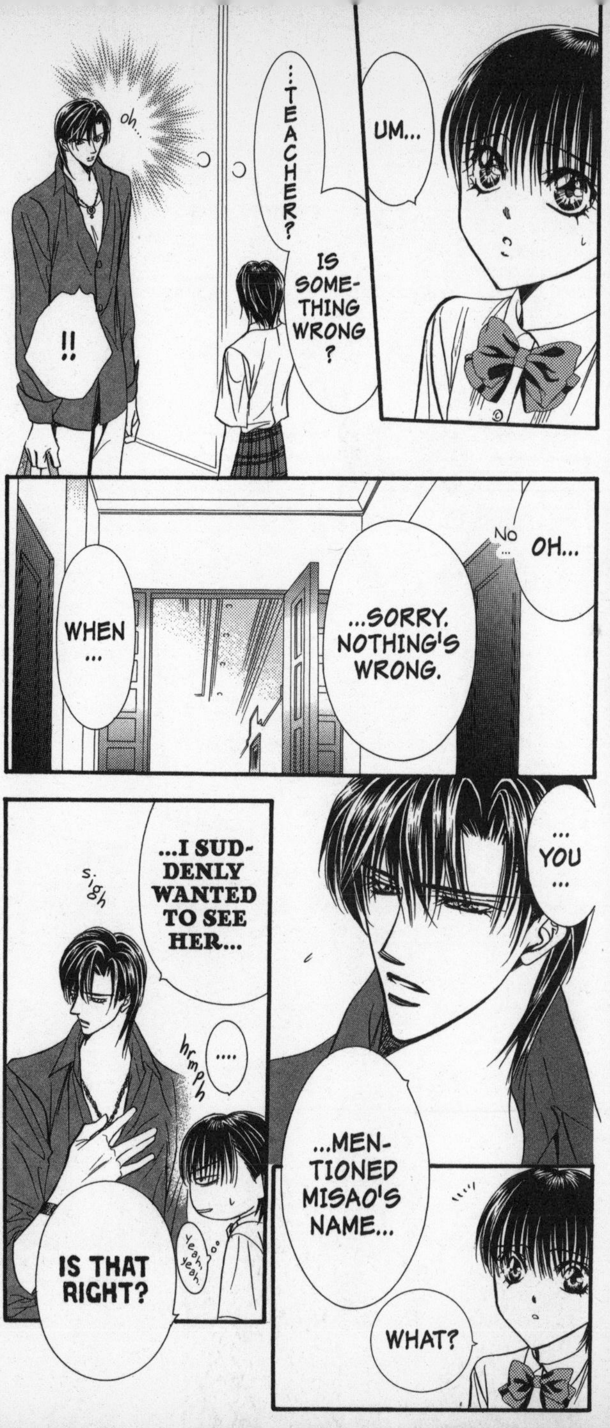
UM...
...TEACHER?
IS SOMETHING WRONG?
oh...
!!
OH...
No...
...SORRY. NOTHING'S WRONG.
WHEN...
...YOU...
...MENTIONED MISAO'S NAME...
WHAT?
...I SUDDENLY WANTED TO SEE HER...
sigh
....
hrmph
IS THAT RIGHT?
Yeah, yeah.

Apology

In this volume, I found it a bother to write "King of the Night" each time, and thought about abbreviating it as "Yaoh." However, I remembered the title of the drama and thought, "Using an abbreviation that's the same as the drama title is not good," so I didn't...I feel that I'm too neurotic myself... yeah...(wry smile)

...By the way...about my apology...the new material for this volume consists only of the title page illustration and four sidebars...unfortunately...I couldn't get around to drawing new illustrations for the pages between the chapters...I really apologize to the readers who read the magazine as well, because there are so few extras...next time...well...probably next time too... correcting the tankobon will probably take a lot of time... But I will do my best to draw new illustrations and fill the sidebars...But...sidebars...what should I write...there are no new characters appearing...hmm... (sweat)...I'll...think of something...

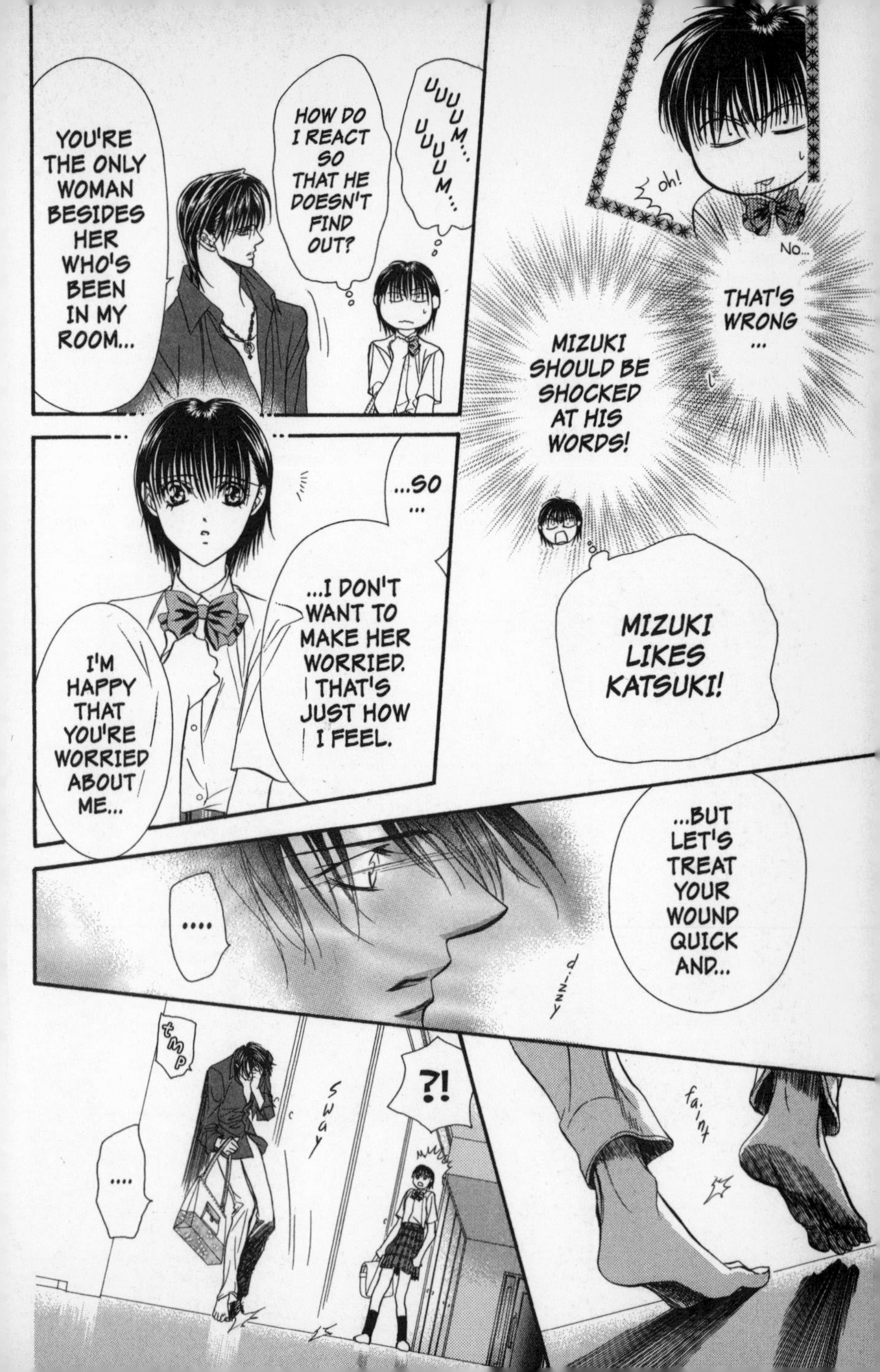
oh!
No...
THAT'S WRONG ...
MIZUKI SHOULD BE SHOCKED AT HIS WORDS!
MIZUKI LIKES KATSUKI!
UUUUM... UUUUM...
HOW DO I REACT SO THAT HE DOESN'T FIND OUT?
YOU'RE THE ONLY WOMAN BESIDES HER WHO'S BEEN IN MY ROOM...
...SO ...
...I DON'T WANT TO MAKE HER WORRIED. THAT'S JUST HOW I FEEL.
I'M HAPPY THAT YOU'RE WORRIED ABOUT ME...
...BUT LET'S TREAT YOUR WOUND QUICK AND...
dizzy
....
faint
?!
sway
tmp
....

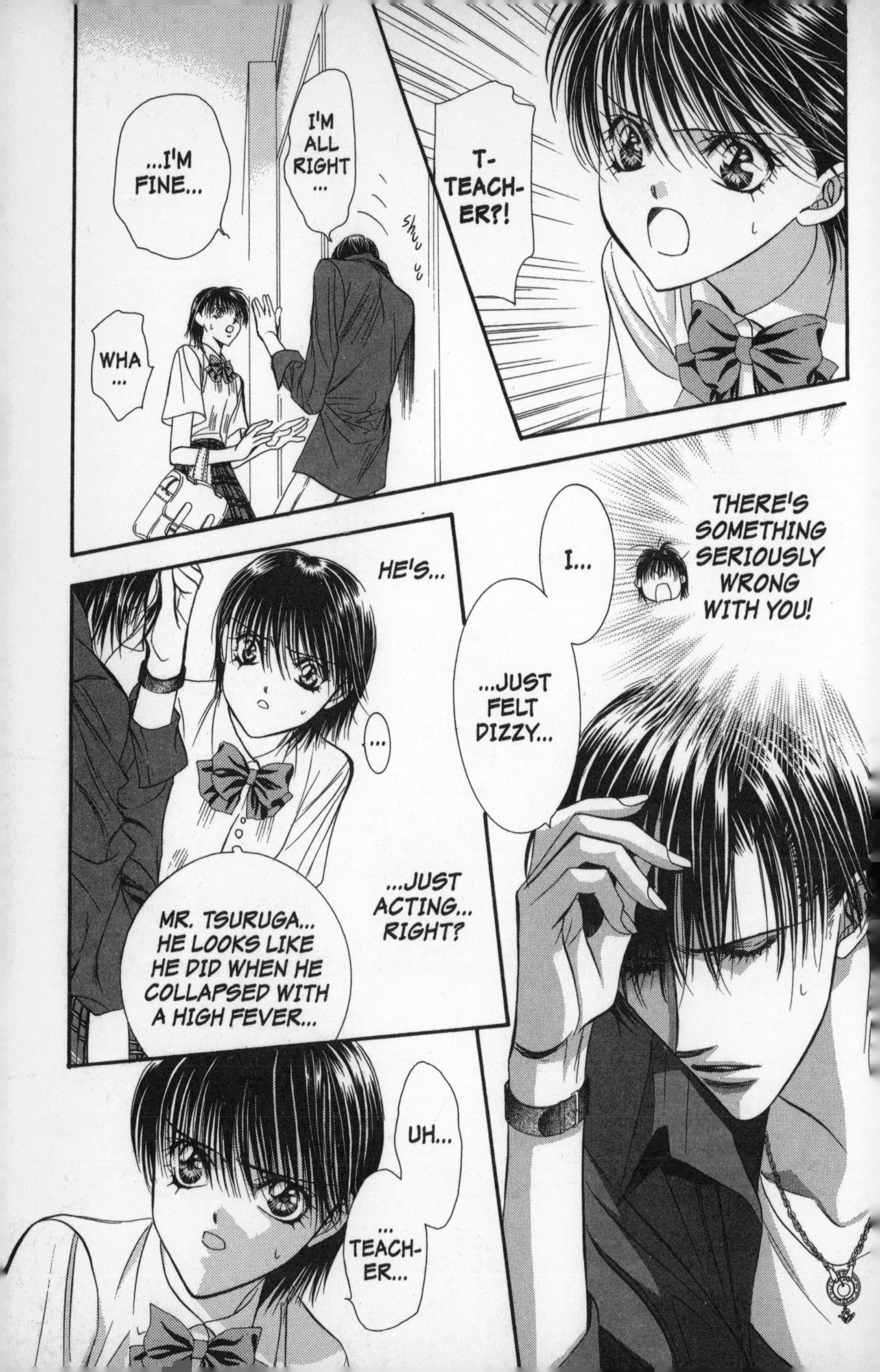
T-TEACHER?!
I'M ALL RIGHT ...
shuu
...I'M FINE...
WHA ...
THERE'S SOMETHING SERIOUSLY WRONG WITH YOU!
I...
...JUST FELT DIZZY...
HE'S...
...
...JUST ACTING... RIGHT?
MR. TSURUGA... HE LOOKS LIKE HE DID WHEN HE COLLAPSED WITH A HIGH FEVER...
UH...
... TEACHER...

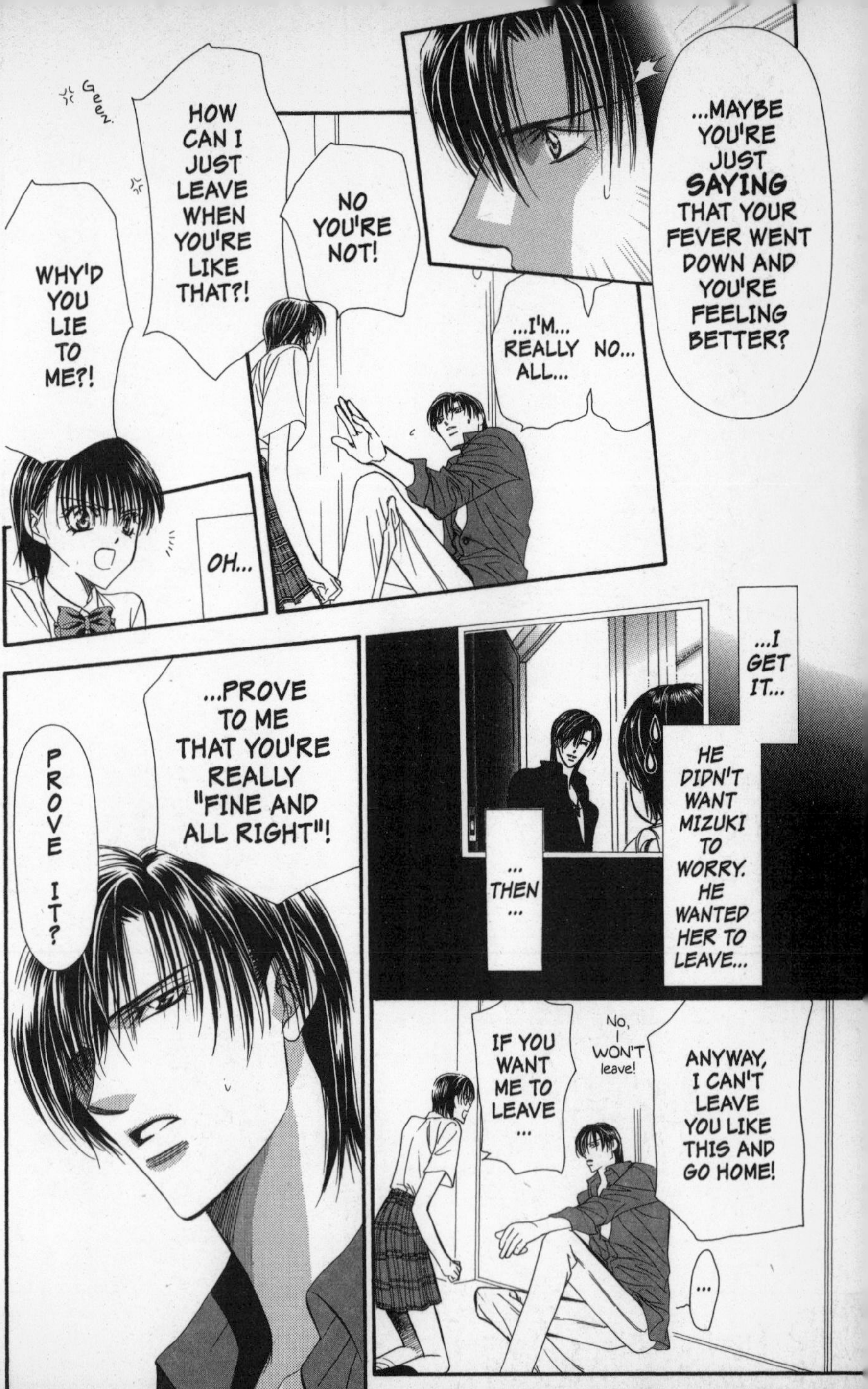
...MAYBE YOU'RE JUST SAYING THAT YOUR FEVER WENT DOWN AND YOU'RE FEELING BETTER?
NO...
...I'M... REALLY ALL...
NO YOU'RE NOT!
HOW CAN I JUST LEAVE WHEN YOU'RE LIKE THAT?!
Geez.
WHY'D YOU LIE TO ME?!
OH...
...I GET IT...
HE DIDN'T WANT MIZUKI TO WORRY. HE WANTED HER TO LEAVE...
...THEN...
ANYWAY, I CAN'T LEAVE YOU LIKE THIS AND GO HOME!
No, I WON'T leave!
IF YOU WANT ME TO LEAVE...
...
...PROVE TO ME THAT YOU'RE REALLY "FINE AND ALL RIGHT"!
PROVE IT?

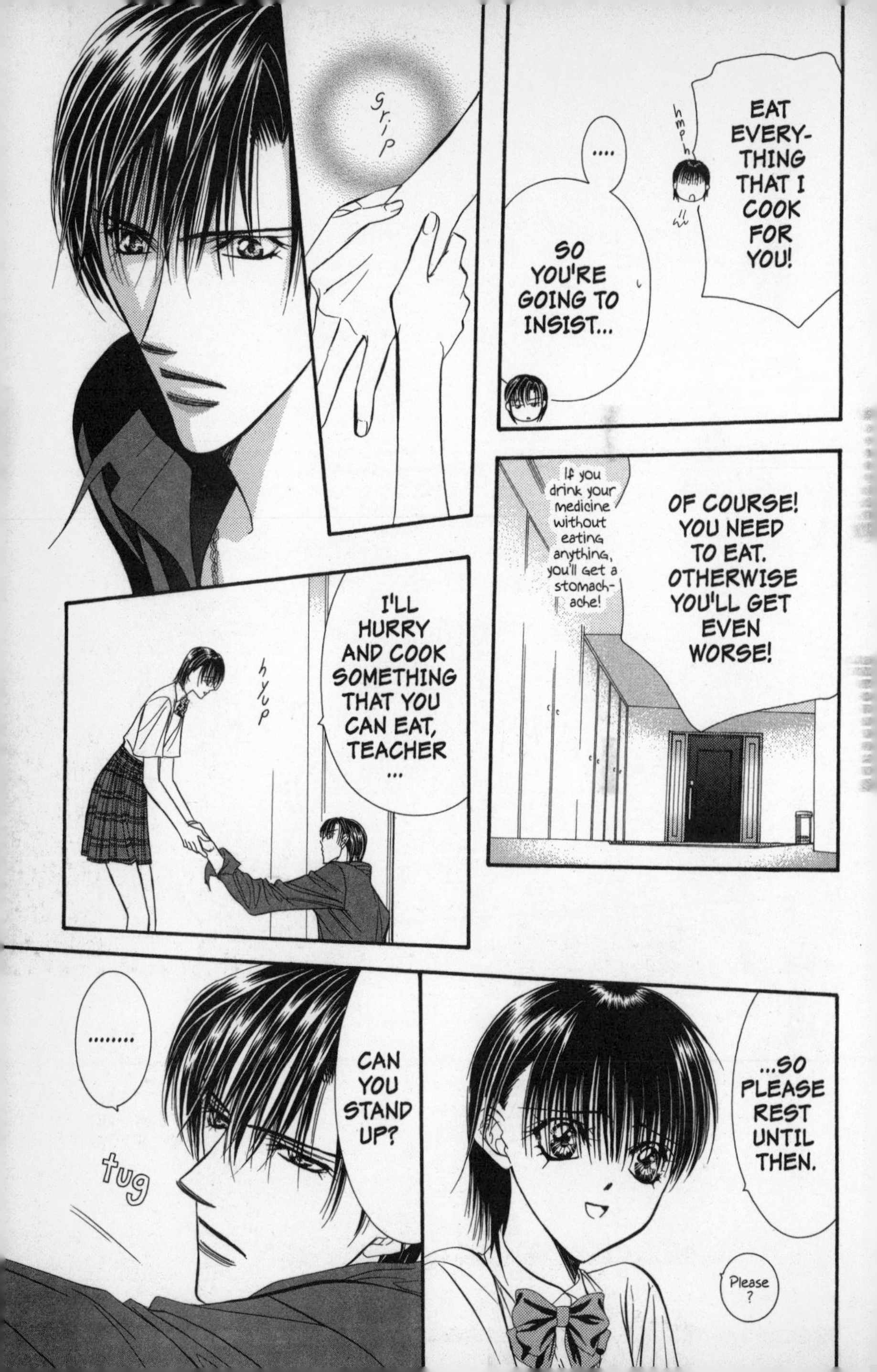
EAT EVERYTHING THAT I COOK FOR YOU!
hmph
....
SO YOU'RE GOING TO INSIST...
grip
OF COURSE! YOU NEED TO EAT. OTHERWISE YOU'LL GET EVEN WORSE!
If you drink your medicine without eating anything, you'll get a stomach-ache!
I'LL HURRY AND COOK SOMETHING THAT YOU CAN EAT, TEACHER ...
hyup
...SO PLEASE REST UNTIL THEN.
Please ?
CAN YOU STAND UP?
....
tug

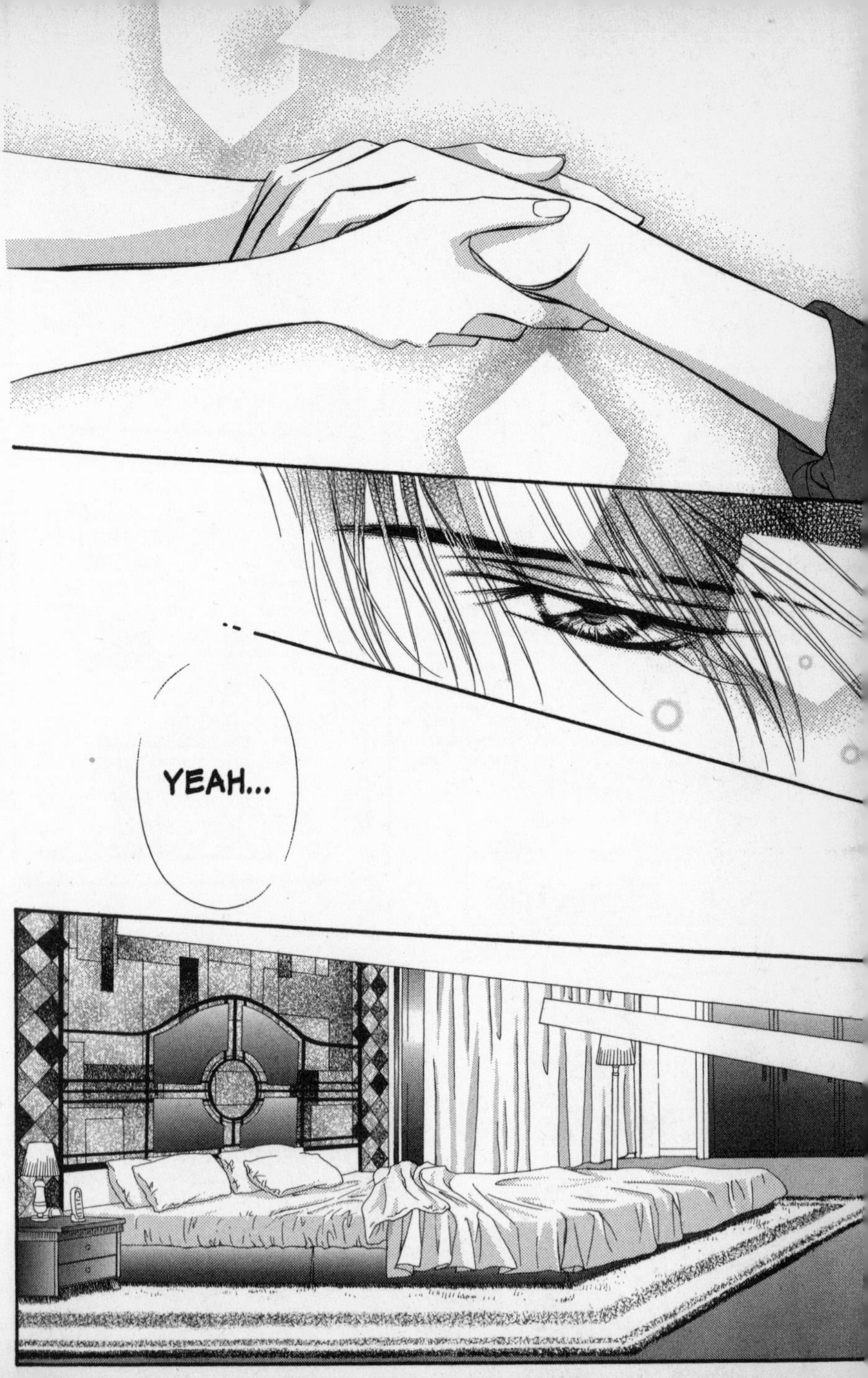
YEAH...

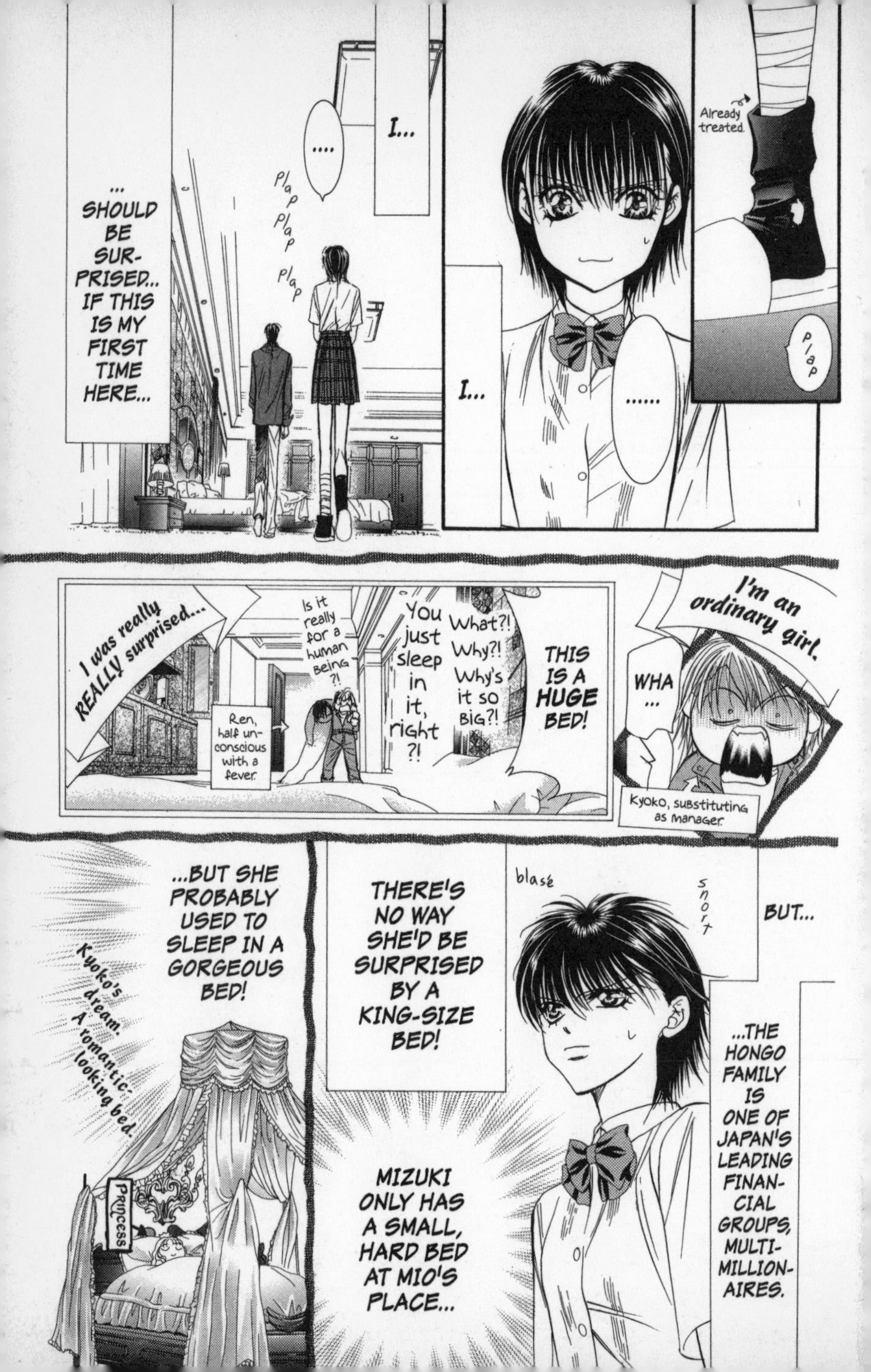
Already treated.
plap
I...
......
I...
....
plap plap plap
... SHOULD BE SURPRISED... IF THIS IS MY FIRST TIME HERE...
I'm an ordinary girl.
WHA...
Kyoko, substituting as manager.
THIS IS A HUGE BED!
What?! Why?! Why's it so BIG?!
You just sleep in it, right?!
Is it really for a human being?!
I was really REALLY surprised...
Ren, half unconscious with a fever.
BUT...
snort
blasé
...THE HONGO FAMILY IS ONE OF JAPAN'S LEADING FINANCIAL GROUPS, MULTI-MILLIONAIRES.
THERE'S NO WAY SHE'D BE SURPRISED BY A KING-SIZE BED!
MIZUKI ONLY HAS A SMALL, HARD BED AT MIO'S PLACE...
...BUT SHE PROBABLY USED TO SLEEP IN A GORGEOUS BED!
Kyoko's dream. A romantic-looking bed.
Princess

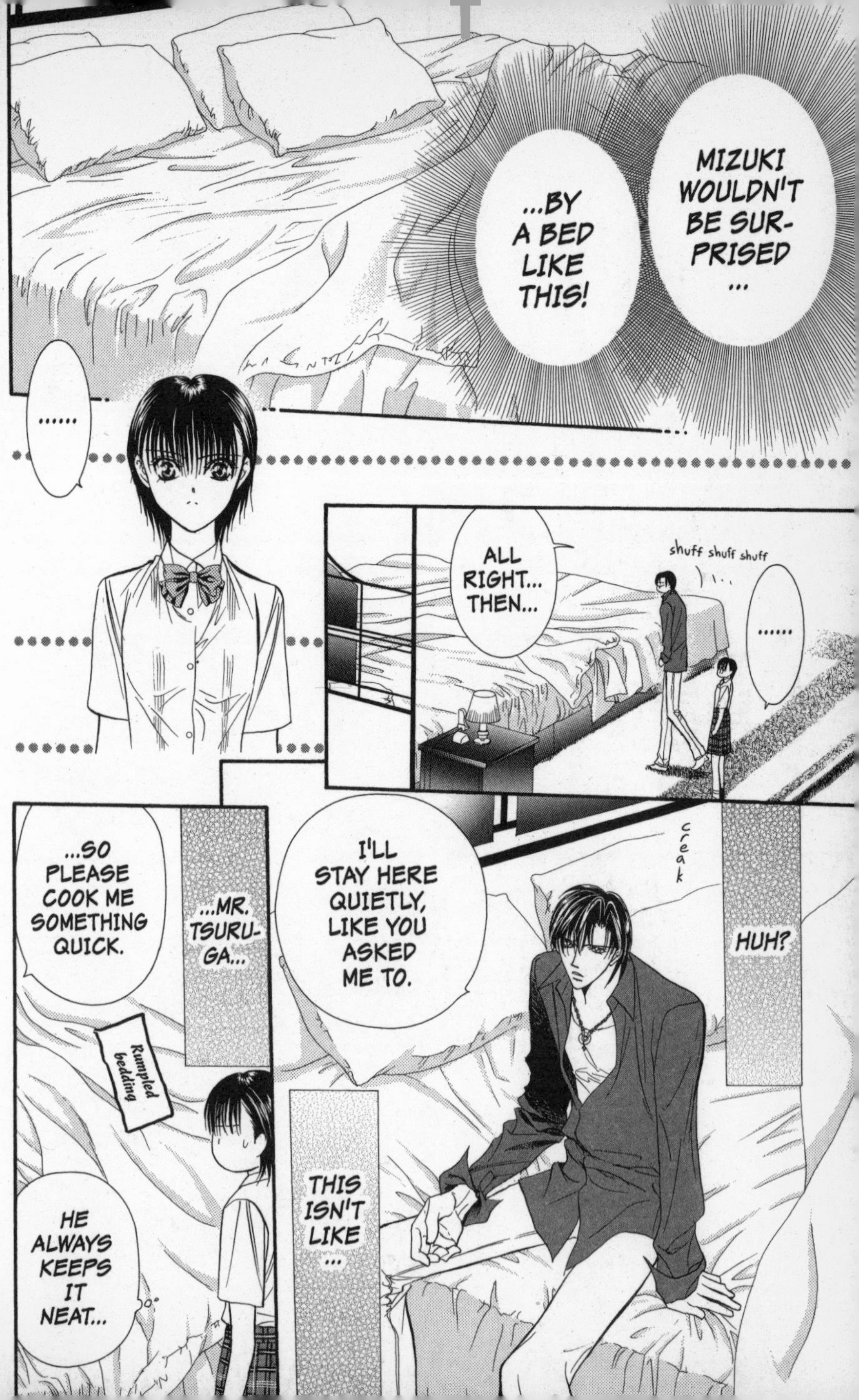
MIZUKI WOULDN'T BE SUR-PRISED ...
...BY A BED LIKE THIS!
......
shuff shuff shuff
ALL RIGHT... THEN...
......
creak
HUH?
I'LL STAY HERE QUIETLY, LIKE YOU ASKED ME TO.
...MR. TSURU-GA...
...SO PLEASE COOK ME SOMETHING QUICK.
Rumpled bedding
THIS ISN'T LIKE ...
HE ALWAYS KEEPS IT NEAT...

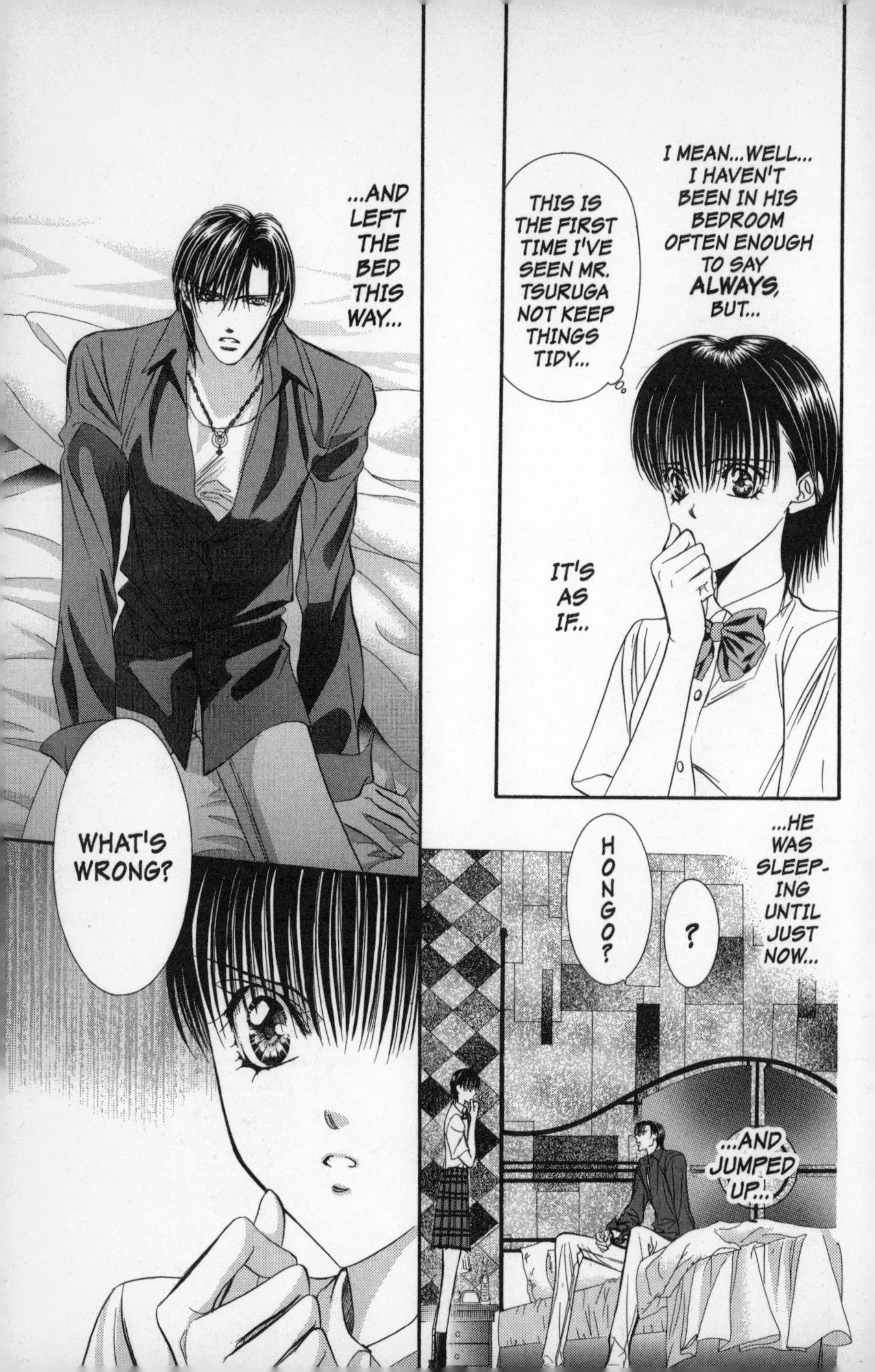
I MEAN...WELL... I HAVEN'T BEEN IN HIS BEDROOM OFTEN ENOUGH TO SAY ALWAYS, BUT...
THIS IS THE FIRST TIME I'VE SEEN MR. TSURUGA NOT KEEP THINGS TIDY...
IT'S AS IF...
...HE WAS SLEEP-ING UNTIL JUST NOW...
?
HONGO?
...AND JUMPED UP...
...AND LEFT THE BED THIS WAY...
WHAT'S WRONG?

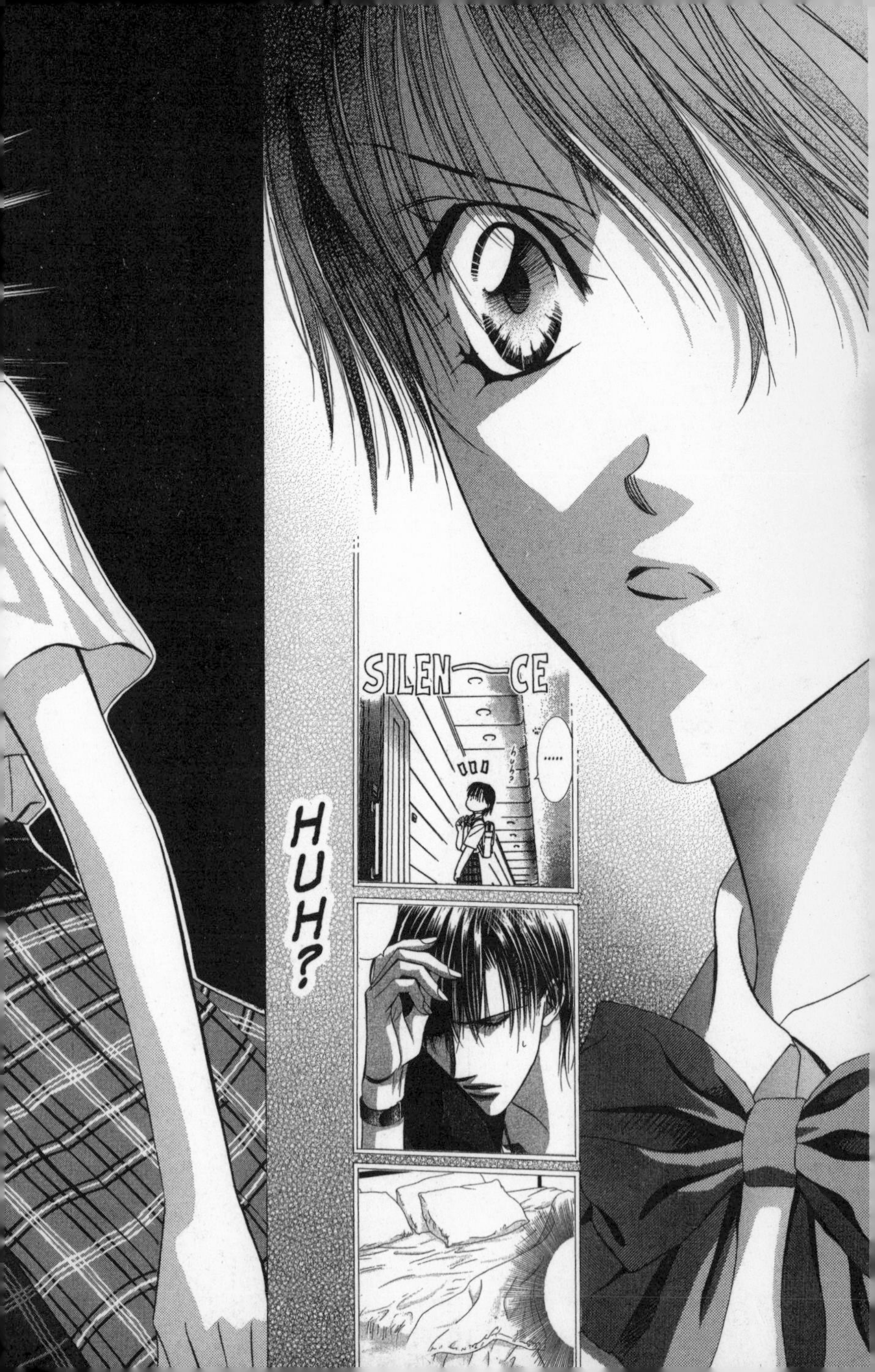
SILEN—CE
......
HUH?

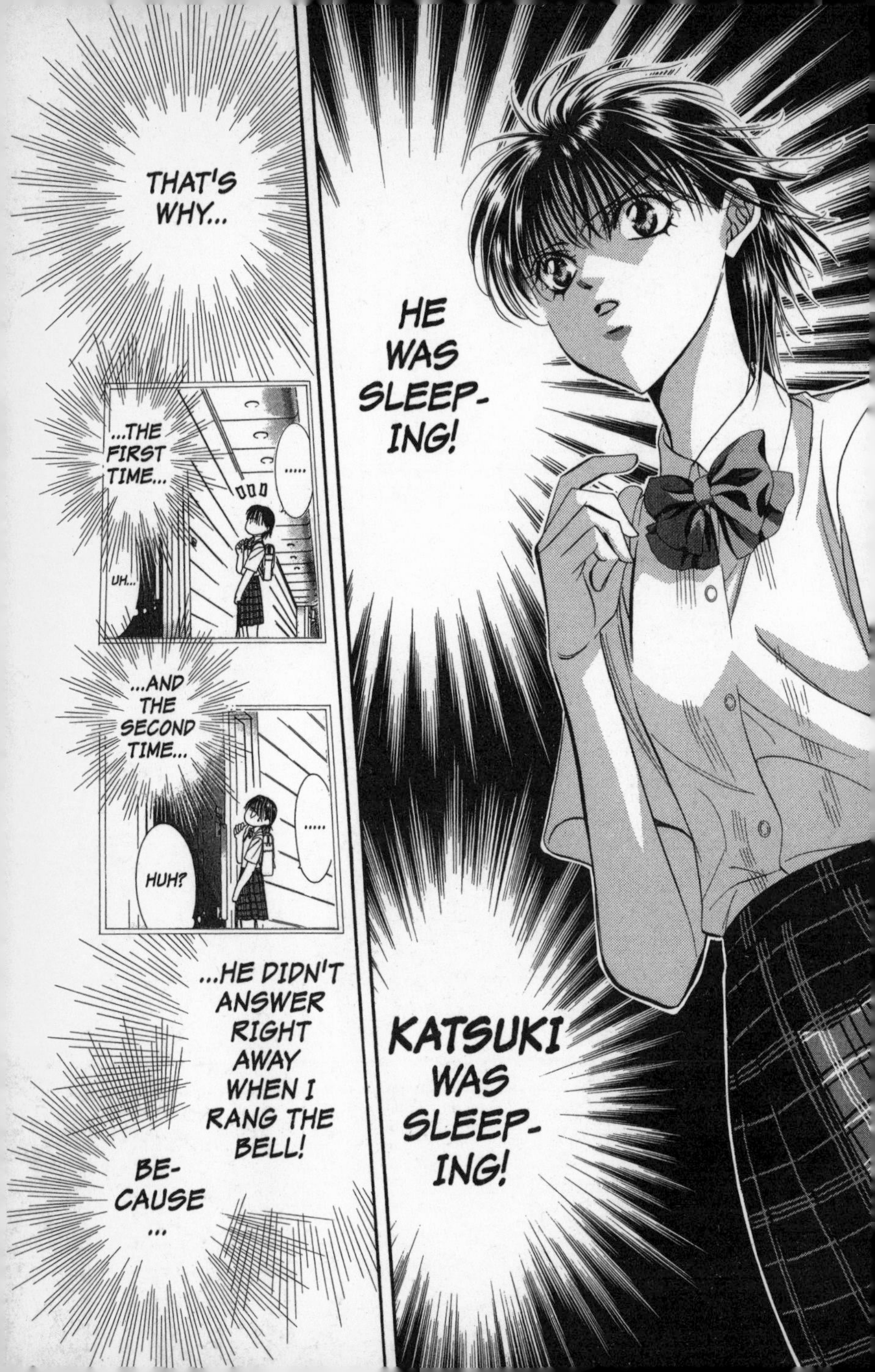
THAT'S WHY...
...THE FIRST TIME...
.....
UH...
...AND THE SECOND TIME...
.....
HUH?
...HE DIDN'T ANSWER RIGHT AWAY WHEN I RANG THE BELL!
BE-CAUSE ...
HE WAS SLEEP-ING!
KATSUKI WAS SLEEP-ING!

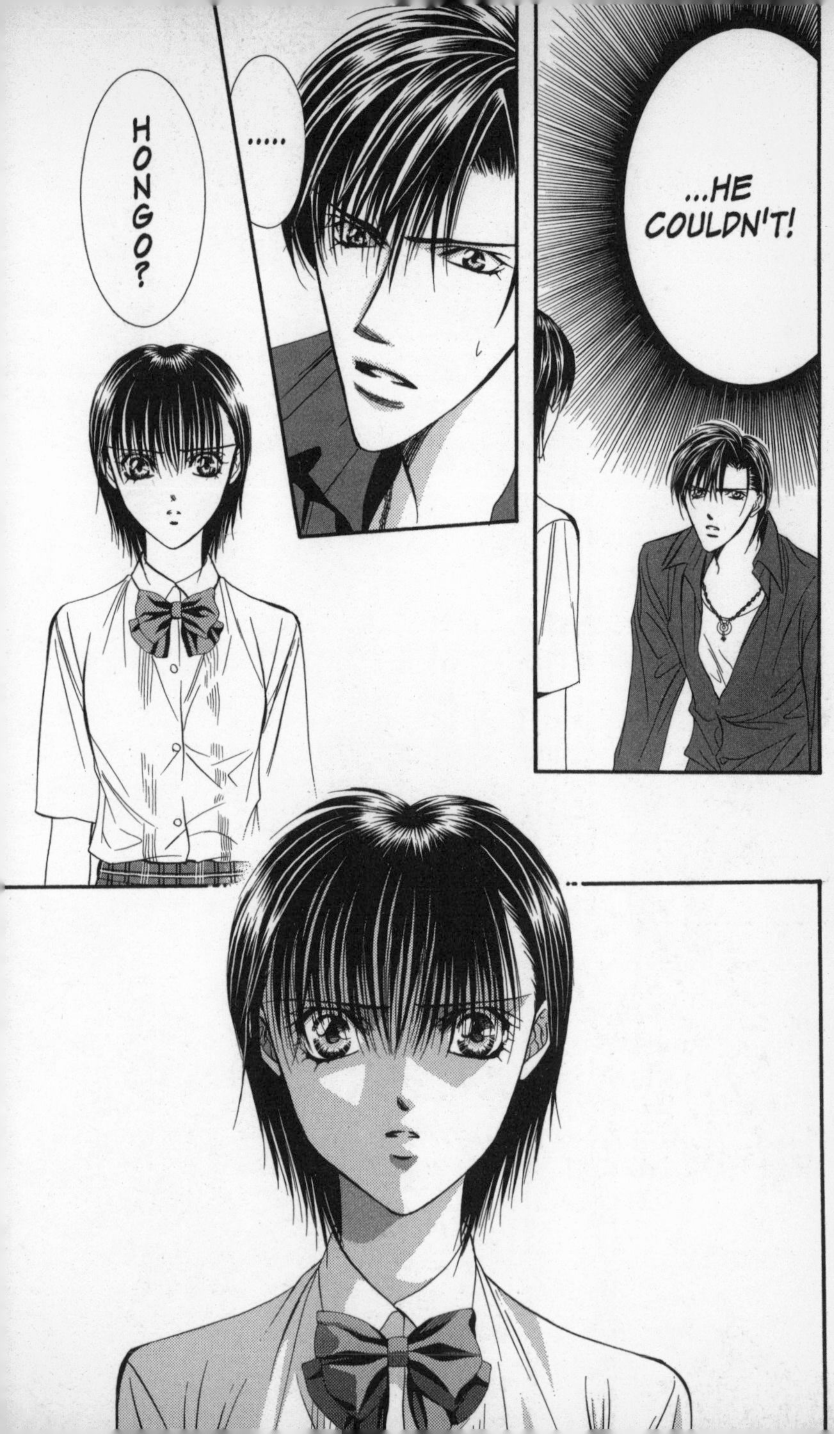
...HE COULDN'T!
......
HONGO?

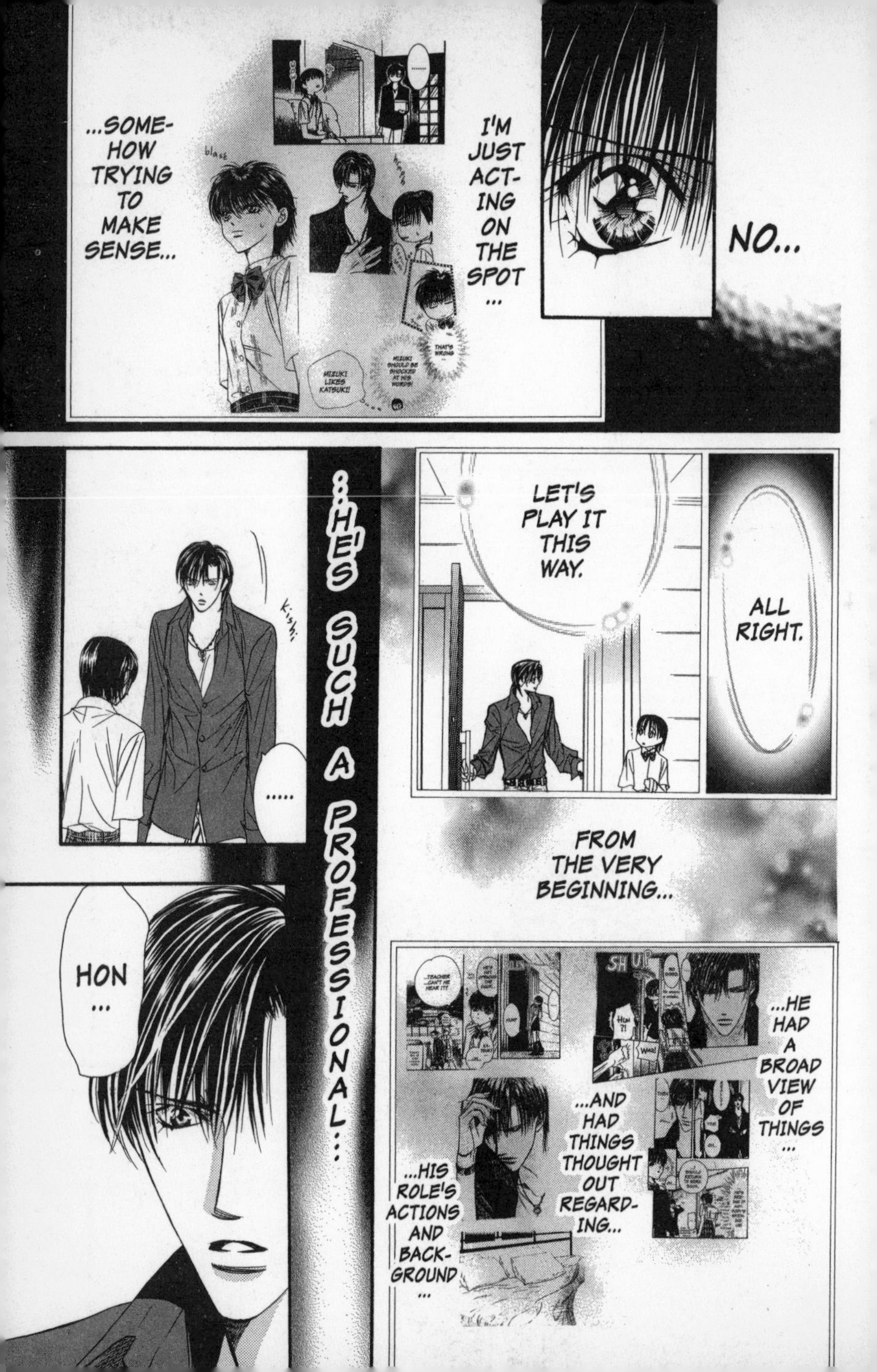
NO...
I'M JUST ACTING ON THE SPOT...
...SOMEHOW TRYING TO MAKE SENSE...
blast
NO.
THAT'S WRONG...
MIZUKI SHOULD BE SHOCKED AT HIS WORDS!
MIZUKI LIKES KATSUKI!
ALL RIGHT.
LET'S PLAY IT THIS WAY.
FROM THE VERY BEGINNING...
...HE HAD A BROAD VIEW OF THINGS...
...AND HAD THINGS THOUGHT OUT REGARDING...
...HIS ROLE'S ACTIONS AND BACKGROUND...
...HE'S SUCH A PROFESSIONAL...
kishi
.....
HON...

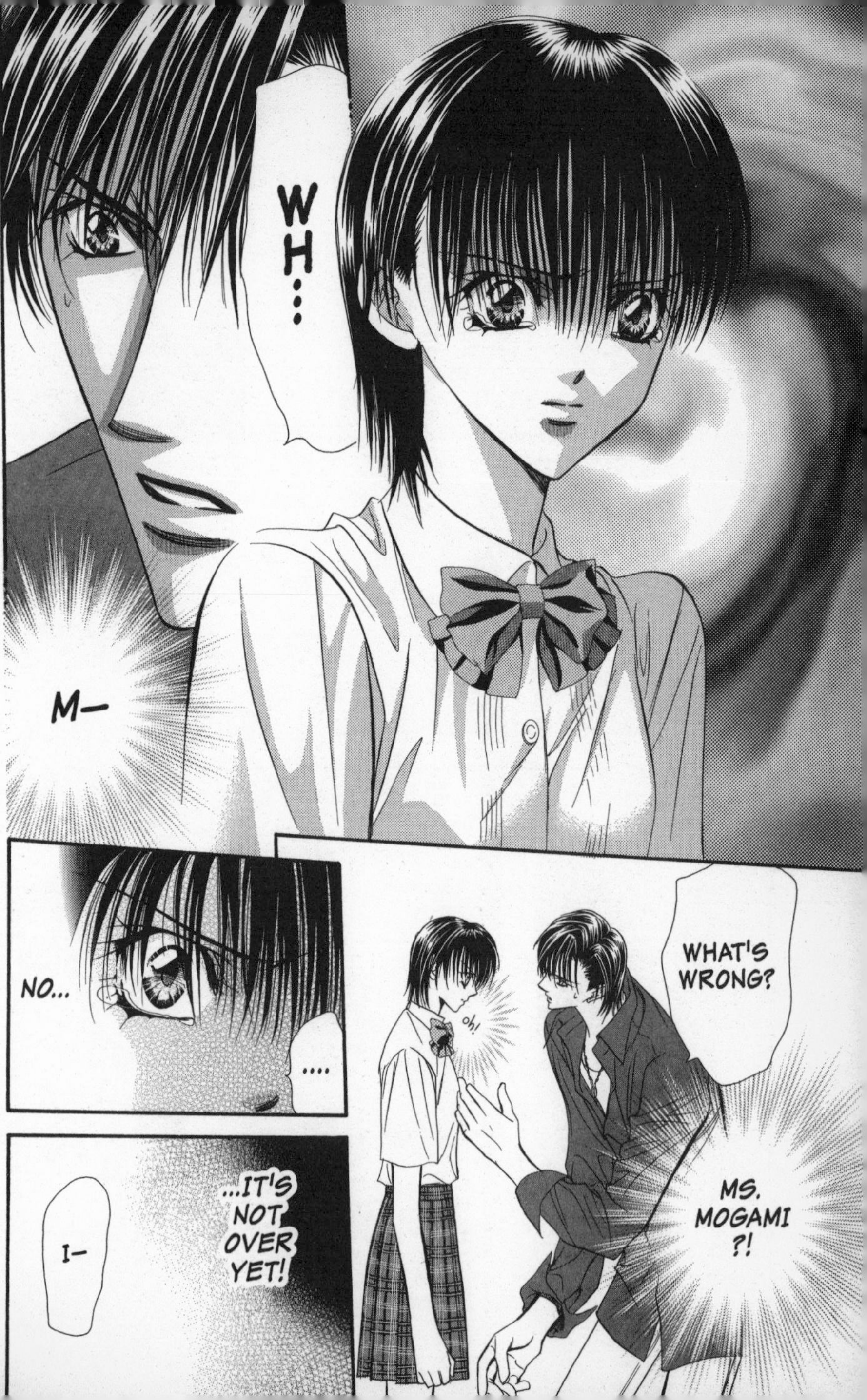
WH...
M—
WHAT'S WRONG?
oh!
MS. MOGAMI ?!
NO...
....
...IT'S NOT OVER YET!
I—

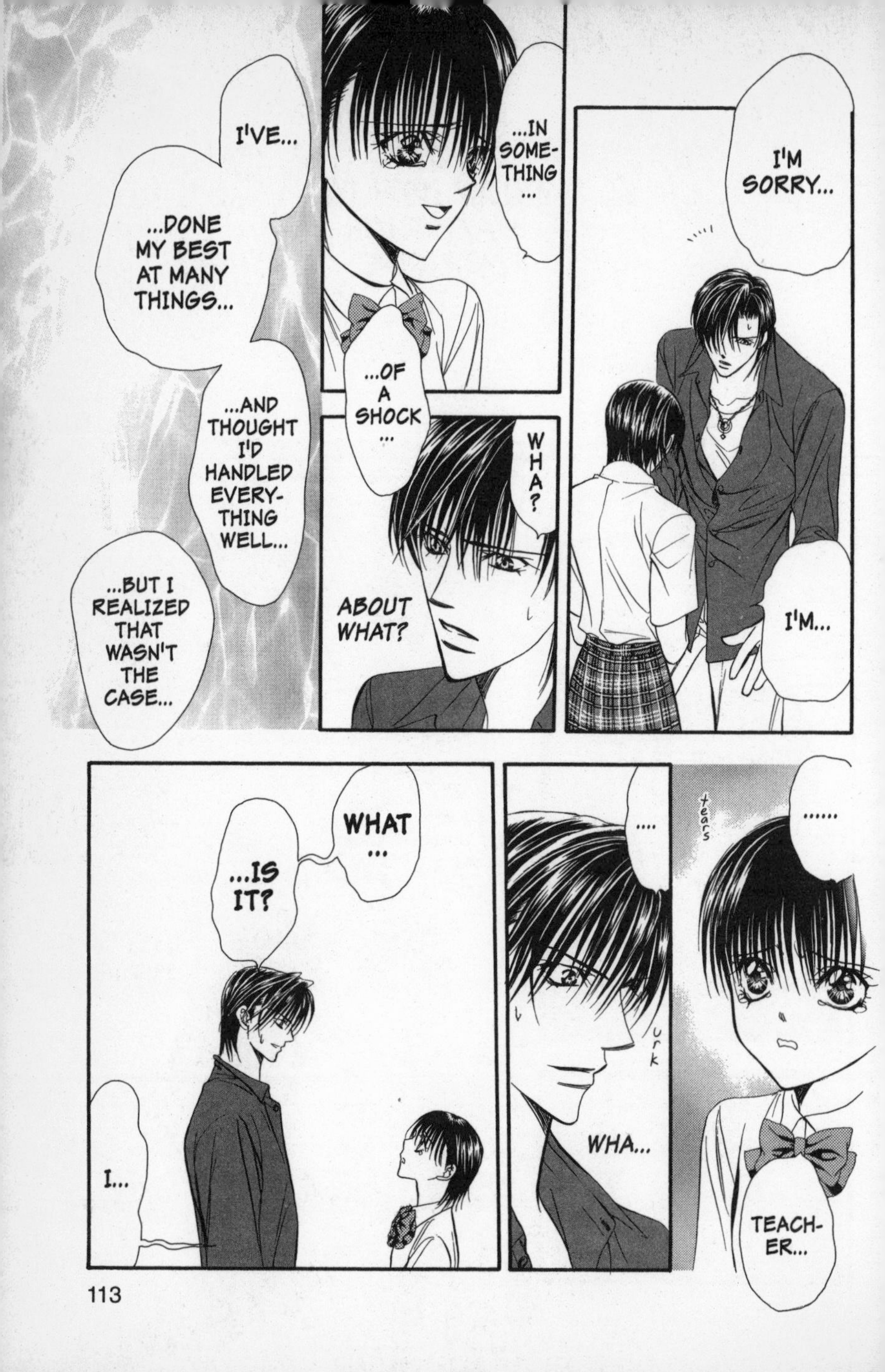
I'M SORRY...
I'M...
...IN SOMETHING...
...OF A SHOCK...
WHA?
ABOUT WHAT?
I'VE...
...DONE MY BEST AT MANY THINGS...
...AND THOUGHT I'D HANDLED EVERYTHING WELL...
...BUT I REALIZED THAT WASN'T THE CASE...
......
tears
TEACHER...
....
urk
WHA...
WHAT...
...IS IT?
I...

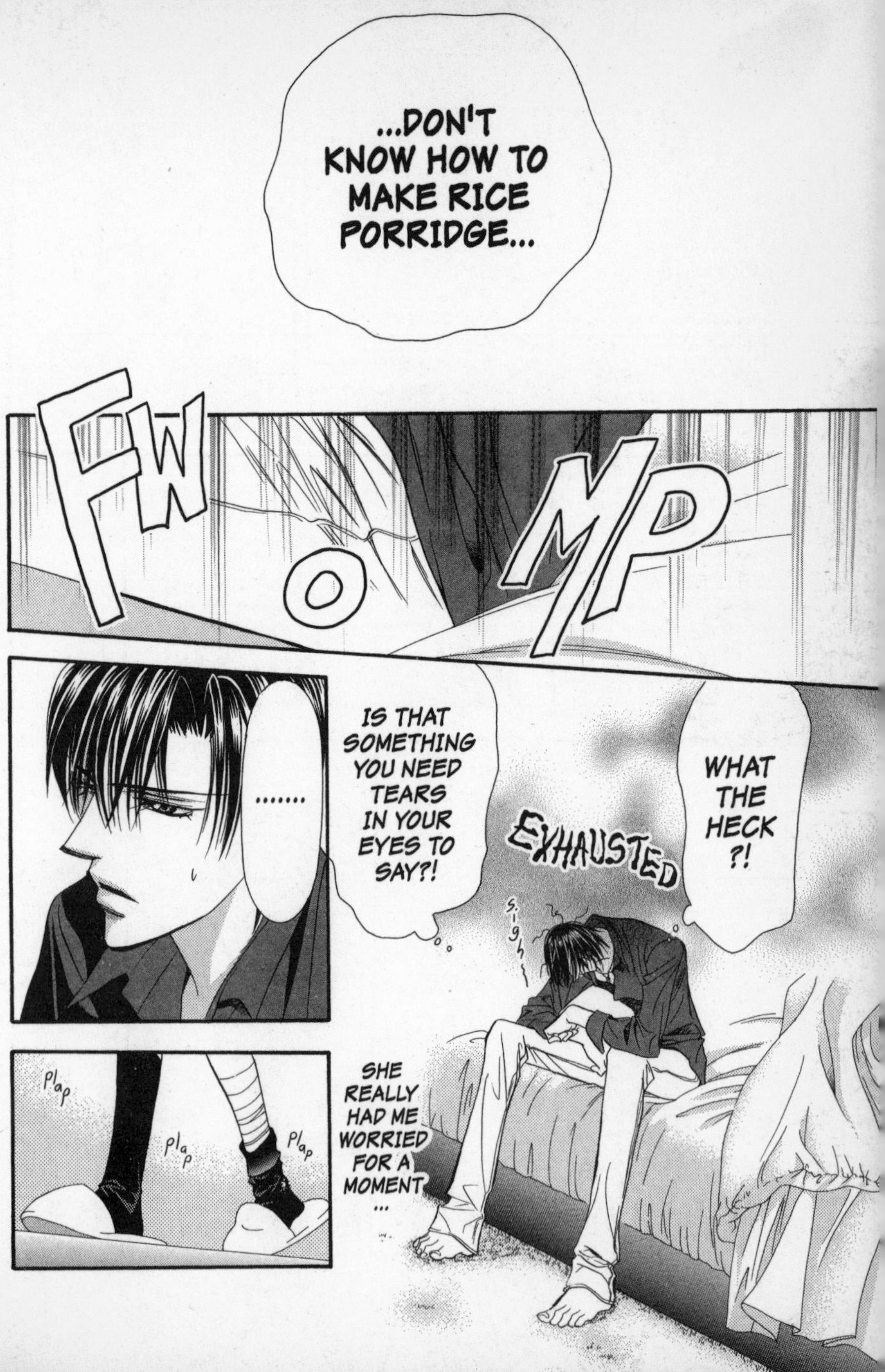
...DON'T KNOW HOW TO MAKE RICE PORRIDGE...
FWOMP
WHAT THE HECK?!
EXHAUSTED
sigh
IS THAT SOMETHING YOU NEED TEARS IN YOUR EYES TO SAY?!
SHE REALLY HAD ME WORRIED FOR A MOMENT...
....
plap
plap
plap

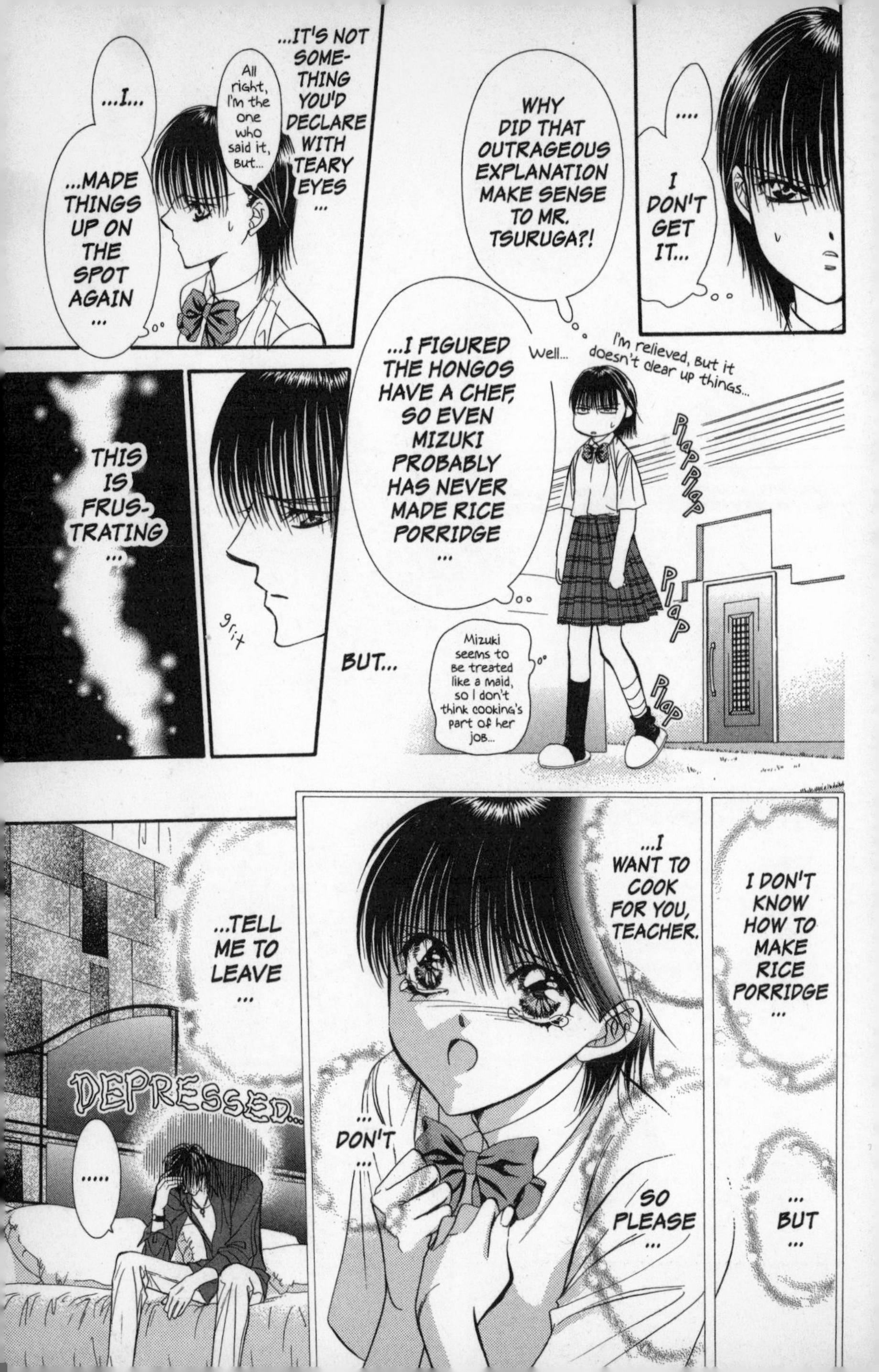
....
I DON'T GET IT...
WHY DID THAT OUTRAGEOUS EXPLANATION MAKE SENSE TO MR. TSURUGA?!
...IT'S NOT SOMETHING YOU'D DECLARE WITH TEARY EYES...
All right, I'm the one who said it, but...
...I...
...MADE THINGS UP ON THE SPOT AGAIN...
I'm relieved, but it doesn't clear up things...
Well...
...I FIGURED THE HONGOS HAVE A CHEF, SO EVEN MIZUKI PROBABLY HAS NEVER MADE RICE PORRIDGE...
Plap Plap
Plap
Plap
BUT...
Mizuki seems to be treated like a maid, so I don't think cooking's part of her job...
grit
THIS IS FRUSTRATING...
I DON'T KNOW HOW TO MAKE RICE PORRIDGE...
...BUT...
...I WANT TO COOK FOR YOU, TEACHER.
SO PLEASE...
...DON'T...
...TELL ME TO LEAVE...
DEPRESSED...
......

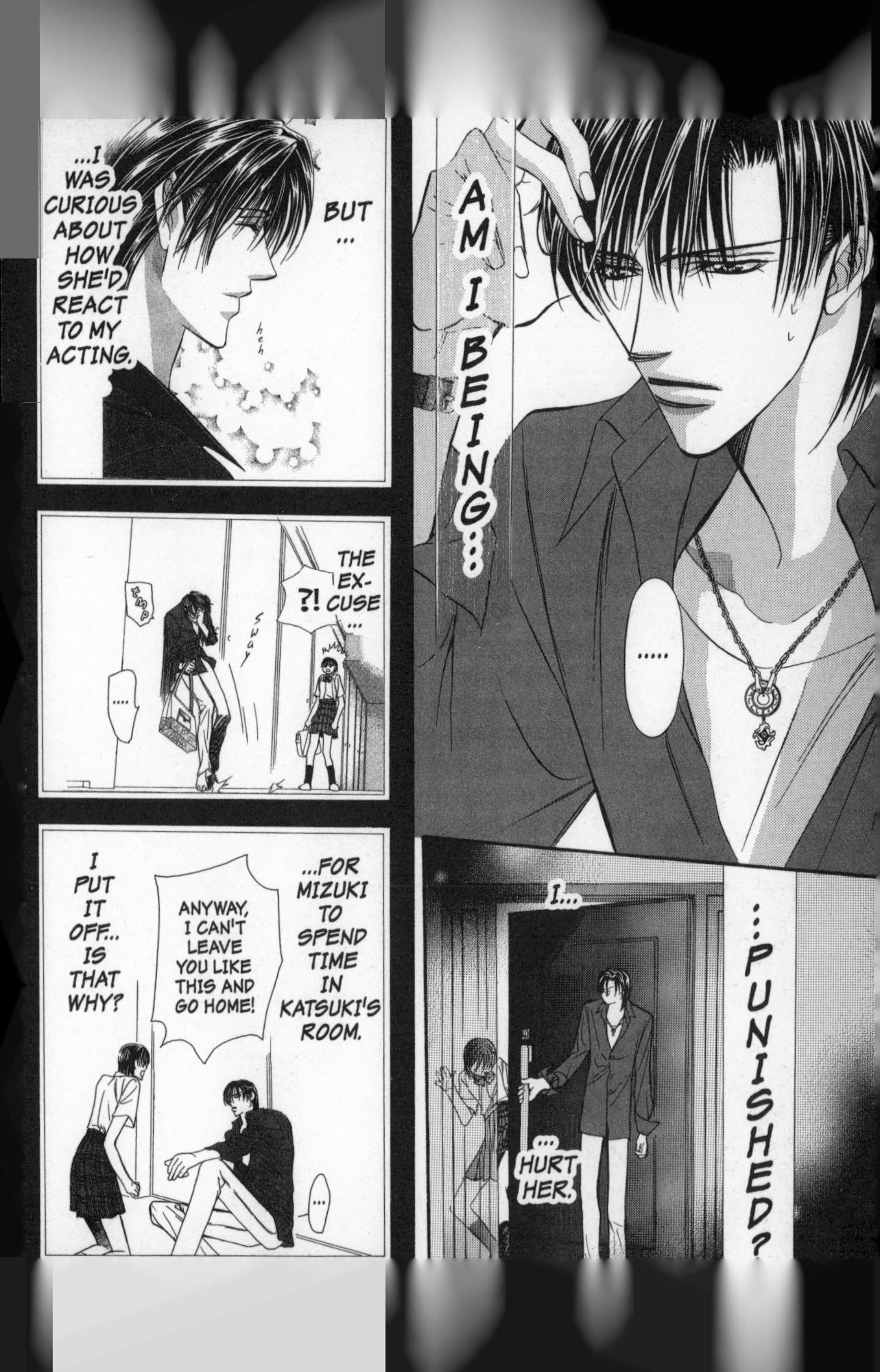
AM I BEING...
.....
...I WAS CURIOUS ABOUT HOW SHE'D REACT TO MY ACTING.
BUT ...
heh
THE EX-CUSE ...
?!
tmp
sway
.....
I...
...PUNISHED?
...HURT HER.
...FOR MIZUKI TO SPEND TIME IN KATSUKI'S ROOM.
ANYWAY, I CAN'T LEAVE YOU LIKE THIS AND GO HOME!
I PUT IT OFF... IS THAT WHY?
...

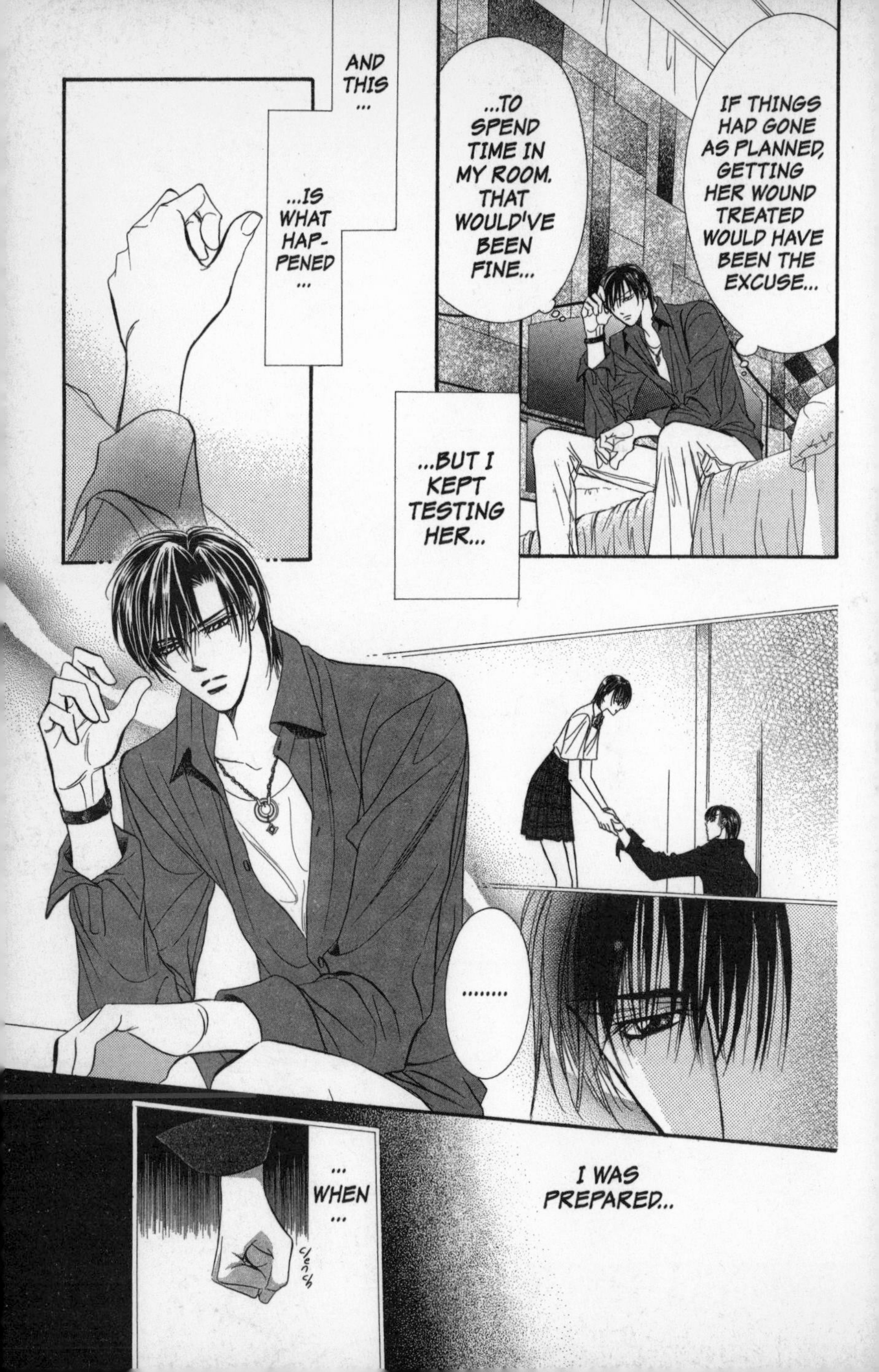
IF THINGS HAD GONE AS PLANNED, GETTING HER WOUND TREATED WOULD HAVE BEEN THE EXCUSE...
...TO SPEND TIME IN MY ROOM. THAT WOULD'VE BEEN FINE...
...BUT I KEPT TESTING HER...
AND THIS...
...IS WHAT HAP-PENED...
....
I WAS PREPARED...
...WHEN...
clench

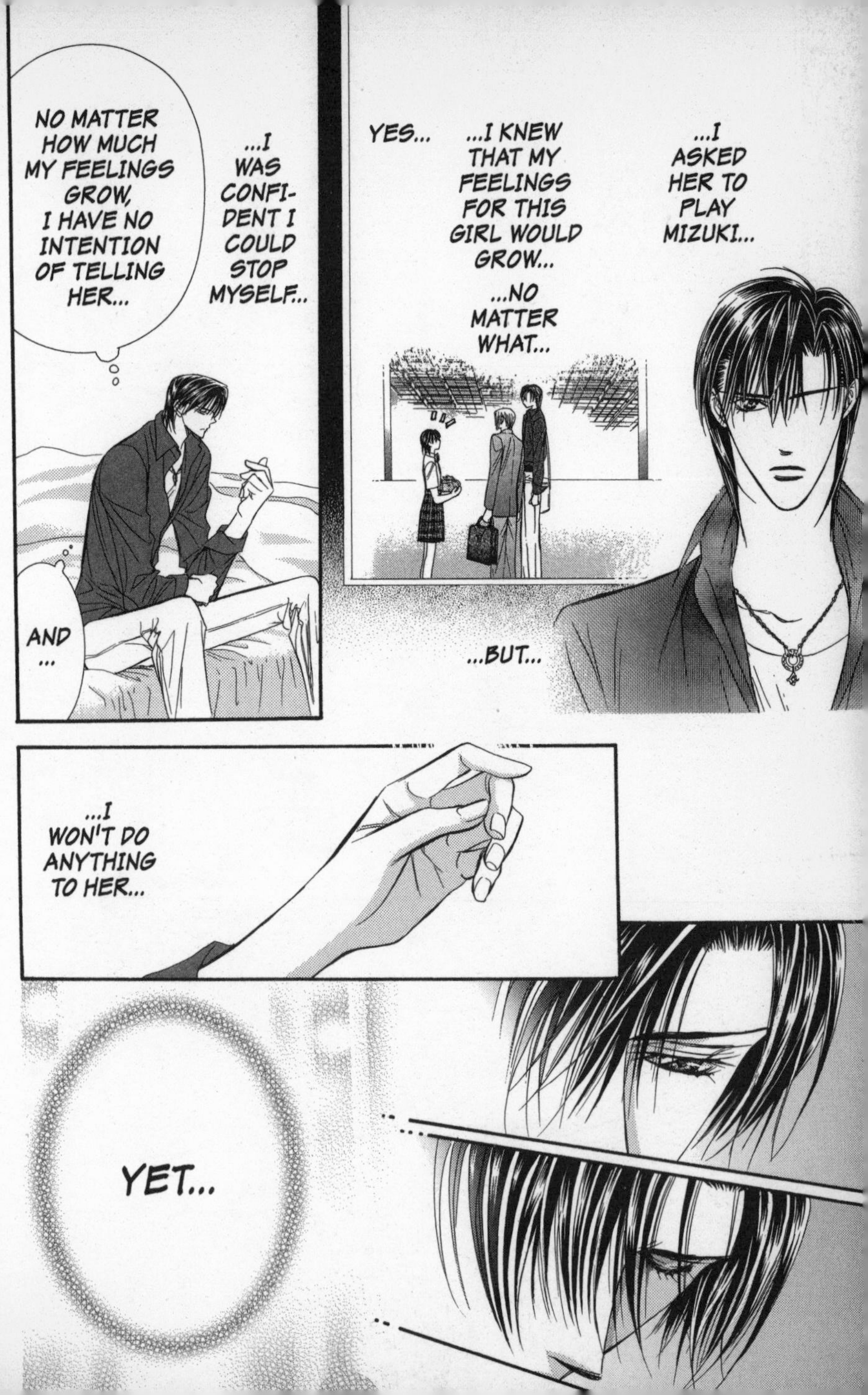

...I ASKED HER TO PLAY MIZUKI...
...I KNEW THAT MY FEELINGS FOR THIS GIRL WOULD GROW...
YES...
...NO MATTER WHAT...
...BUT...
...I WAS CONFI-DENT I COULD STOP MYSELF...
NO MATTER HOW MUCH MY FEELINGS GROW, I HAVE NO INTENTION OF TELLING HER...
AND ...
...I WON'T DO ANYTHING TO HER...
YET...

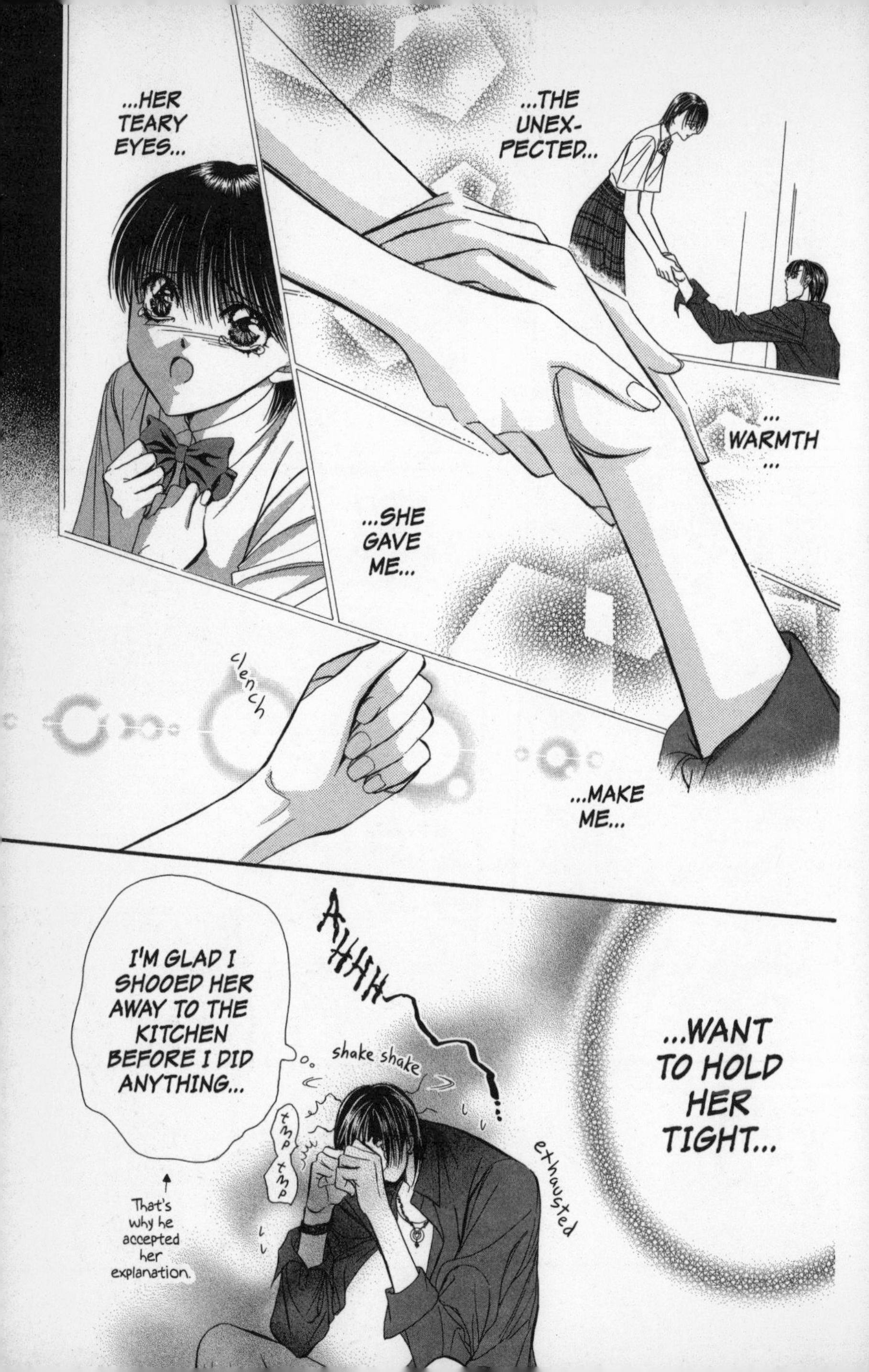
...THE UNEX-PECTED...
...WARMTH...
...HER TEARY EYES...
...SHE GAVE ME...
clench
...MAKE ME...
...WANT TO HOLD HER TIGHT...
AHHHH
shake shake
exhausted
tmp tmp
I'M GLAD I SHOOED HER AWAY TO THE KITCHEN BEFORE I DID ANYTHING...
That's why he accepted her explanation.

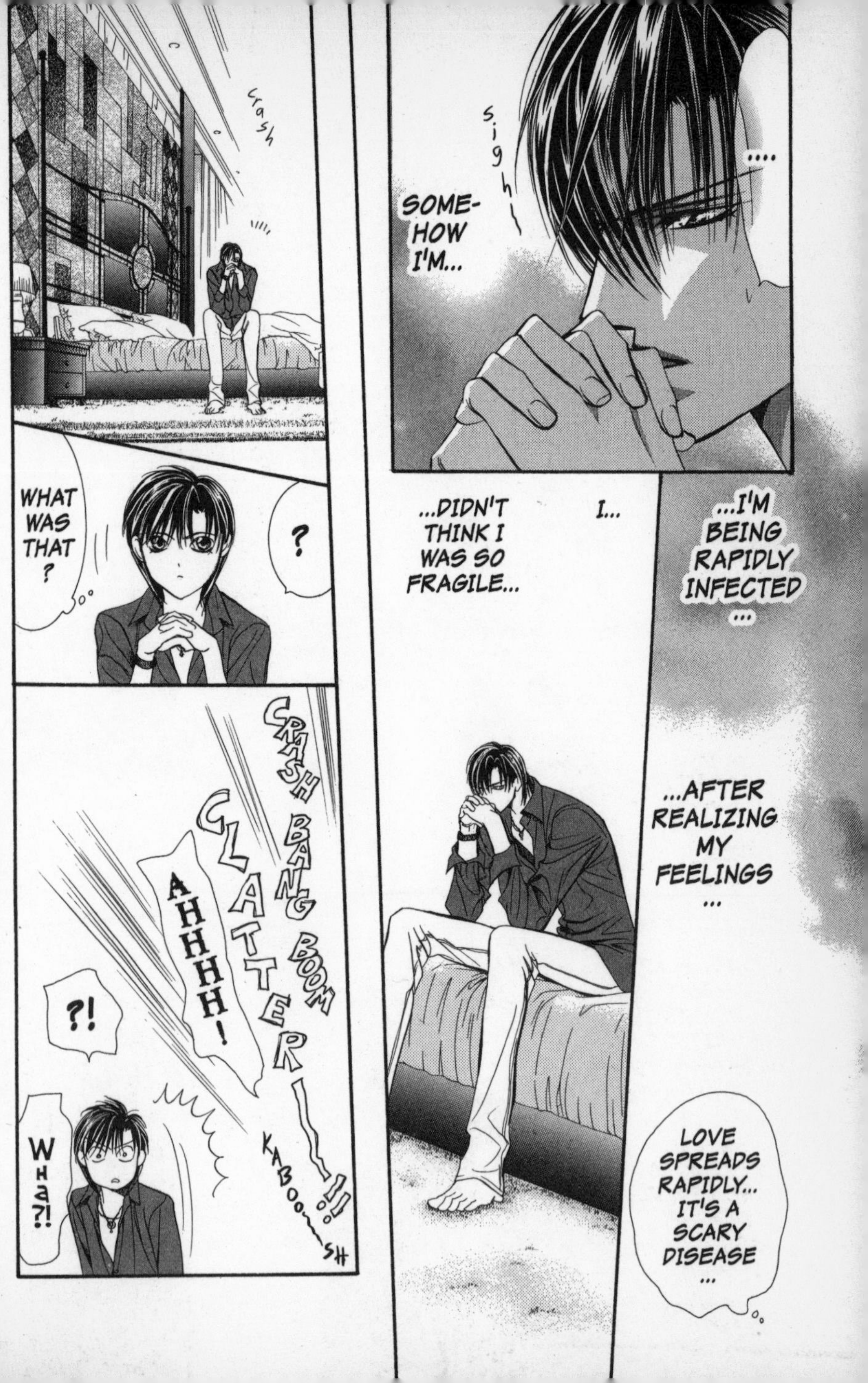
....
sigh
SOME-HOW I'M...
...I'M BEING RAPIDLY INFECTED...
...AFTER REALIZING MY FEELINGS...
I...
...DIDN'T THINK I WAS SO FRAGILE...
LOVE SPREADS RAPIDLY... IT'S A SCARY DISEASE...
crash
?
WHAT WAS THAT?
CRASH BANG BOOM
CLATTER!
AHHHH!
?!
KABOO~SH!!
Wha?!

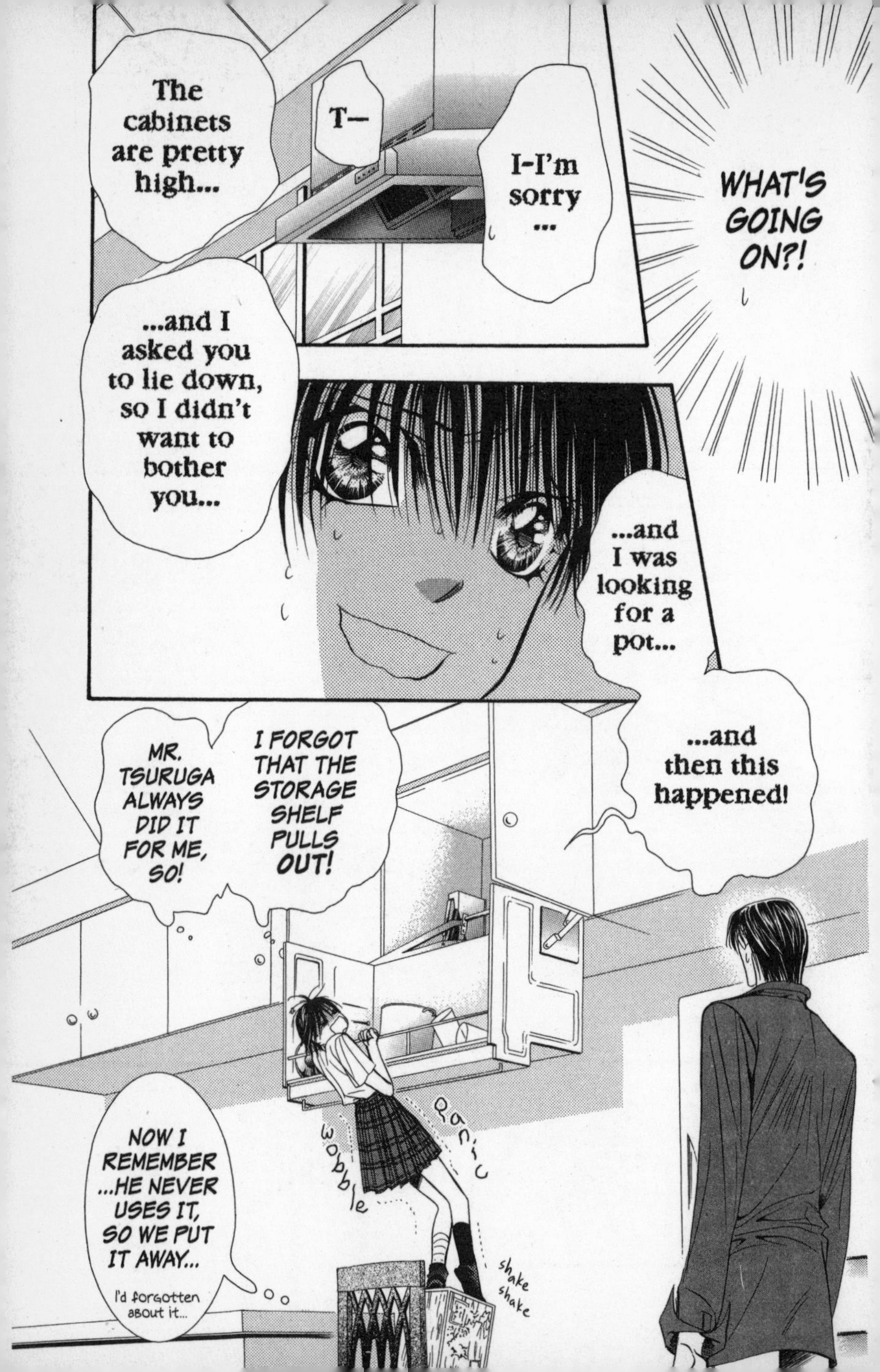
WHAT'S GOING ON?!
I-I'm sorry...
T—
The cabinets are pretty high...
...and I asked you to lie down, so I didn't want to bother you...
...and I was looking for a pot...
...and then this happened!
I FORGOT THAT THE STORAGE SHELF PULLS OUT!
MR. TSURUGA ALWAYS DID IT FOR ME, SO!
shake shake
wobble
NOW I REMEMBER ...HE NEVER USES IT, SO WE PUT IT AWAY...
I'd forgotten about it...

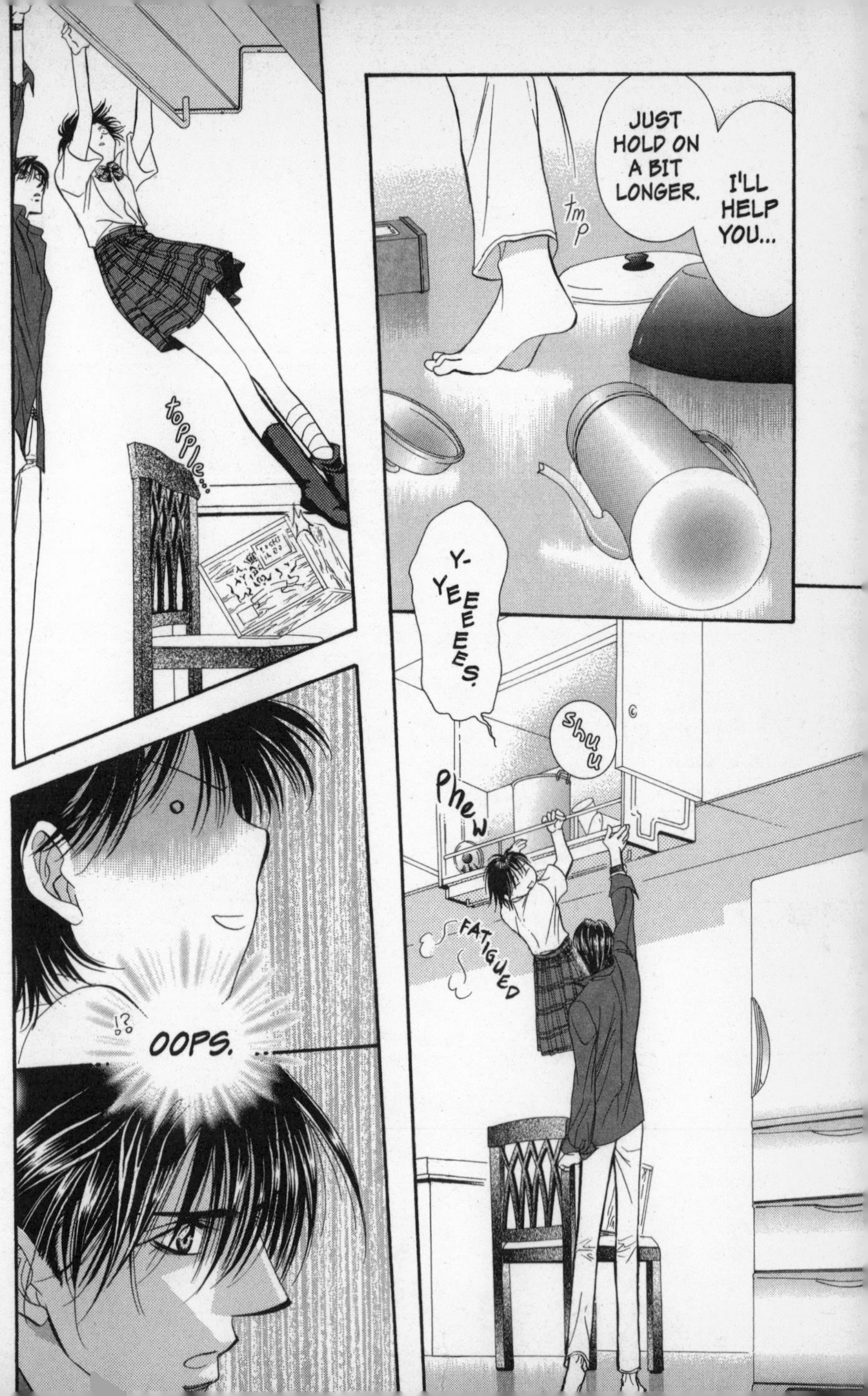
JUST HOLD ON A BIT LONGER.
I'LL HELP YOU...
tmp
topple...
Y-YEEEEES.
Shuu
Phew
FATIGUED
!?
OOPS.

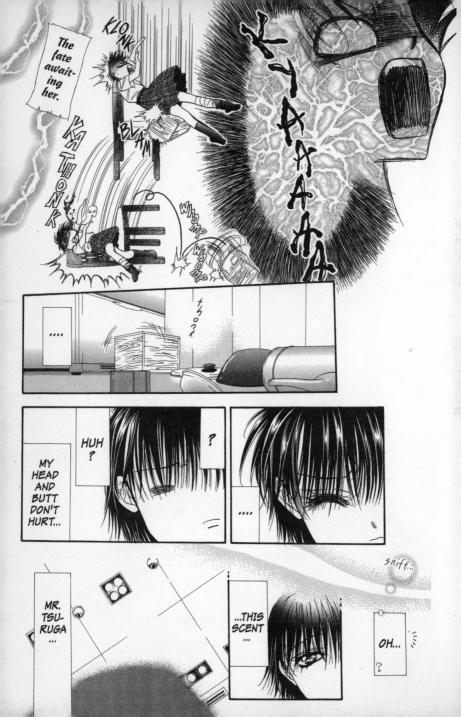

The fate awaiting her.

KLONK

KYAAAAA

KATHONK

BLAM

WHOMP WHOMP

thonk

....

HUH?

MY HEAD AND BUTT DON'T HURT...

?

....

sniff...

MR. TSURUGA...

...THIS SCENT...

OH... ?

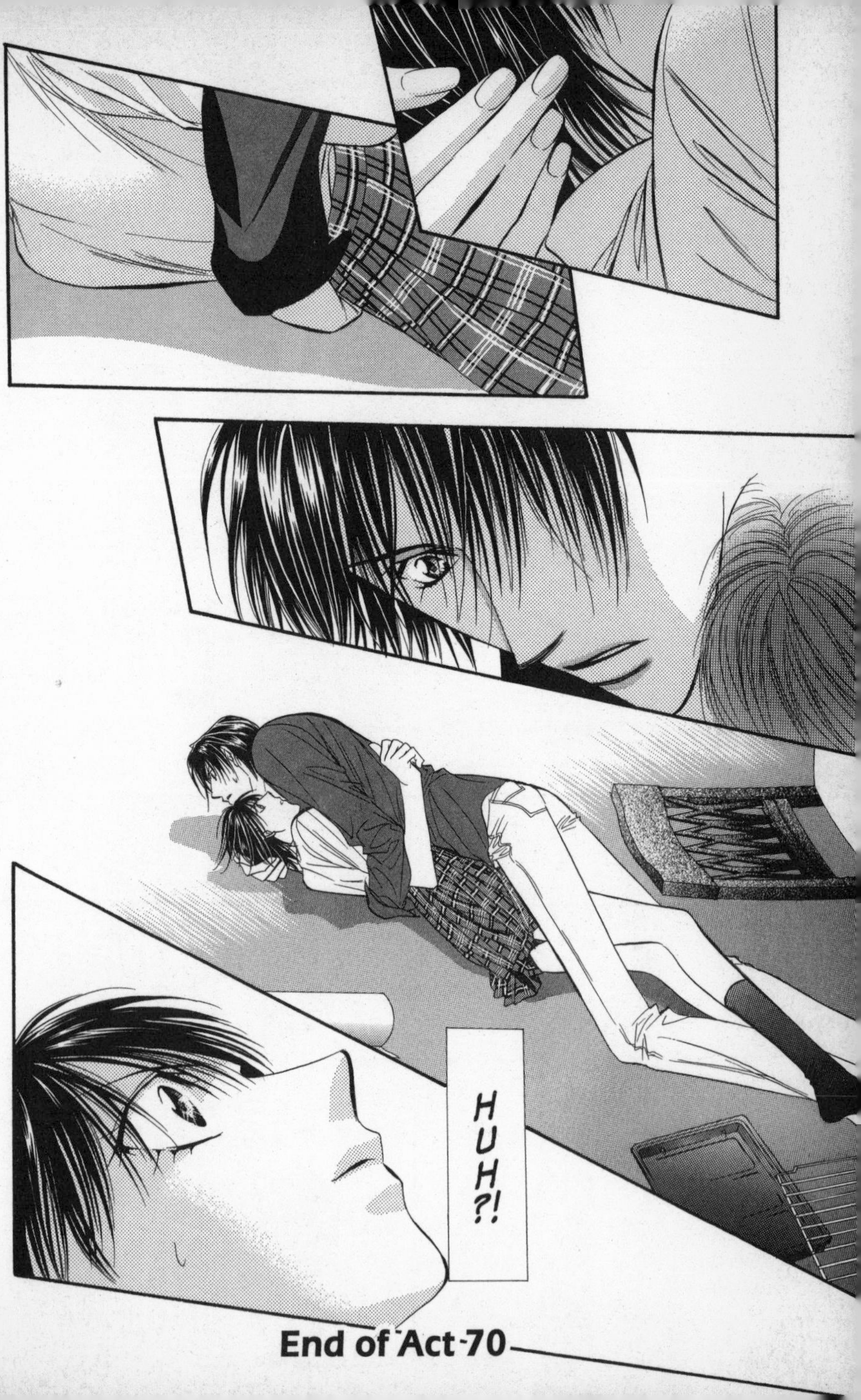
HUH?!

End of Act 70

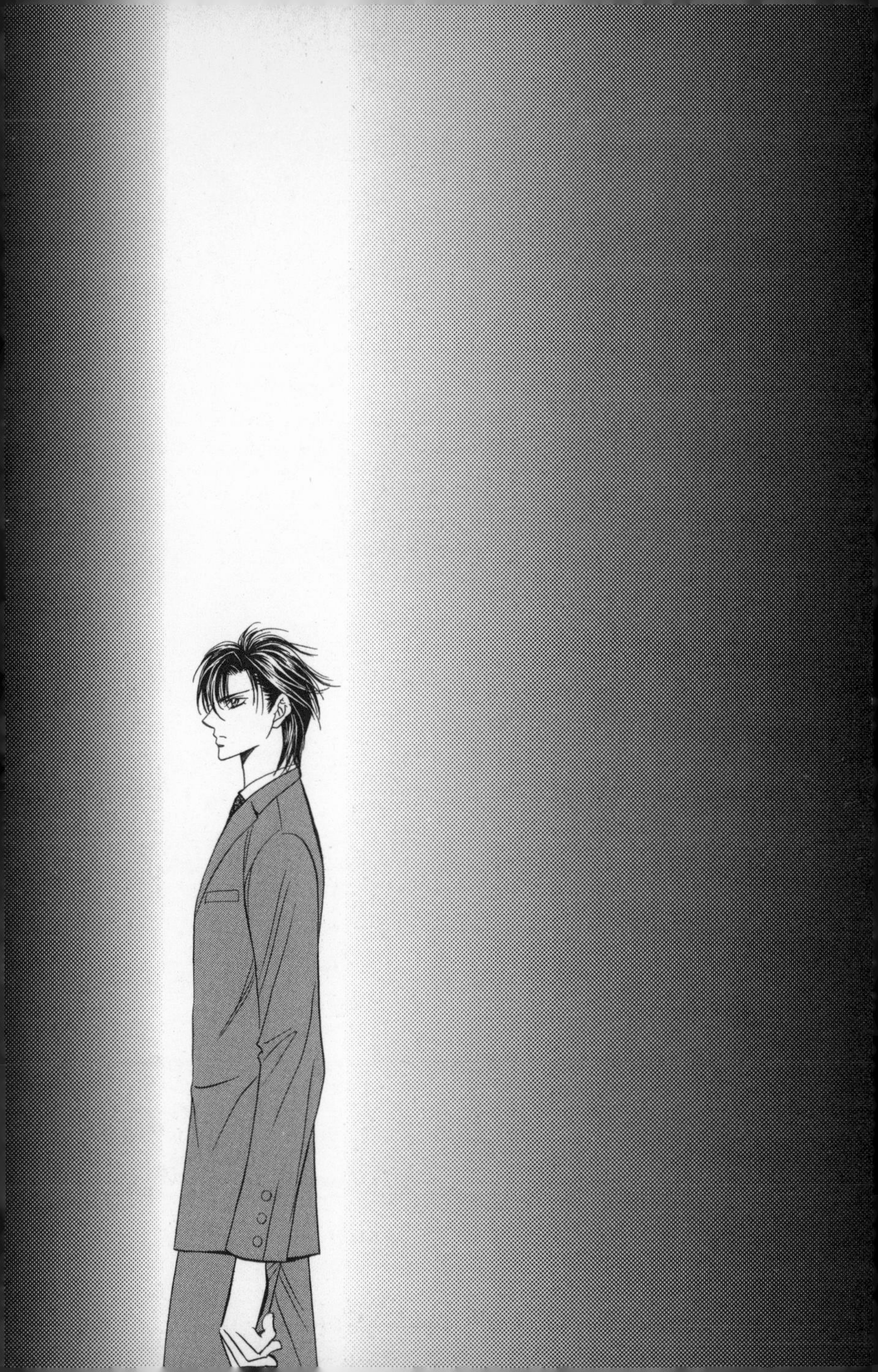

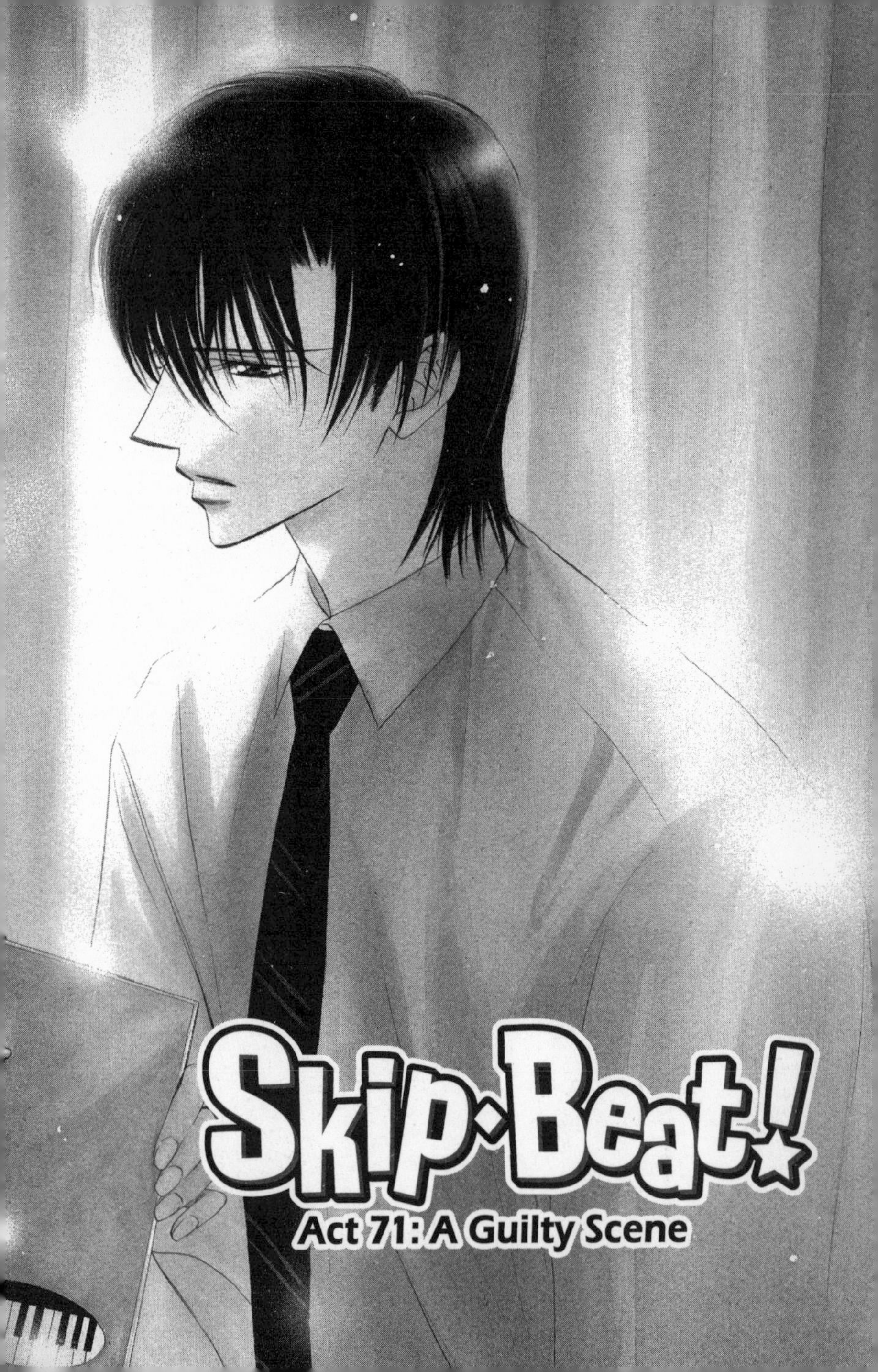
Skip·Beat!
Act 71: A Guilty Scene

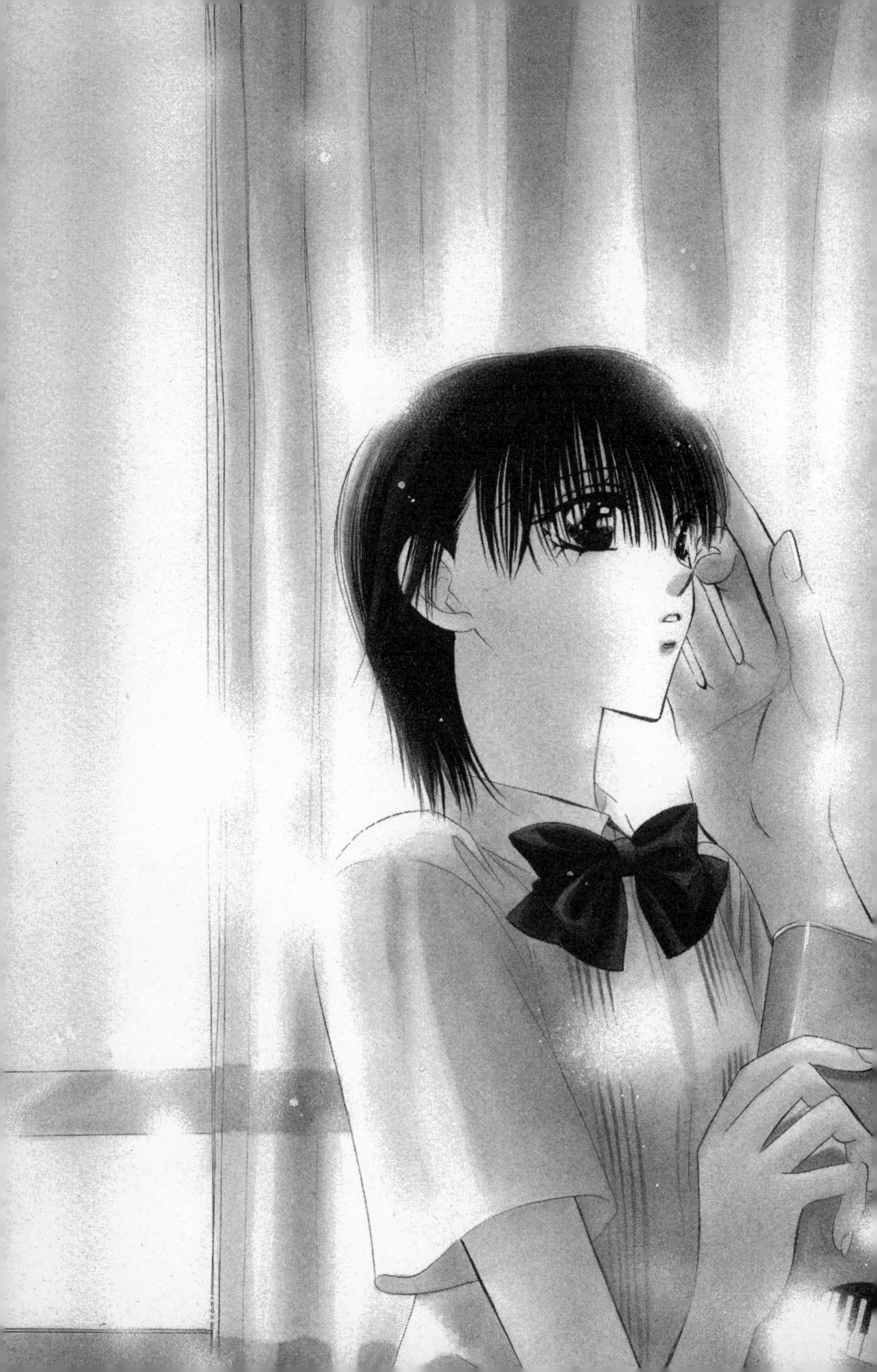

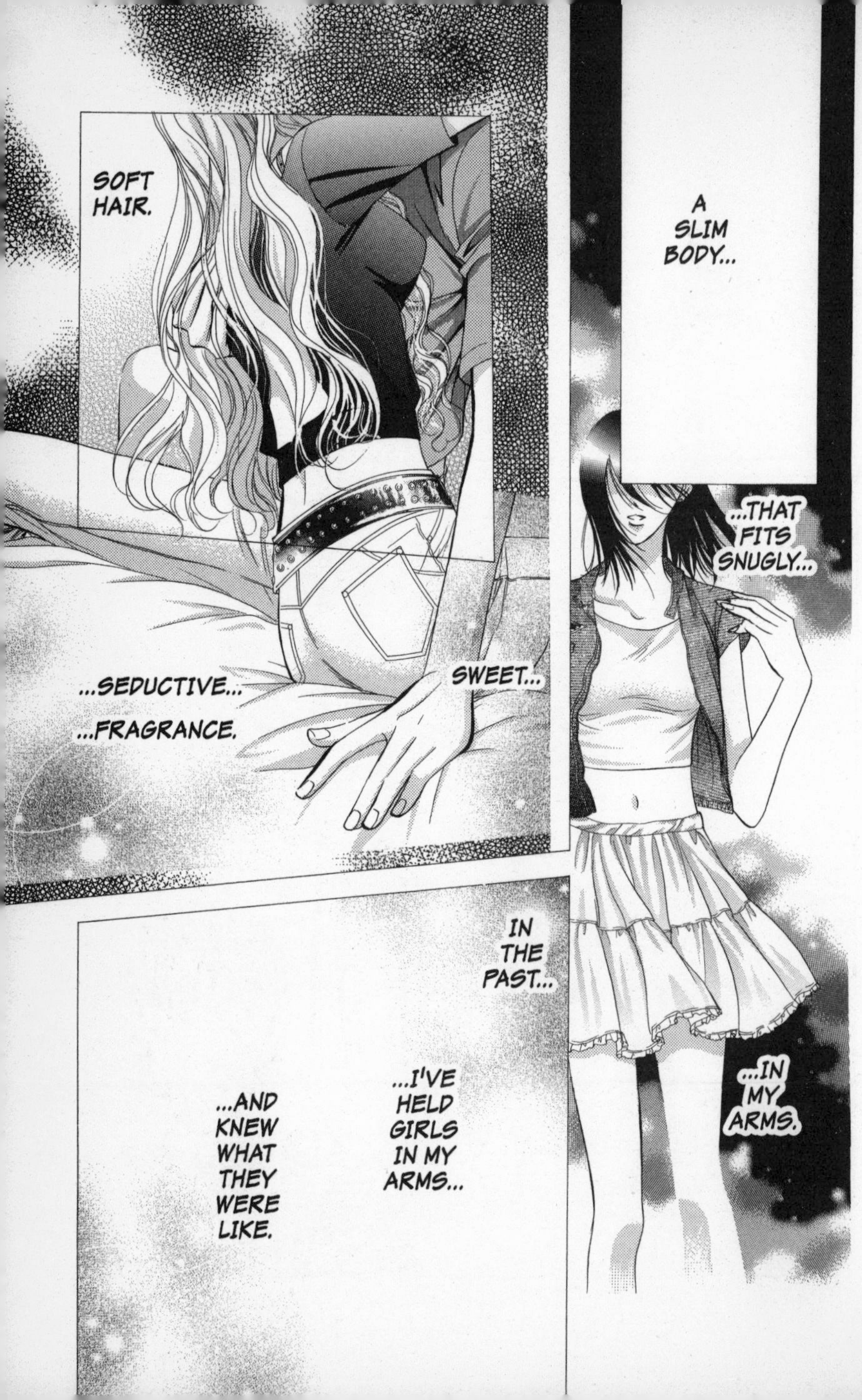
A SLIM BODY...
...THAT FITS SNUGLY...
...IN MY ARMS.
SOFT HAIR.
SWEET...
...SEDUCTIVE...
...FRAGRANCE.
IN THE PAST...
...I'VE HELD GIRLS IN MY ARMS...
...AND KNEW WHAT THEY WERE LIKE.

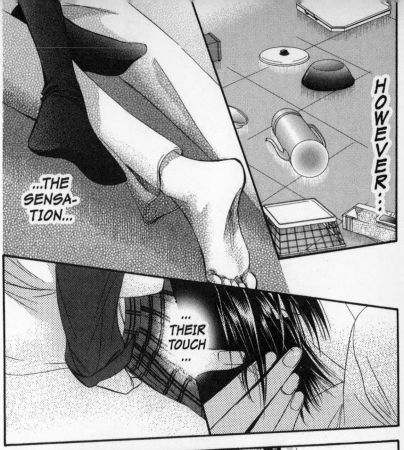

HOWEVER...

...THE SENSA-TION...

...THEIR TOUCH...

...THEIR FRA-GRANCE...

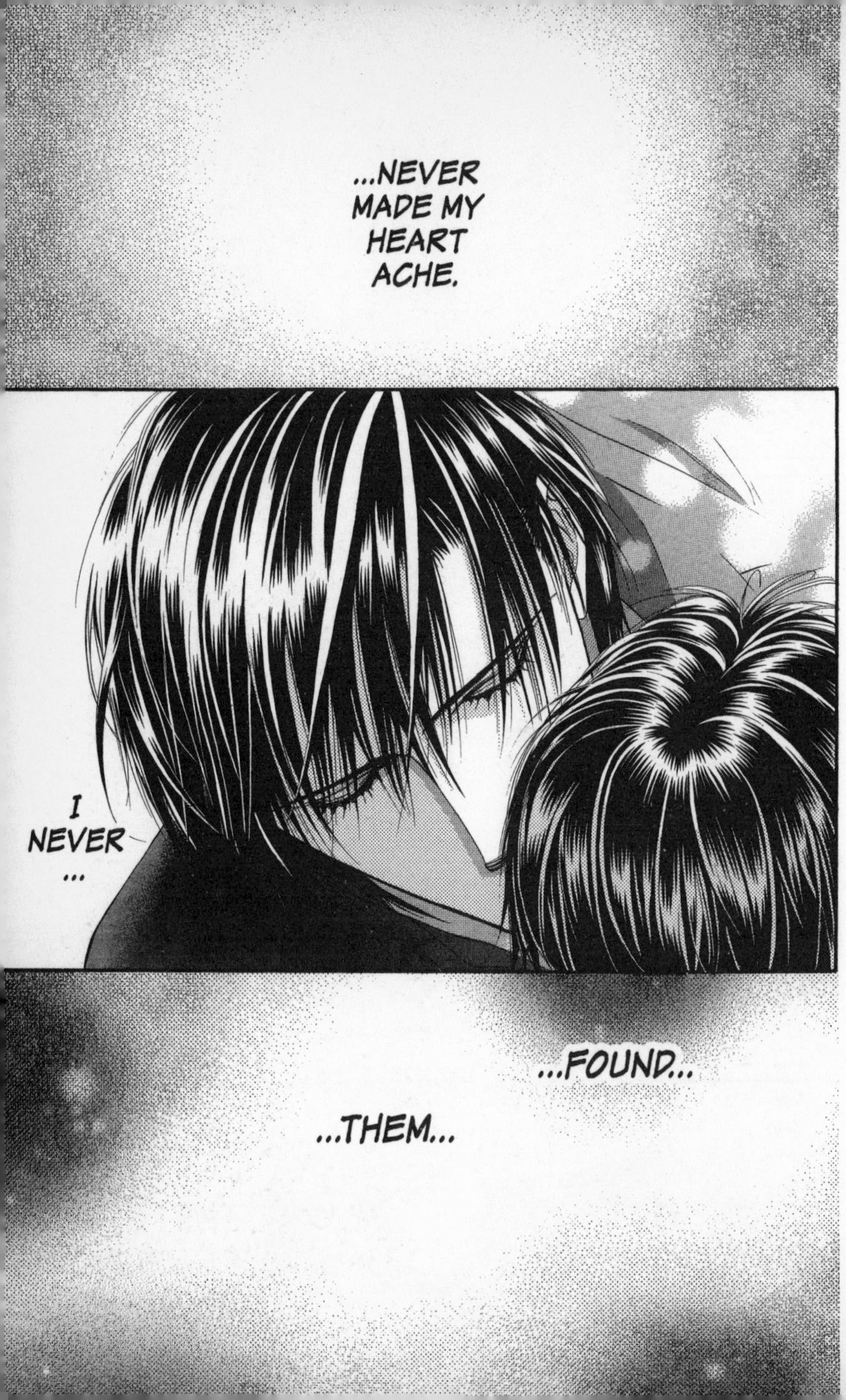
...NEVER MADE MY HEART ACHE.
I NEVER ...
...FOUND...
...THEM...

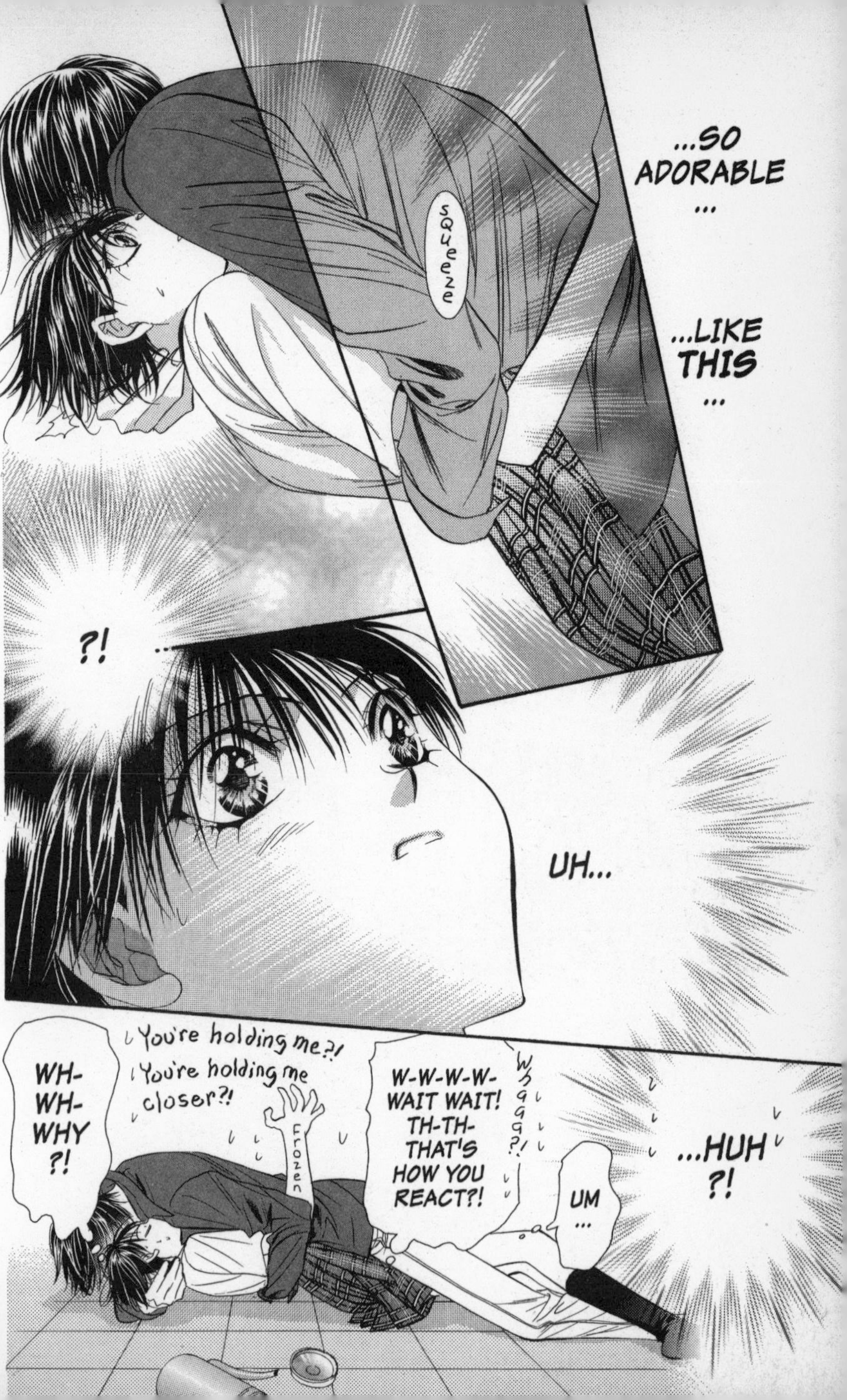
...SO ADORABLE ...
squeeze
...LIKE THIS ...
...
?!
UH...
...HUH ?!
UM ...
Whaggg?!
W-W-W-W-WAIT WAIT! TH-TH-THAT'S HOW YOU REACT?!
You're holding me?!
You're holding me closer?!
Frozen
WH-WH-WHY ?!

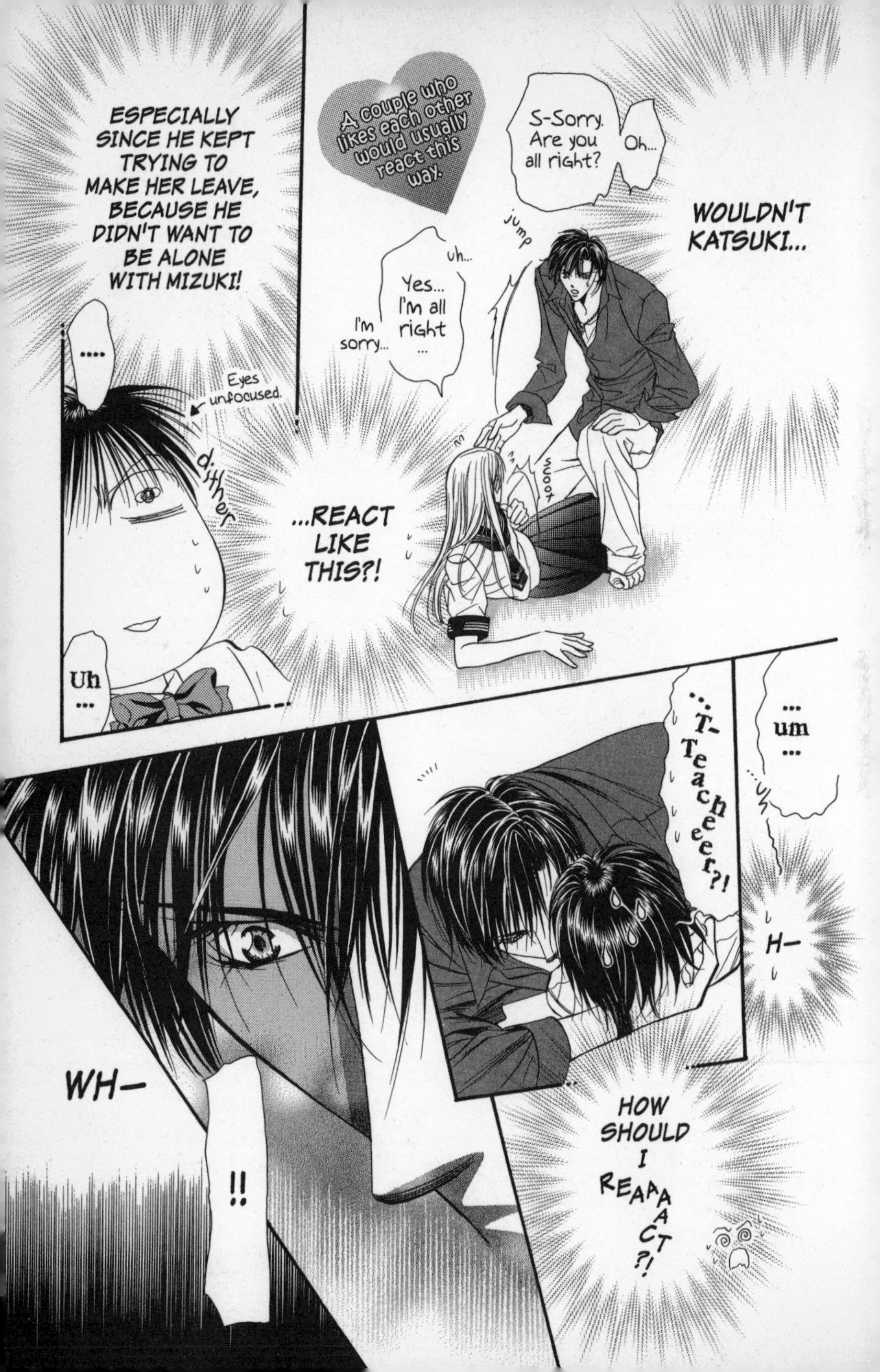
Oh...
S-Sorry. Are you all right?
A couple who likes each other would usually react this way.
WOULDN'T KATSUKI...
jump
uh...
Yes... I'm all right ...
I'm sorry...
...REACT LIKE THIS?!
ESPECIALLY SINCE HE KEPT TRYING TO MAKE HER LEAVE, BECAUSE HE DIDN'T WANT TO BE ALONE WITH MIZUKI!
....
Eyes unfocused.
dither
Uh ...
... um ...
...uh
H-
...T-Teacheer?!
HOW SHOULD I REAAAACT?!
WH-
!!

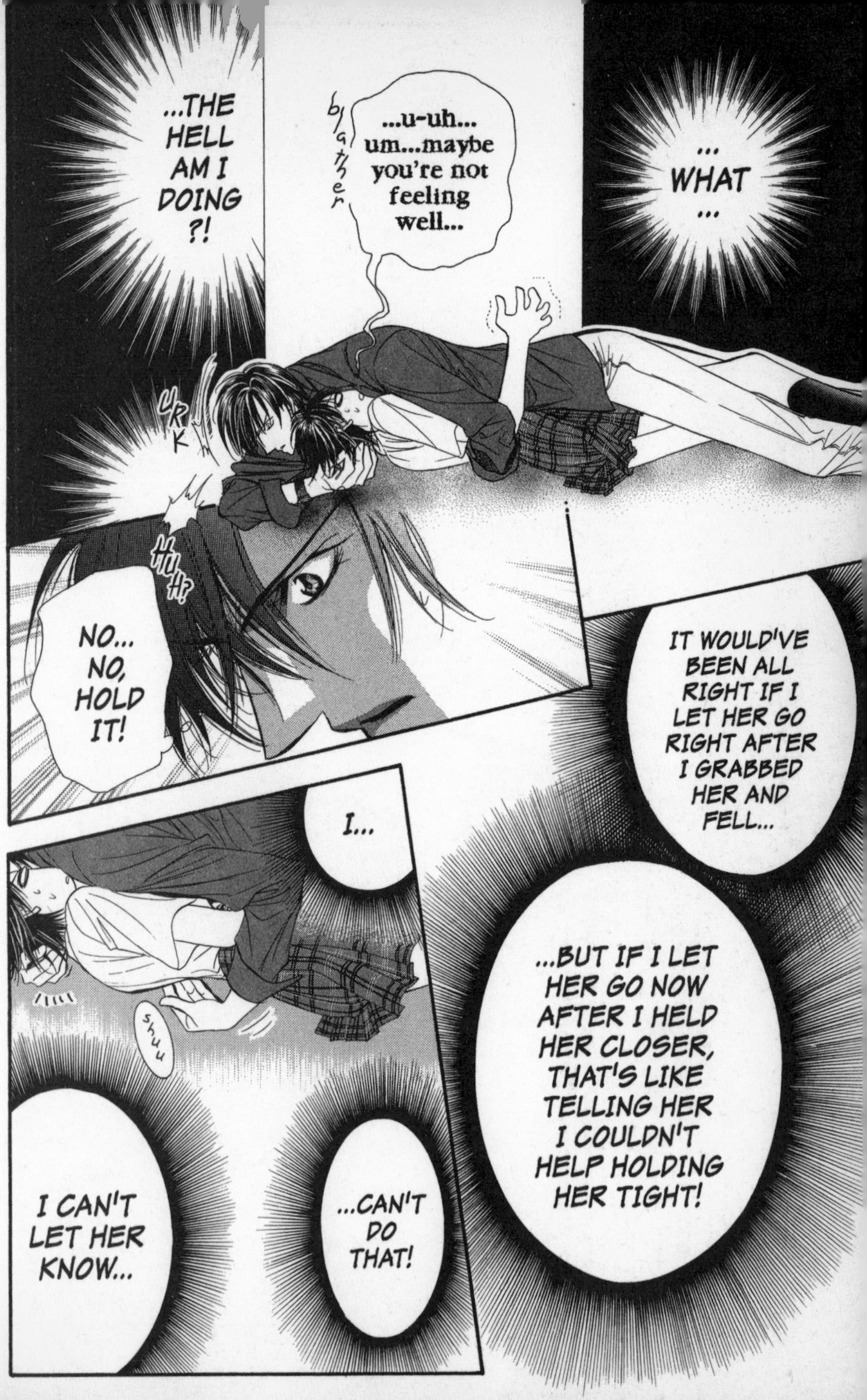
... WHAT ...
...u-uh... um...maybe you're not feeling well...
blather
...THE HELL AM I DOING ?!
URK
HUH?
NO... NO, HOLD IT!
IT WOULD'VE BEEN ALL RIGHT IF I LET HER GO RIGHT AFTER I GRABBED HER AND FELL...
I...
...BUT IF I LET HER GO NOW AFTER I HELD HER CLOSER, THAT'S LIKE TELLING HER I COULDN'T HELP HOLDING HER TIGHT!
shuu
...CAN'T DO THAT!
I CAN'T LET HER KNOW...

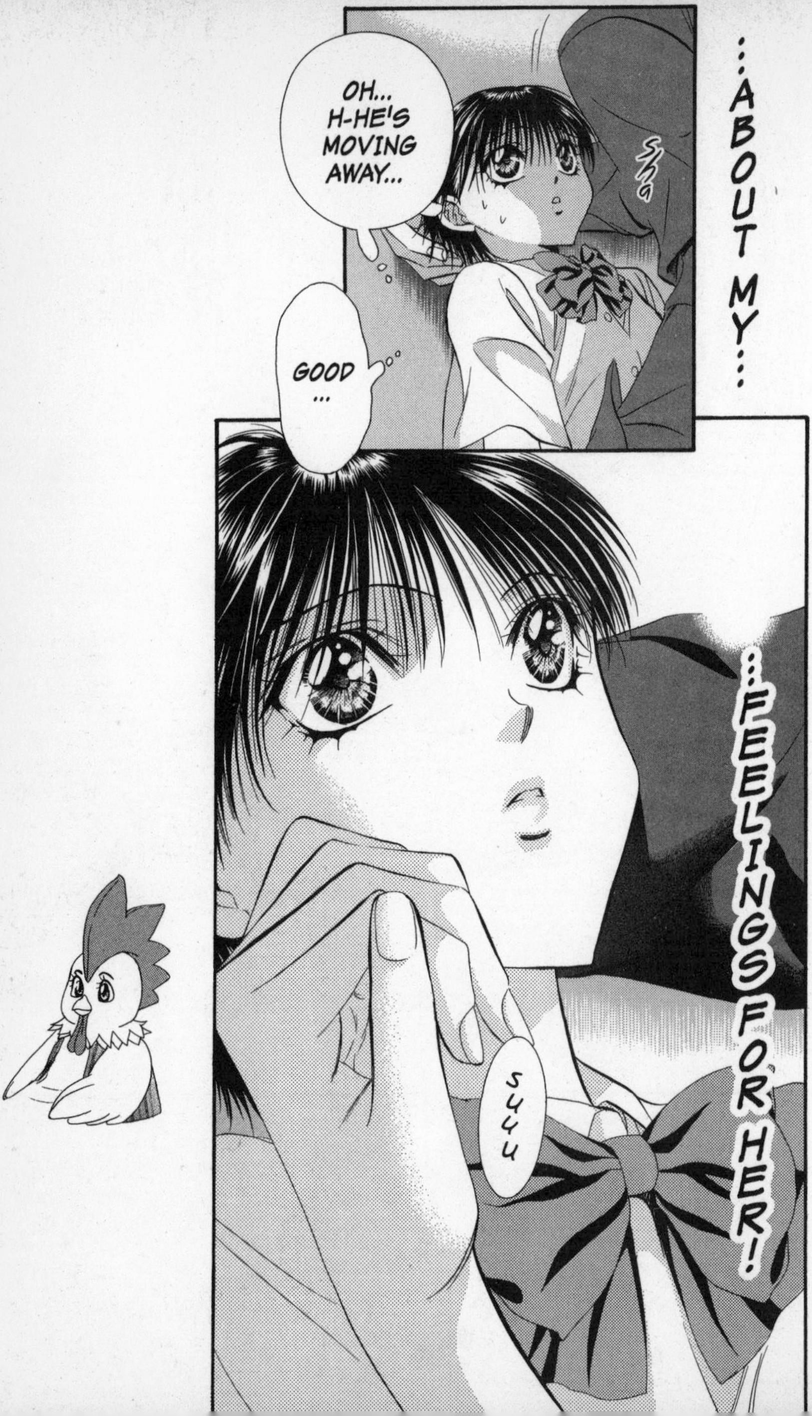
...ABOUT MY...
Sha
OH... H-HE'S MOVING AWAY...
GOOD...
...FEELINGS FOR HER!
SUUU

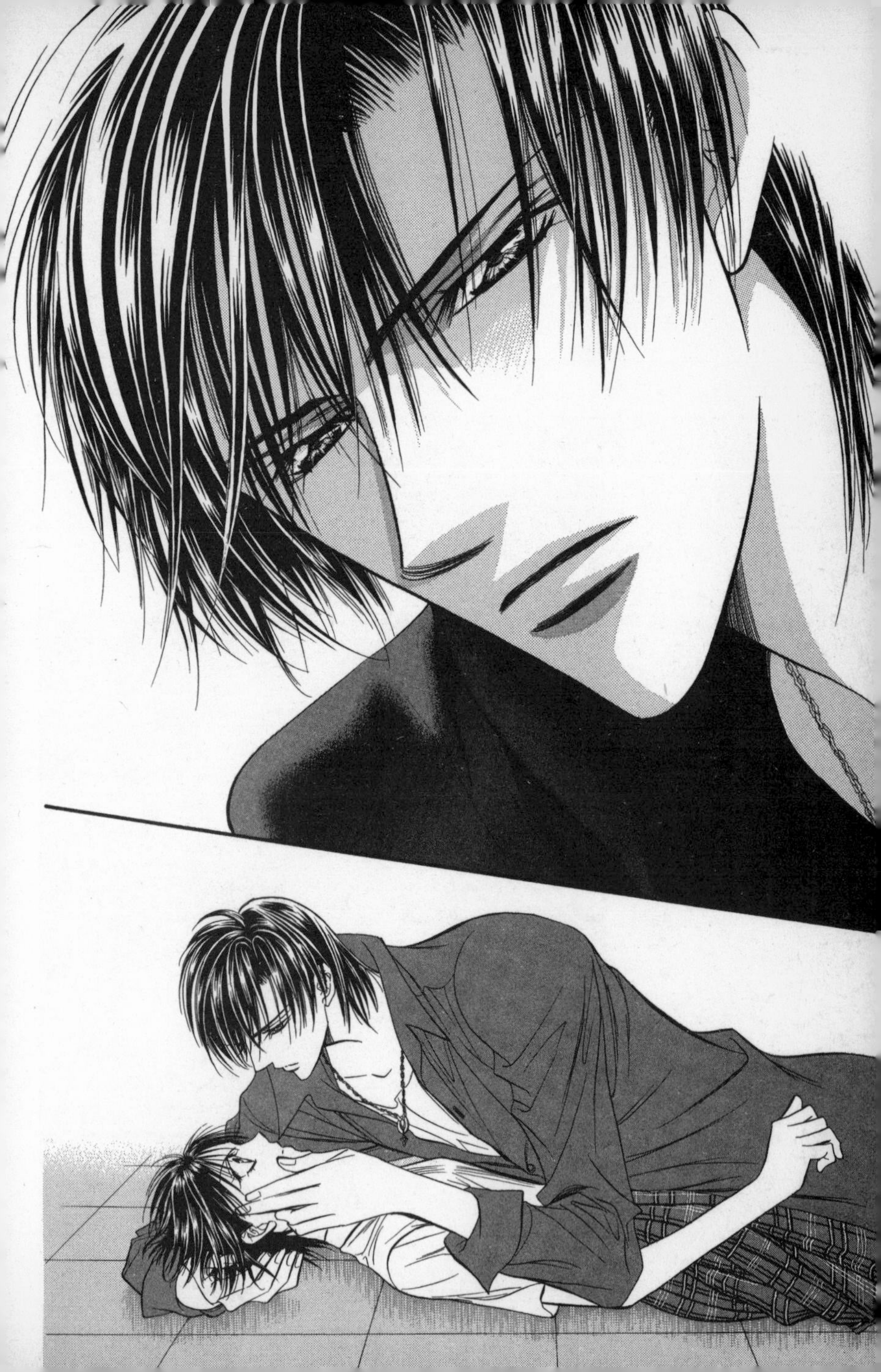

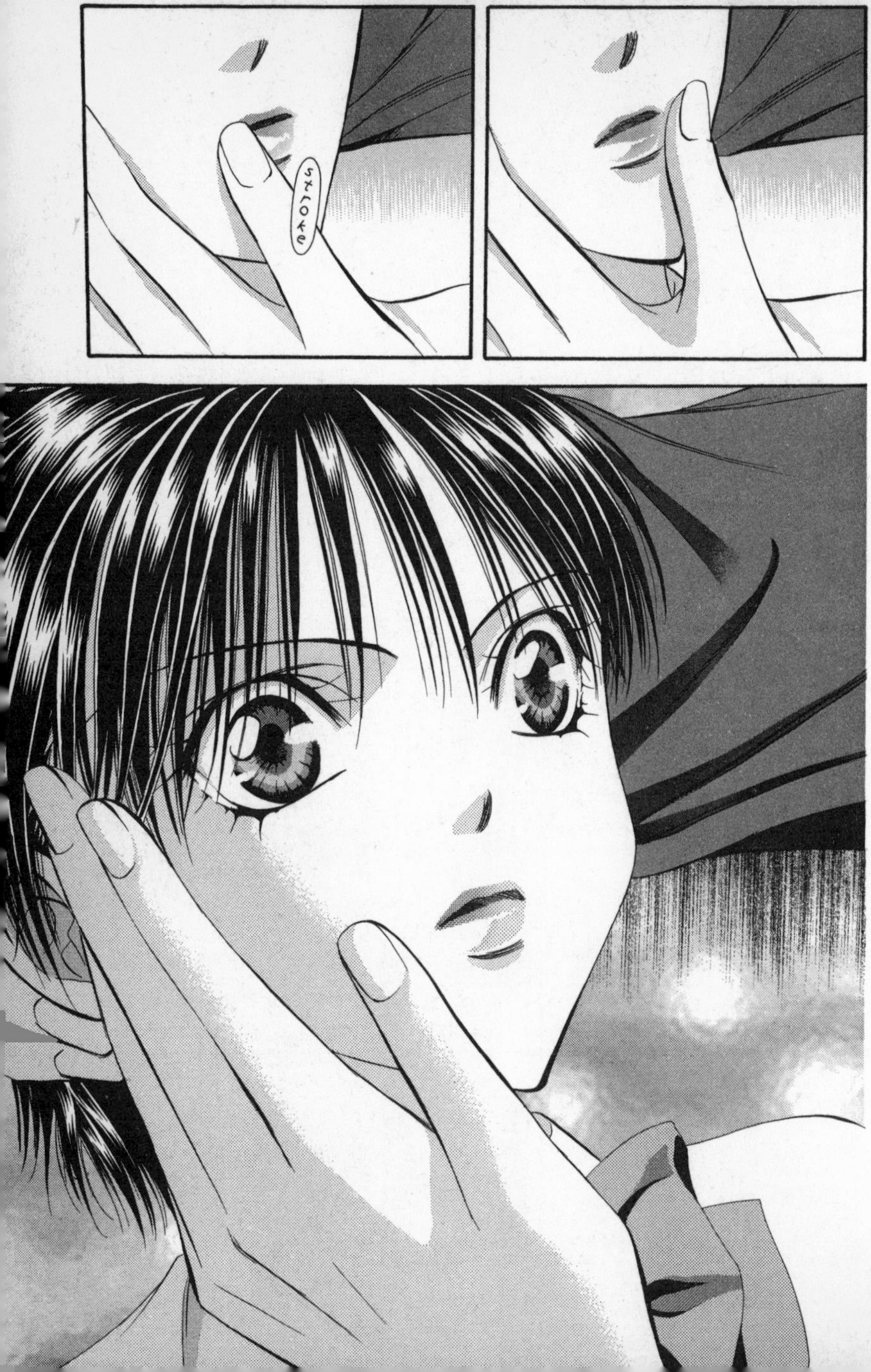
stroke

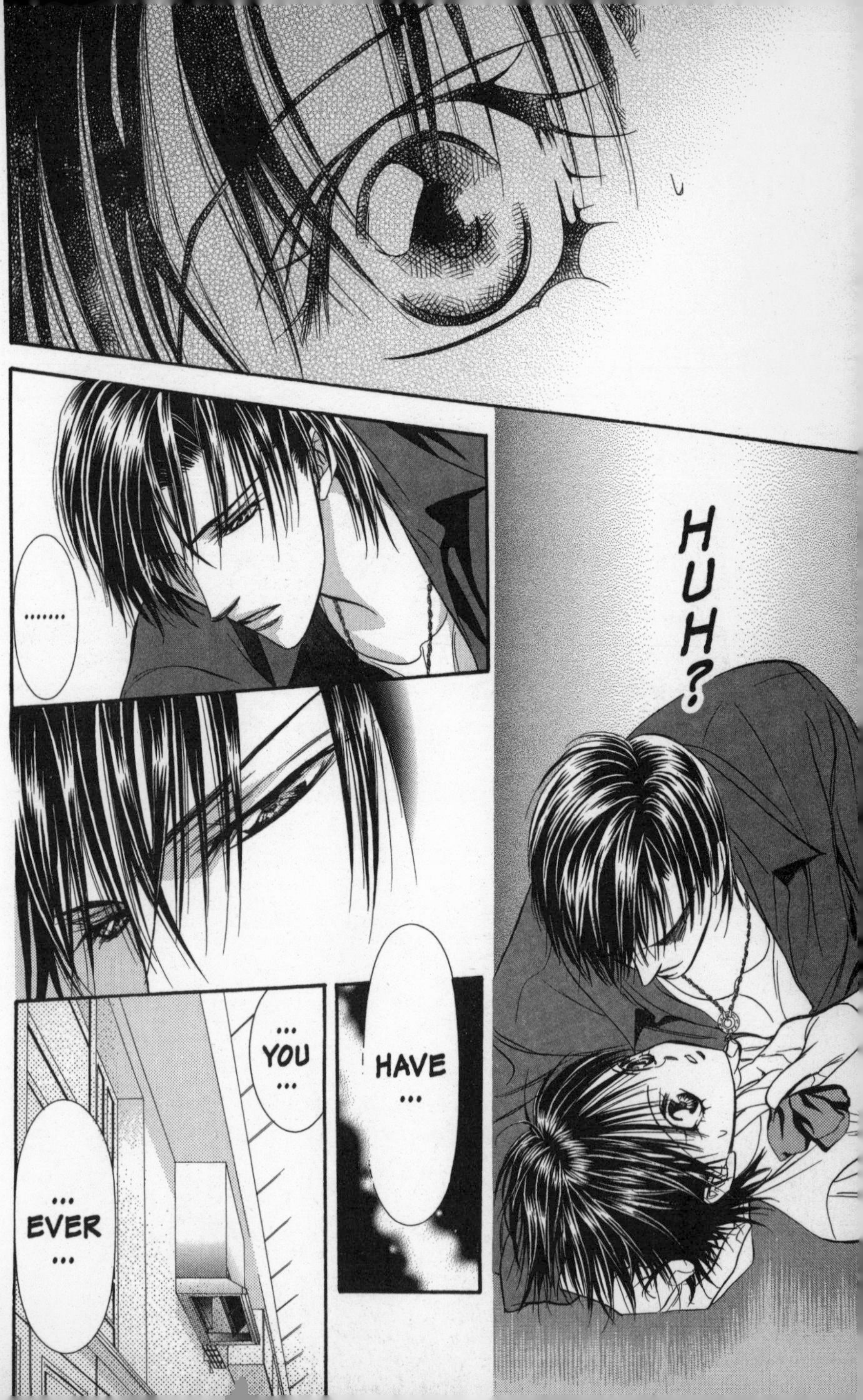
HUH?
....
HAVE ...
... YOU ...
... EVER ...

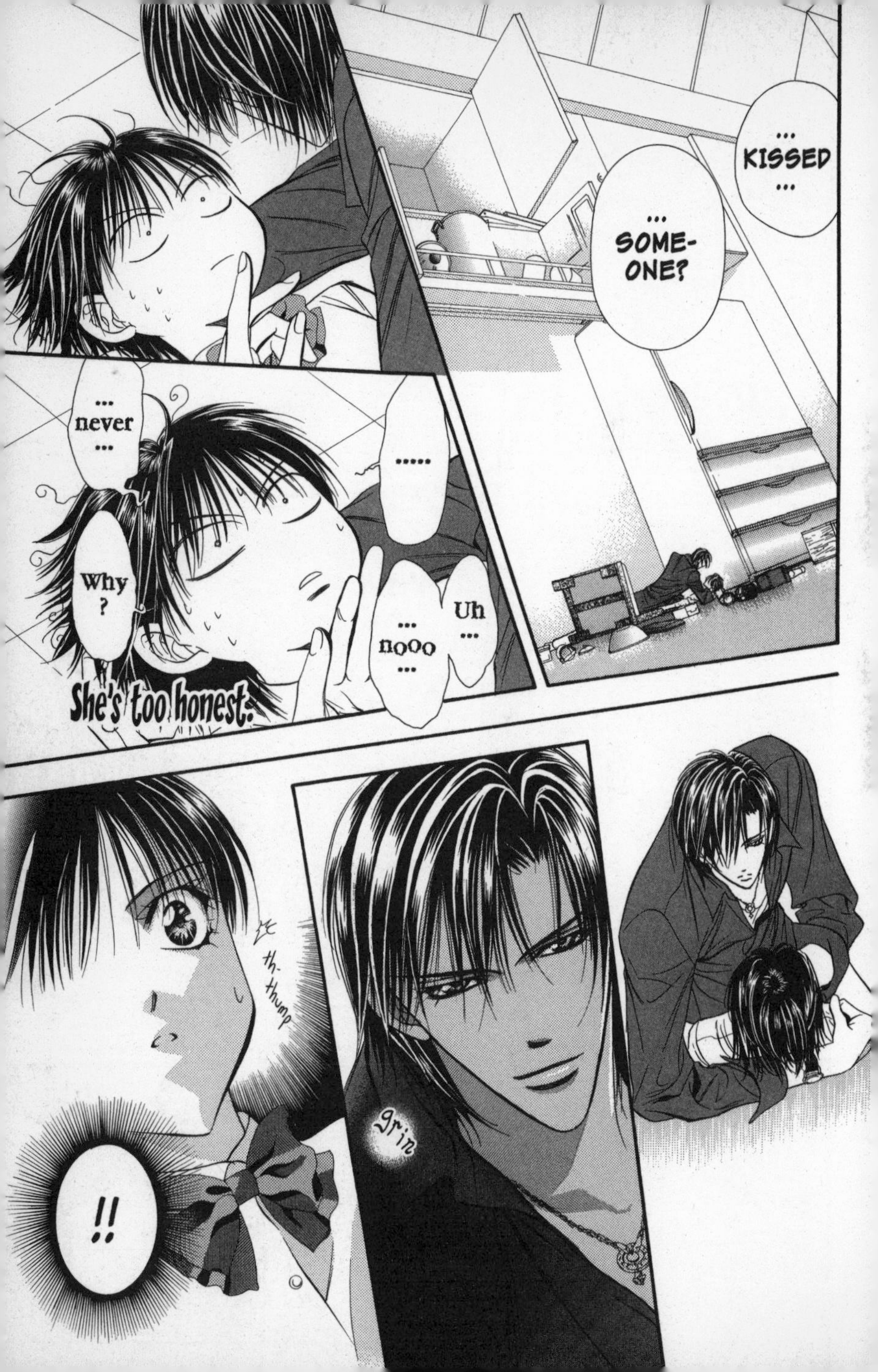
...KISSED...
...SOME-ONE?
......
Uh...
...nooo...
...never...
Why?
She's too honest.
grin
th-thump
!!

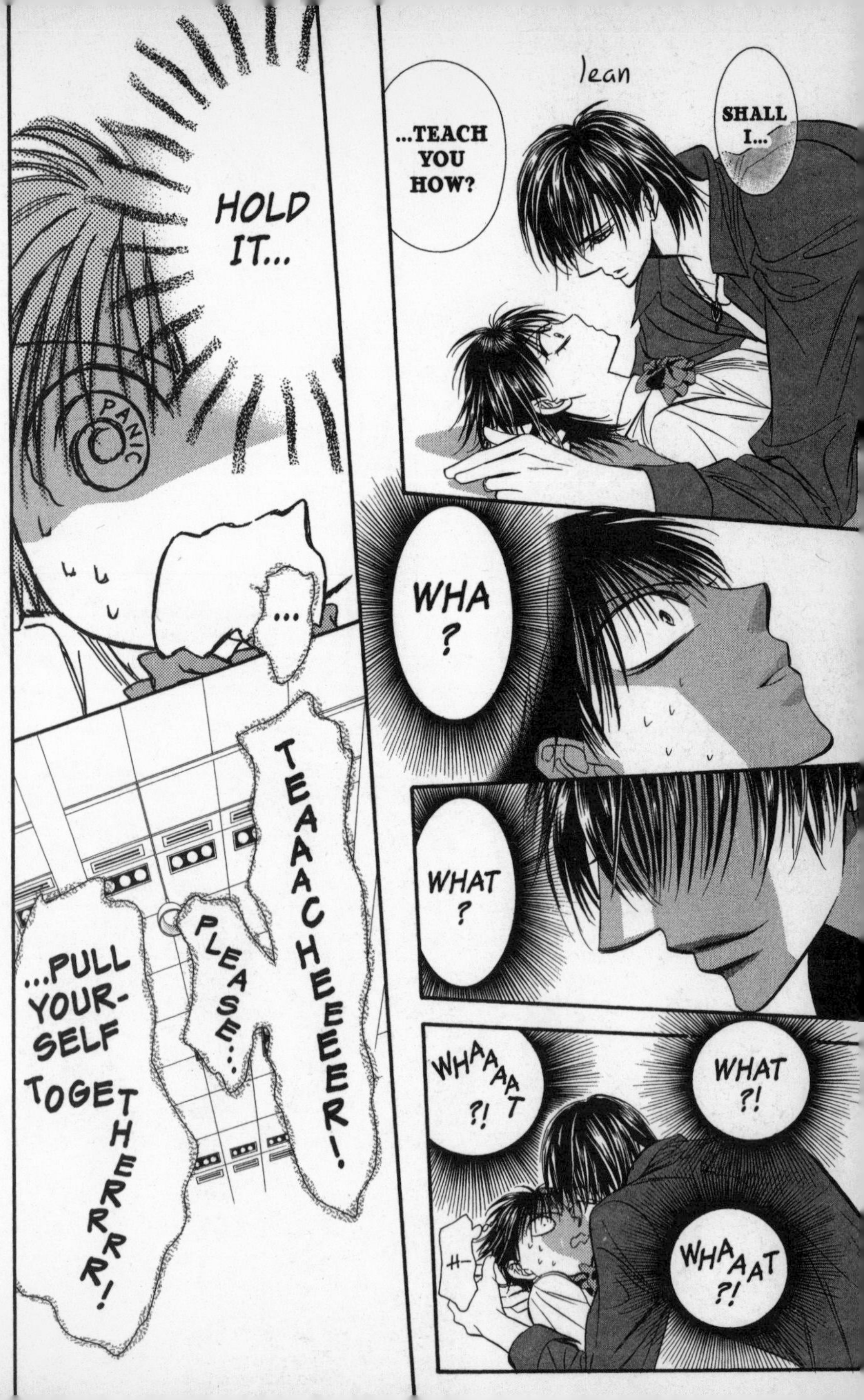
SHALL I...
lean
...TEACH YOU HOW?
WHA?
WHAT?
WHAT?!
WHAAAAT?!
H-
WHAAAT?!
HOLD IT...
PANIC
...
TEAAACHEEEER!
PLEASE...
...PULL YOURSELF TOGETHERRRR!

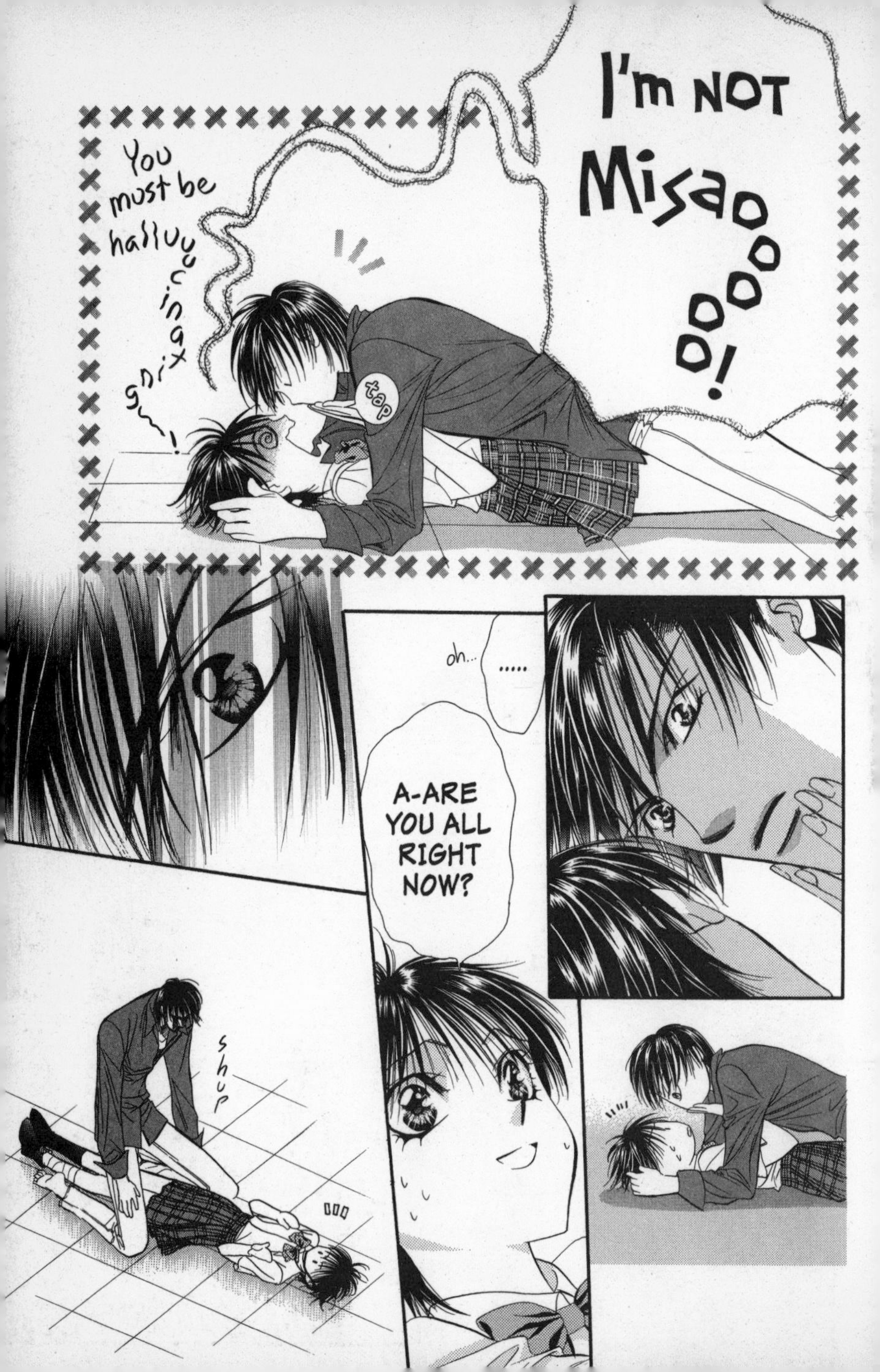
I'm NOT Misaooooo!
tap
You must be halluucinating~!
oh...
.....
A-ARE YOU ALL RIGHT NOW?
shup

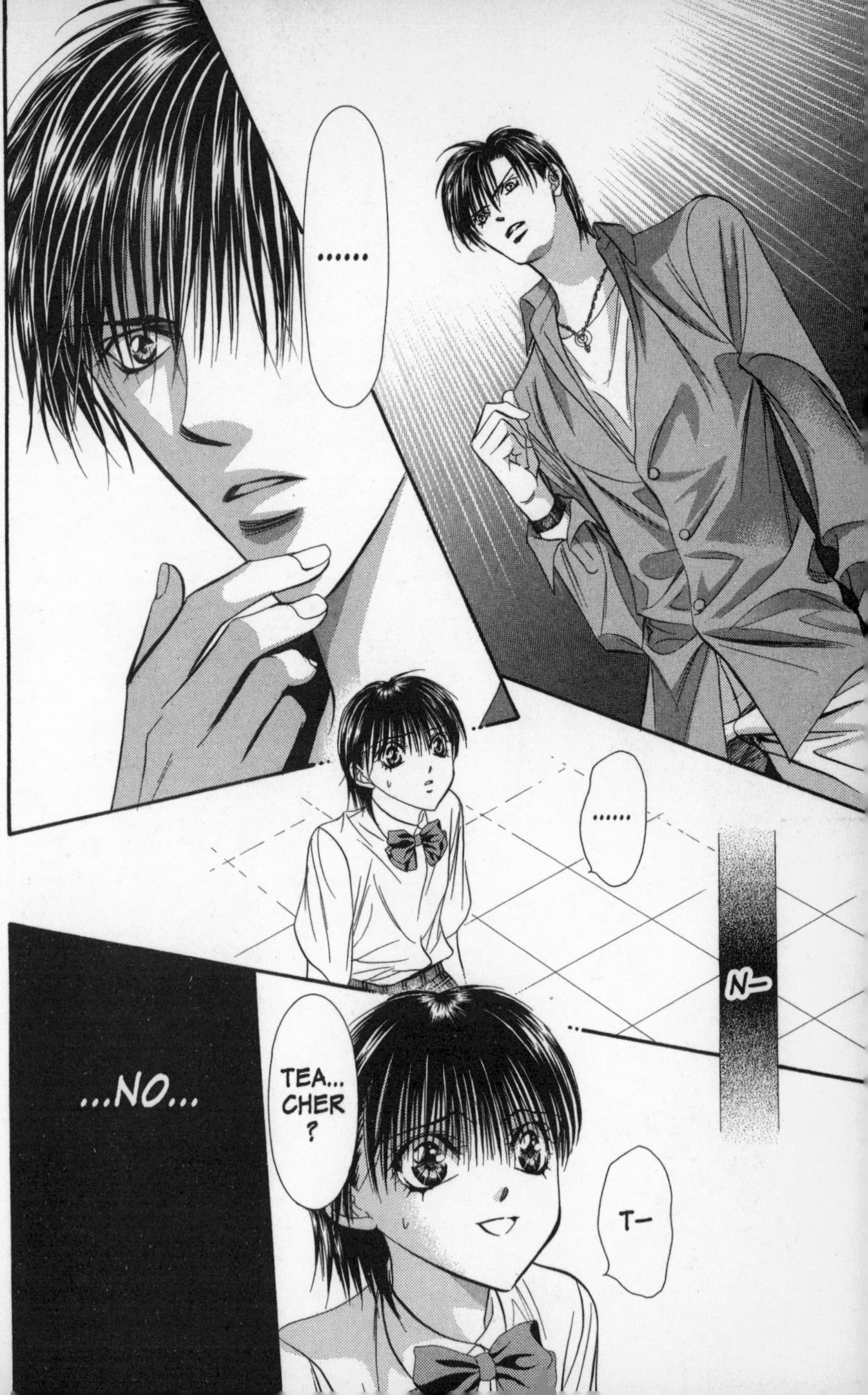
......
......
N—
T—
TEA... CHER ?
...NO...

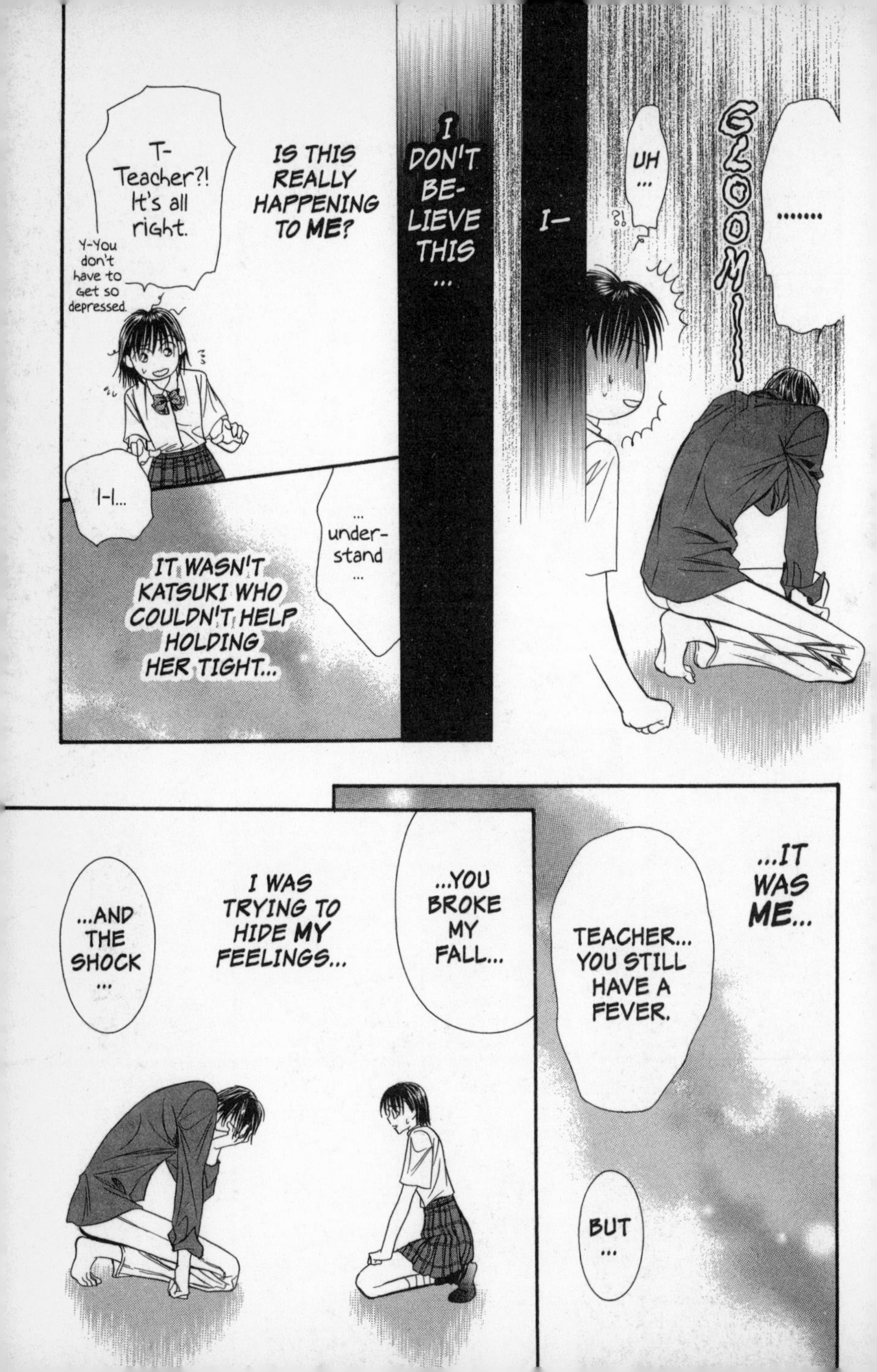

....
GLOOM!
UH ...
?!
I—
I DON'T BE-LIEVE THIS ...
IS THIS REALLY HAPPENING TO ME?
T-Teacher?! It's all right.
Y-You don't have to get so depressed.
... under-stand ...
I-I...
IT WASN'T KATSUKI WHO COULDN'T HELP HOLDING HER TIGHT...
...IT WAS ME...
TEACHER... YOU STILL HAVE A FEVER.
BUT ...
...YOU BROKE MY FALL...
I WAS TRYING TO HIDE MY FEELINGS...
...AND THE SHOCK ...

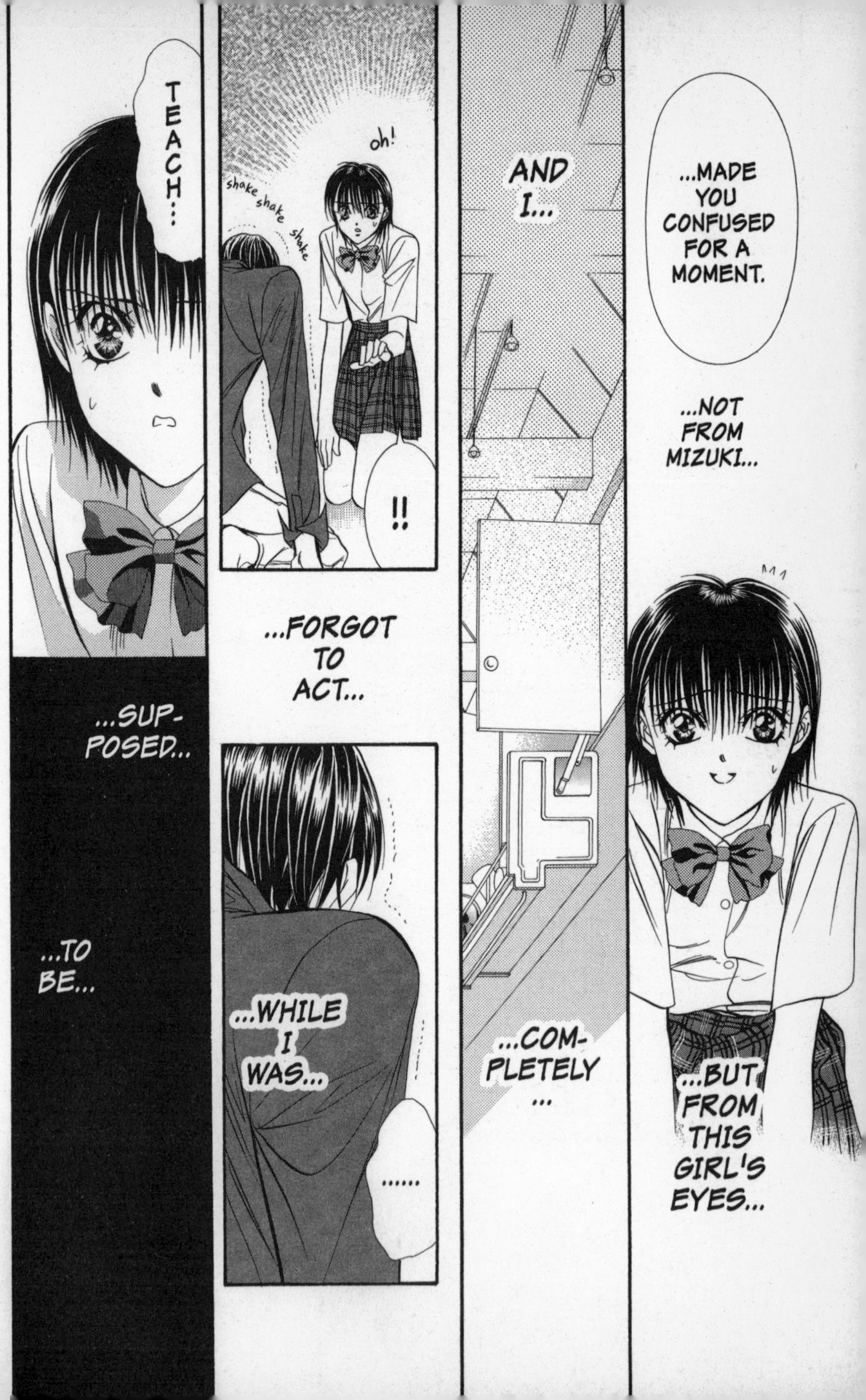
...MADE YOU CONFUSED FOR A MOMENT.
...NOT FROM MIZUKI...
...BUT FROM THIS GIRL'S EYES...
AND I...
...COM-PLETELY ...
oh!
shake shake shake
!!
...FORGOT TO ACT...
...WHILE I WAS...
......
TEACH...
...SUP-POSED...
...TO BE...

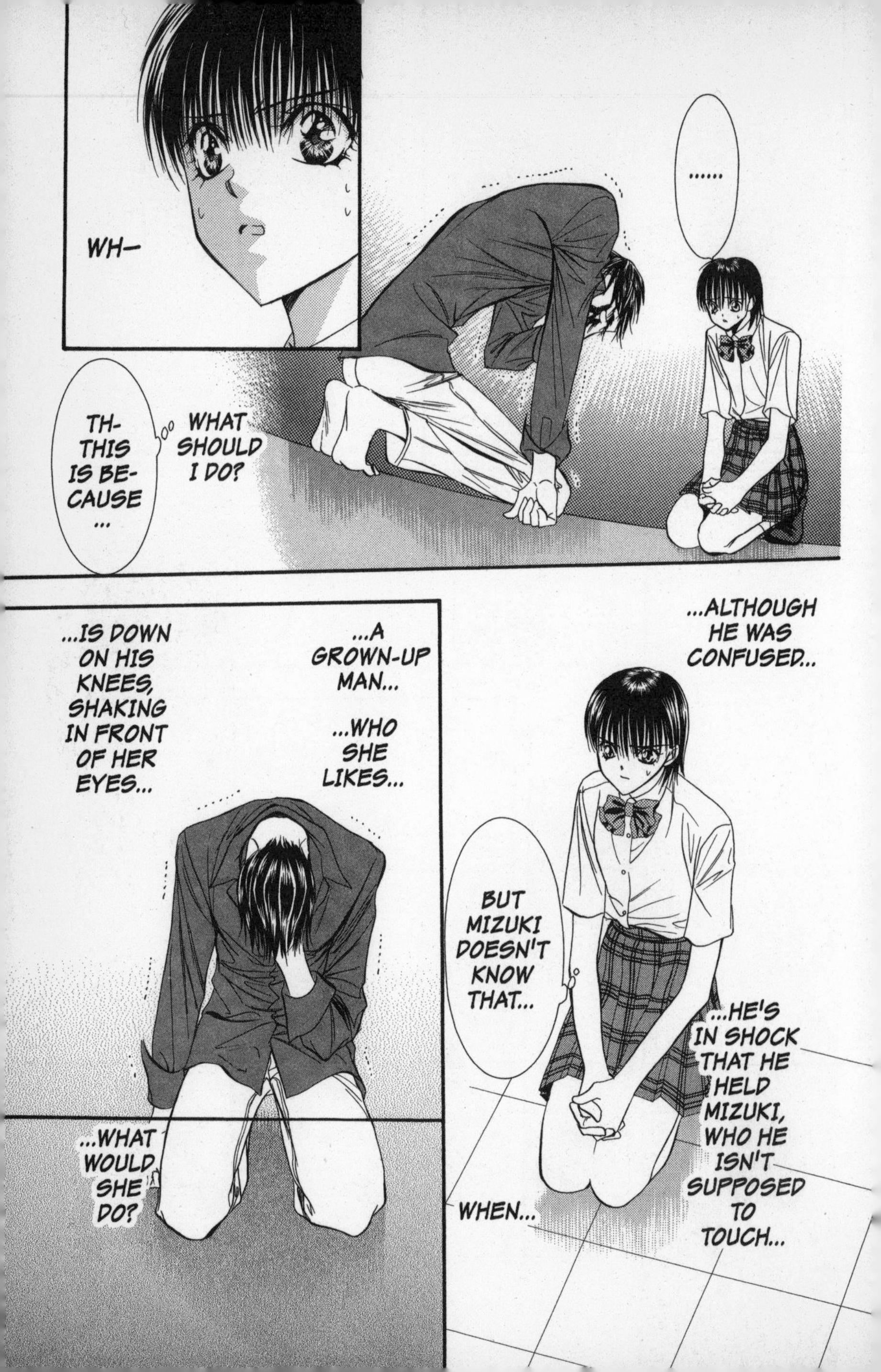
......
WH—
WHAT SHOULD I DO?
TH- THIS IS BE- CAUSE ...
...ALTHOUGH HE WAS CONFUSED...
...HE'S IN SHOCK THAT HE HELD MIZUKI, WHO HE ISN'T SUPPOSED TO TOUCH...
BUT MIZUKI DOESN'T KNOW THAT...
WHEN...
...A GROWN-UP MAN...
...WHO SHE LIKES...
...IS DOWN ON HIS KNEES, SHAKING IN FRONT OF HER EYES...
...WHAT WOULD SHE DO?

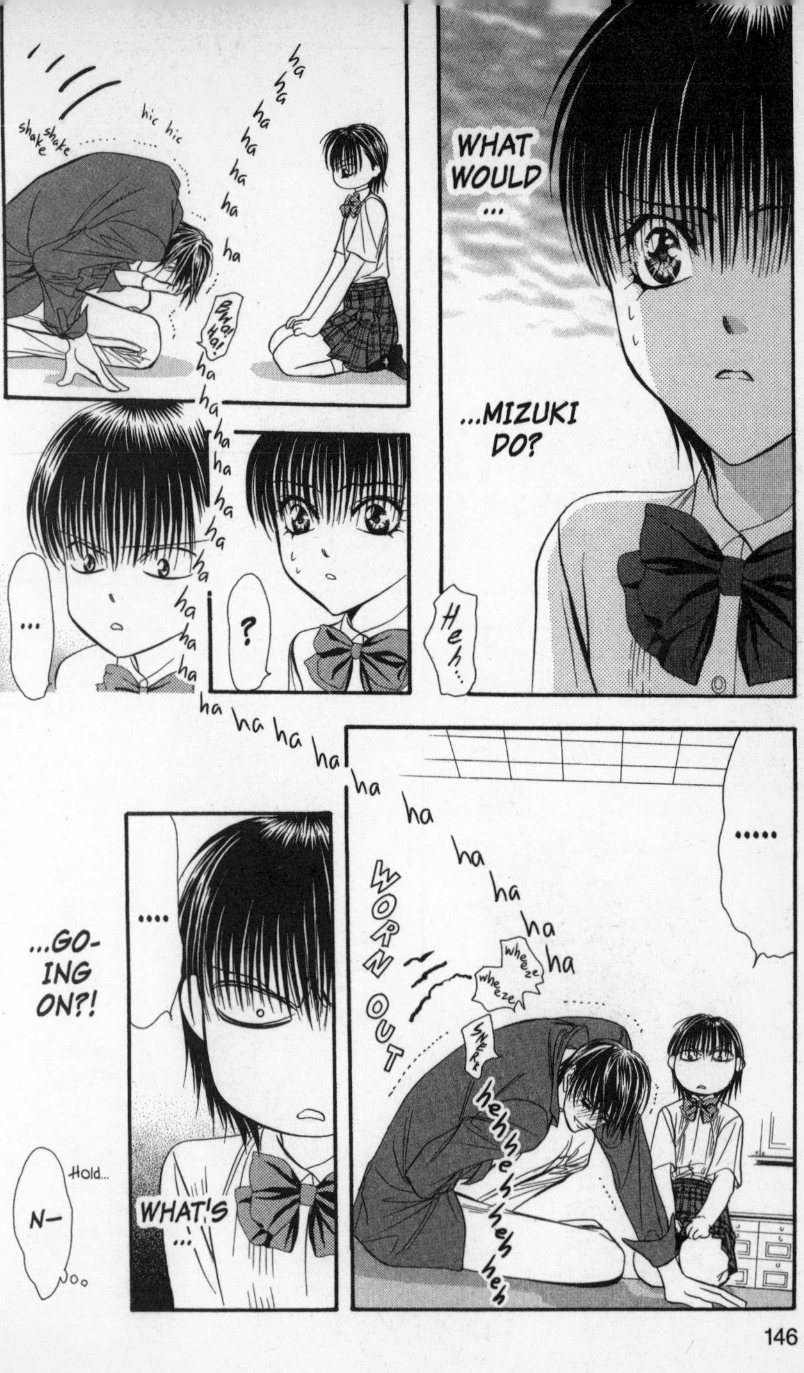
WHAT WOULD ...
...MIZUKI DO?
Heh...
ha ha ha ha ha ha ha ha
hic hic
shake shake
BWA HA!
ha ha ha ha ha ha ha ha ha ha ha
?
...
ha ha ha ha ha ha ha ha ha ha ha
.....
WORN OUT
wheeze wheeze
SNERK
heh heh heh heh heh
....
...GO-ING ON?!
WHAT'S ...
Hold...
N—
Noo

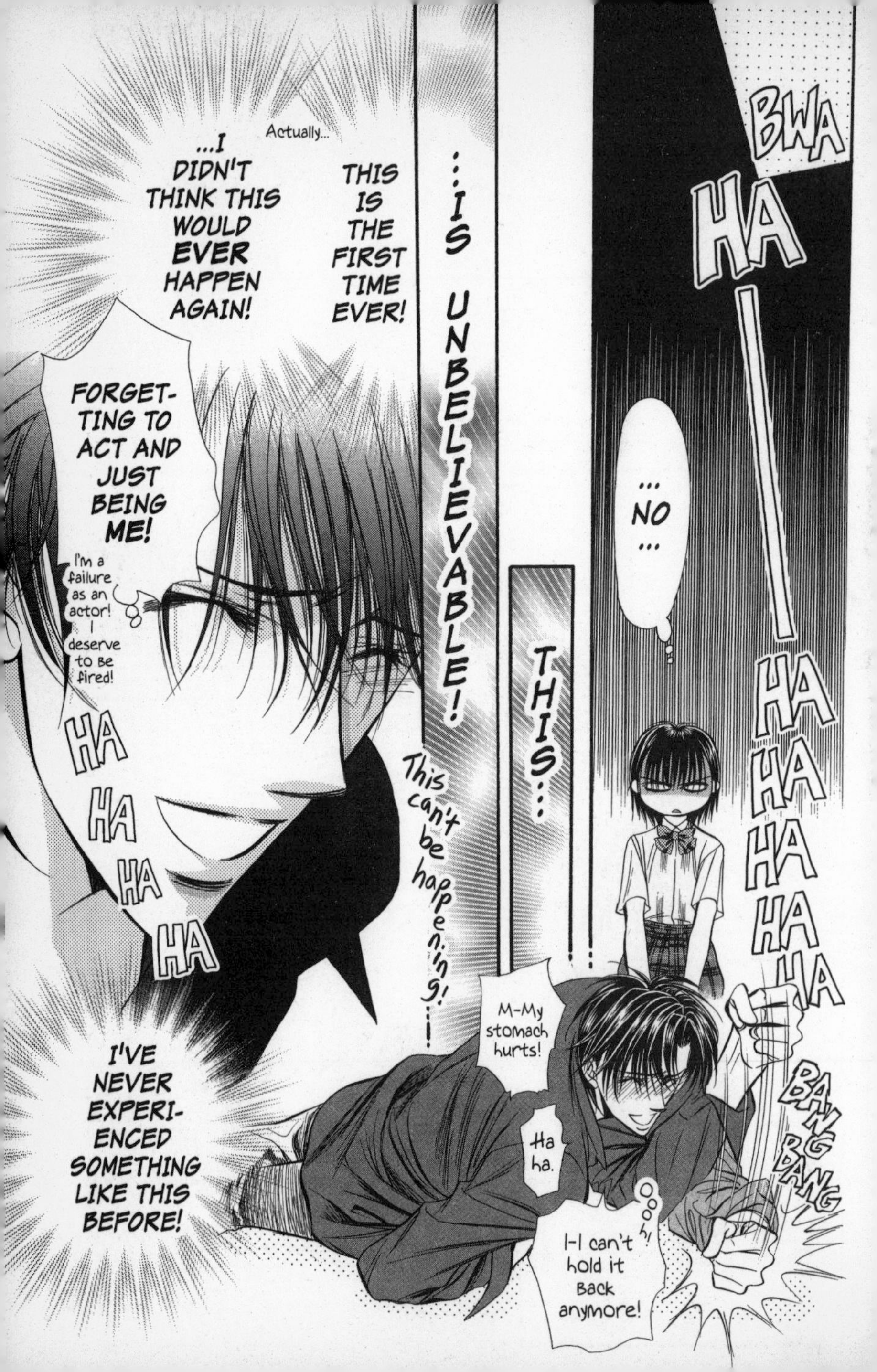
BWAHA HA
...NO...
HA HA HA HA HA
THIS...
M-My stomach hurts!
BANG BANG
Ha ha.
Oooh!
I-I can't hold it back anymore!
...IS UNBELIEVABLE!
This can't be happening!
THIS IS THE FIRST TIME EVER!
Actually...
...I DIDN'T THINK THIS WOULD EVER HAPPEN AGAIN!
FORGETTING TO ACT AND JUST BEING ME!
I'm a failure as an actor! I deserve to be fired!
HA HA HA HA
I'VE NEVER EXPERIENCED SOMETHING LIKE THIS BEFORE!

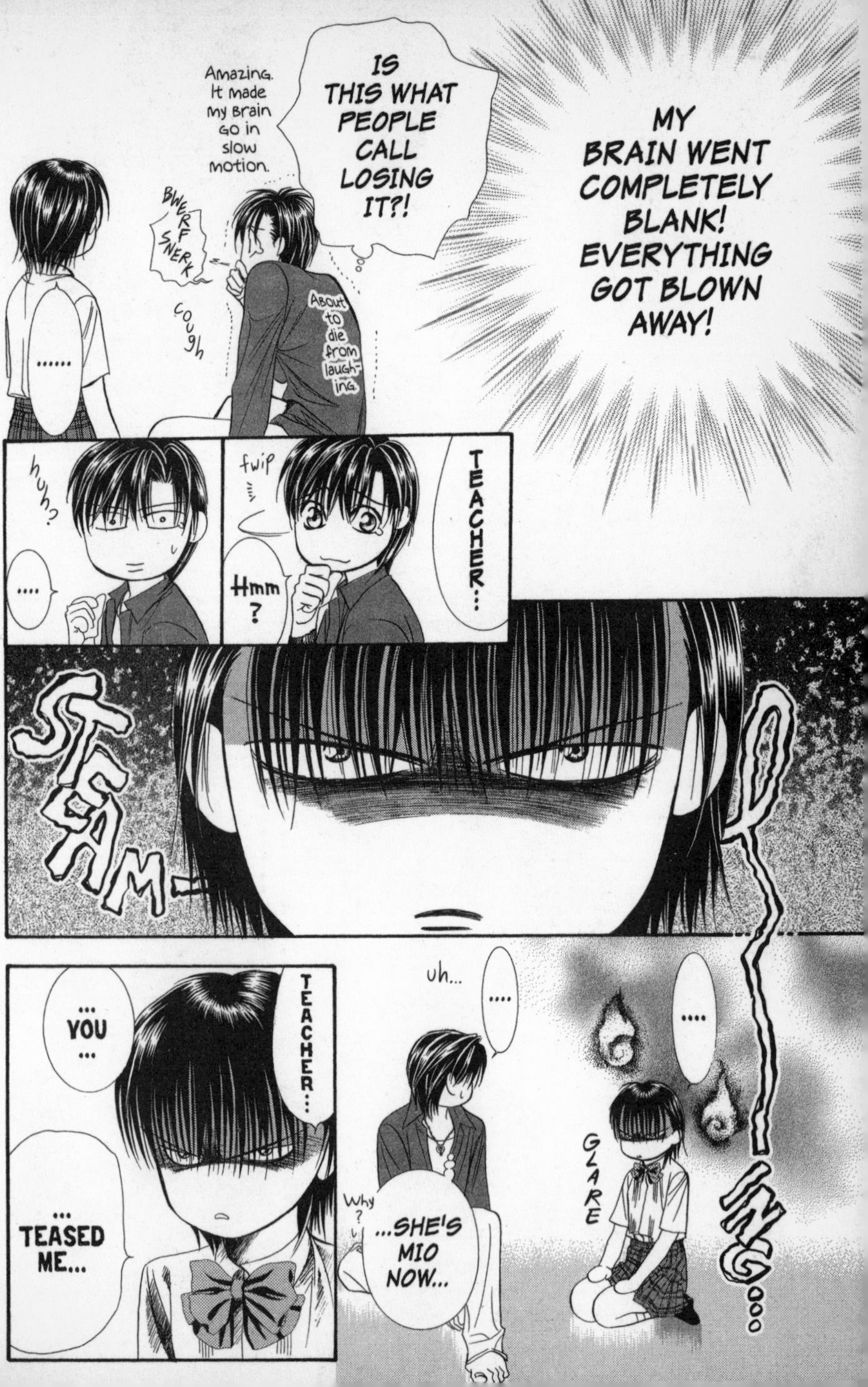
MY BRAIN WENT COMPLETELY BLANK! EVERYTHING GOT BLOWN AWAY!
IS THIS WHAT PEOPLE CALL LOSING IT?!
Amazing. It made my brain go in slow motion.
BWERF SNERK
cough
About to die from laughing.
......
TEACHER...
fwip
Hmm ?
huh?
....
STEAM-
ING...
....
....
uh...
GLARE
Why ?
...SHE'S MIO NOW...
TEACHER...
... YOU ...
... TEASED ME...

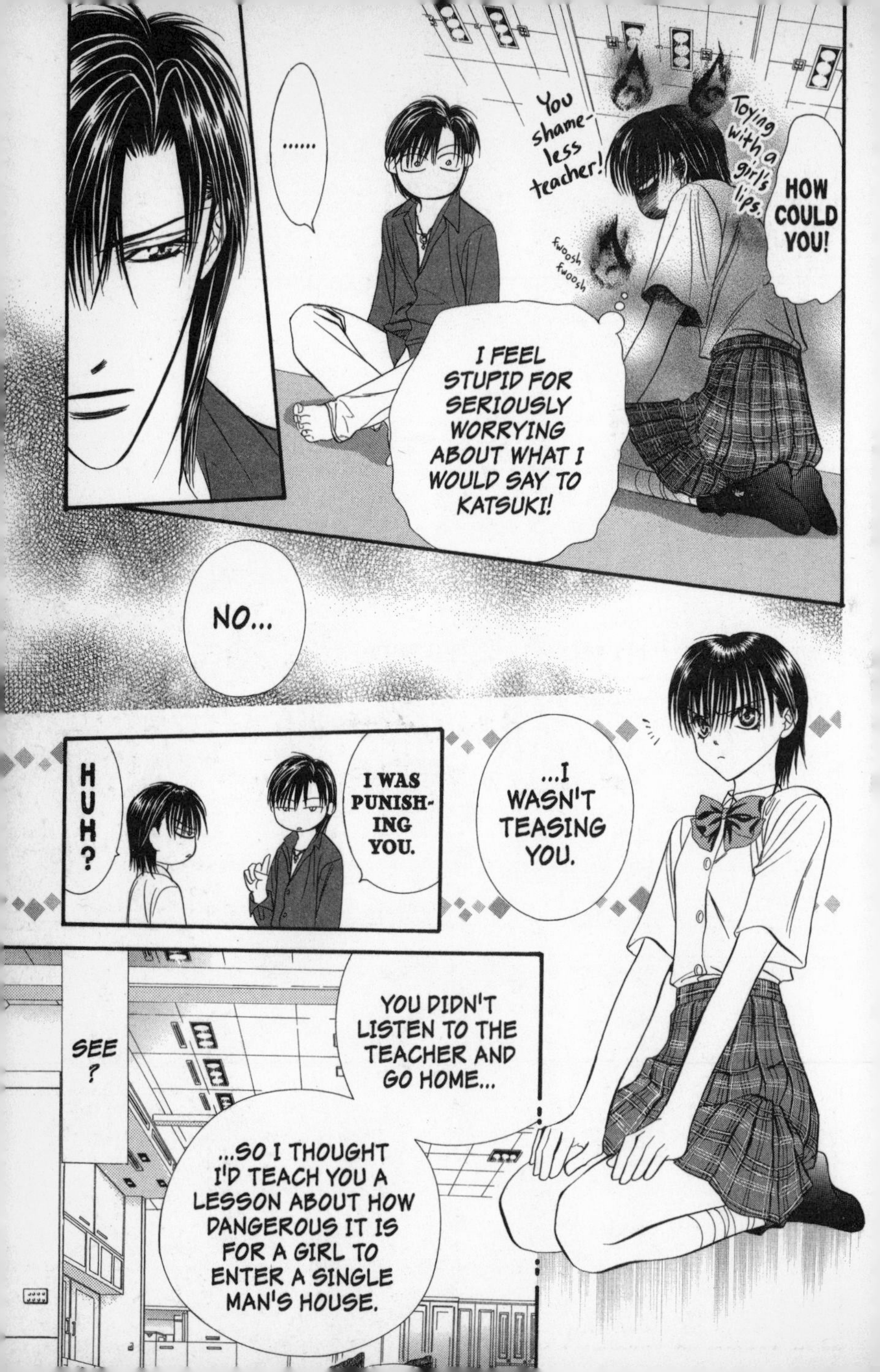
HOW COULD YOU!
Toying with a girl's lips.
You shame-less teacher!
fwoosh fwoosh
I FEEL STUPID FOR SERIOUSLY WORRYING ABOUT WHAT I WOULD SAY TO KATSUKI!
......
NO...
...I WASN'T TEASING YOU.
I WAS PUNISH-ING YOU.
HUH?
YOU DIDN'T LISTEN TO THE TEACHER AND GO HOME...
...SO I THOUGHT I'D TEACH YOU A LESSON ABOUT HOW DANGEROUS IT IS FOR A GIRL TO ENTER A SINGLE MAN'S HOUSE.
SEE?

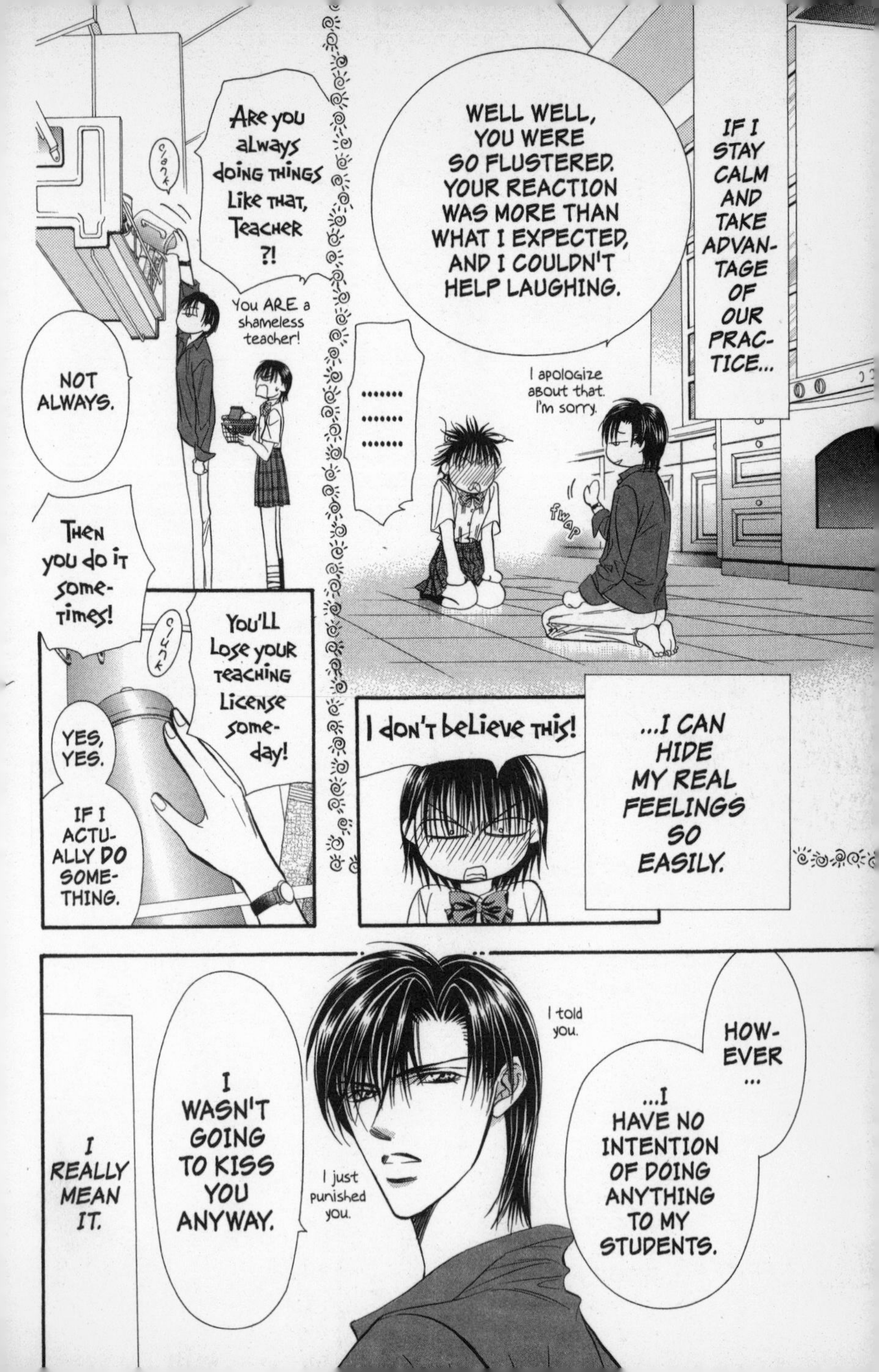
IF I STAY CALM AND TAKE ADVANTAGE OF OUR PRACTICE...
WELL WELL, YOU WERE SO FLUSTERED. YOUR REACTION WAS MORE THAN WHAT I EXPECTED, AND I COULDN'T HELP LAUGHING.
I apologize about that. I'm sorry.
....
fwap
...I CAN HIDE MY REAL FEELINGS SO EASILY.
I don't believe this!
Are you always doing things like THAT, Teacher?!
clank
You ARE a shameless teacher!
NOT ALWAYS.
Then you do it sometimes!
You'll lose your teaching license someday!
clunk
YES, YES.
IF I ACTUALLY DO SOMETHING.
HOW-EVER...
...I HAVE NO INTENTION OF DOING ANYTHING TO MY STUDENTS.
I told you.
I WASN'T GOING TO KISS YOU ANYWAY.
I just punished you.
I REALLY MEAN IT.

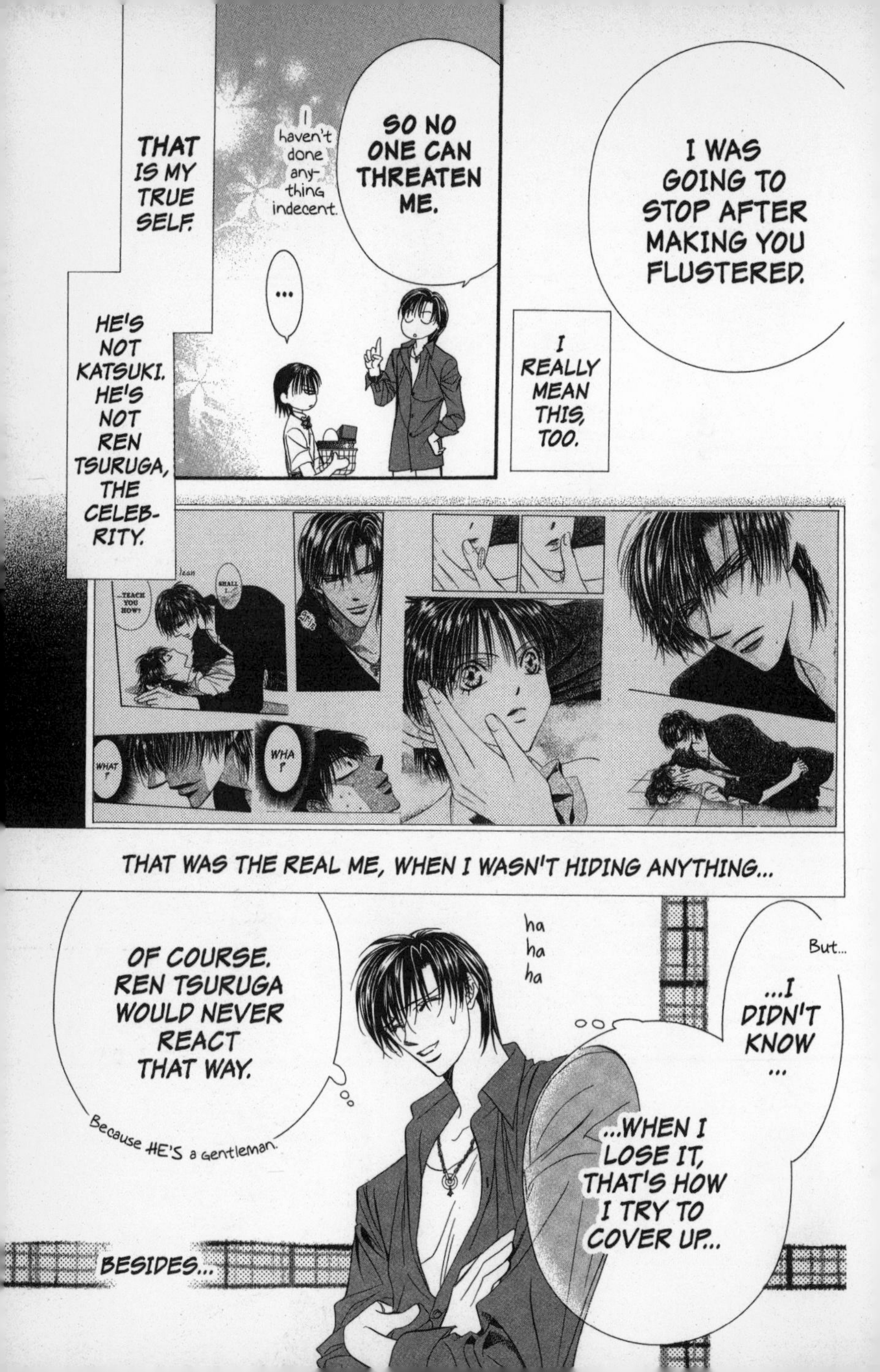
I WAS GOING TO STOP AFTER MAKING YOU FLUSTERED.
I REALLY MEAN THIS, TOO.
SO NO ONE CAN THREATEN ME.
I haven't done anything indecent.
...
THAT IS MY TRUE SELF.
HE'S NOT KATSUKI. HE'S NOT REN TSURUGA, THE CELEBRITY.
lean
SHALL I...
...TEACH YOU HOW?
WHA?
WHAT?
THAT WAS THE REAL ME, WHEN I WASN'T HIDING ANYTHING...
But...
...I DIDN'T KNOW...
...WHEN I LOSE IT, THAT'S HOW I TRY TO COVER UP...
ha ha ha
OF COURSE. REN TSURUGA WOULD NEVER REACT THAT WAY.
Because HE'S a gentleman.
BESIDES...

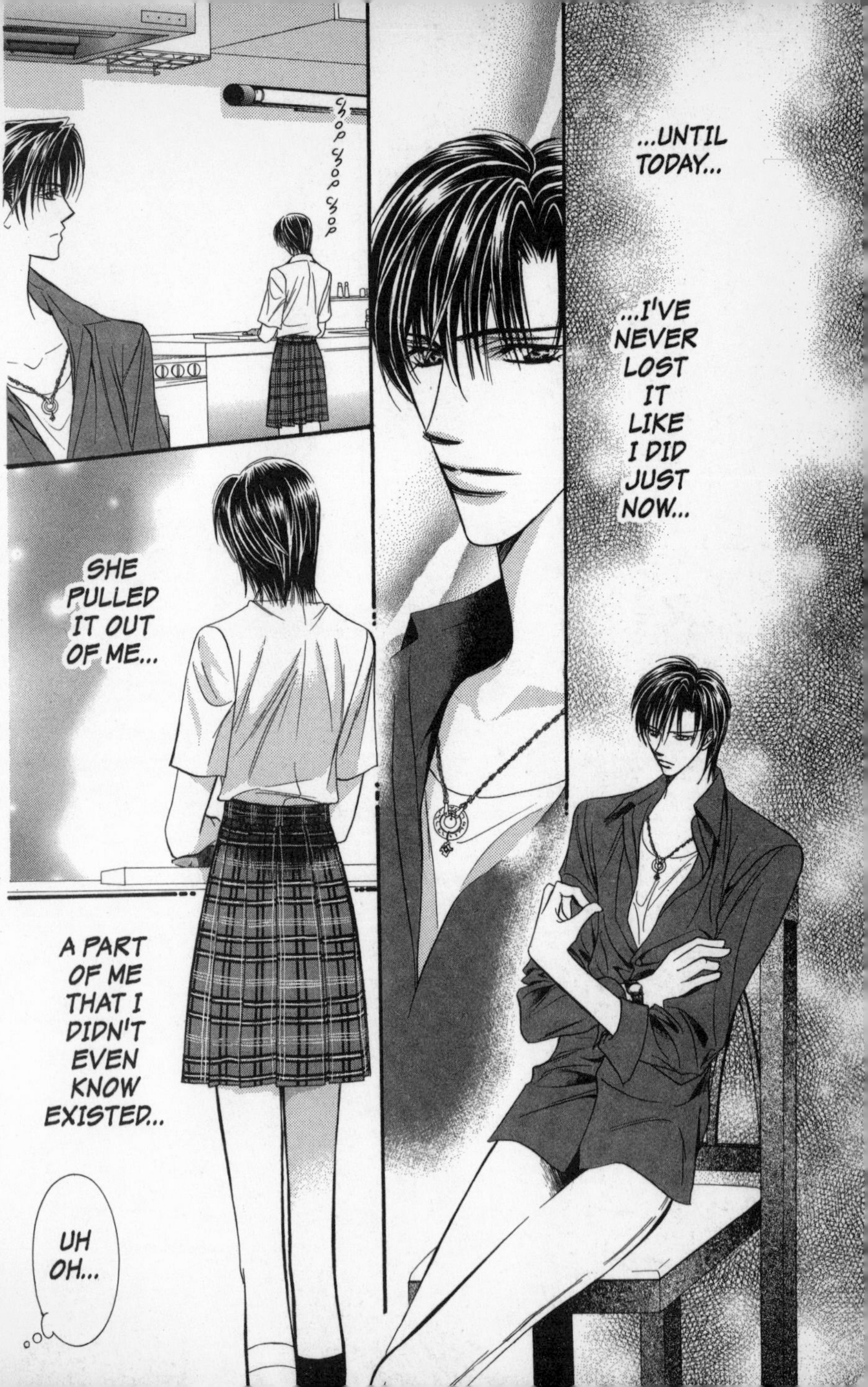
...UNTIL TODAY...
...I'VE NEVER LOST IT LIKE I DID JUST NOW...
chop chop chop
SHE PULLED IT OUT OF ME...
A PART OF ME THAT I DIDN'T EVEN KNOW EXISTED...
UH OH...

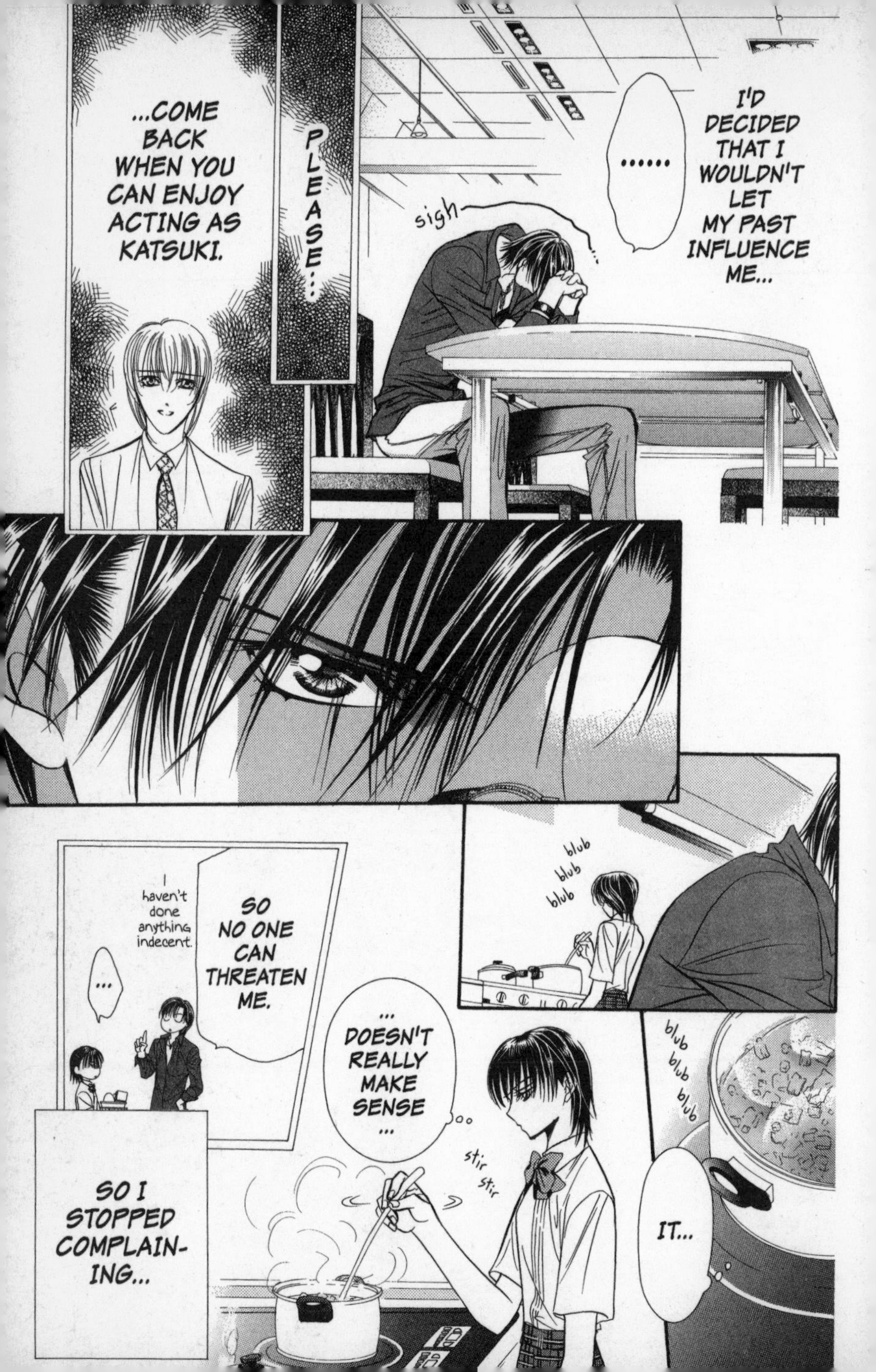
I'D DECIDED THAT I WOULDN'T LET MY PAST INFLUENCE ME...
......
sigh
PLEASE...
...COME BACK WHEN YOU CAN ENJOY ACTING AS KATSUKI.
blub blub blub
I haven't done anything indecent.
SO NO ONE CAN THREATEN ME.
...
blub blub blub
IT...
...DOESN'T REALLY MAKE SENSE...
stir stir
SO I STOPPED COMPLAIN-ING...

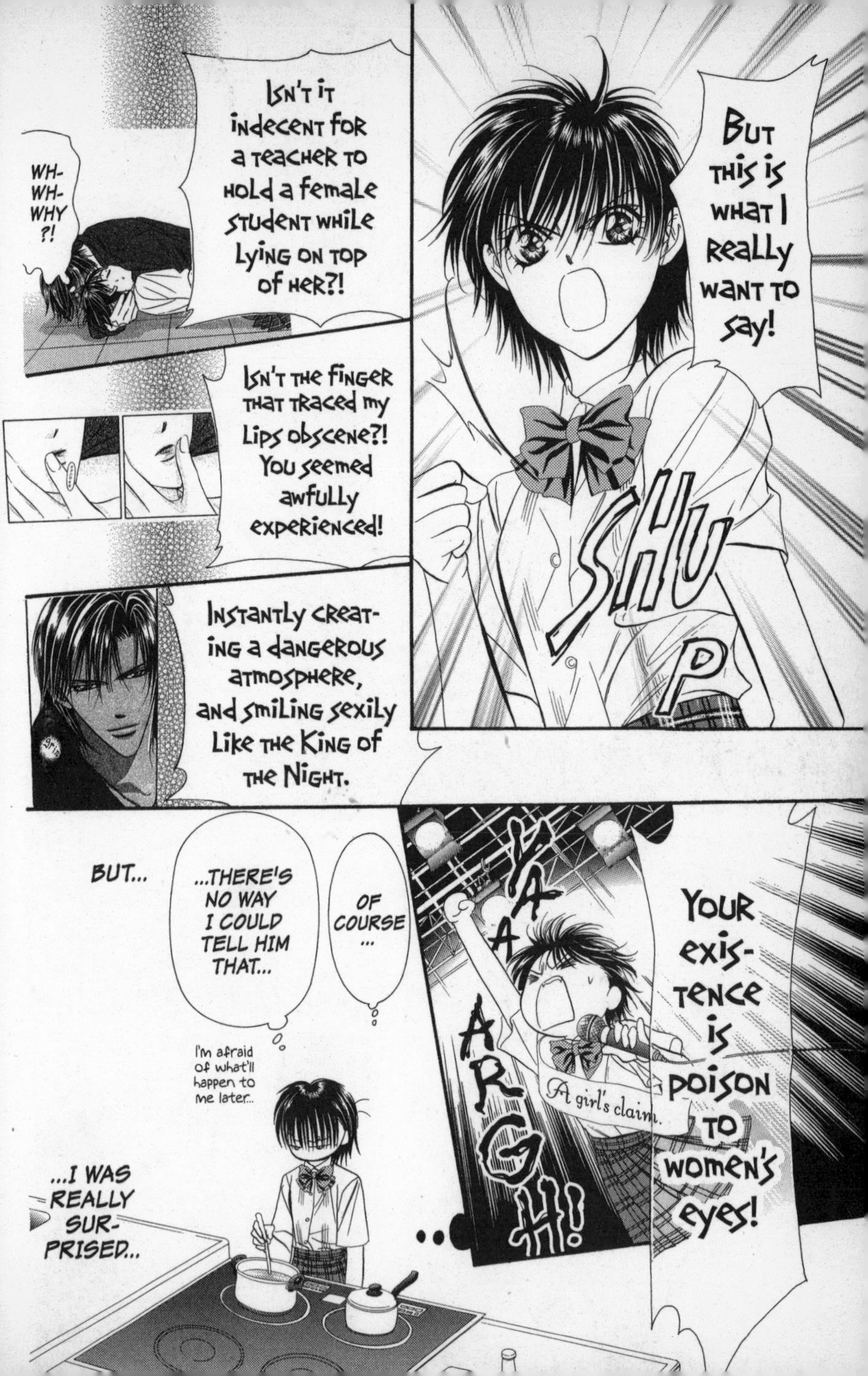
But this is what I really want to say!
SHUP
Isn't it indecent for a teacher to hold a female student while lying on top of her?!
WH-WH-WHY?!
Isn't the finger that traced my lips obscene?! You seemed awfully experienced!
Instantly creating a dangerous atmosphere, and smiling sexily like the King of the Night.
Your existence is poison to women's eyes!
YAAAARGH!
A girl's claim.
..
OF COURSE...
...THERE'S NO WAY I COULD TELL HIM THAT...
BUT...
I'm afraid of what'll happen to me later...
...I WAS REALLY SURPRISED...

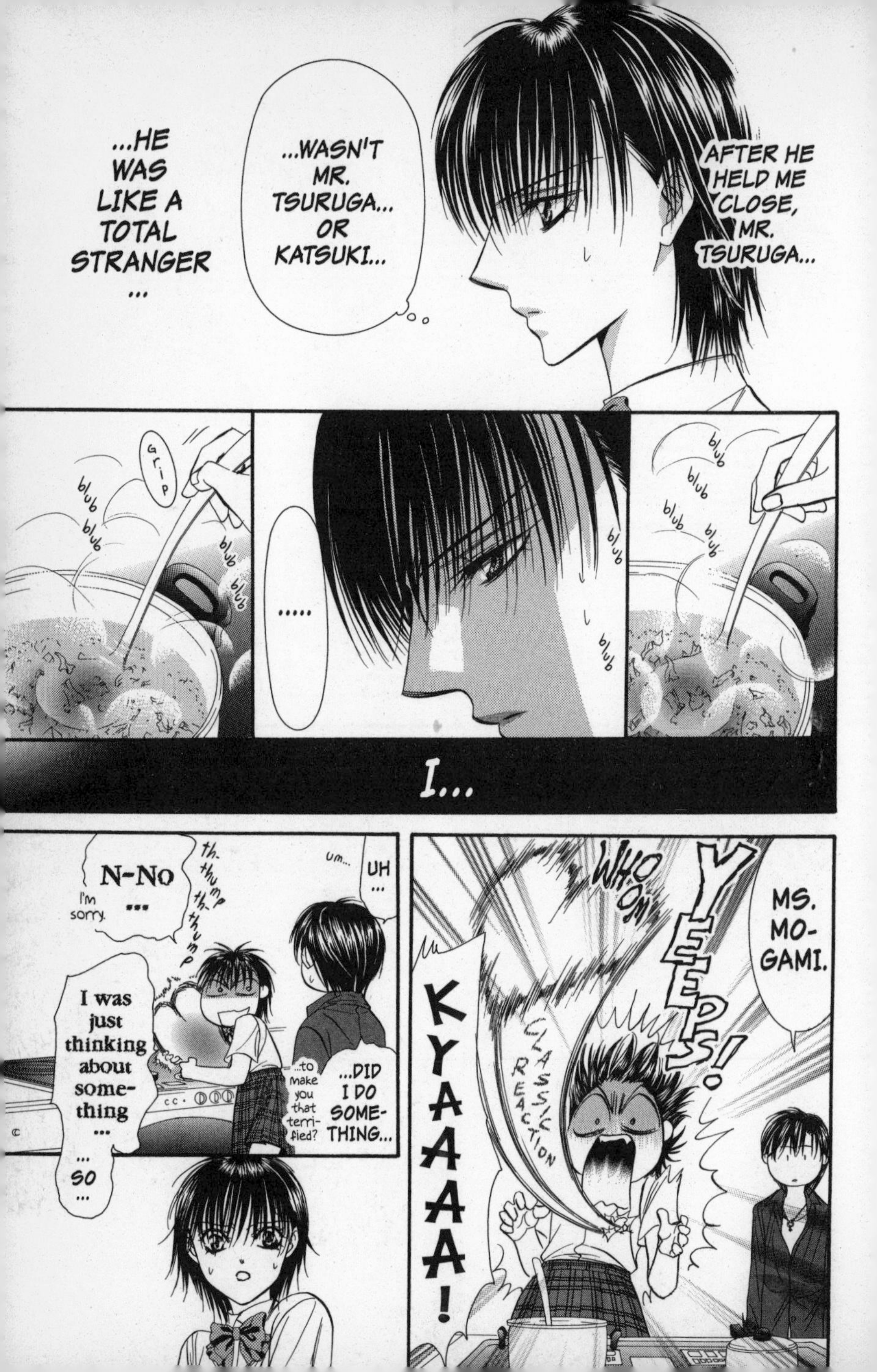
AFTER HE HELD ME CLOSE, MR. TSURUGA...
...WASN'T MR. TSURUGA... OR KATSUKI...
...HE WAS LIKE A TOTAL STRANGER ...
blub blub blub blub
......
blub blub
grip
blub blub blub blub
I...
MS. MO-GAMI.
YIEEEPS!
WHOOM
CLASSIC REACTION
KYAAAA!
UH ...
um...
th-thump th-thump
N-No ...
I'm sorry.
...DID I DO SOME-THING...
...to make you that terri-fied?
I was just thinking about some-thing ...
... SO ...

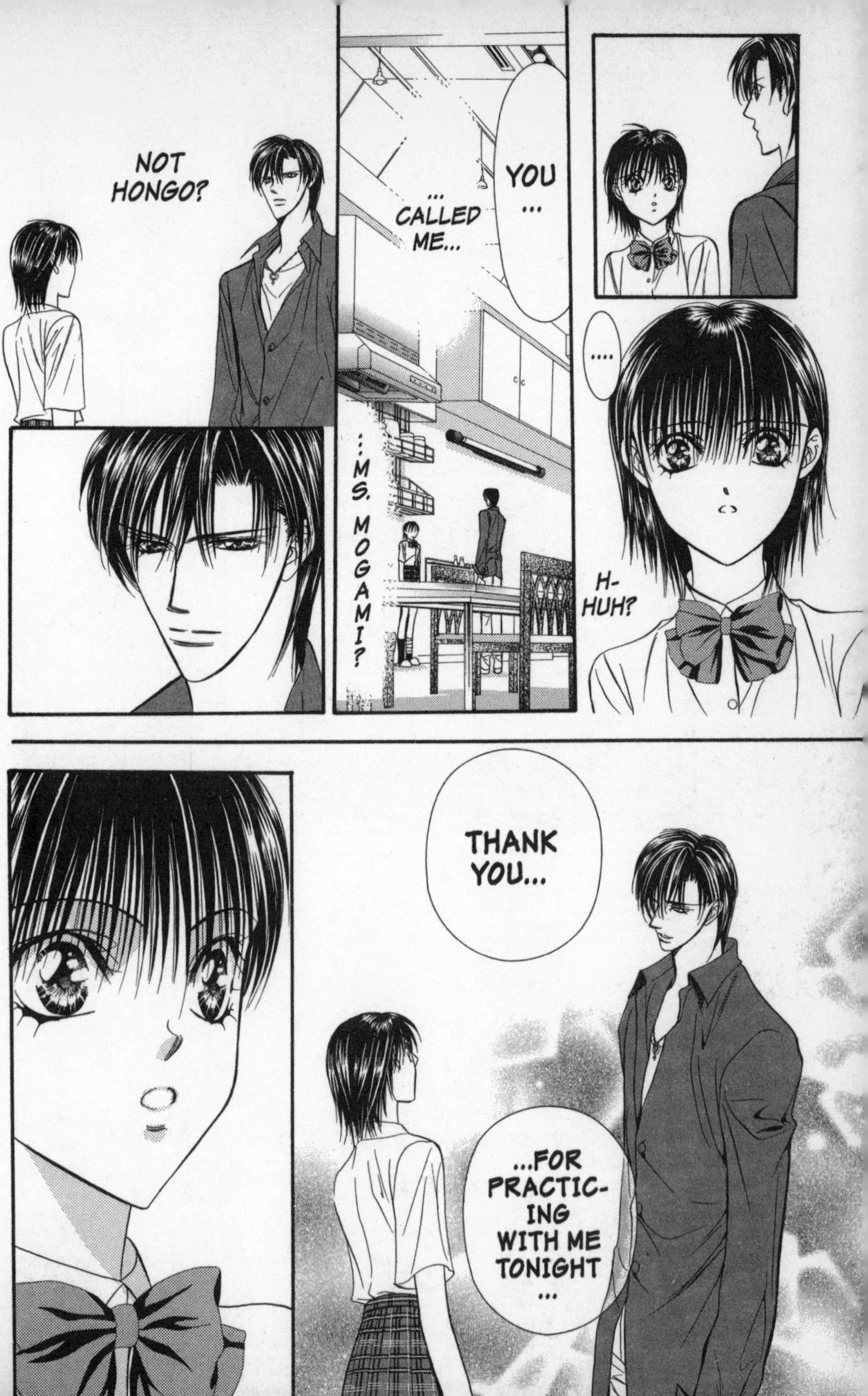
....
H-HUH?
YOU ...
... CALLED ME...
...MS. MOGAMI?
NOT HONGO?
THANK YOU...
...FOR PRACTIC-ING WITH ME TONIGHT ...

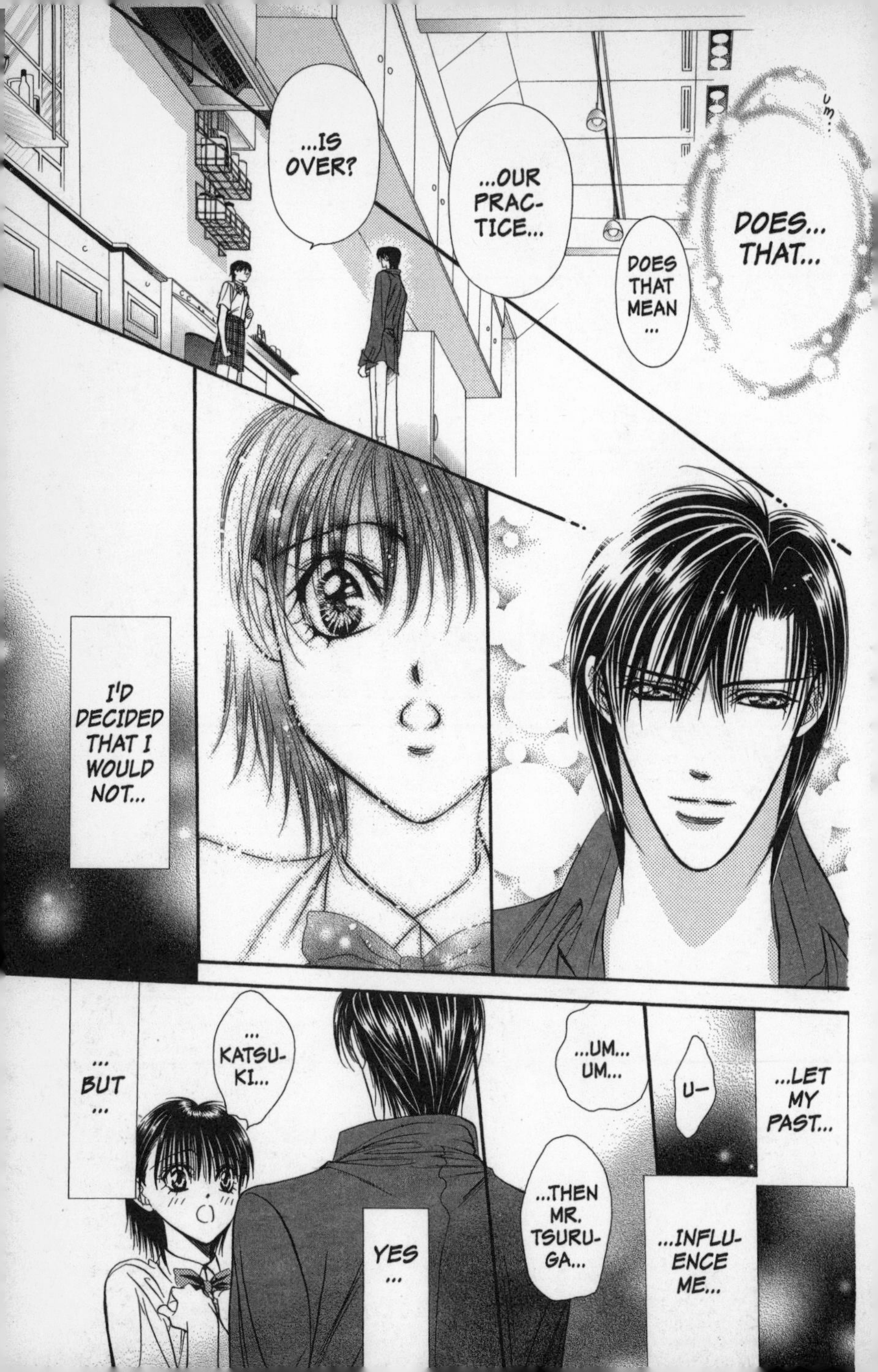
UM...
DOES... THAT...
DOES THAT MEAN ...
...OUR PRAC- TICE...
...IS OVER?
I'D DECIDED THAT I WOULD NOT...
...LET MY PAST...
...INFLU- ENCE ME...
U–
...UM... UM...
...THEN MR. TSURU- GA...
YES ...
... KATSU- KI...
... BUT ...

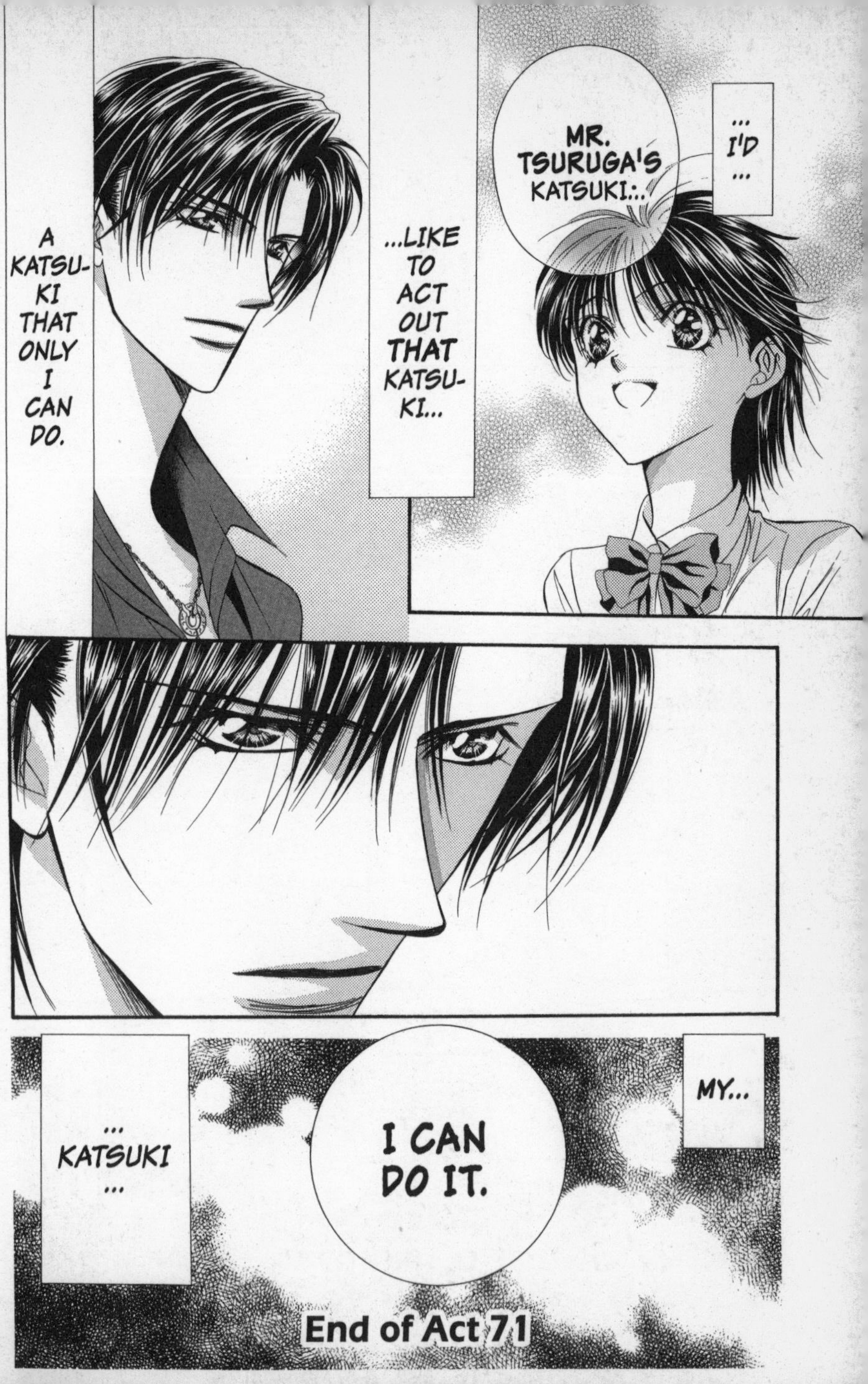
... I'D ...
MR. TSURUGA'S KATSUKI...
...LIKE TO ACT OUT THAT KATSU-KI...
A KATSU-KI THAT ONLY I CAN DO.
MY...
I CAN DO IT.
... KATSUKI ...
End of Act 71

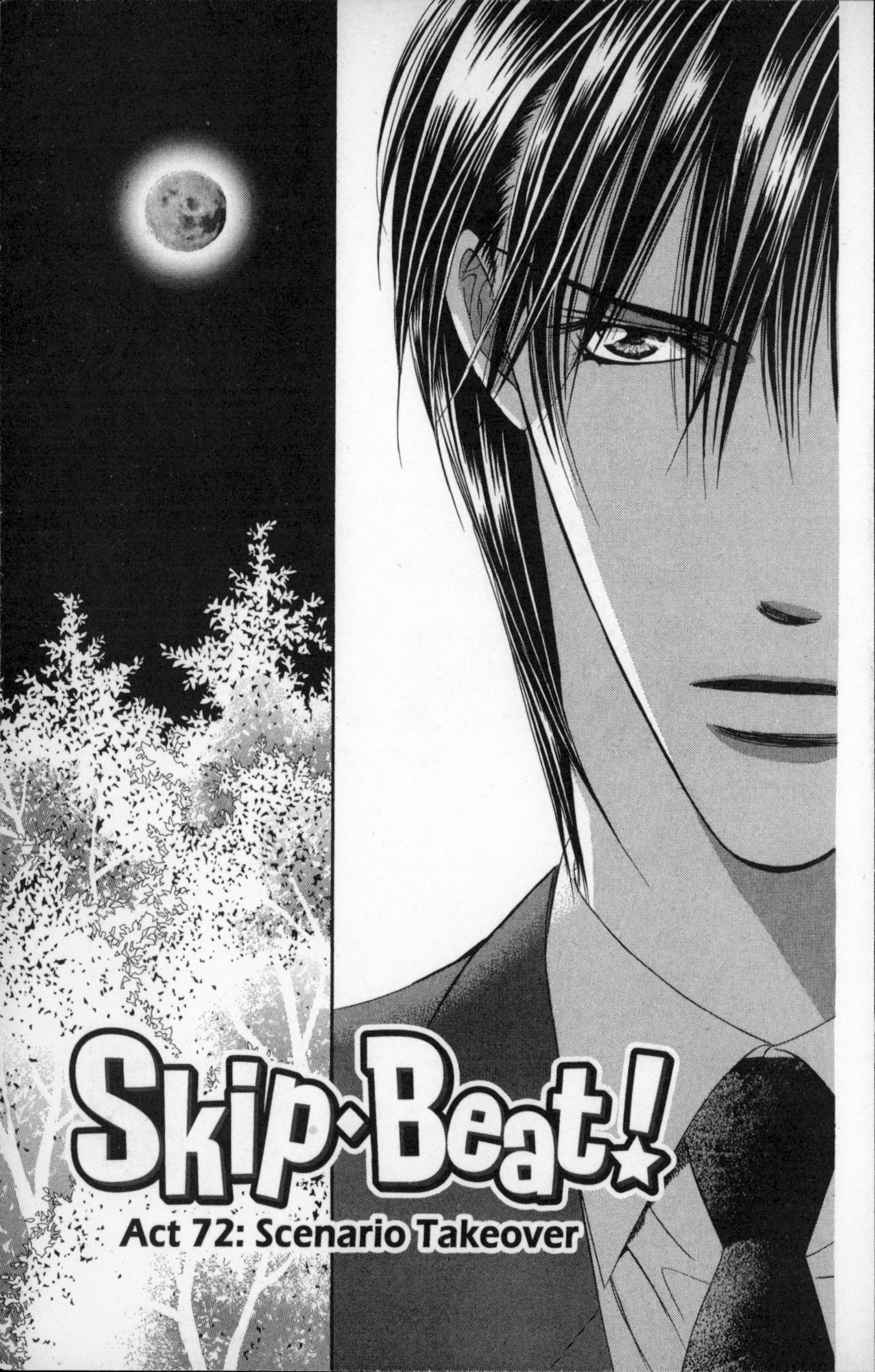
Skip·Beat!
Act 72: Scenario Takeover

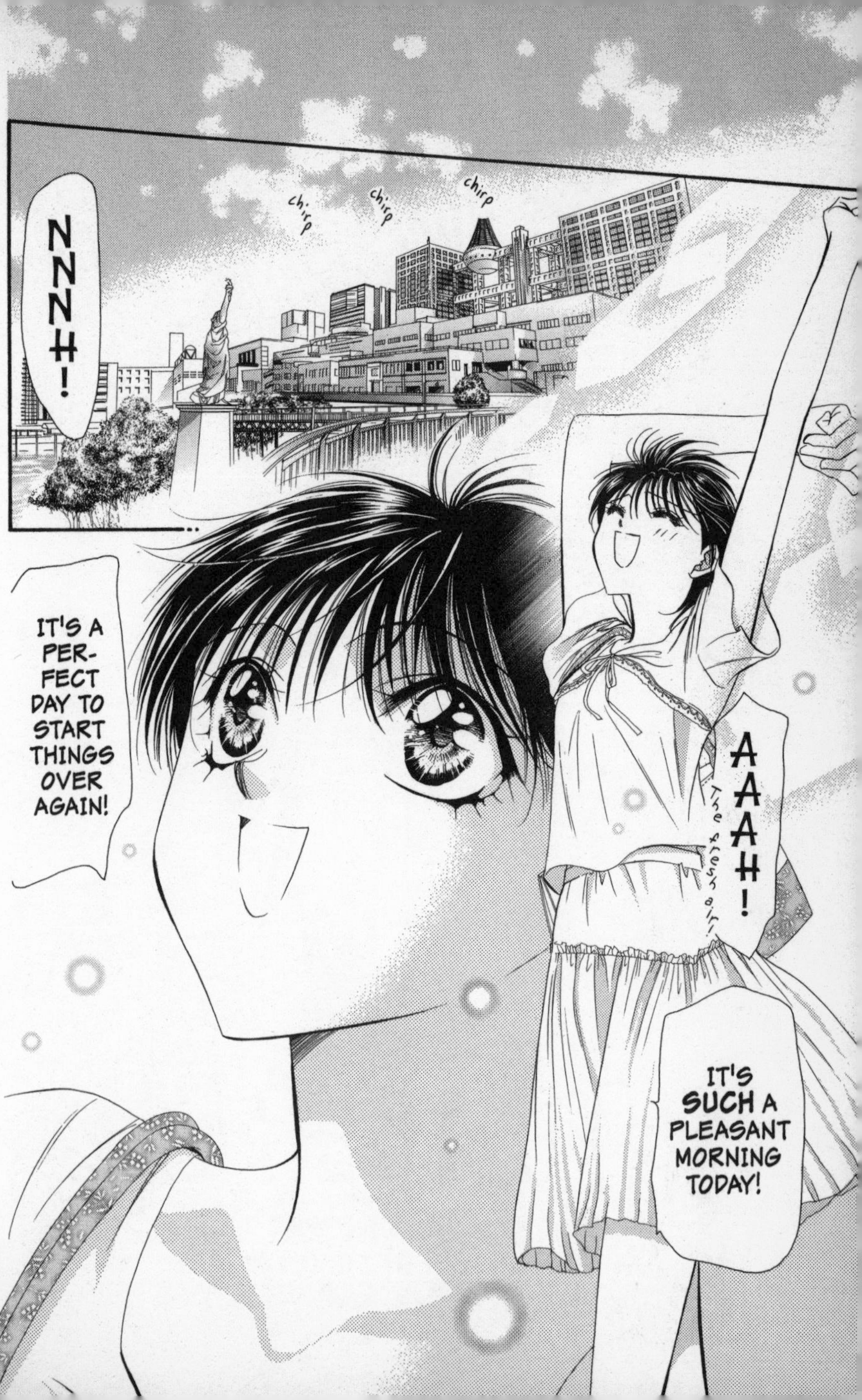
chirp
chirp
chirp
NNNH!
AAAH!
The fresh air!
IT'S SUCH A PLEASANT MORNING TODAY!
IT'S A PER-FECT DAY TO START THINGS OVER AGAIN!

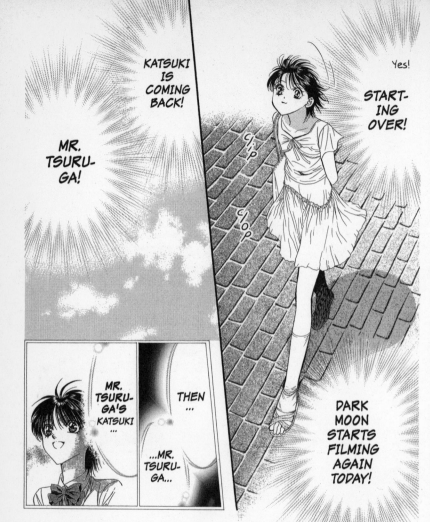

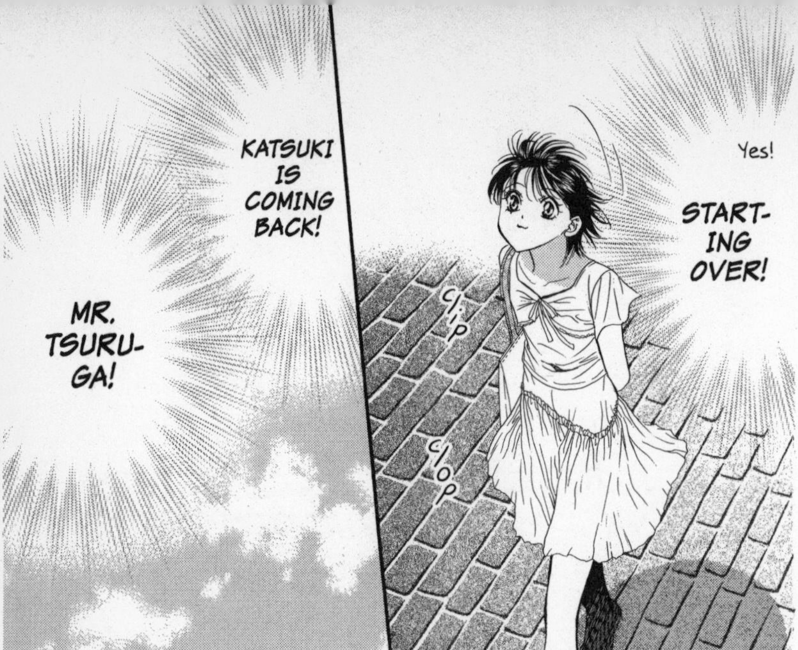
Yes!
START-ING OVER!
clip
clop
DARK MOON STARTS FILMING AGAIN TODAY!
KATSUKI IS COMING BACK!
MR. TSURU-GA!
THEN ...
...MR. TSURU-GA...
MR. TSURU-GA'S KATSUKI ...

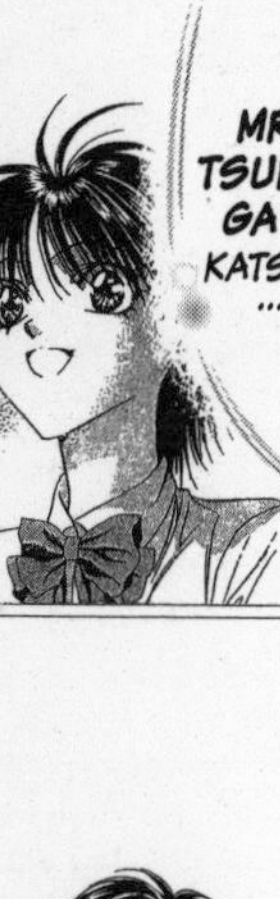

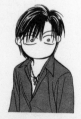

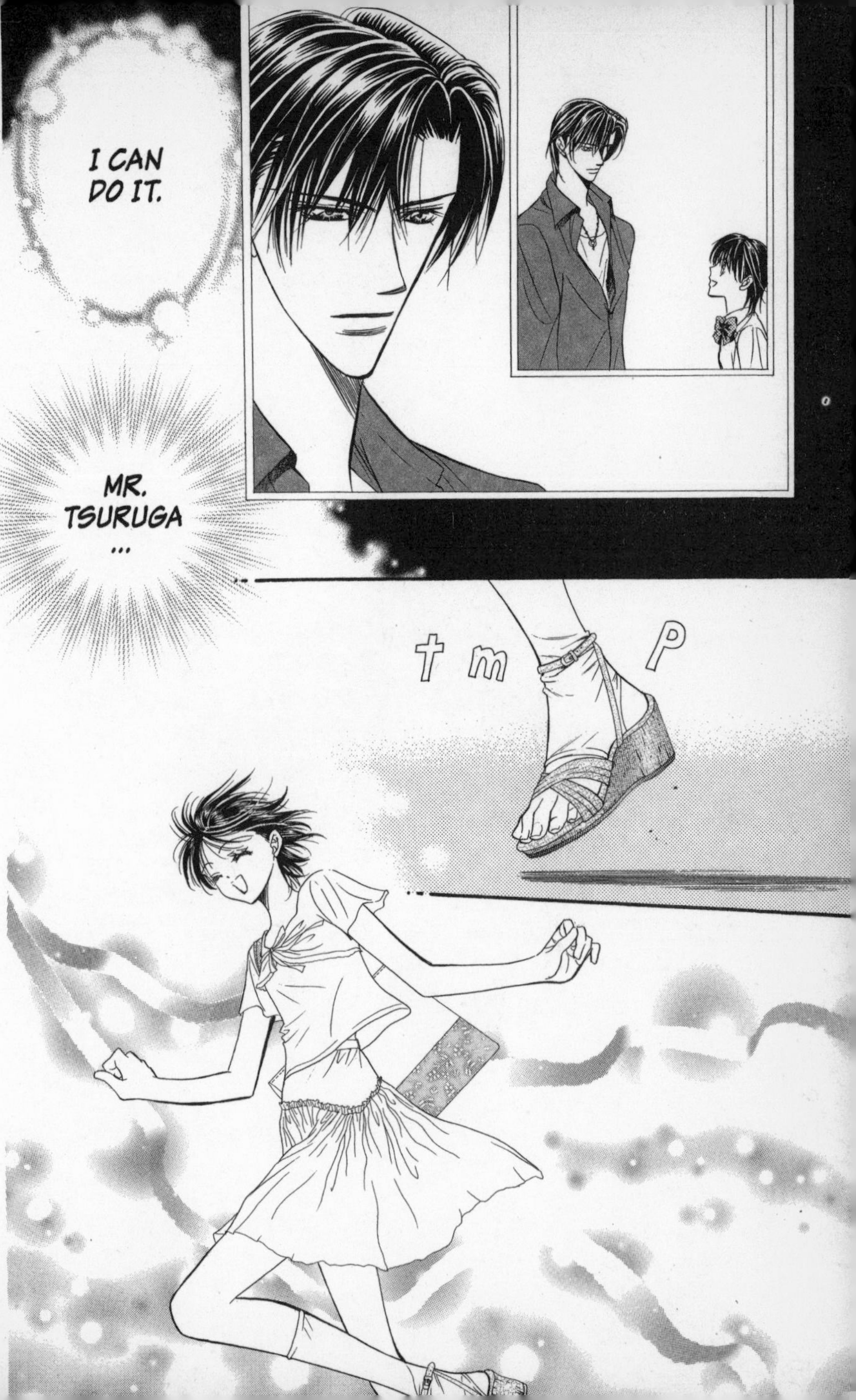
I CAN DO IT.
MR. TSURUGA ...
tmp

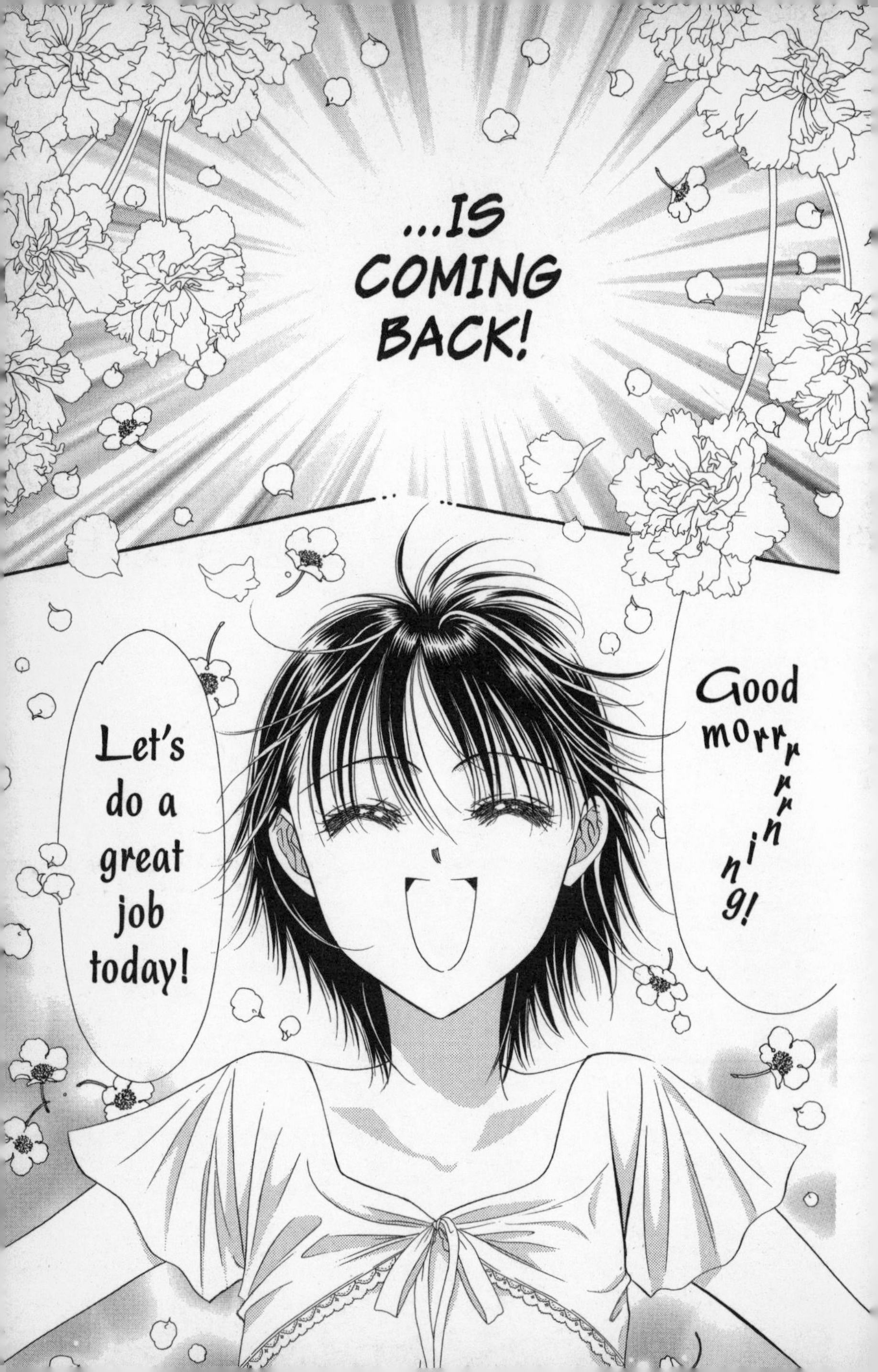
...IS COMING BACK!
Good morrrrrning!
Let's do a great job today!

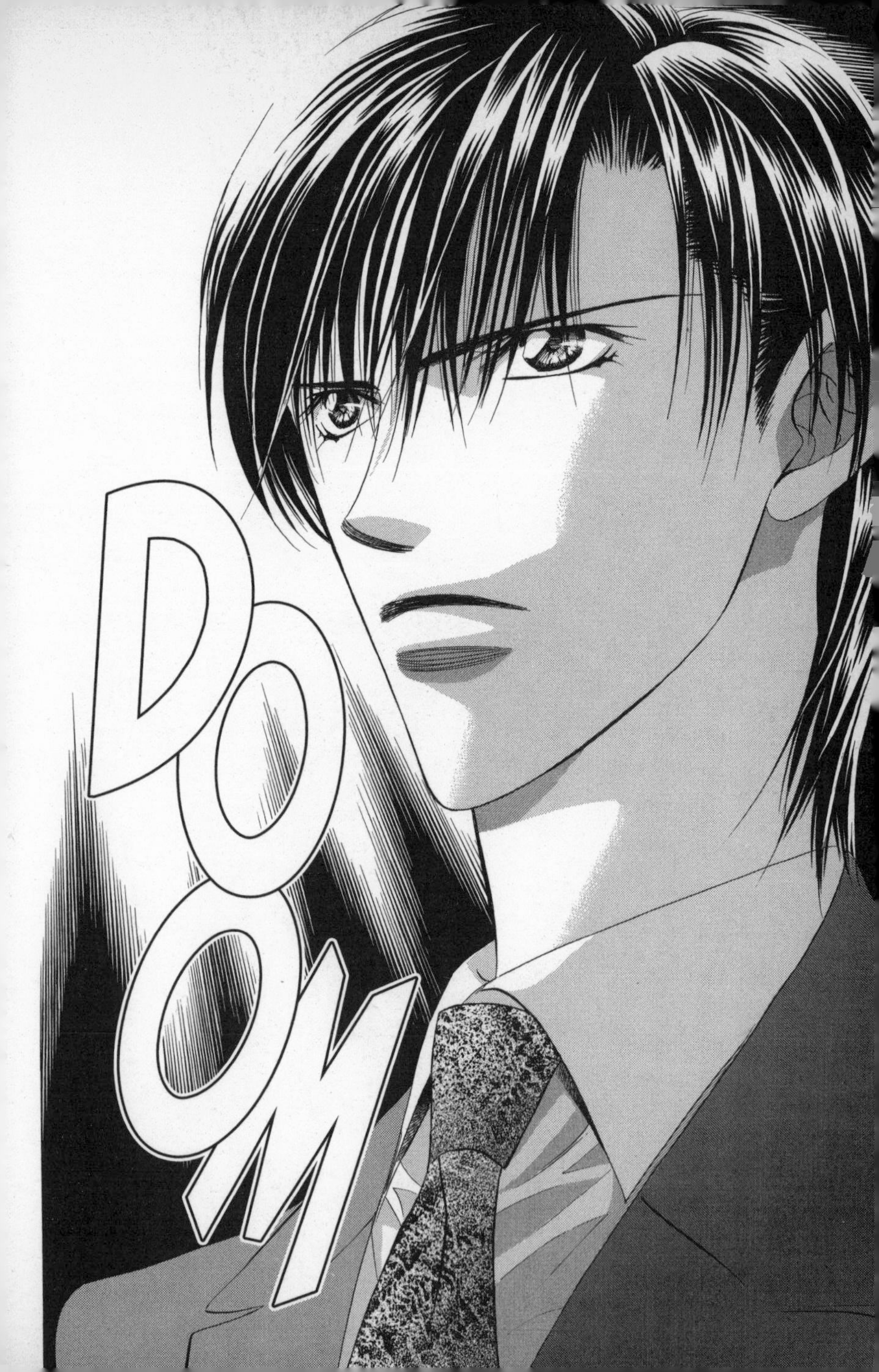
DOOM

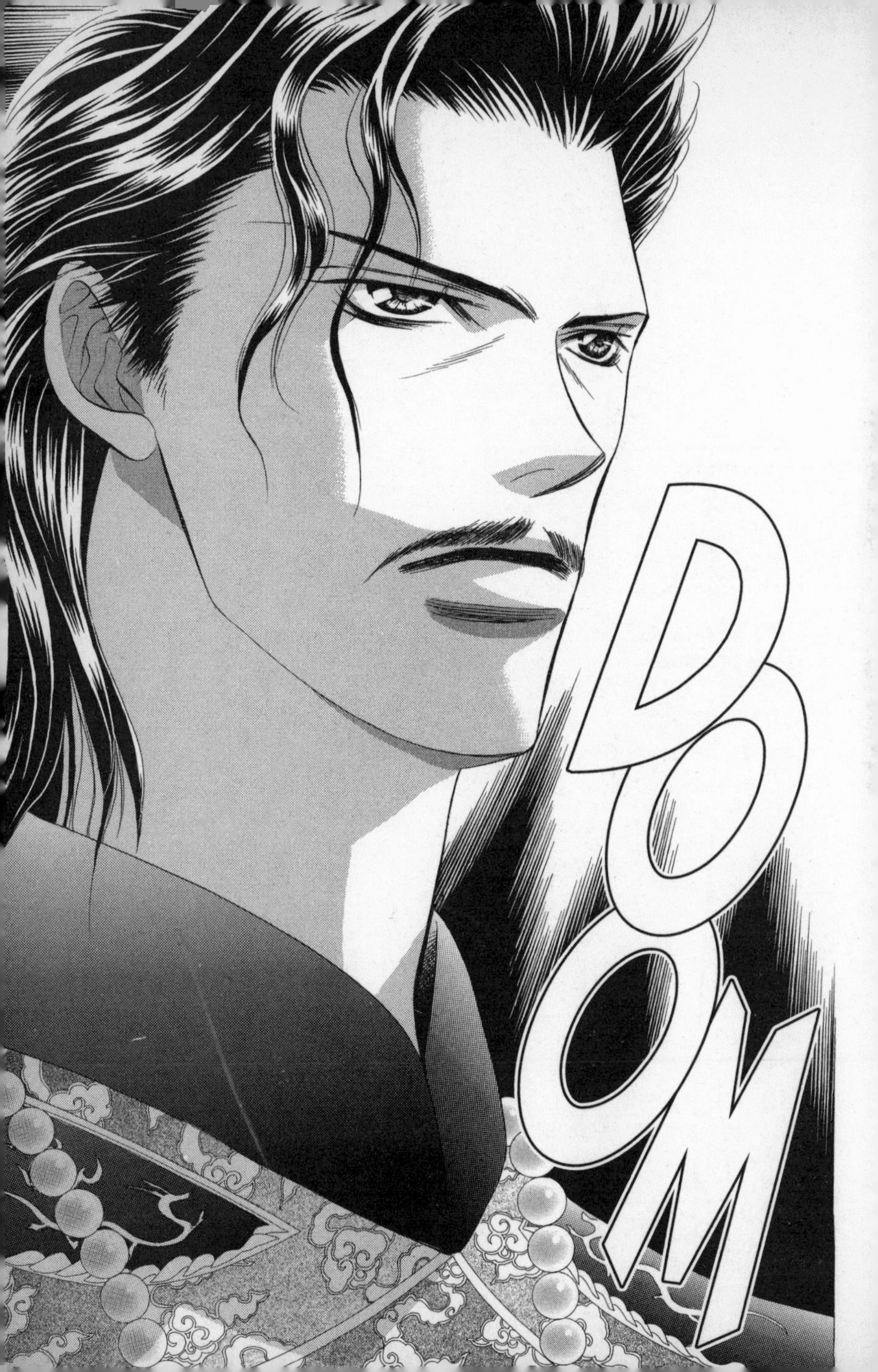
DOOM

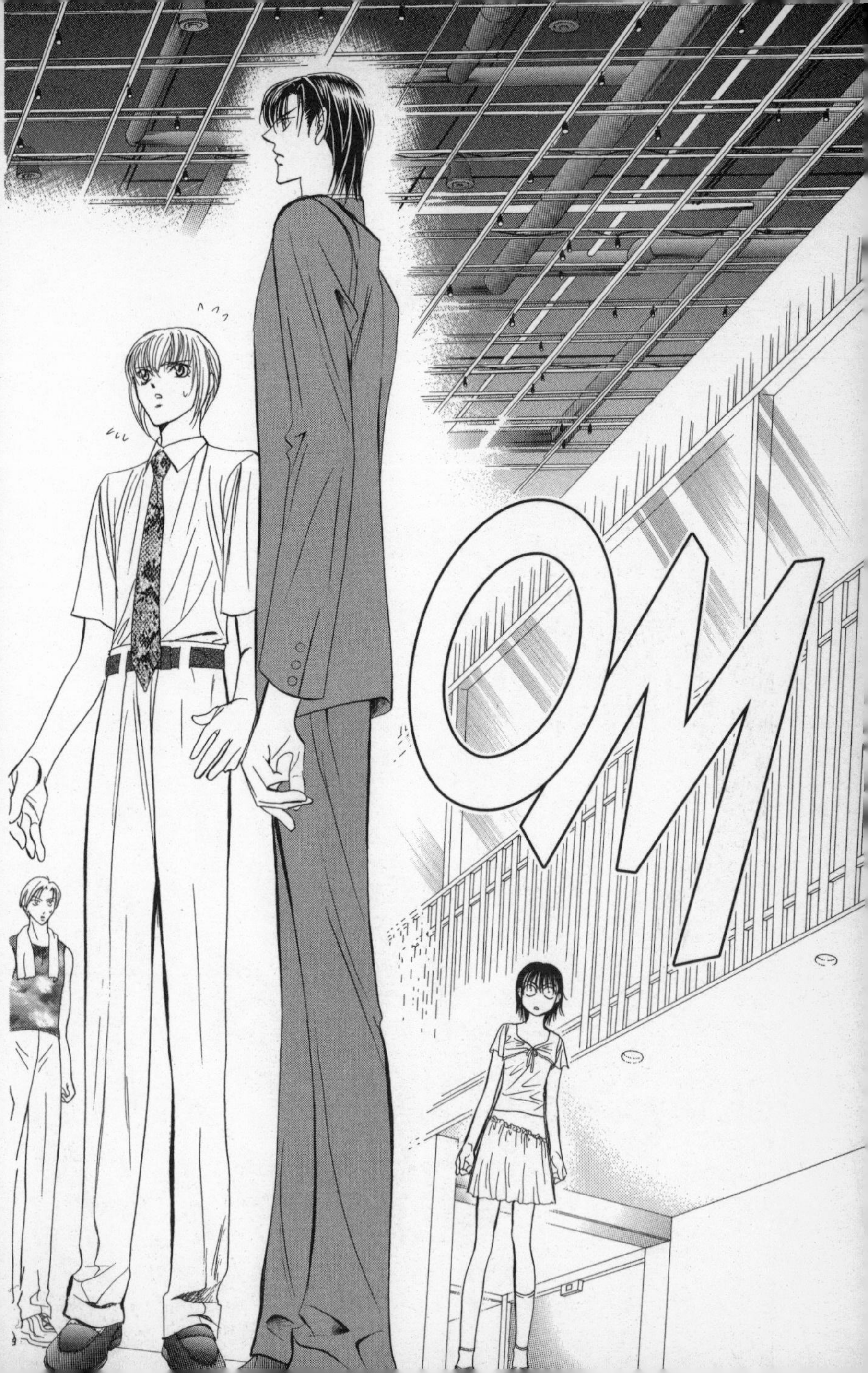

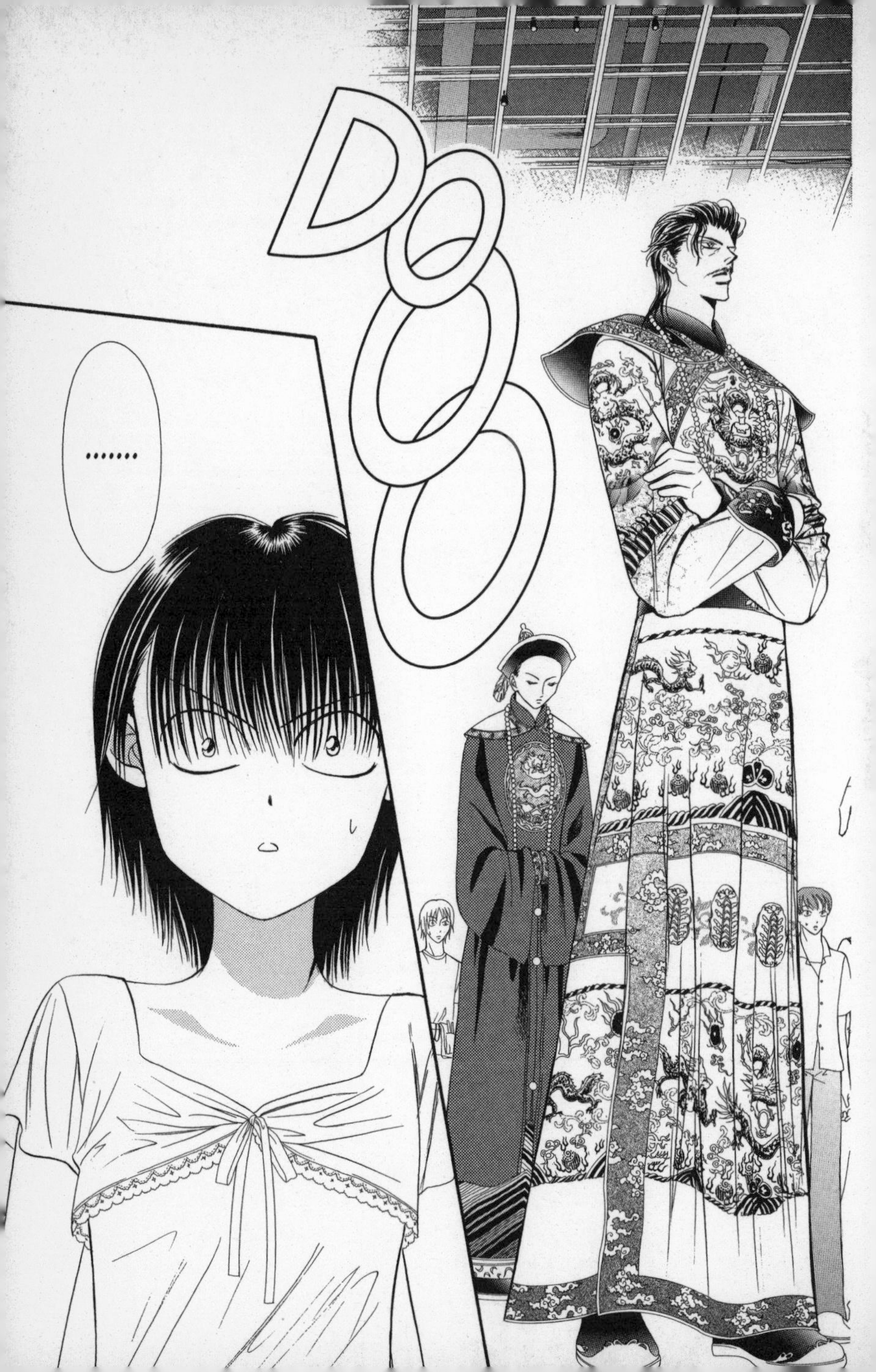
DOOOO
....

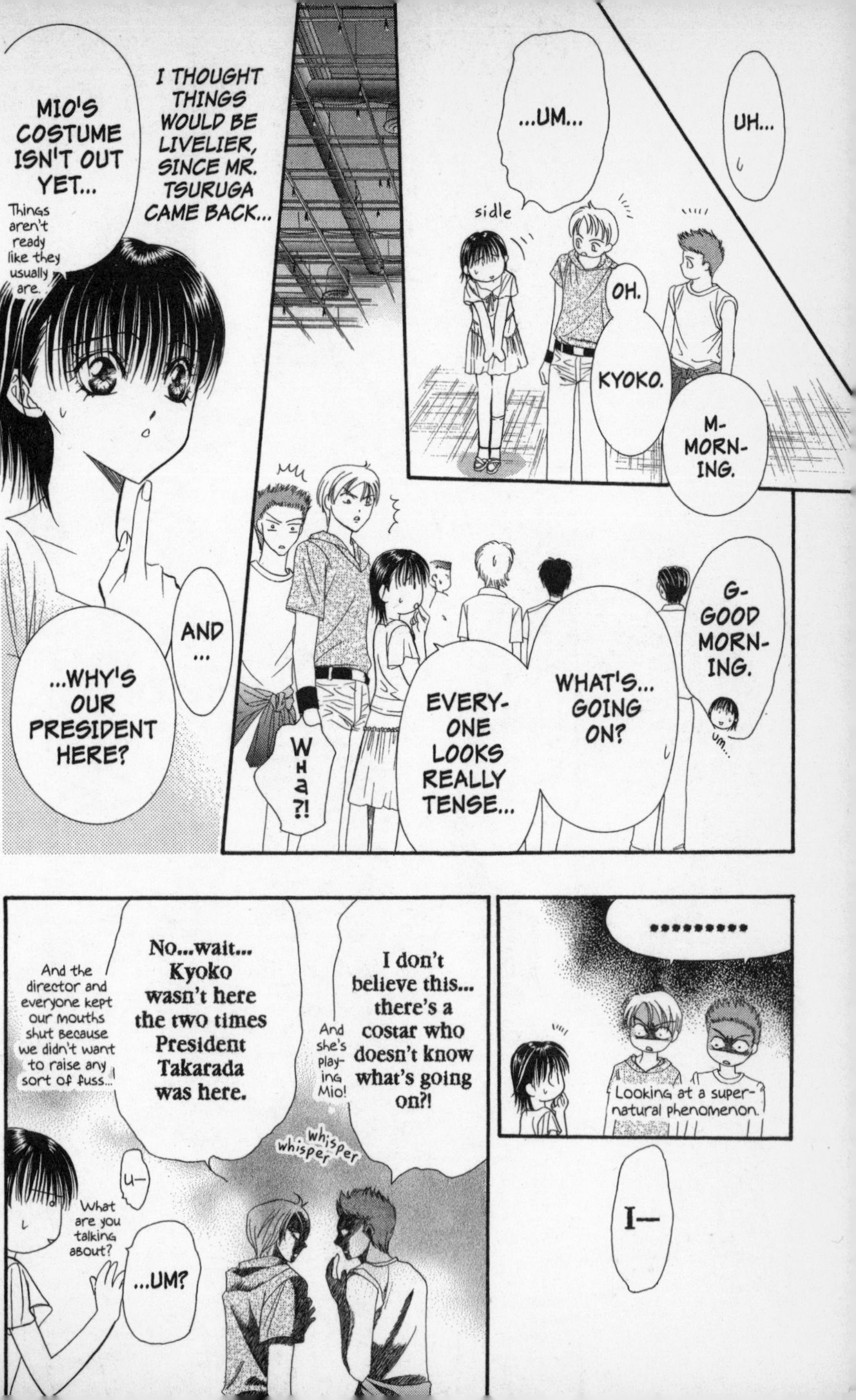
UH...
...UM...
sidle
OH.
KYOKO.
M-MORNING.
G-GOOD MORNING.
um...
WHAT'S... GOING ON?
EVERYONE LOOKS REALLY TENSE...
Wha?!
I THOUGHT THINGS WOULD BE LIVELIER, SINCE MR. TSURUGA CAME BACK...
MIO'S COSTUME ISN'T OUT YET...
Things aren't ready like they usually are.
AND...
...WHY'S OUR PRESIDENT HERE?
....
Looking at a supernatural phenomenon.
I—
I don't believe this... there's a costar who doesn't know what's going on?!
And she's playing Mio!
No...wait... Kyoko wasn't here the two times President Takarada was here.
And the director and everyone kept our mouths shut because we didn't want to raise any sort of fuss...
whisper whisper
U—
What are you talking about?
...UM?

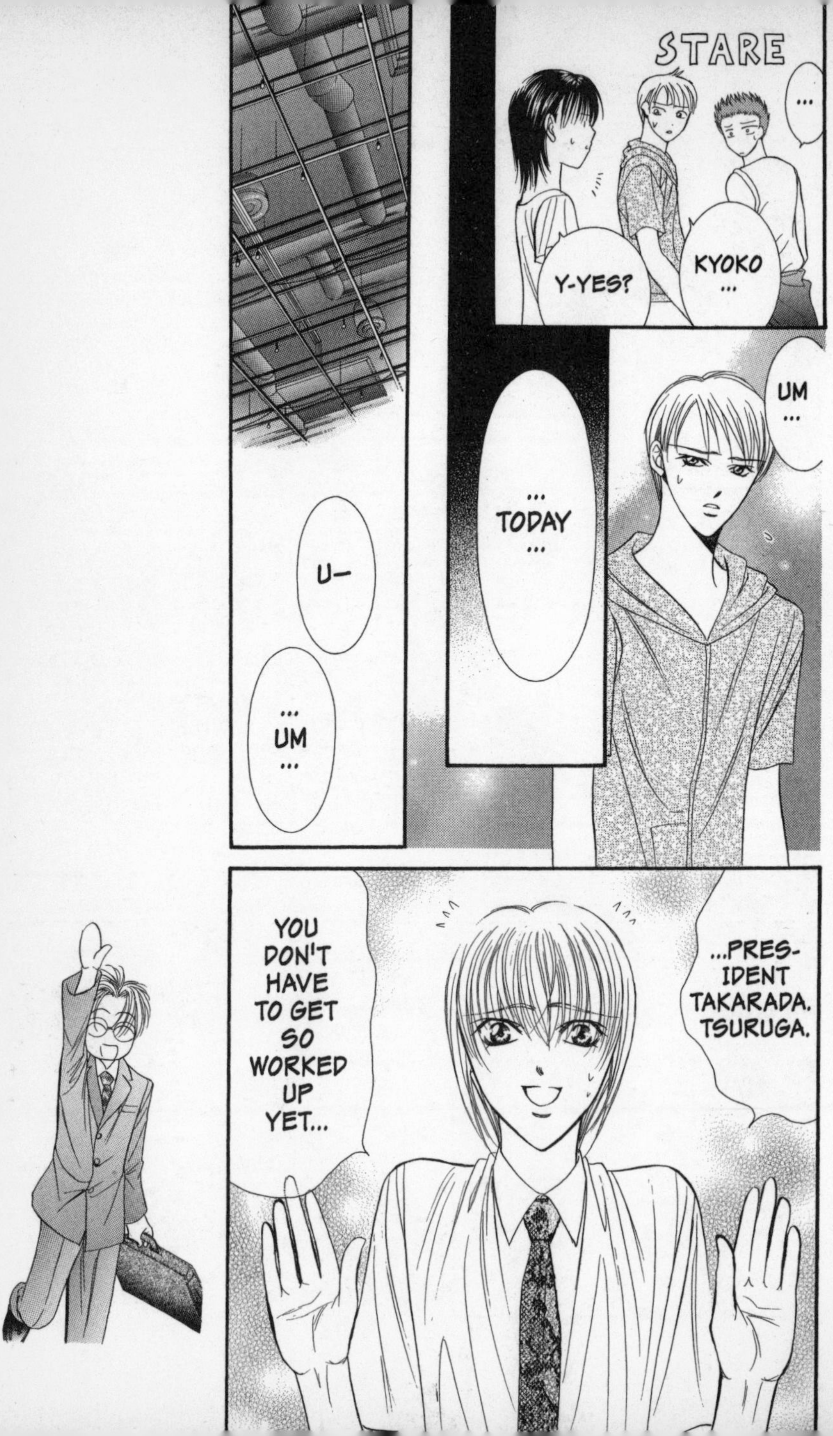
STARE
...
KYOKO ...
Y-YES?
UM ...
... TODAY ...
U—
... UM ...
...PRES- IDENT TAKARADA. TSURUGA.
YOU DON'T HAVE TO GET SO WORKED UP YET...

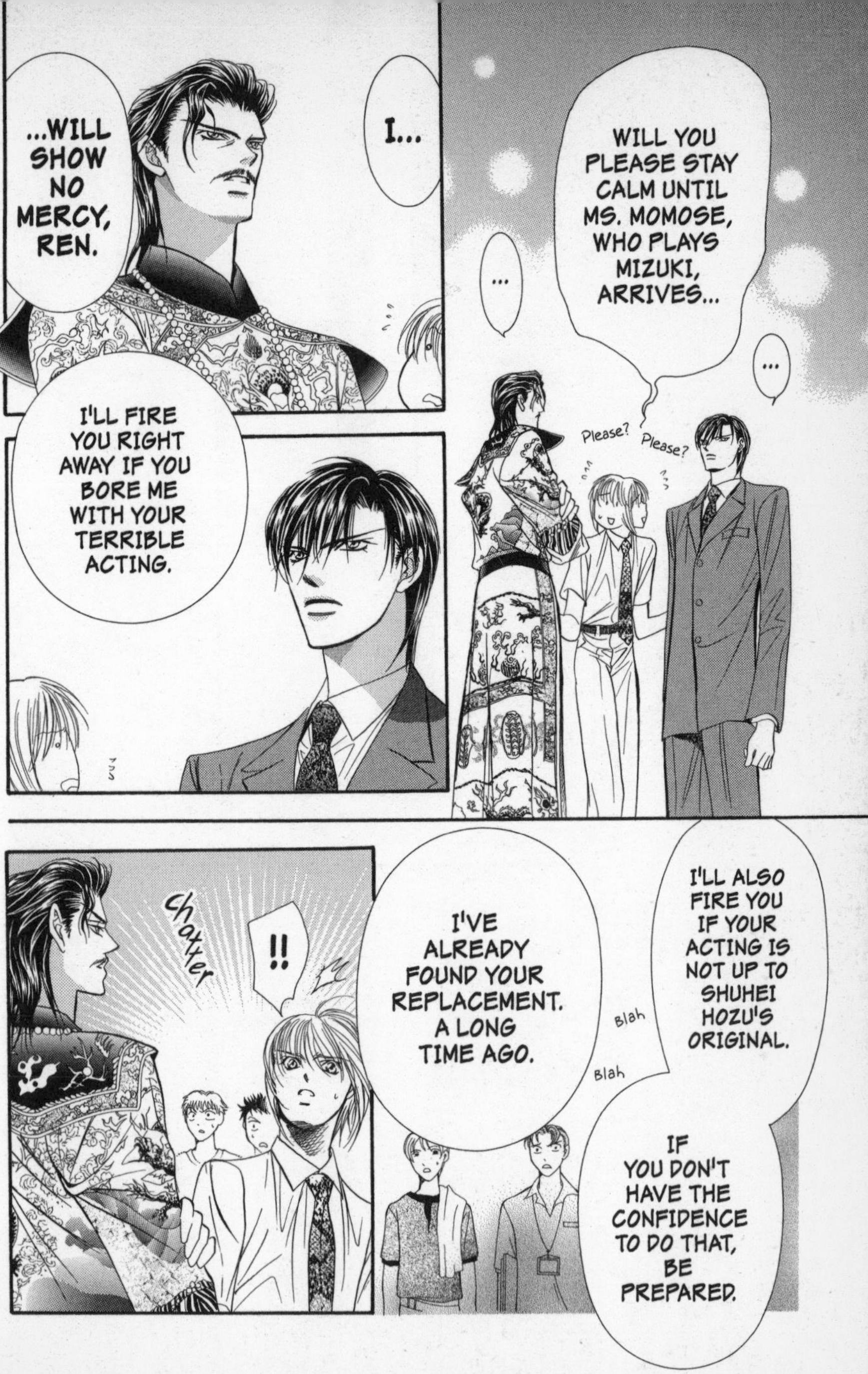
WILL YOU PLEASE STAY CALM UNTIL MS. MOMOSE, WHO PLAYS MIZUKI, ARRIVES...
...
...
Please?
Please?
I...
...WILL SHOW NO MERCY, REN.
I'LL FIRE YOU RIGHT AWAY IF YOU BORE ME WITH YOUR TERRIBLE ACTING.
I'LL ALSO FIRE YOU IF YOUR ACTING IS NOT UP TO SHUHEI HOZU'S ORIGINAL.
IF YOU DON'T HAVE THE CONFIDENCE TO DO THAT, BE PREPARED.
Blah
Blah
I'VE ALREADY FOUND YOUR REPLACEMENT. A LONG TIME AGO.
!!
chatter

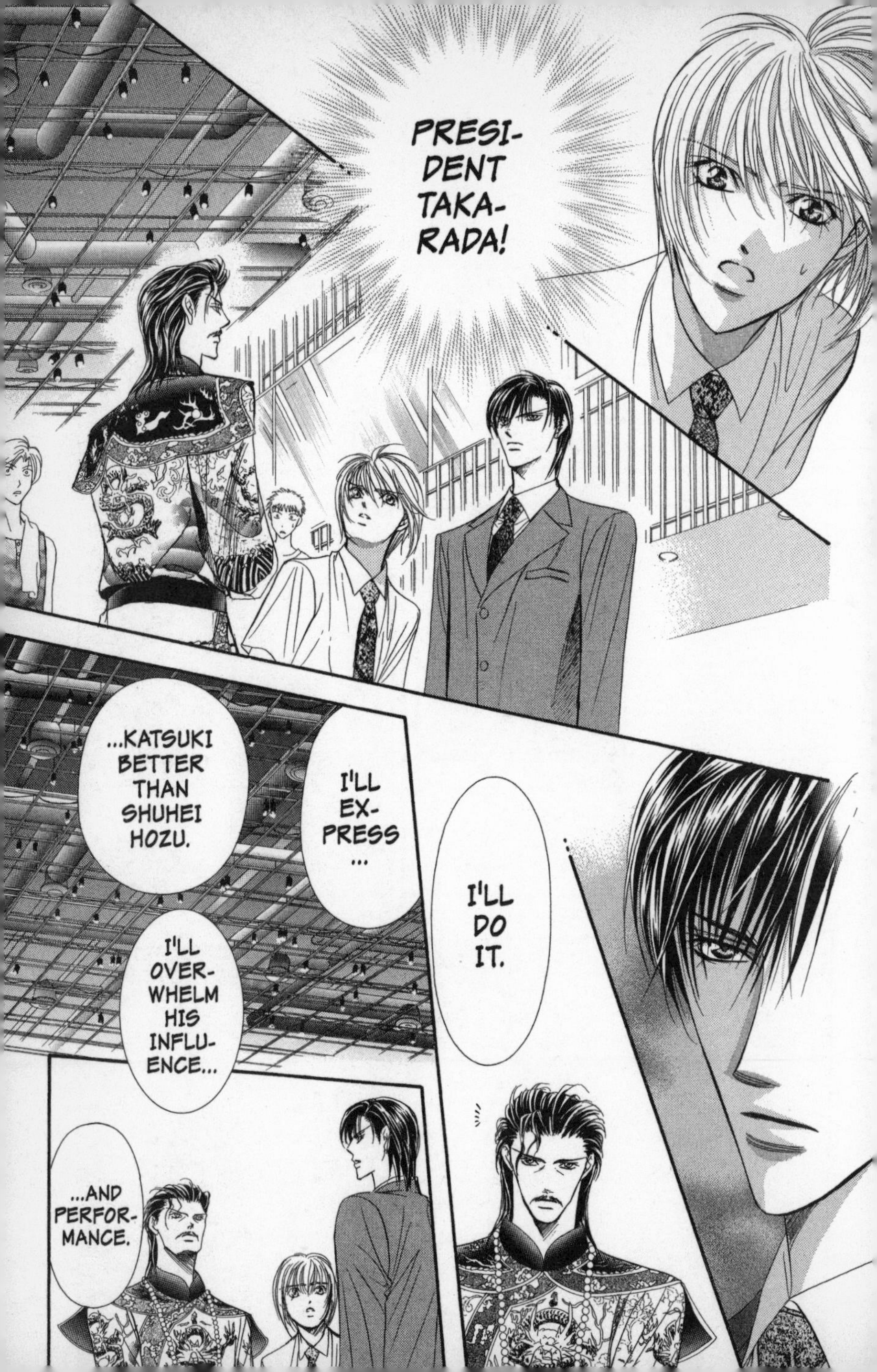
PRESI-DENT TAKA-RADA!
I'LL DO IT.
I'LL EX-PRESS...
...KATSUKI BETTER THAN SHUHEI HOZU.
I'LL OVER-WHELM HIS INFLU-ENCE...
...AND PERFOR-MANCE.

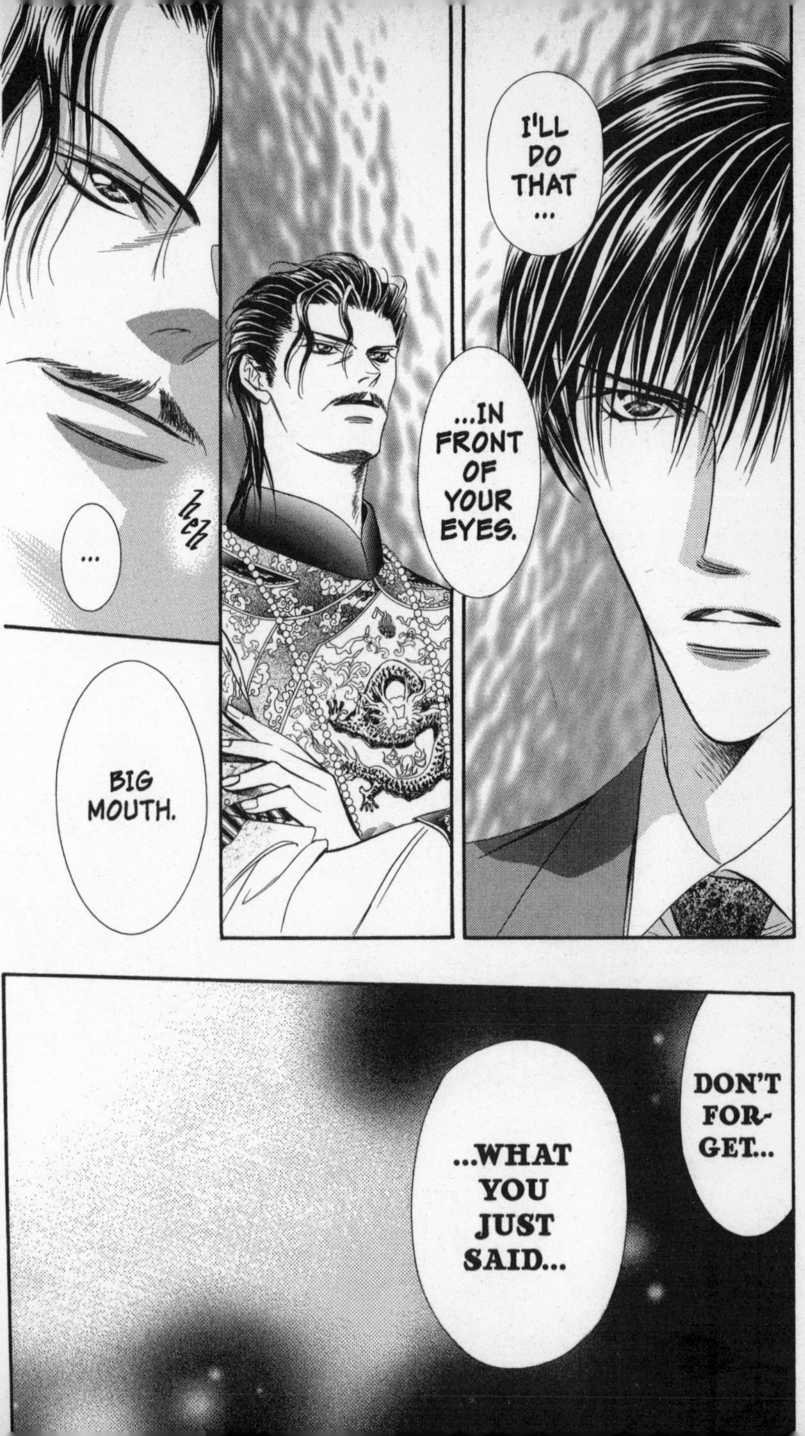
I'LL DO THAT ...
...IN FRONT OF YOUR EYES.
...
BIG MOUTH.
DON'T FOR-GET...
...WHAT YOU JUST SAID...

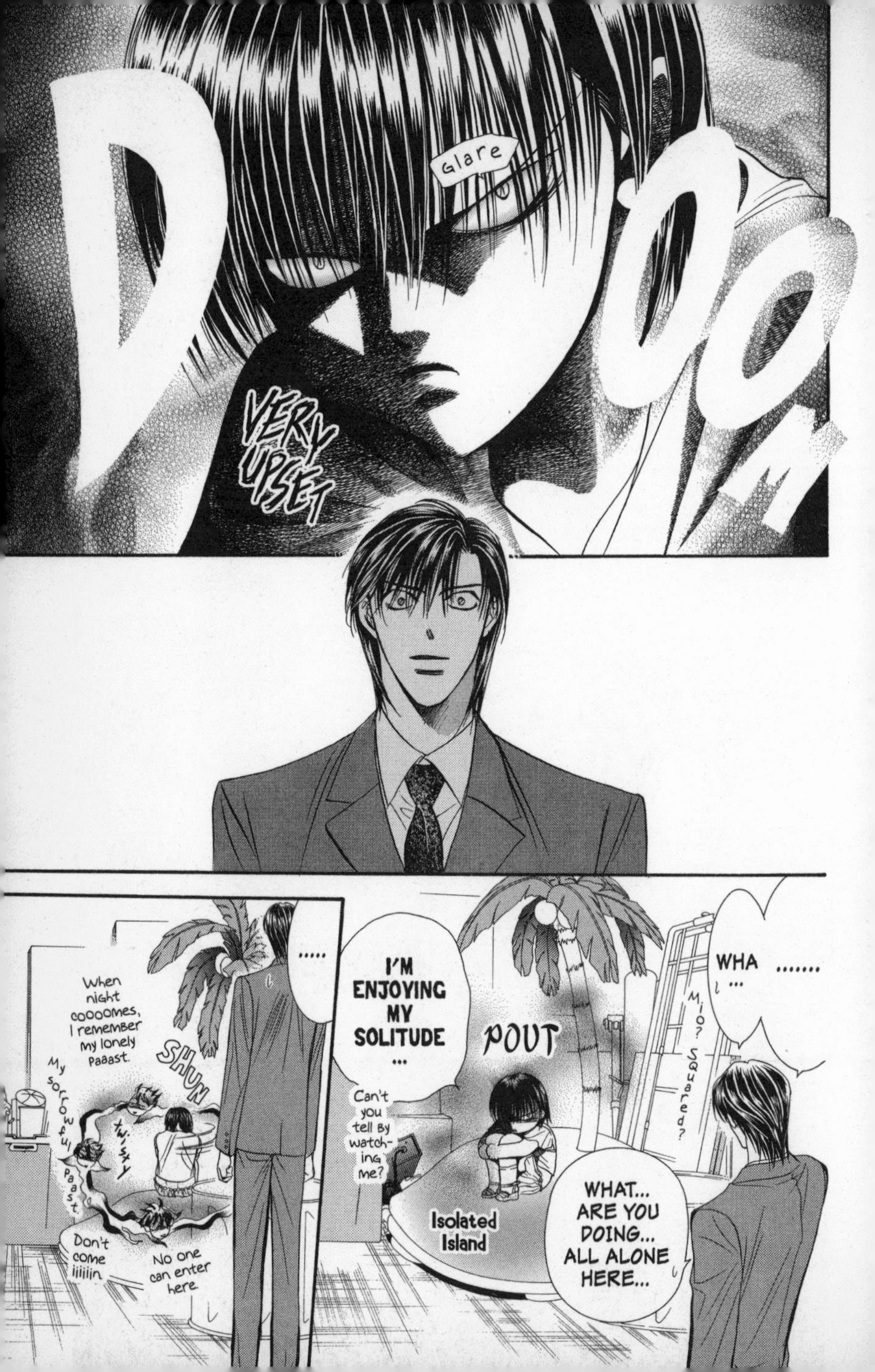

Glare
DOOM
VERY UPSET
WHA ...
....
Mio? Squared?
WHAT... ARE YOU DOING... ALL ALONE HERE...
POUT
I'M ENJOYING MY SOLITUDE ...
Can't you tell by watching me?
Isolated Island
.....
When night cooooomes, I remember my lonely paaast.
SHUN
My sorrowful paaast.
twisty
Don't come iiiiiin.
No one can enter here.

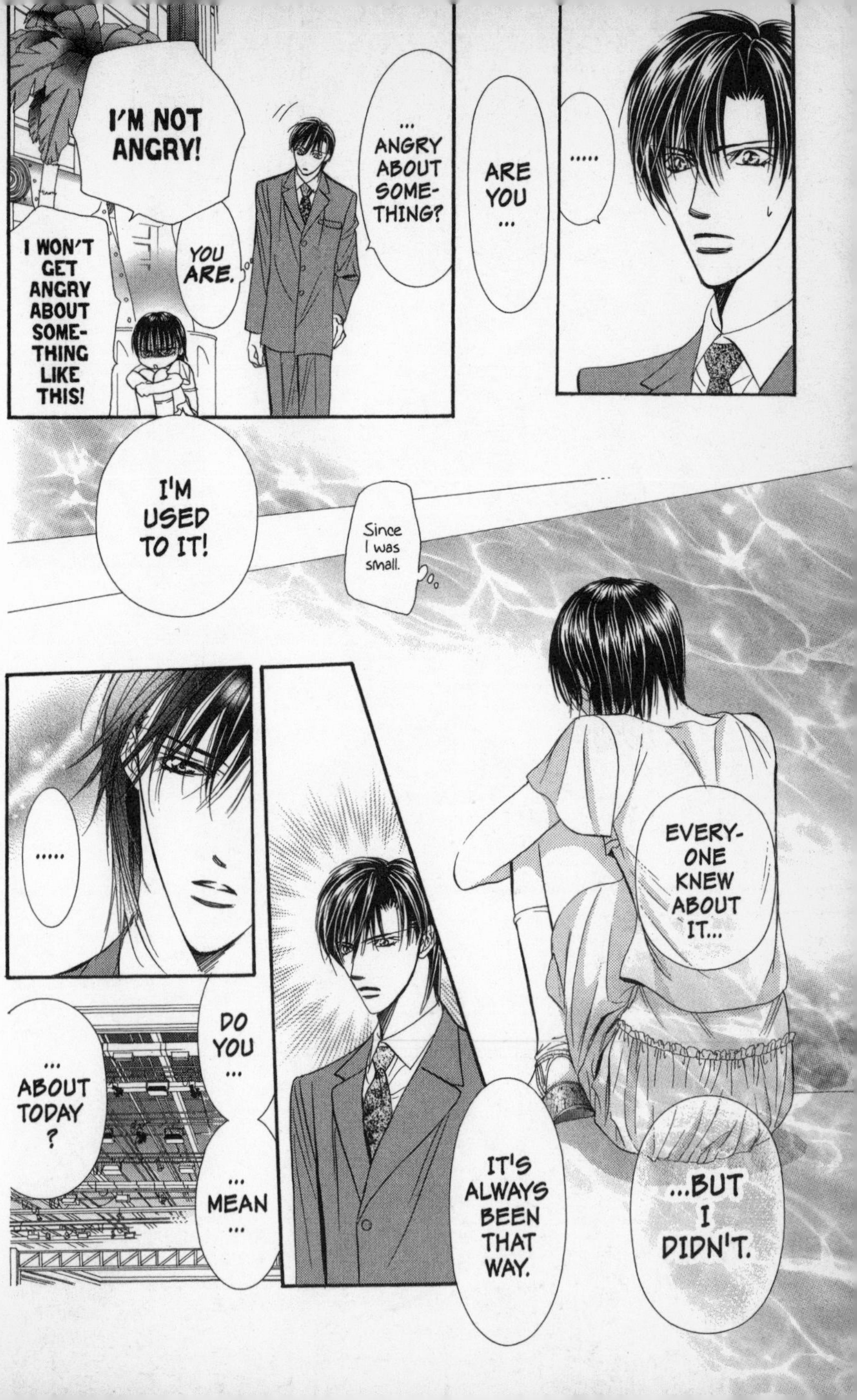
.....
ARE YOU ...
... ANGRY ABOUT SOME-THING?
YOU ARE.
I'M NOT ANGRY!
I WON'T GET ANGRY ABOUT SOME-THING LIKE THIS!
I'M USED TO IT!
Since I was small.
EVERY-ONE KNEW ABOUT IT...
...BUT I DIDN'T.
IT'S ALWAYS BEEN THAT WAY.
.....
DO YOU ...
... MEAN ...
... ABOUT TODAY ?

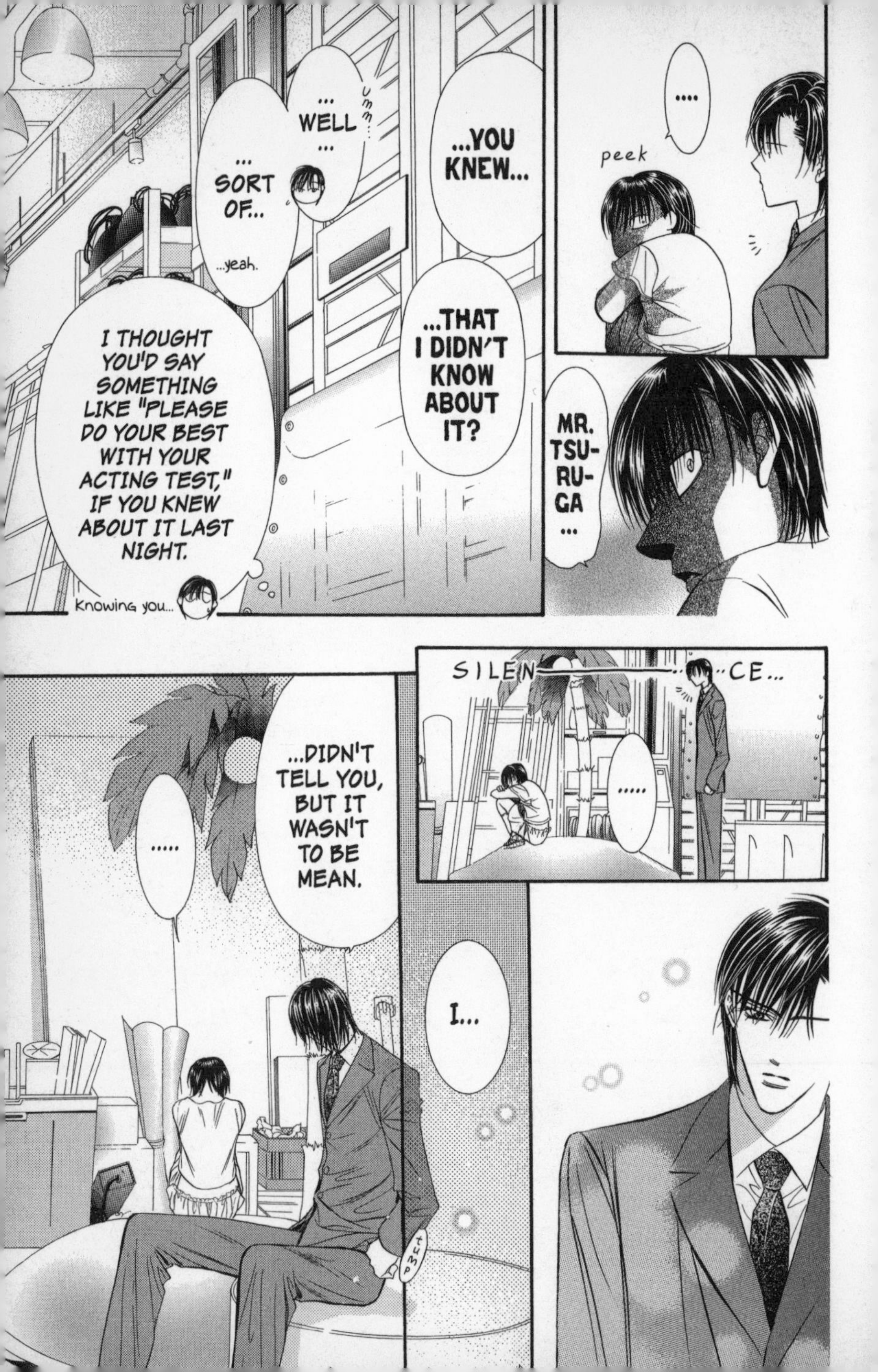
....
peek
MR. TSURUGA...
...YOU KNEW...
...THAT I DIDN'T KNOW ABOUT IT?
... WELL ...
umm...
... SORT OF...
...yeah.
I THOUGHT YOU'D SAY SOMETHING LIKE "PLEASE DO YOUR BEST WITH YOUR ACTING TEST," IF YOU KNEW ABOUT IT LAST NIGHT.
Knowing you...
SILEN——CE...
.....
I...
...DIDN'T TELL YOU, BUT IT WASN'T TO BE MEAN.
.....
THUMP

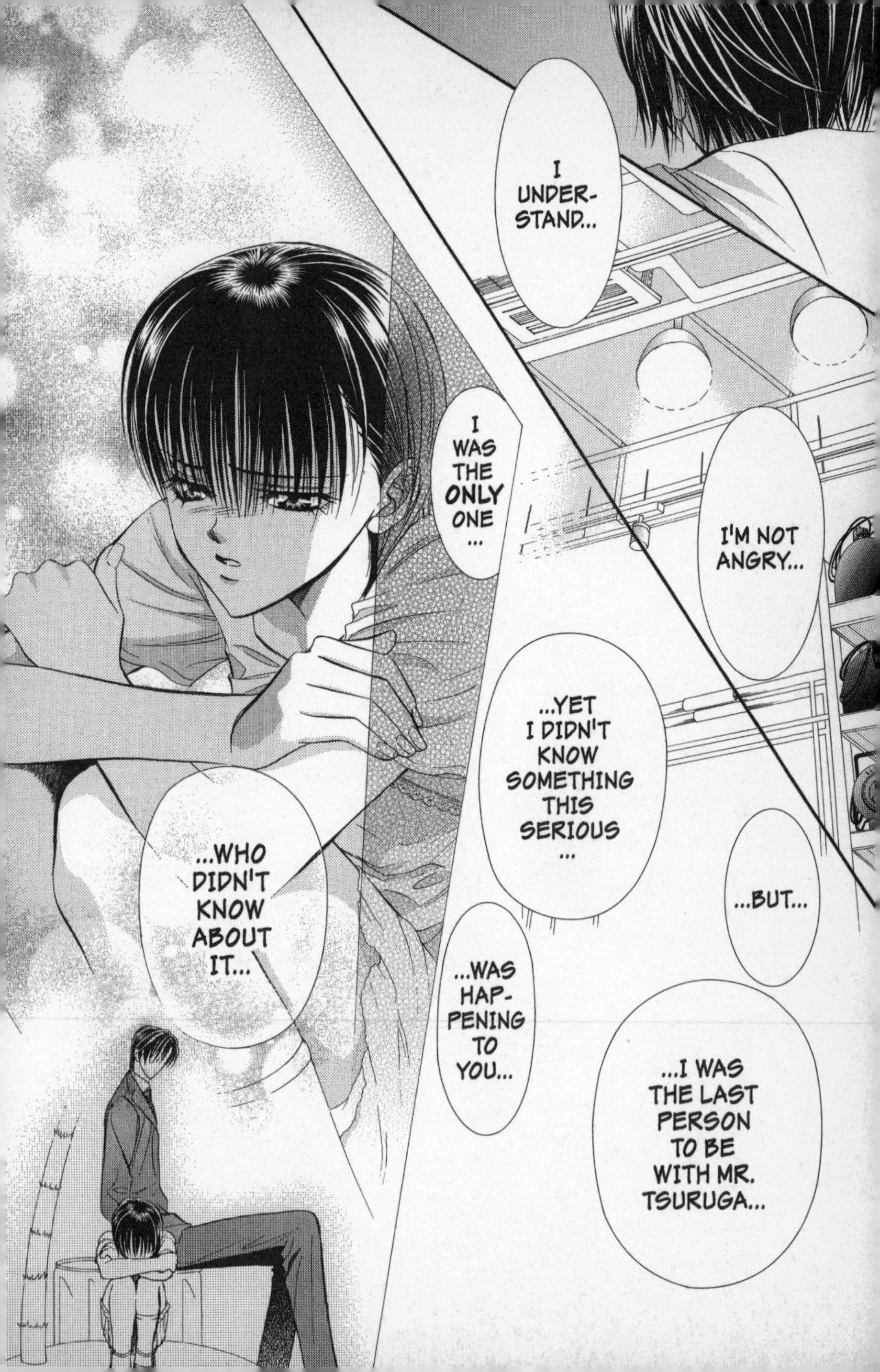
I UNDERSTAND...
I'M NOT ANGRY...
...BUT...
...I WAS THE LAST PERSON TO BE WITH MR. TSURUGA...
...YET I DIDN'T KNOW SOMETHING THIS SERIOUS...
...WAS HAPPENING TO YOU...
I WAS THE ONLY ONE...
...WHO DIDN'T KNOW ABOUT IT...

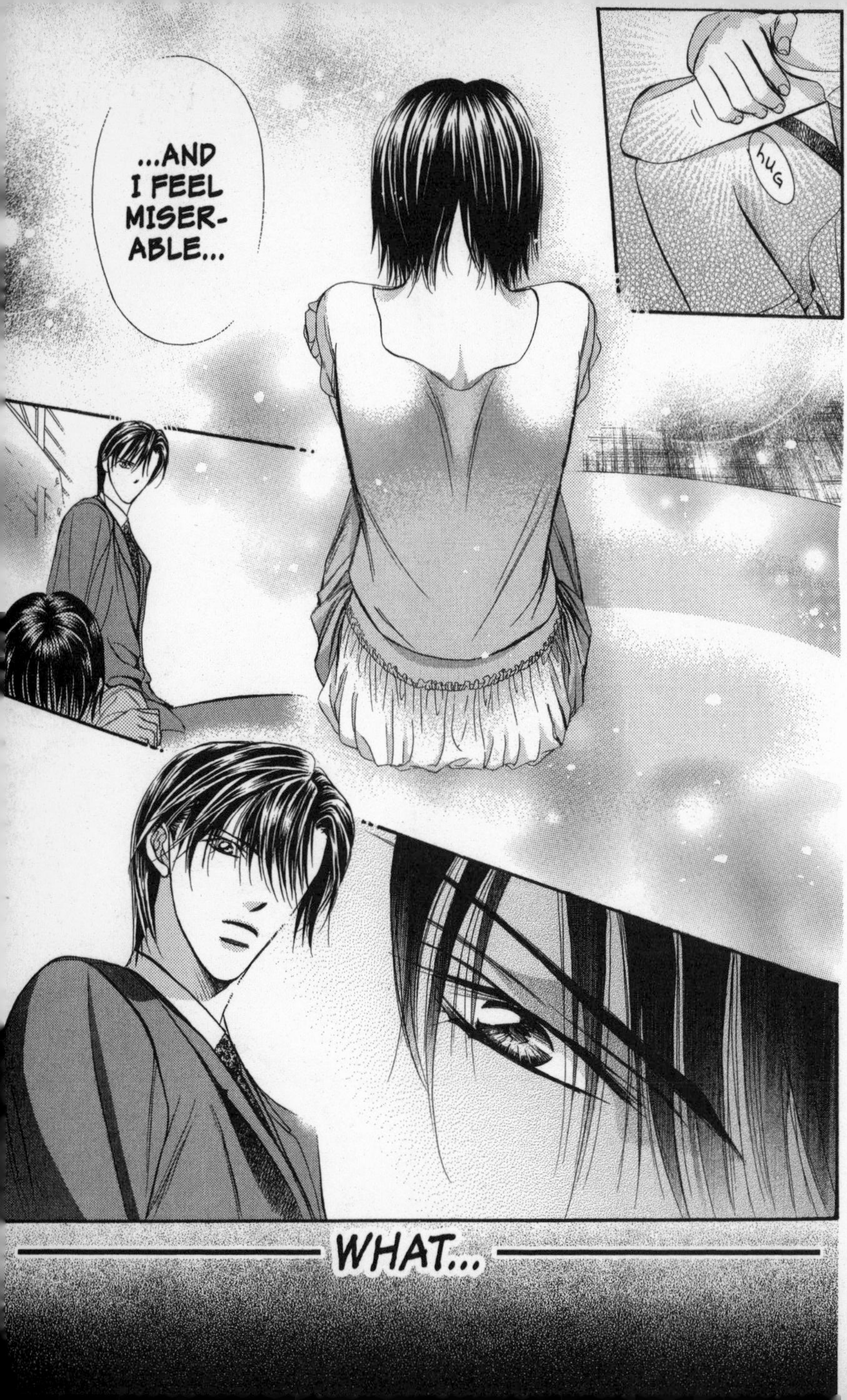
hug
...AND I FEEL MISER-ABLE...
WHAT...

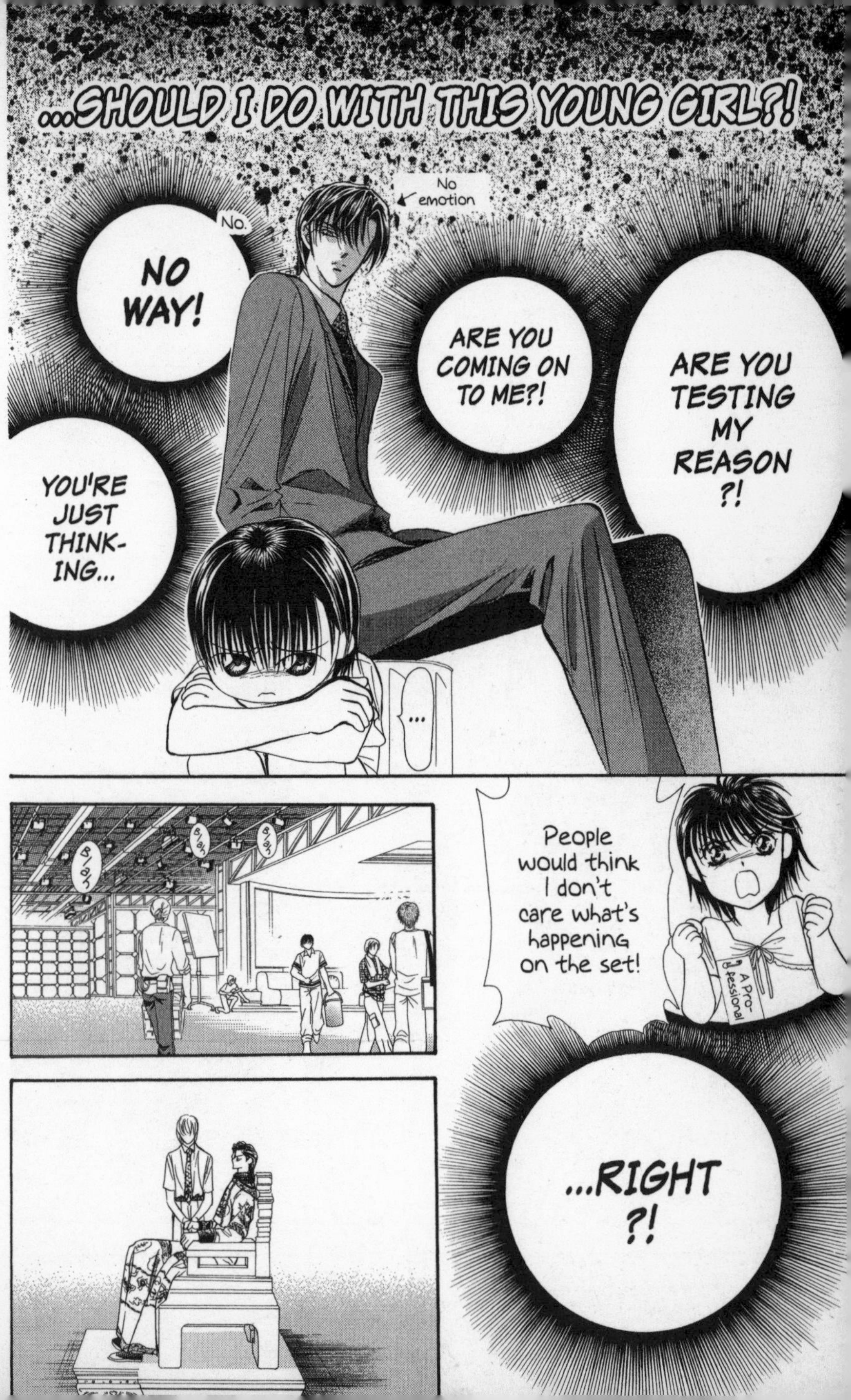
...SHOULD I DO WITH THIS YOUNG GIRL?!
ARE YOU TESTING MY REASON ?!
ARE YOU COMING ON TO ME?!
No emotion
No.
NO WAY!
YOU'RE JUST THINKING...
...
People would think I don't care what's happening on the set!
A Professional
Blah
Blah
Blah
...RIGHT ?!

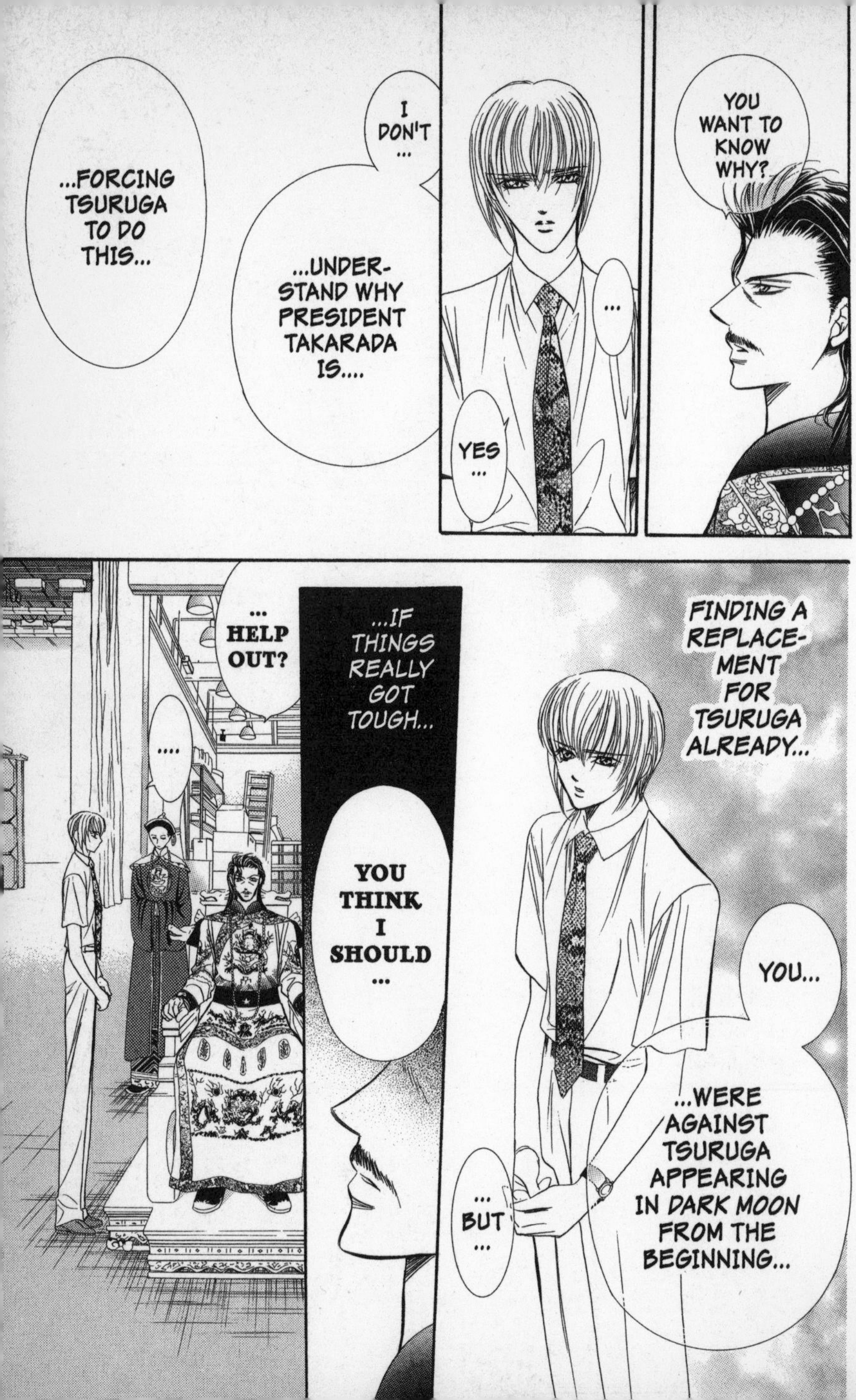
YOU WANT TO KNOW WHY?
...
YES ...
I DON'T ...
...UNDER-STAND WHY PRESIDENT TAKARADA IS....
...FORCING TSURUGA TO DO THIS...
FINDING A REPLACE-MENT FOR TSURUGA ALREADY...
YOU...
...WERE AGAINST TSURUGA APPEARING IN DARK MOON FROM THE BEGINNING...
... BUT ...
...IF THINGS REALLY GOT TOUGH...
YOU THINK I SHOULD ...
... HELP OUT?
....

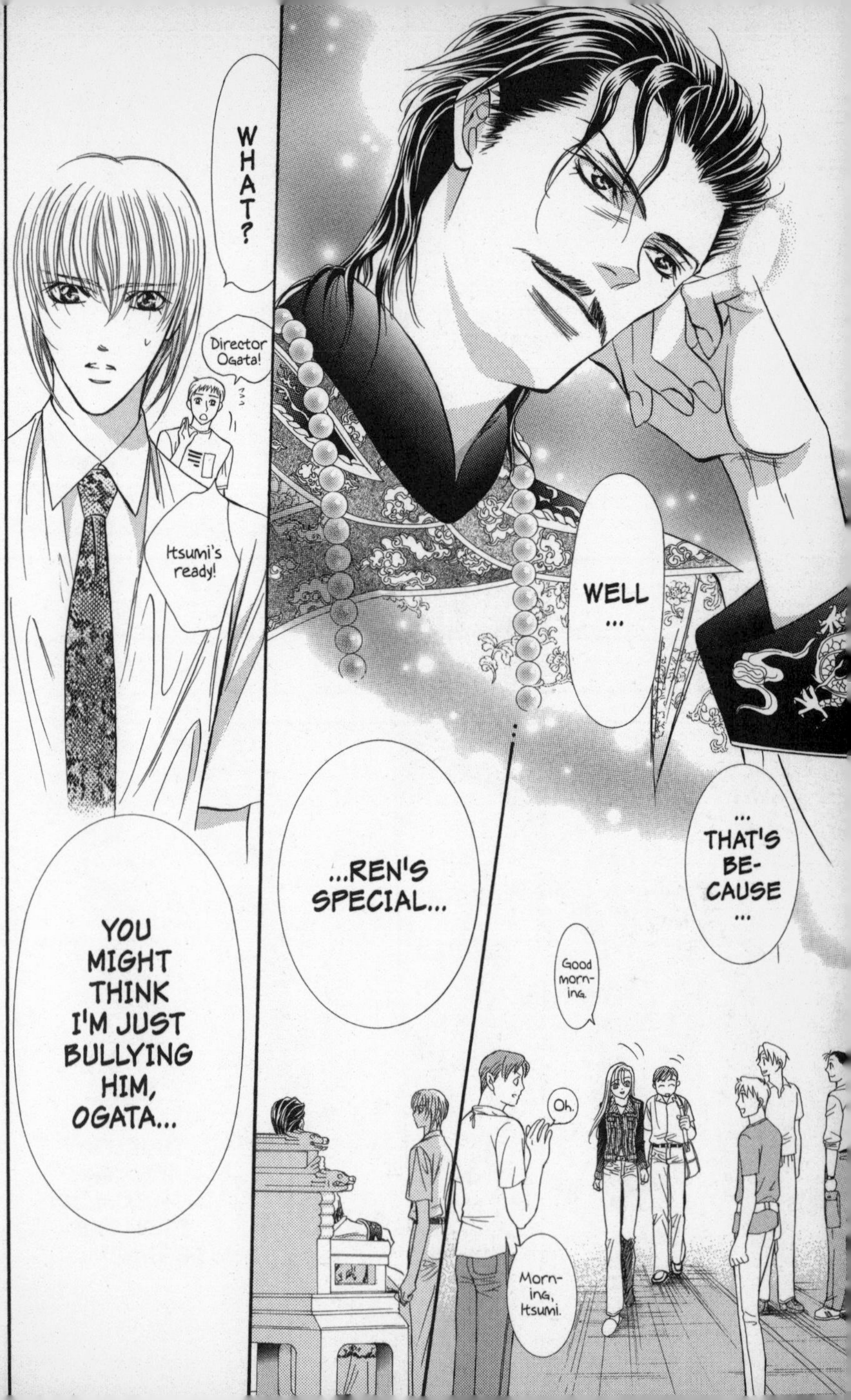
WELL ...
... THAT'S BE-CAUSE ...
...REN'S SPECIAL...
Good morn-ing.
Oh.
Morn-ing, Itsumi.
WHAT?
Director Ogata!
Itsumi's ready!
YOU MIGHT THINK I'M JUST BULLYING HIM, OGATA...

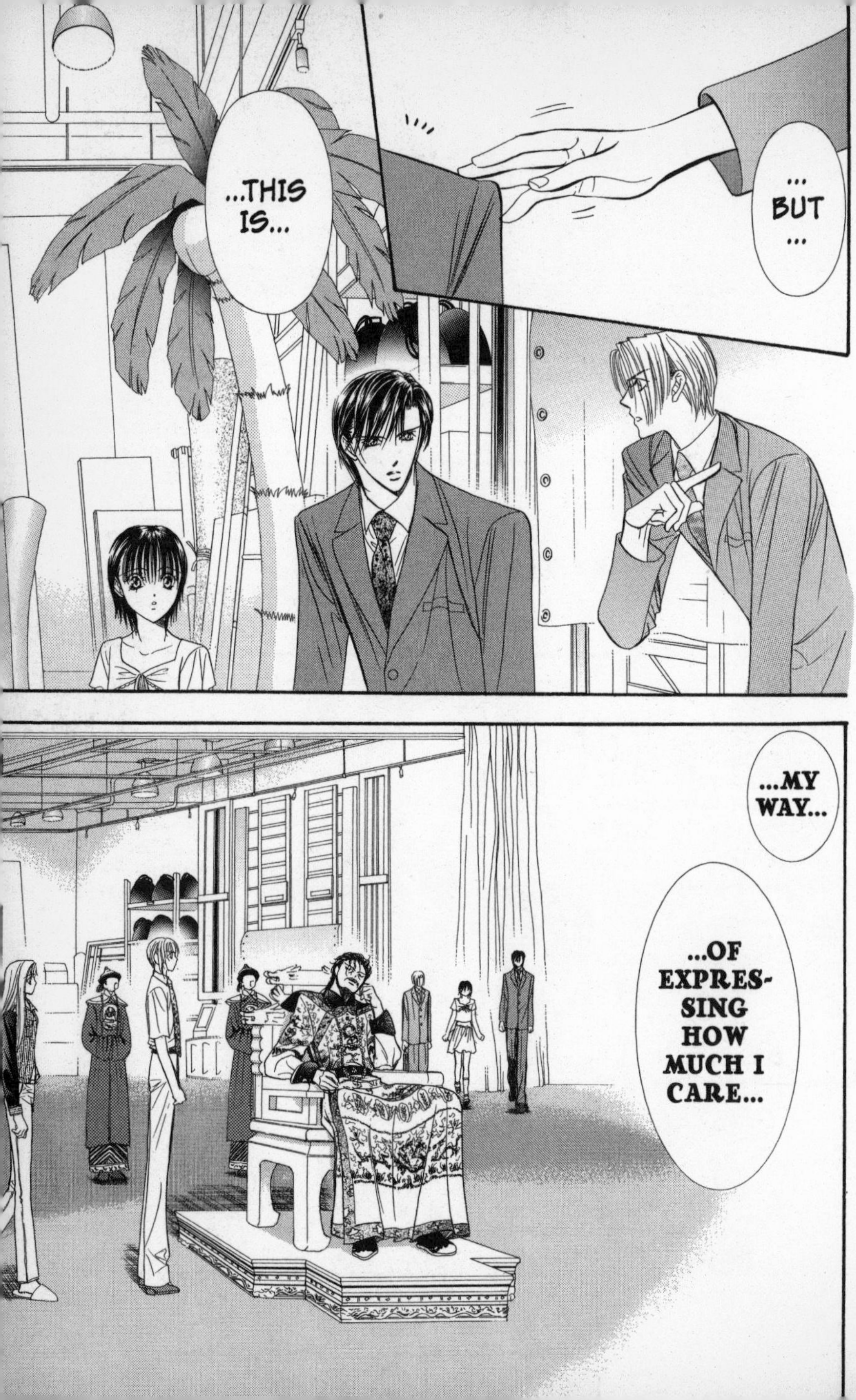
...BUT...
...THIS IS...
...MY WAY...
...OF EXPRES-SING HOW MUCH I CARE...

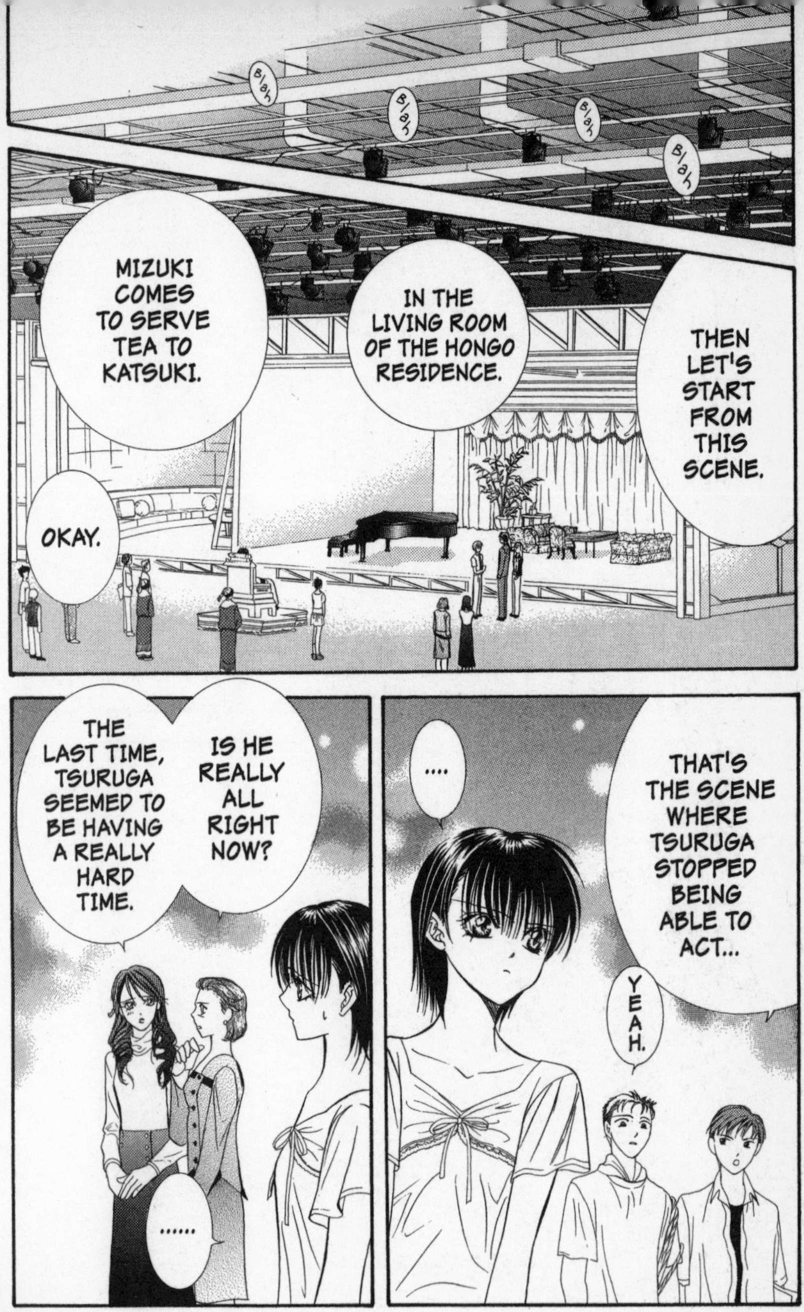
Blah
Blah
Blah
Blah
THEN LET'S START FROM THIS SCENE.
IN THE LIVING ROOM OF THE HONGO RESIDENCE.
MIZUKI COMES TO SERVE TEA TO KATSUKI.
OKAY.
THAT'S THE SCENE WHERE TSURUGA STOPPED BEING ABLE TO ACT...
....
YEAH.
IS HE REALLY ALL RIGHT NOW?
THE LAST TIME, TSURUGA SEEMED TO BE HAVING A REALLY HARD TIME.
......

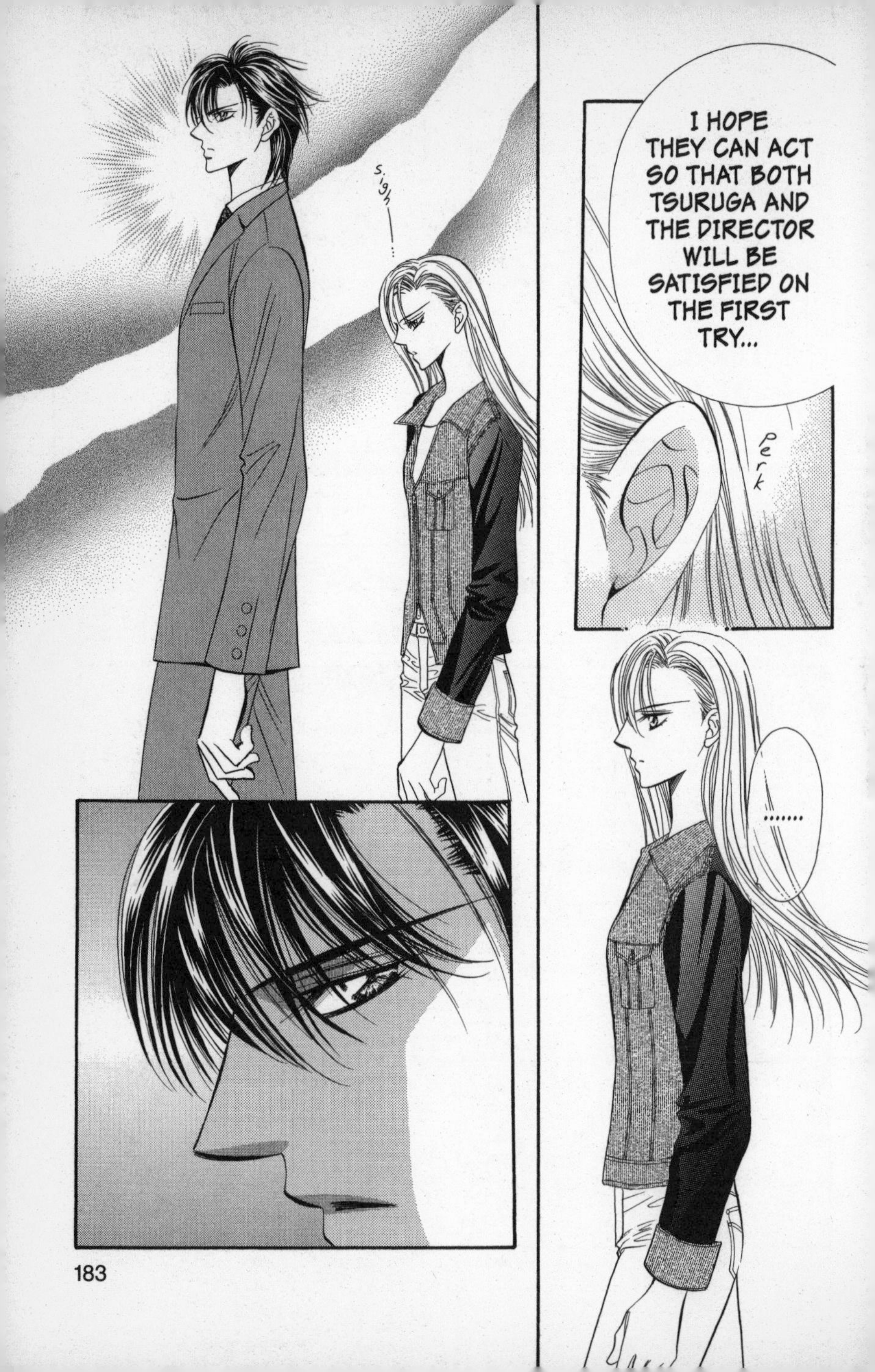
I HOPE THEY CAN ACT SO THAT BOTH TSURUGA AND THE DIRECTOR WILL BE SATISFIED ON THE FIRST TRY...
Perk
....
sigh...

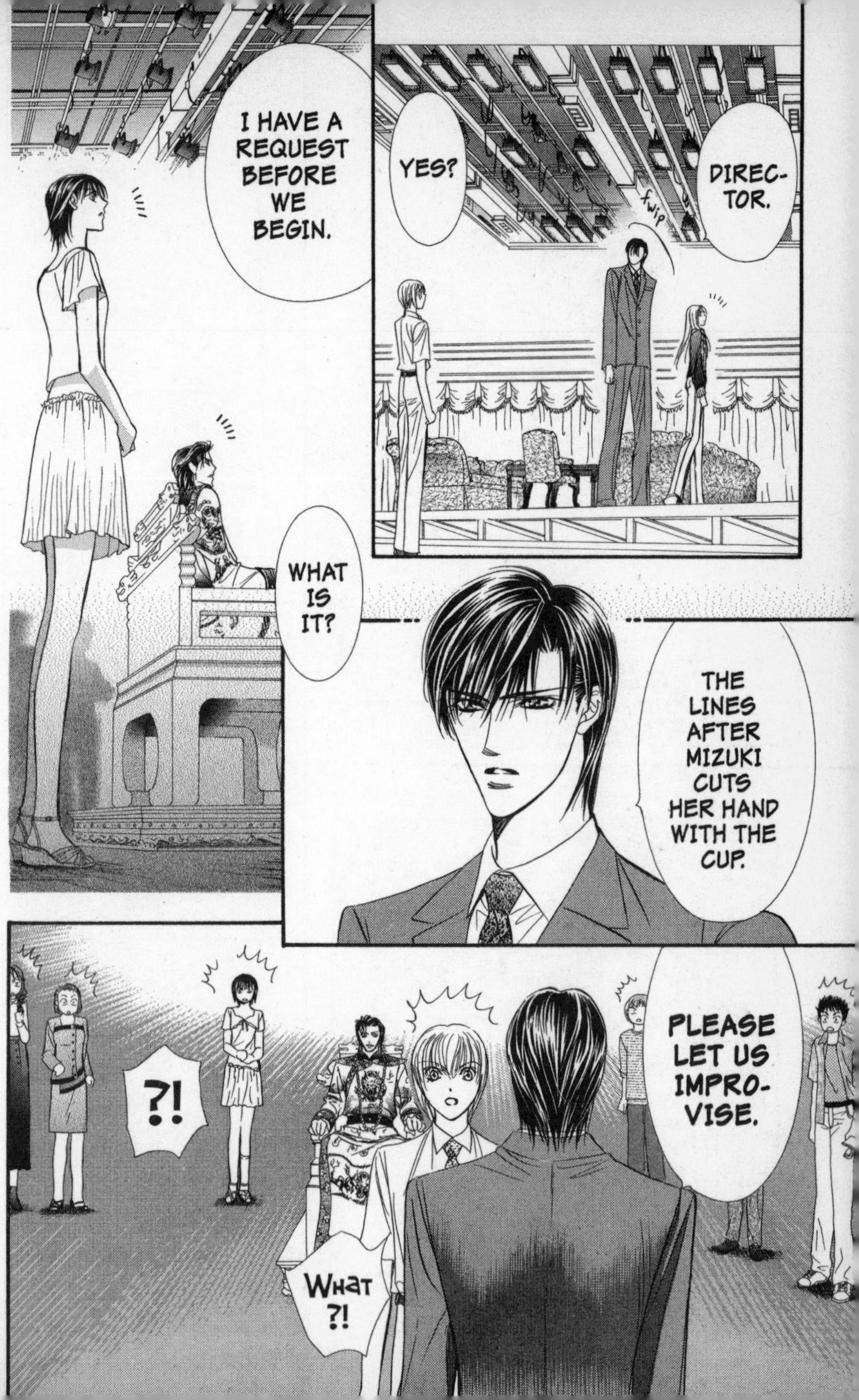
DIREC-
TOR.
fwip
YES?
I HAVE A REQUEST BEFORE WE BEGIN.
WHAT IS IT?
THE LINES AFTER MIZUKI CUTS HER HAND WITH THE CUP.
PLEASE LET US IMPRO-
VISE.
?!
WHAT ?!

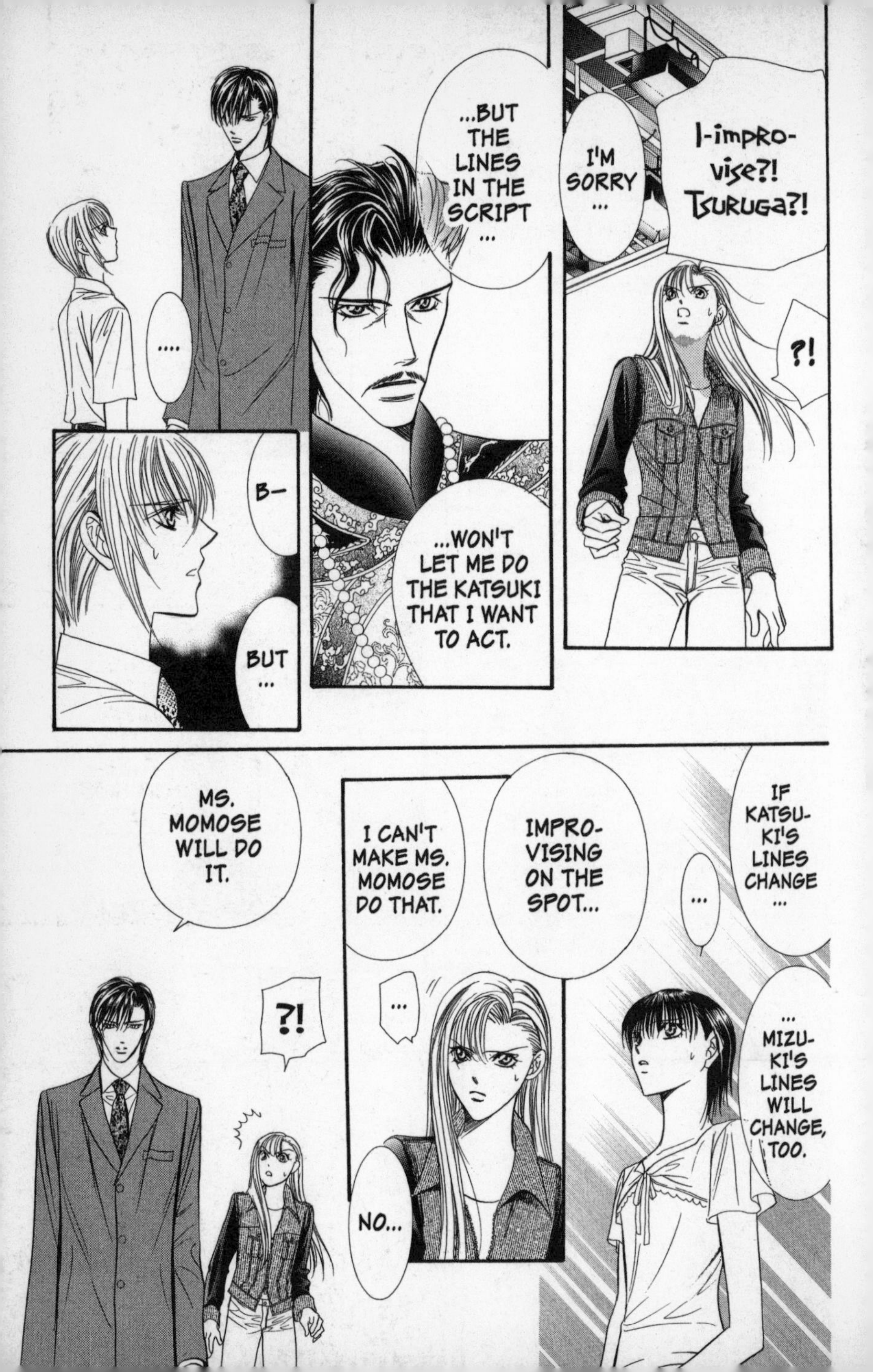
I-impro-vise?! Tsuruga?!
I'M SORRY ...
?!
...BUT THE LINES IN THE SCRIPT ...
...WON'T LET ME DO THE KATSUKI THAT I WANT TO ACT.
....
B—
BUT ...
IF KATSU-KI'S LINES CHANGE ...
...
... MIZU-KI'S LINES WILL CHANGE, TOO.
IMPRO-VISING ON THE SPOT...
I CAN'T MAKE MS. MOMOSE DO THAT.
...
NO...
MS. MOMOSE WILL DO IT.
?!

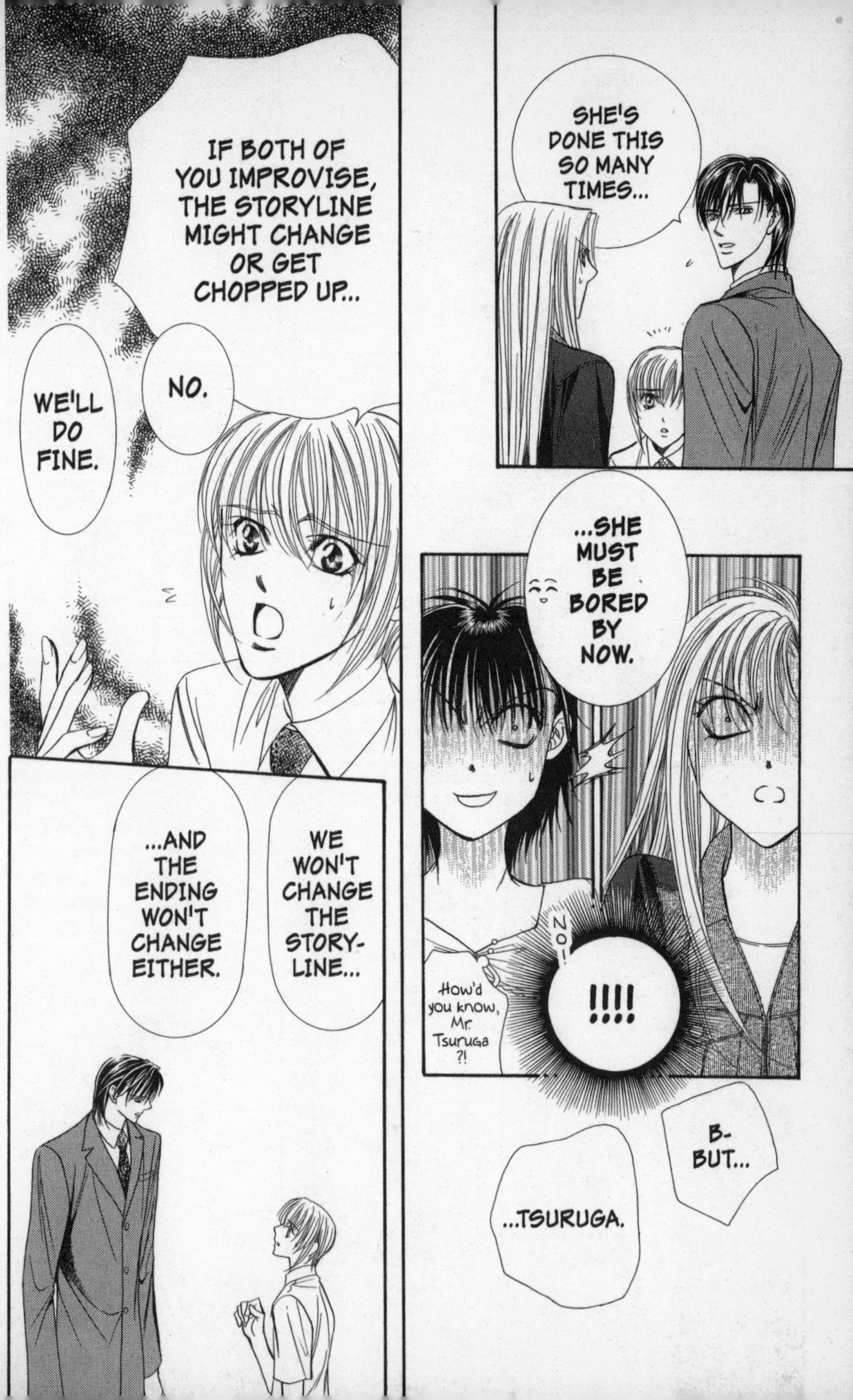
SHE'S DONE THIS SO MANY TIMES...
...SHE MUST BE BORED BY NOW.
NO!
!!!!
How'd you know, Mr. Tsuruga?!
B-BUT...
...TSURUGA.
IF BOTH OF YOU IMPROVISE, THE STORYLINE MIGHT CHANGE OR GET CHOPPED UP...
NO.
WE'LL DO FINE.
WE WON'T CHANGE THE STORY-LINE...
...AND THE ENDING WON'T CHANGE EITHER.

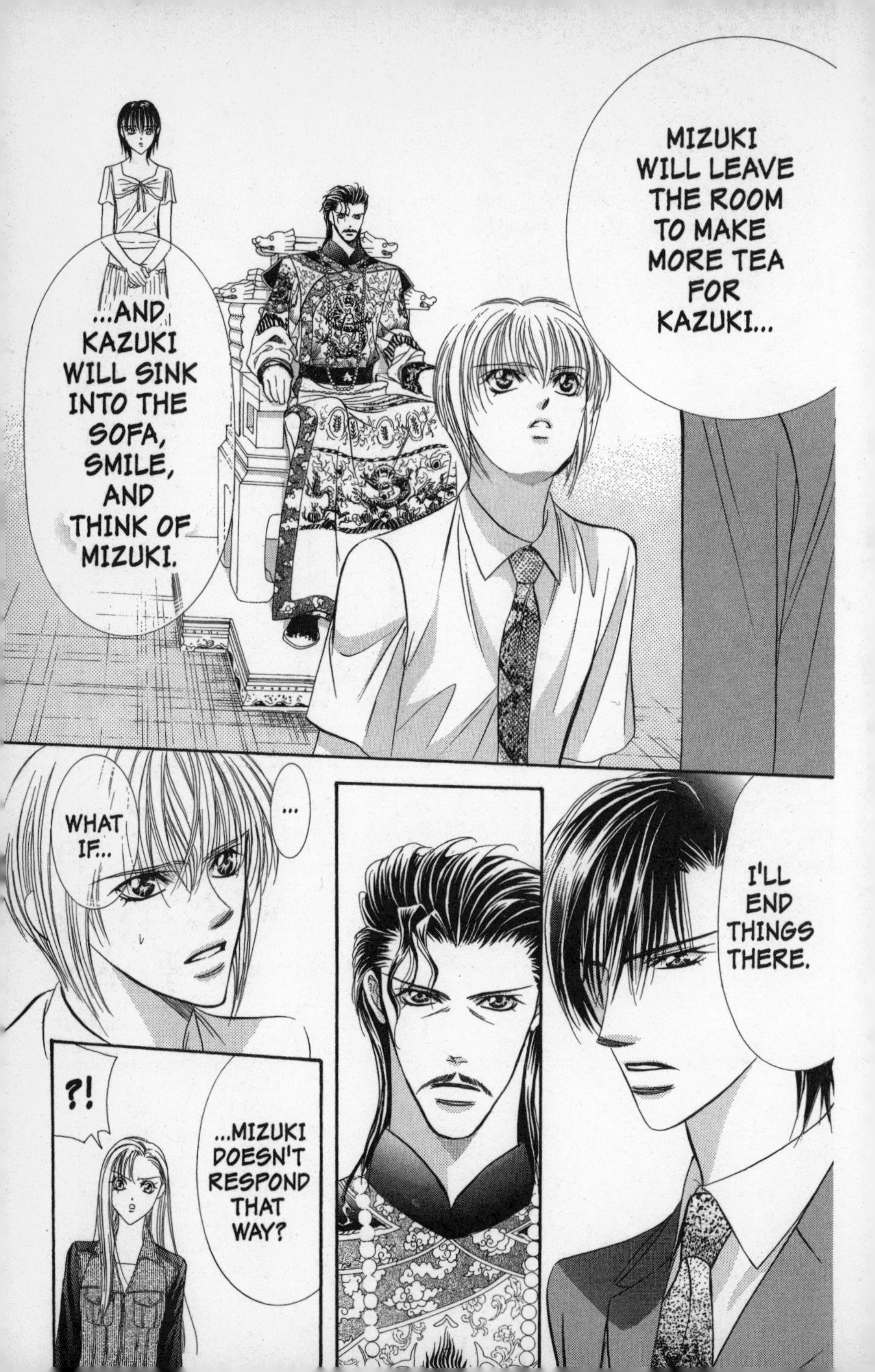
MIZUKI WILL LEAVE THE ROOM TO MAKE MORE TEA FOR KAZUKI...
...AND KAZUKI WILL SINK INTO THE SOFA, SMILE, AND THINK OF MIZUKI.
I'LL END THINGS THERE.
...
WHAT IF...
...MIZUKI DOESN'T RESPOND THAT WAY?
?!

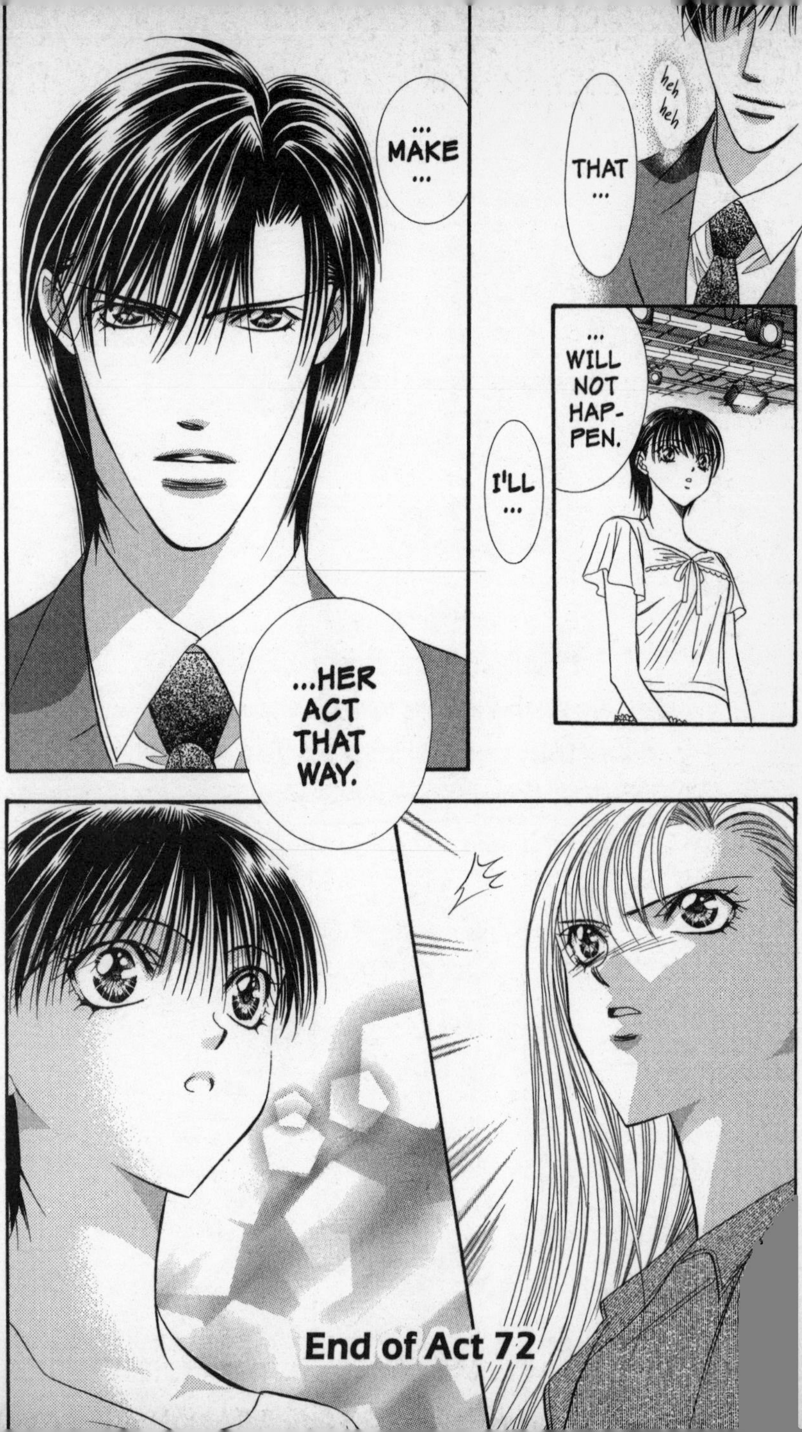
heh heh
THAT ...
... WILL NOT HAP-PEN.
I'LL ...
... MAKE ...
...HER ACT THAT WAY.
End of Act 72

Yoshiki Nakamura is
originally from Tokushima prefecture.
She started drawing manga in elementary
school, which eventually led to her 1993 debut of
Yume de Au yori Suteki (Better than Seeing in
a Dream) in *Hana to Yume* magazine. Her other
works include the basketball series *Saint Love,*
MVP wa Yuzurenai (Can't Give Up MVP),
Blue Wars, and *Tokyo Crazy Paradise,* a
series about a female bodyguard
in 2020 Tokyo.

SKIP·BEAT!
Vol. 12
The Shojo Beat Manga Edition

STORY AND ART BY YOSHIKI NAKAMURA

English Translation & Adaptation/Tomo Kimura
Touch-up Art & Lettering/Sabrina Heep
Cover Design/Yukiko Whitley
Interior Design/Izumi Evers
Editor/Pancha Diaz

Editor in Chief, Books/Alvin Lu
Editor in Chief, Magazines/Marc Weidenbaum
VP of Publishing Licensing/Rika Inouye
VP of Sales/Gonzalo Ferreyra
Sr. VP of Marketing/Liza Coppola
Publisher/Hyoe Narita

Printed in Canada

Published by VIZ Media, LLC
P.O. Box 77010
San Francisco, CA 94107

Shojo Beat Manga Edition
10 9 8 7 6 5 4 3 2 1
First printing, May 2008

store.viz.com

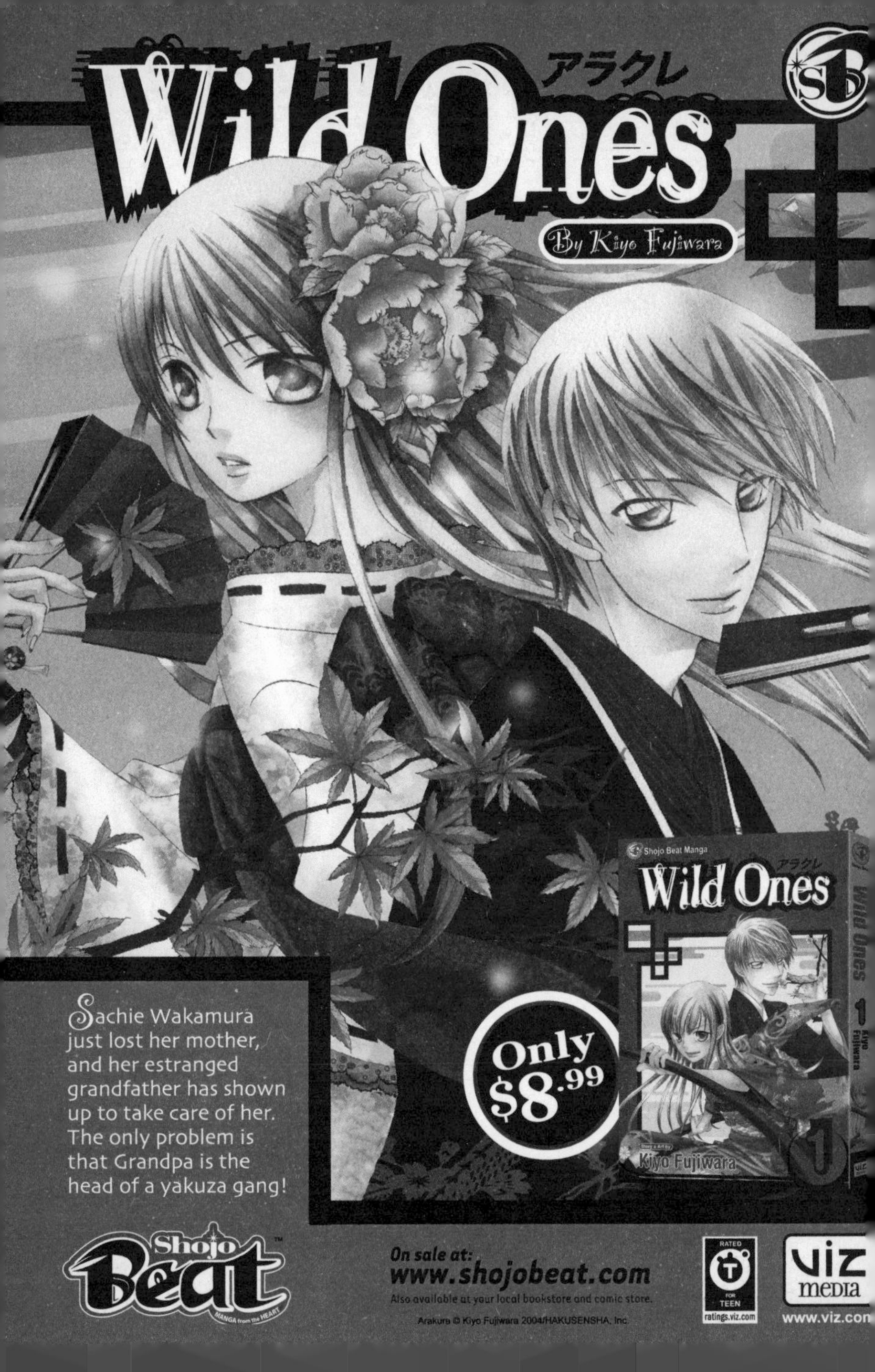

Wild Ones
アラクレ
By Kiyo Fujiwara
Sachie Wakamura just lost her mother, and her estranged grandfather has shown up to take care of her. The only problem is that Grandpa is the head of a yakuza gang!
Only $8.99
Shojo Beat Manga
Wild Ones
アラクレ
Kiyo Fujiwara
Shojo Beat
MANGA from the HEART
On sale at:
www.shojobeat.com
Also available at your local bookstore and comic store.
Arakura © Kiyo Fujiwara 2004/HAKUSENSHA, Inc.
RATED T FOR TEEN
ratings.viz.com
VIZ media
www.viz.com

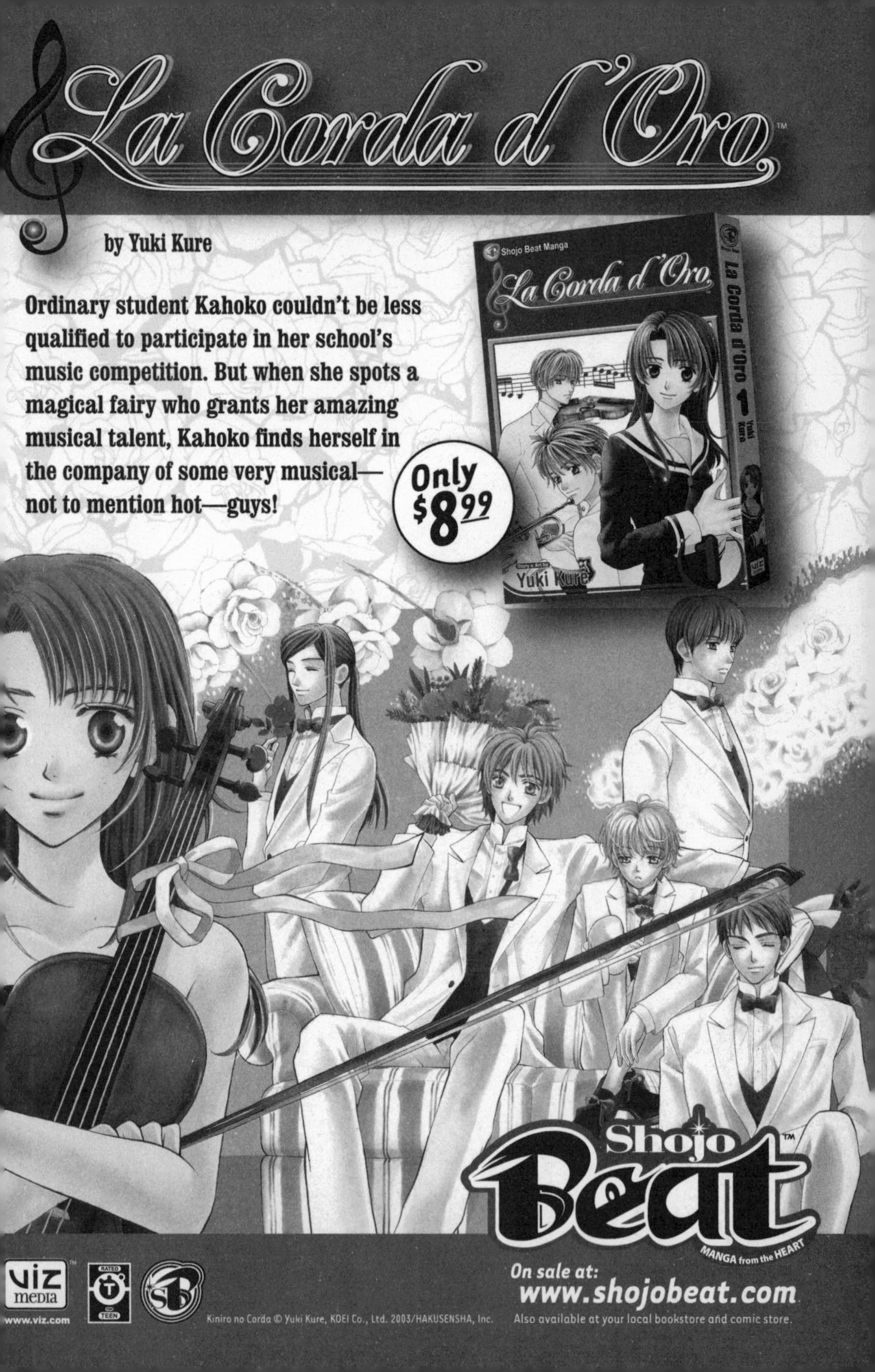

La Corda d'Oro™
by Yuki Kure
Ordinary student Kahoko couldn't be less qualified to participate in her school's music competition. But when she spots a magical fairy who grants her amazing musical talent, Kahoko finds herself in the company of some very musical—not to mention hot—guys!
Only $8.99
Shojo Beat Manga
La Corda d'Oro
Yuki Kure
Shojo Beat™
MANGA from the HEART
On sale at:
www.shojobeat.com
Also available at your local bookstore and comic store.
viz media
www.viz.com
RATED T TEEN
Kiniro no Corda © Yuki Kure, KOEI Co., Ltd. 2003/HAKUSENSHA, Inc.

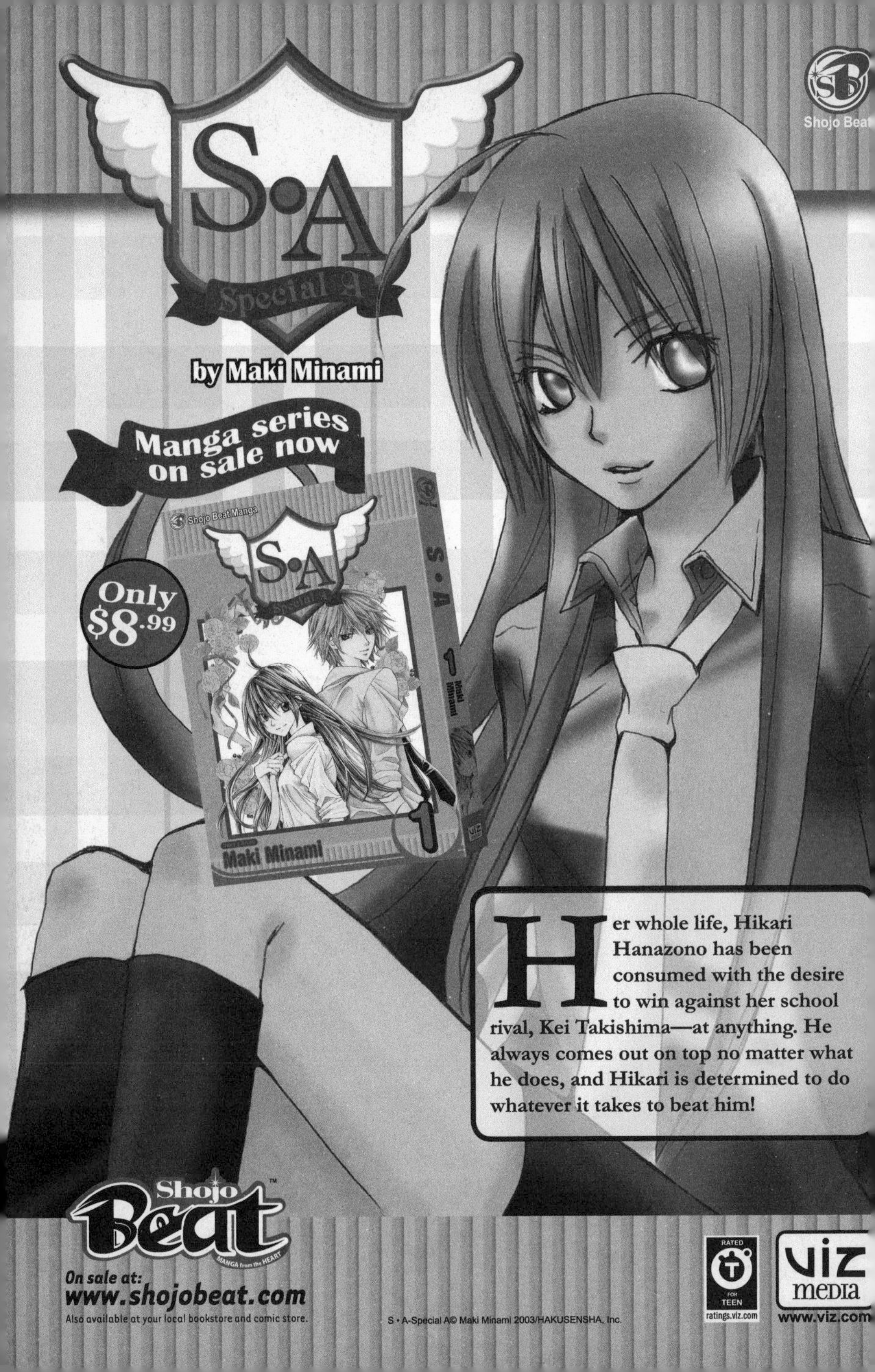
Shojo Beat
S•A
Special A
by Maki Minami
Manga series on sale now
Shojo Beat Manga
S•A
1
Maki Minami
Only $8.99
Her whole life, Hikari Hanazono has been consumed with the desire to win against her school rival, Kei Takishima—at anything. He always comes out on top no matter what he does, and Hikari is determined to do whatever it takes to beat him!
Shojo Beat™
MANGA from the HEART
On sale at:
www.shojobeat.com
Also available at your local bookstore and comic store.
S • A-Special A© Maki Minami 2003/HAKUSENSHA, Inc.
RATED
T
FOR TEEN
ratings.viz.com
VIZ media
www.viz.com

zine!

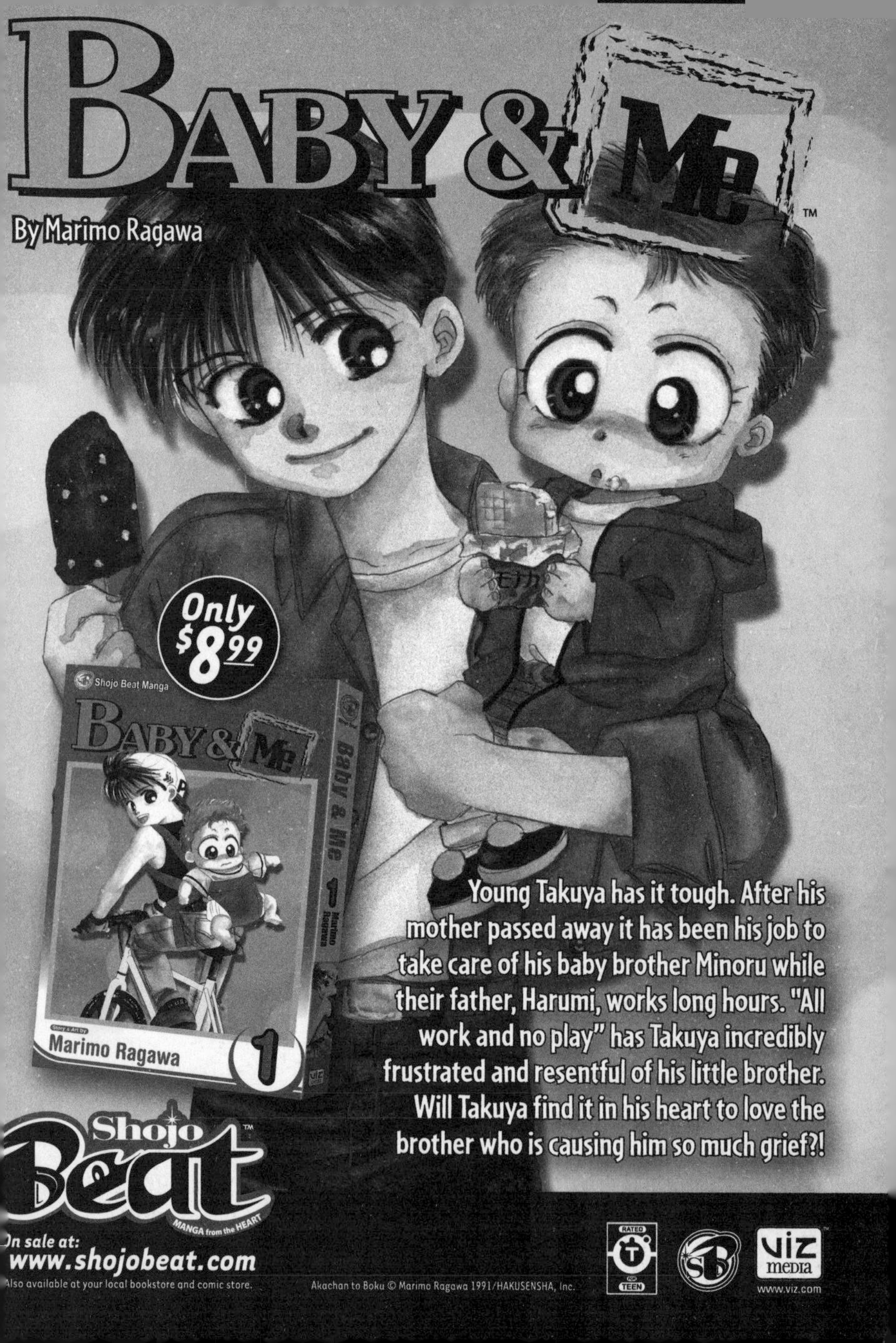
BABY & ME™
By Marimo Ragawa
Only $8.99
Shojo Beat Manga
BABY & ME
Story & Art by
Marimo Ragawa
1
Young Takuya has it tough. After his mother passed away it has been his job to take care of his baby brother Minoru while their father, Harumi, works long hours. "All work and no play" has Takuya incredibly frustrated and resentful of his little brother. Will Takuya find it in his heart to love the brother who is causing him so much grief?!
Shojo Beat™
MANGA from the HEART
On sale at:
www.shojobeat.com
Also available at your local bookstore and comic store.
Akachan to Boku © Marimo Ragawa 1991/HAKUSENSHA, Inc.
RATED T FOR TEEN
VIZ media
www.viz.com

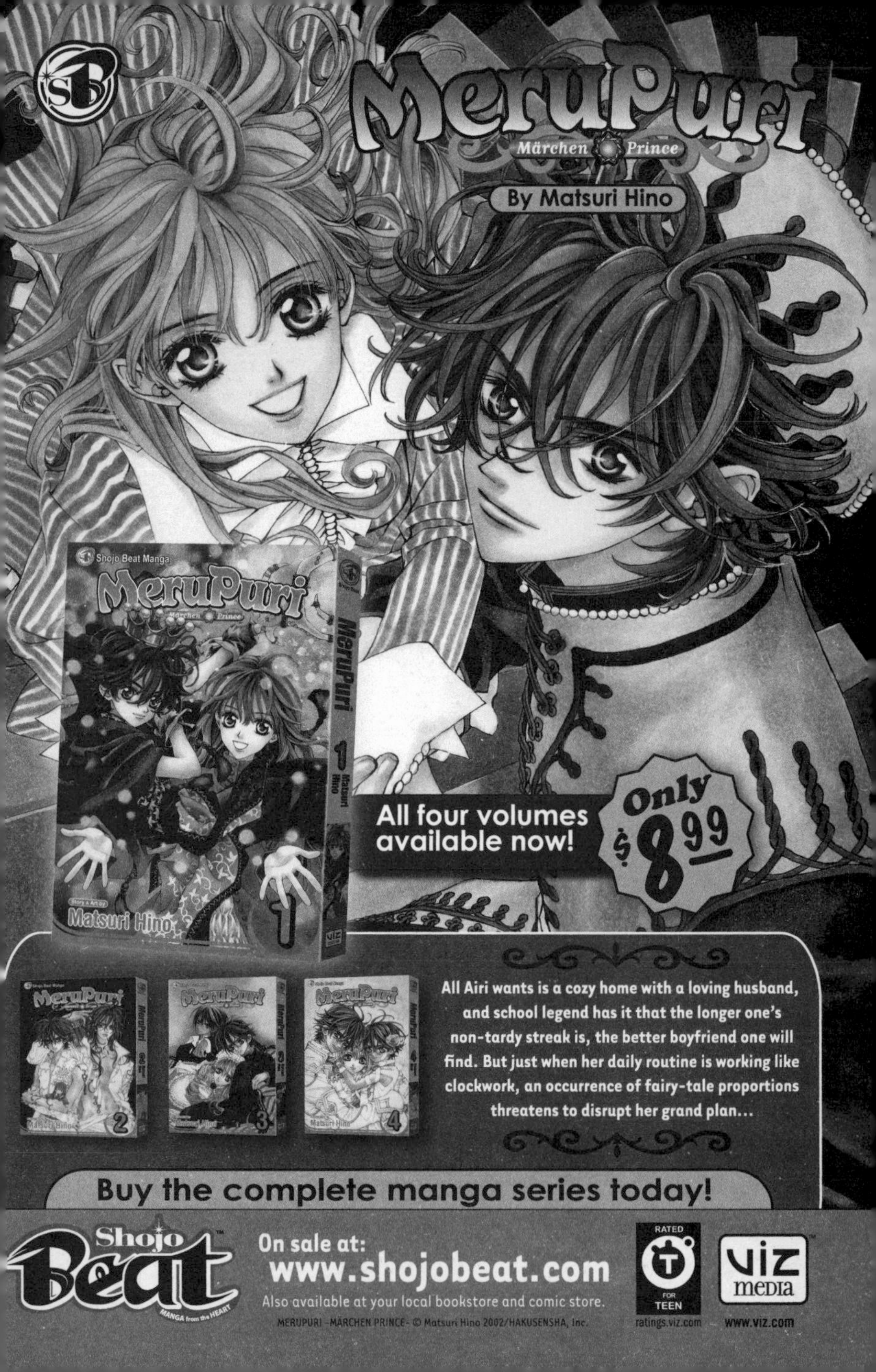
MeruPuri
Märchen Prince
By Matsuri Hino
Shojo Beat Manga
MeruPuri
Märchen Prince
Story & Art by
Matsuri Hino
All four volumes available now!
Only $8.99
All Airi wants is a cozy home with a loving husband, and school legend has it that the longer one's non-tardy streak is, the better boyfriend one will find. But just when her daily routine is working like clockwork, an occurrence of fairy-tale proportions threatens to disrupt her grand plan...
Buy the complete manga series today!
Shojo Beat
MANGA from the HEART
On sale at:
www.shojobeat.com
Also available at your local bookstore and comic store.
MERUPURI -MÄRCHEN PRINCE- © Matsuri Hino 2002/HAKUSENSHA, Inc.
RATED T FOR TEEN
ratings.viz.com
VIZ media
www.viz.com

Tell us what about Shojo Beat Manga!

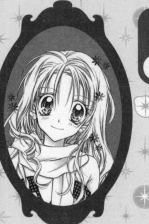

Our survey is now available online. Go to:

shojobeat.com/mangasurvey

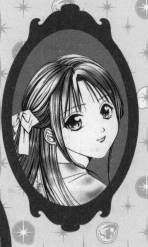

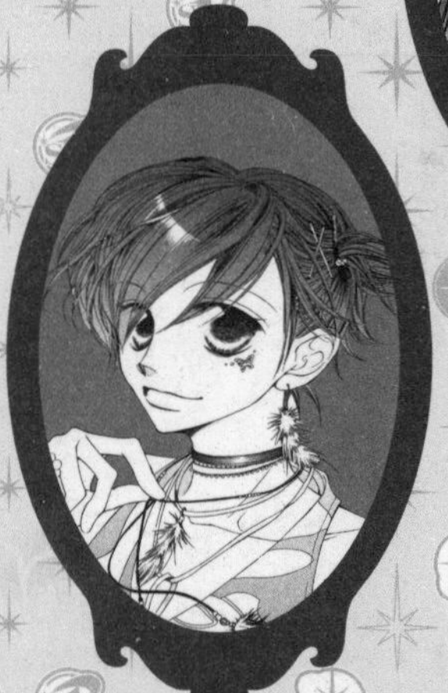

Help us make our product offerings better!

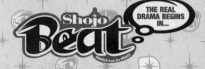

VIZ media

Shojo Beat
MANGA from the HEART
THE REAL DRAMA BEGINS IN...